# Abruzzo
## History and Art Guide

**ABRUZZO • History and Art Guide**

EDITORIAL PROJECT
Giovanni Tavano

GRAPHICS PROJECT AND PAGE-UP
Roberto Monasterio

EDITORIAL TEAM
Marialuce Latini, Ugo Esposito,
Roberto Monasterio, Giovanni Tavano,
All editorial material used herein is the literary
property of CARSA Edizioni srl

ENGLISH TRANSLATION PROJECT MANAGER
Angela Arnone

PHOTOGRAPHY
CARSA Edizioni Archives
(Giovanni Cocco, Luca Del Monaco,
Paolo Iammarrone, Barbara Miozza,
Marco Minoliti, Roberto Monasterio,
Sonia Ricchezza, Giovanni Tavano),
Archivio Arcidiocesi Chieti-Vasto, Archivio
Museo Civico di Sulmona, Archivio Parco
Nazionale d'Abruzzo, Lazio e Molise, Archivio
Soprintendenza Archeologica dell'Abruzzo,
Archivio www.paesaggidabruzzo.com
(Paolo Baglioni, Marco Cingolani,
Cristofaro Sante Di Giovanni, Giuseppe Paoletti,
Stefano Scarsella, Giovanni Sfarra,
Gennaro Staniscia, Antonella Taddei,
Giancarlo Vetrone, Luca Zappacosta)
Ezio Burri, Massimo Capaldi,
Roberto Colacioppo, Maurizio D'Antonio,
Giovanni Lattanzi, Domenico Mariano,
Edoardo Micati, Antonio Porto, Mauro Vitale.

*Printed in May 2020, in*
*Grafica 080, Modugno (BA)*

© Copyright 2003
**CARSA Edizioni, Pescara - Italy**
**Second edition: May 2020**
All Rights Reserved

**ISBN 978-88-501-0389-8**

**CARSA Edizioni**

PRESIDENT
Roberto Di Vincenzo

CEO, ART DIRECTOR
Giovanni Tavano

MANAGING EDITOR
Oscar Buonamano

PICTURE EDITOR,
PRODUCTION MANAGER
Roberto Monasterio

DISTRIBUTION MANAGER
Alessio Mariano

HEAD OFFICES AND EDITORIAL OFFICES
Piazza Salvador Allende, 4
65128 Pescara • Italia
www.carsaedizioni.it
www.carsa.it

1. Cover: Rocca Calascio (AQ) castle; Capoturchino trabocco, San Vito Chietino; the Italic sculpture called the "Warrior of Capestrano", an exhibit at Chieti's Museo Archeologico Nazionale.

# Abruzzo
## History and Art Guide

Edited by Marialuce Latini

# INDEX

**11**    Abruzzo: A Great, Permanent Open-Air Museum

## 35    L'AQUILA and province

**37**    **The City**

**53**    **Upper Aterno Valley**
Poggio di Roio, Lucoli, Tornimparte, Coppito, Scoppito, Preturo, S. Vittorino, Cavallari, Pizzoli, Barete, Cagnano Amiterno, Montereale, Capitignano, Campotosto

**61**    **Rocche Plateau**
Civita di Bagno, Ocre, Rocca di Cambio, Rocca di Mezzo, Ovindoli, Secinaro, Gagliano Aterno

**67**    **Subequano Valley**
Fossa, S. Eusanio Forconese, Villa S. Angelo, S. Demetrio ne' Vestini, Stiffe, Fagnano Alto, Fontecchio, Tione degli Abruzzi, Acciano, Goriano Valli, Roccapreturo, Molina Aterno, Castelvecchio Subequo, Castel di Ieri, Goriano Sicoli

**79**    **Gran Sasso and the Navelli Plain**
Bazzano, Paganica, Tempera, Pescomaggiore, Filetto, Camarda, Assergi, Poggio Picenze, Barisciano, S. Stefano di Sessanio, Calascio, Rocca Calascio, Castel del Monte, Villa S. Lucia, Ofena, Castelvecchio Calvisio, Carapelle Calvisio, S. Pio delle Camere, Castelnuovo, Prata d'Ansidonia, S. Nicandro, Caporciano, Bominaco, Civitaretenga, Navelli, Capestrano, Collepietro, S. Benedetto in Perillis

**101**    **Valle Peligna and the Cinque Miglia Plateau**
Corfinio, Raiano, Vittorito, Prezza, Pratola Peligna, Roccacasale, Sulmona, Badia Morronese, Introdacqua, Bugnara, Pettorano sul Gizio, Rocca Pia, Rivisondoli, Roccaraso, Pietransieri, Ateleta, Castel di Sangro, Pescocostanzo, Cansano, Campo di Giove, Pacentro

**127**    **Fucino Basin and Marsican Abruzzo**
Magliano dei Marsi, Massa d'Albe, Scurcola Marsicana, Avezzano, Luco dei Marsi, Trasacco, Collelongo, Villavallelonga, Ortucchio, S. Benedetto dei Marsi, Pescina, Collarmele, Cerchio, Aielli, Celano

**145**    **Piana del Cavaliere and the River Liri Valley**
Oricola, Rocca di Botte, Pereto, Carsoli, Pietrasecca, Tagliacozzo, Cappadocia, Castellafiume, Capistrello, Canistro, Civitella Roveto, Civita D'Antino, Morino, S. Vincenzo Valle Roveto, Balsorano

**155**    **Sagittario Valley and Abruzzo – Lazio – Molise National Park**
Cocullo, Anversa degli Abruzzi, Castrovalva, Villalago, Scanno, Villetta Barrea, Civitella Alfedena, Barrea, Alfedena, Scontrone, Opi, Pescasseroli, Bisegna, Ortona dei Marsi, Gioia dei Marsi, Lecce dei Marsi

## 169    CHIETI and province

**171**    **The City**

**181**    **The Hills Between the River Alento and the River Foro**
Casalincontrada, Bucchianico, Villamagna, Ripa Teatina, Torrevecchia Teatina, S. Giovanni Teatino

**185**    **From the Aventino to the Sangro**
Casoli, Altino, Roccascalegna, Gessopalena, Torricella Peligna, Montenerodomo, Colledimacine

**193**    **Lanciano, Town and Territory**
Lanciano, Frisa, Castelfrentano, S. Eusanio del Sangro, Filetto, Vacri, Ari, Giuliano Teatino, Canosa Sannita, Crecchio, Poggiofiorito, Arielli, Orsogna, Treglio, Mozzagrogna, S. Maria Imbaro

**203**    **Vasto and Hinterland**
Vasto, S. Salvo, Lentella, Fresagrandinaria, Dogliola, Tufillo, Celenza sul Trigno, S. Giovanni Lipioni, Castelguidone, Schiavi d'Abruzzo, Castiglione Messer Marino, Torrebruna, Carunchio, Fraine, Roccaspinalveti, Montazzoli, Liscia, Palmoli, San Buono, Guilmi, Carpineto Sinello, Furci, Gissi, Casalanguida, Cupello, Monteodorisio, Villalfonsina

| 219 | **Sangro River Valley**
Perano, Archi, Tornareccio, Atessa, Bomba, Colledimezzo, Pietraferrazzana, Monteferrante, Roio del Sangro, Rosello, Borrello, Quadri, Pizzoferrato, Gamberale, Fallo, Civitaluparella, Villa S. Maria, Montelapiano, Montebello sul Sangro, Pennadomo |

| 229 | **Guardiagrele and Mount Majella**
Roccamontepiano, Pretoro, Rapino, Fara Filiorum Petri, Casacanditella, S. Martino sulla Marrucina, Guardiagrele, Pennapiedimonte, Palombaro, Fara S. Martino, Civitella Messer Raimondo, Lama dei Peligni, Taranta Peligna, Lettopalena, Palena |

| 243 | **The Coast from Francavilla to Casalbordino**
Francavilla al Mare, Miglianico, Tollo, Ortona, S. Vito Chietino, Fossacesia, Rocca S. Giovanni, Torino di Sangro, Paglieta, Casalbordino, Pollutri |

## 255 — PESCARA and province

| 257 | **The City** |

| 267 | **The Coast Meets the Hills**
Montesilvano, Cappelle sul Tavo, Spoltore, Moscufo, Pianella |

| 271 | **Penne and the Vestino area**
Città S. Angelo, Elice, Picciano, Penne, Loreto Aprutino, Collecorvino |

| 281 | **Nora River Valley**
Cepagatti, Nocciano, Catignano, Vicoli, Civitaquana, Cugnoli |

| 285 | **The Pescara Valley and its Historic Abbeys**
Rosciano, Alanno, Pietranico, Torre de' Passeri, Castiglione a Casauria, Popoli, Tocco da Casauria, Scafa, Turrivalignani, Manoppello Scalo |

| 295 | **National Parks in the Pescara District**
Manoppello, Serramonacesca, Lettomanoppello, San Valentino in Abruzzo Citeriore, Abbateggio, Roccamorice, Bolognano, Salle, Caramanico Terme, Sant'Eufemia a Majella, Bussi sul Tirino, Pescosansonesco, Corvara, Brittoli, Carpineto della Nora, Civitella Casanova, Villa Celiera, Montebello di Bertona, Farindola |

## 311 — TERAMO and province

| 313 | **The City** |

| 323 | **The Coast from Martinsicuro to Silvi**
Martinsicuro, Alba Adriatica, Tortoreto, Giulianova, Roseto degli Abruzzi, Montepagano, Pineto, Silvi |

| 331 | **Vibrata and Salinello River Valleys**
Colonnella, Controguerra, Ancarano, S. Egidio alla Vibrata, Faraone, Civitella del Tronto, Valle Castellana, S. Omero, Torano Nuovo, Nereto, Corropoli |

| 343 | **Tordino Valley**
Montone, Mosciano Sant'Angelo, Bellante, Campli, Torricella Sicura, Rocca Santa Maria, Cortino, Crognaleto |

| 351 | **From the Vomano Valley to Gran Sasso**
Morro d'Oro, Notaresco, Castellalto, Castelbasso, Canzano, Montegualtieri, Cellino Attanasio, Cermignano, Penna S. Andrea, Basciano, Castel Castagna, Castelli, Isola del Gran Sasso, Colledara, Tossicia, Montorio al Vomano, Fano Adriano, Pietracamela |

| 365 | **Fino River Valley**
Atri, Castilenti, Castiglione Messer Raimondo, Montefino, Bisenti, Arsita |

| 374 | Table of Insights / Table of Districts |
| 382 | Bibliography |
| 384 | Photographic references |

# Exploring Abruzzo

What are the distinctive features and peculiarities of Abruzzo? Where does the region's originality lie? Why is it unique, particular, exclusive, and what makes it different from any other region? Why should it be visited and explored? There are countless special characteristics, as we will see, but the chief reason that comes to mind now is that this region is intact and unfamiliar, so it is one of the few still able to gratify visitors with the priceless satisfaction of discovery, of innate intuition.

First of all, the sheer extent of nature here: Abruzzo's three national parks, a regional park and over thirty nature reserves account for one third of its area and make it the greenest region in Europe. Moreover, its habitat contains 75% of the entire continent's flora and fauna species: an astonishing fact that delineates a precise regional identity.

Then there is its territory: most of it pristine, a pure anthology of Italian landscapes, above all a seamless concentrate of Alpine and Mediterranean ecosystems. The 130km of coastline are counterbalanced by the two highest peaks in the Apennines (Gran Sasso and Majella), connected by the peninsula's mightiest, most complex system of mountain plateaux: Abruzzo could be called the "Tibet of Italy".

Even in the Middle Ages this was the natural backdrop to the Abruzzo landscape, which has changed very little on the whole, and which makes it so special. An ancient landscape, of great humanity even in its most rugged traits, rooted in our memory like a fairy tale.

Finally, its history, etched in the thousand castles that still watch over and dominate these timeless landscapes; the Medieval abbeys, in whose industrious silence the austere Christian spirit of this region was forged; its mountain pastures, travelled over the millennia by shepherds and their flocks; in the one hundred incredible hermitages where nature and faith continue to unite, now as in the past; in the multitude of picturesque villages, each clustered around its church, its tower, its castle. Not the history we find written in books, but the story told by the landscapes, the church façades, the ancient traditions, the unsophisticated, gentle candour of its people.

So, the time has come to begin to explore this land of Abruzzo. It will be a memorable experience for those who seek to scratch the surface and turn the pages of memory.

The Editor

2. Facing page: Gran Sasso d'Italia mountain chain.

3–6. Left, top to below: Cerrano coastal tower; the River Pescara (PE); Campo Imperatore plateau (AQ); Punta Aderci marine reserve (CH).

# Abruzzo
## A great, permanent open-air museum

Abruzzo is a region that knows about preservation. No better concept could sum up the spirit and nature of this region. Discovering its stunning landscapes, strolling through its historic, stately towns and age-old hilltop villages, the immediate impression is that the region has successfully preserved many of its original characteristics, and that the pristine environment and ancient human settlement constitute an extraordinary and perfect achievement. Abruzzo's magic also – above all – lies in the measured equilibrium between the landscape still dominated by nature and the stratified human presence, creating the system of small villages dotted across the territory, the architectural might of churches, castles, mansions, priceless works of art, countless expressions of arts and crafts, and venerable crop and sheep farming traditions. For the mindful, enthusiastic visitor, the door opens to a discovery of Abruzzo and a quest to find the intrinsic traits that make this region so splendid, and in many ways, so unique.

7. Rocca Calascio castle with the church of Santa Maria della Pietà and the Majella massif in the background.

## The Settlements of Abruzzo: Enchanting Nobility.

First of them all: L'Aquila, with its legendary ninety-nine churches, founded in the thirteenth century, its colossal sixteenth-century fortress still intact. Then Chicti, the region's major archaeological museum district, "Teate" for the Marrucino people, with ancient remains scattered around today's city centre. Teramo, with its lovely cathedral and the well-preserved remains of ancient Interamnia. Pescara, birthplace of Gabriele D'Annunzio and Ennio Flaiano, a modern business city and tourist resort, home to the leading ethnographic museum in the region, Museo delle Genti d'Abruzzo. Astonishing artistic fervour swept over towns like Pescocostanzo, a Baroque jewel, with the Santa Maria del Colle collegiate and the old town's splendid buildings, where many expressions of ancient craft traditions still flourish, like goldsmithing, blacksmithing, woodcarving, lacemaking. Or Sulmona, the town of the sugared almond, vaunting a charming old centre and the splendid Annunziata complex, the city's iconic monument. Then Popoli, with the famous Cantelmo Taverna Ducale and excellent churches. Penne, the "brick town". Campli, known for its historic arcades and examples of handsome lay and religious architecture. Atri deserves a special mention, its origins lost in the mists of time, birthplace of the artist Andrea Delitio, the region's greatest artist of the 1400s, his supreme masterpiece surviving in the frescoes of the cathedral presbytery. Castelli, a village nestling on Gran Sasso's Teramo slope, where the noble potter's art flourished and rose to international fame thanks to its excellent majolica makers. Lanciano, the town of the "Eucharistic Miracle", still boasting the walls and towers of an ancient fortified town, and its splendid Santa Maria Maggiore, one of Abruzzo's few examples of Burgundian Cistercian architecture. Guardiagrele, the lovely town in the foothills of Mount Majella, where crafts are still a thriving reality. Giulianova, with its unusual octagonal cathedral. Aristocratic Vasto, beloved of the Marquises d'Avalos. Ortona, whose majestic cliff-top castle basks

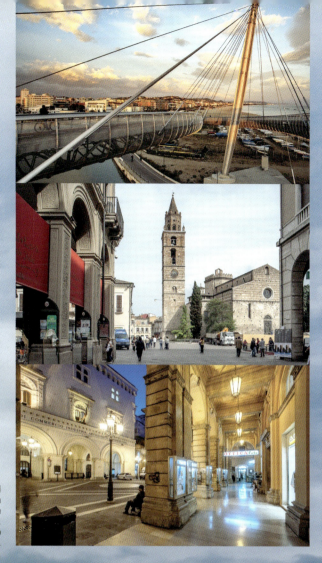

in a romantic aura. All equally enchanting destinations: coastal Abruzzo with its many attractions, small towns where seaside tourism and port activities are all still on a human scale. Sandy beaches and rocky reefs are the hallmark features of the region's coast, the fascinating landscape still unspoiled. Seek out the towering "trabocchi" in that section of coast connecting Ortona to San Salvo, for these historic fishing platforms reaching out to sea now symbolize the protection of this strip of shoreline.

8–10. Right, top to below: Ponte del Mare, Pescara; cathedral of Santa Maria Assunta, Teramo; Piazza Giambattista Vico, Chieti.
11. Below: night view of Palazzo dell'Emiciclo, L'Aquila.

# Humans have always been present in Abruzzo,

and there is proof in the Valle Giumentina, near Caramanico Terme (PE), a site dating back 300,000 years. However, Abruzzo's ethnic and cultural matrix can be identified most clearly in the ages of Bronze and Iron, with the arrival of the Indo-European races, a group of shepherd-farmers of warrior inclination, the forebears of the Italic tribes who spread across Abruzzo.

Thus, a combined crop and stock farming economy evolved and consolidated in the centuries that followed, influenced by the mountainous terrain and characterized by transhumance. When Rome was at the height of its power, magnificent towns developed, often built over existing Italic settlements, and with monumental forums, baths, temples, theatres and amphitheatres, whose remains can still be admired at Amiternum (AQ), Iuvanum (CH), Alba Fucens (AQ), Peltuinum (AQ). Many of these towns were destroyed or abandoned with the decline of the Empire, but Medieval towns then emerged on the remains of some of the more significant Roman urban structures.

In the past, the protohistoric site at Campovalano brought to light extraordinary items, now displayed in the museum in Campli (TE); more recently, new excavations revealed some perfectly preserved sites like Paludi di Celano (AQ), a village of pile-dwellings and annexed prehistoric necropolis, or the Fossa (AQ) necropolis where Hellenistic chamber

tombs contained intact bone-laminated palls, but there were even older graves, still perfectly delimited by circles and marked by piles of stones, dating back to the ninth century BC! Abruzzo's icon, the renowned Warrior of Capestrano, is an exceptional funeral statuette, now in Chieti Archaeological Museum. It was found by chance during a 1935 excavation and is considered one of the most significant archaeological testimonies of indigenous culture in Adriatic regions.

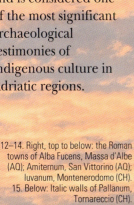

12–14. Right, top to below: the Roman towns of Alba Fucens, Massa d'Albe (AQ); Amiternum, San Vittorino (AQ); Iuvanum, Montenerodomo (CH).
15. Below: Italic walls of Pallanum, Tornareccio (CH).

**Many thousands of years of sheep farming conditioned the region in numerous ways**: the morphology of both the natural and agricultural landscape, the position and urban layout of settlements, the ancient communication routes. Transhumance – the ancient seasonal migration of shepherds and flocks from the Apennine pastures to the Puglia's Tavoliere plain along the sheep tracks – has been a constant in Abruzzo history since the Punic Wars, and in Roman times was even legislated. In 2019, the practice of Transhumance was officially recognized by UNESCO as intangible cultural heritage.

Regional territory still shows the traces of that back and forth of humans and flocks: sections of the ancient sheep track are still visible, for instance on the Navelli plain, cutting through the relics of ancient towns like Peltuinum, marking the legs of the journey. The extensive plateau, famous for its precious excellent saffron, is now dotted with the enigmatic presence of the sheep-track churches: simple, isolated architectures that served as refuges for shepherds on their long, exhausting trudge down to Puglia. Along the sheep tracks, the compact Medieval villages whose stark stone architecture hugs high slopes, the houses huddled together to create a border that protected the settlements with an extremely efficient defensive structure. These communities had their own special wealth, evident in the astounding standard of architecture with its numerous traces of art and possible chiefly thanks to the flourishing trade in sheep. Then

there is a singular stretch of mid-mountain Abruzzo, defined by terraces and drystone huts, the patient work of former generations who sought to wrest scraps of land and tiny pastures from the mountain. These tholos huts are numerous even today, especially on Majella, validating Abruzzo's rightful role as one of the Mediterranean areas identified by the presence of drystone constructions, a primitive yet effective building technique.

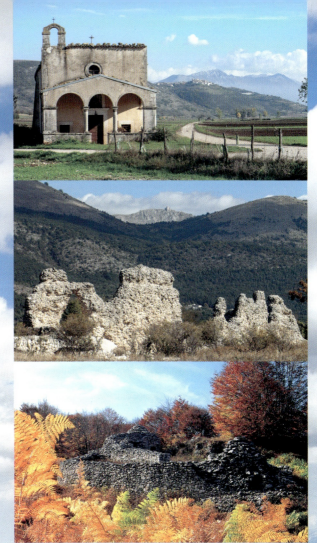

16–18. Right, top to below: the sheep-track church of Santa Maria delle Grazie on the Navelli plain (AQ); the walls of the ancient Roman town of Peltuinum crossed by the L'Aquila–Foggia sheep-track, Prata d'Ansidonia (AQ); La Valletta agricultural tholos hut complex, Passolanciano (CH).
19. Below: a flock grazing on the Campo Imperatore plateau.

20–22. Left, top to below: Celano castle (AQ); Cerrano coastal tower, Pineto (TE); Roccascalegna castle (CH).
23. Below: night view of the towers of Pacentro castle (AQ).

**Abruzzo's one thousand castles are the result of the complex,** fascinating fortification process that spread regularly from the time of the Norman conquest, rooted in a particularly fertile political, cultural and geographical context. Indeed, for many centuries, Abruzzo proliferated with every kind of fortification structure, ranging from simple, archaic towers to more complex, mighty fortresses.

Abruzzo has an extensive legacy of castles, both in number and in type, making this region an outright permanent open-air museum of defensive architecture. Today there are still countless castles, towers, keeps, boundary fortifications, fortresses, fortified villages and urban walls, characterizing the landscape all over Abruzzo, worthy of note.

**The sacred caves scattered throughout the mountains of Abruzzo** are one of the most fascinating aspects of the enduring spirit of this area. Caves are the age-old places where humans communed with Mother Earth. Grotta dei Piccioni, in Bolognano, has brought forth traces of propitiatory fertility rites performed about 6,500 years ago. So this was a sanctuary, just like the countless sacred caves found in the mountains here. Initially Hercules – the most popular divinity of the centre-south's rural world – was worshipped, later replaced by Saint Michael the Archangel, following the arrival of Christianity. The caves dedicated to Saint Michael, also called the "Holy Angel", are dotted along Abruzzo's Apennine ridge. The archangel cult was born in the cave-sanctuary of Mount Sant'Angelo, on the Gargano promontory, in the fifth century, and presumably came to Abruzzo with transhumant shepherds, becoming widespread with the Lombards. For centuries, the mountains of Abruzzo, in particular wild, rugged Majella, served as the perfect retreat for hermits: this was where the mystical experience of Pietro da Morrone (later Pope Celestine V) developed. The enchanting refuges and spectacular caves are a solemn testimony, generated by the mountains even at the highest altitudes, like the extraordinary Celestine hermitage of Sant'Onofrio, carved out of the rock and dominating the Peligna Valley, or the Roccamorice refuge of San Bartolomeo in Legio, laboriously carved from the folds of rock in an extreme act of devotion.

24–26. Left, top to below: Grotta Sant'Angelo hermitage, Palombaro (CH); San Bartolomeo in Legio hermitage, Roccamorice (PE); Grotta Sant'Angelo, Ripe in Civitella del Tronto (TE).
27. Facing page: Grotta Sant'Angelo hermitage, Balsorano (AQ).

**The ancient abbeys speak of the revolution put in place by the Benedictines**, beginning in Abruzzo in San Liberatore a Majella, nestling amidst the Serramonacesca (PE) woods. Applying the rule "ora et labora", the monks drove a vast action of economic, cultural and social reform. The quality of the Romanesque style in Abruzzo rose to the prestigious artistic heights. Subsequently the Cistercians, who were active entrepreneurs, colonizers and reclaimers, also developed a formidable integrated economy system through their monastery network. Abbey complexes, like San Clemente a Casauria (Castiglione a Casauria, PE), or San Giovanni in Venere (Fossacesia, CH) reveal the first hints of local Burgundian Cistercian and stand as austere, vigorous emblems of a monastic presence that translated its total territorial control into stone, frescoes and sculpture.

The monks were able stonemasons and created unique sculptures inside the region's loveliest churches: bas-reliefs, ambos, ciboria and candelabras are the crowning glory of Romanesque and Cistercian architecture. The Middle Ages left a profound impact on Abruzzo; anonymous master painters illustrated its form and colours on the walls of San Pietro ad Oratorium near Capestrano (AQ), and at Santa Maria di Ronzano near Teramo, at Santa Maria ad Cryptas near Fossa (AQ), at San Pellegrino near Bominaco (AQ), now considered some of the most precious cycles of Medieval painting in central-southern Italy.

28–30. Left, top to below: church of Santa Maria in Valleporclaneta, Rosciolo (AQ); abbey of San Bartolomeo della Nora, Carpineto Nora (PE); church of Santa Maria di Ronzano, Castel Castagna (TE).
31. Facing page: the interior of the abbey of San Clemente a Casauria, Castiglione a Casauria (PE).

## The Renaissance's fresh Humanist language

came late to Abruzzo and the new style penetrated slowly, throughout the 1400s. The façade of San Bernardino, in L'Aquila, produced in the 1500s Cola dell'Amatrice was the crowning moment and Renaissance Abruzzo's most significant example. In the vibrant fifteenth century the great local goldsmith and sculptor, Nicola da Guardiagrele established himself, creating monumental processional crucifixes and his masterpiece, the famous Teramo cathedral frontal (1443-8). From 1475 onwards the scene was dominated by sculptor Silvestro dell'Aquila, famous for his delicate polychrome terracotta Virgin Marys and his Saint Sebastian, the masterpiece of Abruzzo sculpture, now in L'Aquila Museum. The most outstanding artwork is by an anonymous hand, a master who worked in the 1420s, frescoing the church of San Silvestro, as well as the famous Beffi Triptych, also in L'Aquila Museum.

Teramo cathedral boasts a splendid fifteenth-century polyptych by Jacobello del Fiore. An unforgettable artist who left significant traces in Abruzzo was Andrea Delitio, a central character of the region's fifteenth-century painting, who produced not only the frescoes in Atri cathedral, but also the colossal Saint Christopher fresco for the portico of Guardiagrele's Santa Maria Maggiore cathedral, his only signed and dated (1473) work.

32–34. Left, top to below: apse frescoes in the church of San Silvestro, L'Aquila; detail of the fresco depicting *St Christopher* in the portico of the church of Santa Maria Maggiore, Guardiagrele (CH); Nicola da Guardiagrele's paliotto, Teramo cathedral.
35. Facing page: detail of Andrea Delitio's frescoes, Atri cathedral (TE).

# Abruzzo's Legacy of 1600s–1700s Masterpieces.

The canvases *Circumcision and Saints Carlo Borromeo and Francis of Assisi*, in Fara San Martino parish church (c. 1612), *Our Lady of Constantinople and Saints*, in the Pescocostanzo Collegiate (1614), and the *Madonna with Saint Francis of Assisi and Patron*, in the Colledimezzo parish church, are all by Tanzio da Varallo, a follower of Caravaggio.
He was one of the most illustrious names in a long series of Lombard presences found in Abruzzo from the fifteenth century onwards, part of the procession of merchants, masons, architects, stucco artists, and painters who were involved above all in modernization of religious buildings, following the trends dictated by new Baroque taste, then prevailing during the reconstruction required after the 1703 and 1706 earthquakes, which devastated mainly L'Aquila and Sulmona.
Several members of the Cicco family, famous Pescocostanzo stonemasons, also made phenomenal achievements in the field of architecture. Norberto Cicco designed and produced the splendid 1710 façade of Sulmona's SS Annunziata church, as well as that of the Santo Spirito church at Badia Morronese, which stands as one of the most complete and exquisite Baroque façades in Abruzzo.
Then, above all in the 1600s–1700s, the art of woodcarving reached its peak, when churches were decorated with sumptuous gilt wood altars, lavish pulpits and elaborate confessionals.
Ceilings and organs were truly spectacular, for instance the wooden ceiling in the Pescocostanzo Collegiate or in the splendid L'Aquila church of San Bernardino, made in 1724–6 by Ferdinando Mosca, of Pescocostanzo.

36. Facing page: the splendid Baroque façade of the SS Annunziata church, Sulmona (AQ).
37. Below: Tanzio da Varallo's canvas, Fara San Martino parish church (CH).

**The nineteenth century was an intense, vibrant time in Abruzzo**, and numerous local artists established themselves locally and beyond regional boundaries.
In Vasto, the four Palizzi brothers were a prime example, training at the Neapolitan school of Realism, as was the man of letters, Gabriele Rossetti, father of the more famous Dante Gabriele Rossetti, founder of the Pre-Raphaelite art movement. Teofilo Patini, born in Castel di Sangro, was a dynamic painter, mindful of the demands of the new century. He dedicated himself to social themes and depicted the troubling aspects of peasant life in his territory.
Abruzzo was always present in the works of Gabriele D'Annunzio: the variety of landscape, the sea, the mountains, art, underpin his writing. Together with painter Francesco Paolo Michetti, musician Francesco Paolo Tosti, and sculptor Costantino Barbella, he founded the famous, late–nineteenth-century artistic circle at the Francavilla "conventino". Michetti became extremely famous for his spectacular depictions of Abruzzo folklore and countryside, as did the famous Caramanico sculptor Nicola D'Antino.
From the end of the 1800s to the present day, a family of artists has emerged for its prolific work in various kinds of art: painting, etching, lithography, pottery, sculpture, and mosaic.
The Cascellas, with father Basilio and his sons Tommaso, Michele and Gioacchino, then Tommaso's sons Andrea and Pietro, and now new generations successfully established outside the region.

38. Facing page: *Iorio's Daughter* by Francesco P. Michetti.
39–41. Right, top to below: Teofilo Patini's *Latte e Vanga*; view of Vasto in a painting by Nicola Palizzi; *Verginelle* by Basilio Cascella.

# Abruzzo, the Green Region: Nature Parks and Protected Areas

Parks are not just fenced-off areas, but tangible proof that a community has acknowledged the intrinsic, undeniable value of a territory. The three national parks (the historic Abruzzo – Lazio – Molise National Park, and the more recent Gran Sasso–Laga Mountains and Majella national parks), and Sirente-Velino Regional Park, as well more than thirty nature reserves and oases, are managed directly by municipalities, by the State Forestry Service, or as joint ventures with environmentalist associations.

With about 30% of its territory under protection Abruzzo has earned the title of "Region of Parks". The sheer variety of lushness of its natural landscapes makes Abruzzo a haven of ecological and environmental values. The particular morphology of inland areas, the gentle subcoastal hills and the marine environments mean truly powerful habitats.

Noble, rugged Gran Sasso, with its white limestone, dominates the Apennines; just beneath the north face of Corno Grande, there is Calderone, the only glacier on the Apennines and the southernmost in all Europe. South of the massif boundless Campo Imperatore stands at 1,800m in altitude.

The Laga Mountains, with their springs, rivers and forests.

Mount Majella, bound to the Morrone massif, soars on the Abruzzo skyline between the sea and the Apennine chain: the mother mountain for local people since time immemorial. From the mountains to the sea, the

42. Facing page: ascent to the summit of Corno Grande overlooking the Adriatic Sea, Gran Sasso – Monti della Laga National Park.
43–45. Right, top to below: Costa dei Trabocchi Park with the Punta Le Morge trabocco, Torino di Sangro (CH); Mottagrossa beach, Casalbordino (CH); Punta Aderci dunes, Vasto (CH).

hills bear evident signs of its ongoing evolution, clay sliding downstream, where the badlands carve out the horizon's contours. With surprising nooks of unspoiled nature lingering along 130km of coastline.

If Villetta Barrea's ranges of Austrian pinewoods speak the "language" of European nature, then endemic species, found only in specific locations, speak the "dialect" of nature: the Marsican iris (Iris marsica); L'Aquila's rare milk-vetch (Astragalus aquilanus); Majella's bindweed (Soldanella minima), gentian (Gentiana magellensis) and buttercup (Ranunculus magellensis), are some of the loveliest, most interesting flora. One of the Abruzzo massif's most famous high-altitude flowers is the Apennine edelweiss (Leontopodium nivale). One of the rarest is the splendid lady's slipper orchid (Cypripedium calceolus) which, on the entire Apennine chain, blossoms only in Abruzzo, Lazio & Molise National Park and on Mount Majella. These mountain habitats, with their perennial snowfields and relict glacial plants, like mountain avens, lady's mantle, snow gentian, slope down to the coast with its Mediterranean maquis of holm-oak and myrtle, passing through mountain pasture, with splendid beech groves and hill woods of durmast and hop hornbeam. Dwarf pine vegetation, virtually unknown elsewhere on the Apennine, is quite widespread only on Majella.

The stars of Abruzzo fauna are certainly the Marsica brown bear, symbol of Abruzzo – Lazio – Molise National Park, the Apennine chamois, symbol of Gran Sasso & Monti della Laga National Park, and the wolf, symbol of Majella National Park.

46–48. Right, top to below: Valle delle Cento Fonti, Gran Sasso – Monti della Laga National Park; Passo San Leonardo in Majella National Park; Prati del Sirente in the Sirente–Velino Regional Park. 49–50. Facing page: a Marsica brown bear; the Aceretta valley in Abruzzo – Lazio – Molise National Park.

# L'Aquila
## and province

# L'Aquila

## The City

It is said that L'Aquila was founded when the Valle dell'Aterno feudatories requested permission from the papal authorities to build a town on the hill that separated the counties of Amiterno and Forcona, near the castle of Acquili (which, of course, gave the future L'Aquila its name), linked to the countless water sources present in the territory. The request came from the desire to free populations in the Aterno valley's fortified villages from the feudal power of the Emperor Frederick II. Thus, the earliest nucleus of the city was established and officially recognized by a diploma issued in 1254, by Swabian king, Konrad IV. L'Aquila was destroyed in 1259 by Manfred, son of Frederick II, and rebuilt thanks to King Charles of Anjou, to express his gratitude for the help received from the Aquilans in the historic battle of Tagliacozzo, which marked the end of Swabian rule and the arrival of the Angevins, in 1268. The urban plan that ensued for reconstruction split the

51. On the previous double page: the city of L'Aquila.
52. Facing page: detail of the high altar in the basilica of San Bernardino.
53. Below: detail of the urban plan of L'Aquila engraved by Jean Bleau (1663).

L'Aquila is built on a hill slope to the left of the River Aterno, against the splendid backdrop of the Gran Sasso d'Italia massif. The city is located on the main route between Naples and Florence, in a strategic position along what was known as the "Via degli Abruzzi", an extremely important road in Medieval Italy. As well as being home to a famous market, for much of the Middle Ages L'Aquila was the economic hub for mountain Abruzzo, gathering, processing and trading sheep and cattle, wool and wool fabric, almonds and saffron. Founded in the 13th century, the city was the start of the L'Aquila–Foggia sheep track and for almost three centuries exercised total control over the territory from which it had flourished. This control was applied through the political and institutional system of the Guilds, including the Woolmakers, founded on the exploitation of sheep-farming resources. The indulgence conceded by Celestine V to the church of Santa Maria di Collemaggio, where he was crowned Pope in 1294, meant that the city became one of the most popular destinations for pilgrimages. The extraordinary beauty of the distinctive surroundings make it easy to understand the importance of sheep farming and the great monastic orders in mapping out what was, and continues to be, a unique landscape in Italy.

city into districts, so the inhabitants of the fortified settlements moving there could build their own houses and a church, replicating their village of origin (the story of the 99 founder villages is a myth). The city was then split into four quarters (quarti), one for each district of immigration and still identifiable today: San Giorgio, with the parish church of Santa Giusta di Bazzano, and Santa Maria with the parish church of Santa Maria di Paganica, which included Forcona; San Pietro with the parish church of San Pietro di Coppito, and San Giovanni with the parish church of San Marciano di Roio, which included Amiterno. Most of the churches built by the founding villages were erected between the late–13th–early–14th centuries. In 1316, the massive urban fortifications were completed, with 86 towers and 12 gates, some of which are still visible.

The old urban layout has noticeable height differences and irregularities that accentuate the city's setting against the marvellous backdrop of L'Aquila's peaks. It is also a treasure trove of artistic gems: precious elements of religious architecture, splendid noble mansions rendered unique by their famous, splendid courtyards and, last but not least, the masterpiece of military architecture constituted by the 16th-century **castle** (*see box on p. 39*). The fortress was never used for important military operations and was seriously damaged during WWII, then in the post-war period the city authorities transferred it from the Defence to the Education department, and after restoration under the superintendent of the time, Chierici, it became the home of the Abruzzo and Molise Monuments and Gallery Superintendency, and the **Abruzzo National Museum** (*see box p. 40*), which documents the region's artistic culture at very high level. Following the 2009 earthquake, the **MUNDA** has been moved to the former slaughterhouse and will stay there until the castle is completely restored. The castle also hosts the Auditorium, the Società Aquilana dei Concerti, a conference room and L'Aquila's National Geophysics Institute observatory.

Not far from the castle, in Piazza Battaglione Alpini L'Aquila, there is the **Fontana Luminosa** fountain sculpture by Nicola d'Antino of Caramanico (1880–1966), who transformed the city's squares and fountains during the 1930s construction wave. The fountain stands at the end of Corso Vittorio Emanuele while the two rounded 1930s buildings that open the "Corso Stretto", with Achille Pintonello's Casa del Combattente to the right and to the left Vincenzo Di Nanna's Palazzo Leone, which form

## L'Aquila Castle

Italy has many fortresses, although few are in a good state of repair, and that of L'Aquila is one of the best. It was built at the highest point of the city, designed by the Spanish military architect Pirro Aloisio Scrivà (who was also entrusted with the two prestigious projects for the building of Castel Sant'Elmo, in Naples), who began work in 1534, during a period of extensive military reinforcement of this area, ordered by Don Pedro da Toledo, appointed viceroy in 1532, during the Spanish dominion of Southern Italy. The entire construction is hallmarked by use of the most modern fortification techniques for that era. The fortress is a square building, with four massive corner bastions with lancet design, combined with curtain walls and original double orillons that were intended to double the number of cannon, increasing flanking fire power. There is a moat, not designed to be flooded, originally crossed by a party-mobile wooden drawbridge, demolished in 1833 and replaced by the current stone bridge, set on piers installed so as to offer no protection to attackers who pushed as far as the moat. We arrive at an entrance marked with its handsome stone portal by Aquilan sculptor Pietro di Stefano, surmounted by the lavish pediment with Charles V's double-headed eagle coat of arms.

The building is set around a square court with an entrance on the south-east side, with a double-order portico on sturdy pillars which, in Scrivà's designs, was probably intended to encircle the entire courtyard. In 1606 and in 1698 several garrison buildings were added, north west and north east respectively, whereas the storey added to the main façade, over the loggia, is of a later date.

The polygonal compound surrounded by ramparts rises steeply out of the moat, which was dug out of the hill spur and produced the material for the surrounding earthwork. The massive walls, sloping upwards for about half of their height, vary from ten metres at the base to five at the top of the curtain walls. Each of the four ramparts has two ample, overlapping casemates, vaulted roofs with a circular opening in the top for discharging smoke; each casemate has a round air space, with a dual function of relieving the weight on lower vaults and multiplying the number of cannons. All the basement casemates have stairs leading to the underlying countermine level, an original defence expedient constituted by a series of tunnels running under the moat and inside the foundation walls, enabling enemy mines to be intercepted.

54. Facing page: Nicola d'Antino's *Fontana Luminosa* fountain.
55. Above: the 16th-century fort.

# Museo Nazionale d'Abruzzo dell'Aquila

The Museum was opened during the restoration and upgrading of the Spanish fortress, under the then Superintendent Umberto Chierici, from 1949 and 1951. The core of the museum's assets came from the collections of the former Civic and Diocesan Museums, which included many of the most representative expressions of regional art. on the first floor we will find Medieval icons and wooden sculptures, and Renaissance masterpieces like L'Aquila cathedral's processional cross by Nicola da Guardiagrele (1434), and the wooden sculpture of St Sebastian by the great Silvestro dell'Aquila, a significant figure in Abruzzo Renaissance sculpture. An especially noteworthy piece is the *Enthroned Madonna and Child* triptych, with side panels of the *Nativity*, *Annunciation to the Shepherds*, *Transit* and *Coronation of the Virgin*, a 15th-century (1410–15) work from Santa Maria del Ponte, in Beffi, near Tione degli Abruzzi. The opus is by an artist known as the Maestro del Trittico di Beffi, a major figure in early-1400s Abruzzo art, today pinpointed by scholars as the Teramo artist Leonardo Di Sabino. The collection of religious art includes pieces by Francesco Montereale, an artist who was very active in L'Aquila in the early 1500s (Room I); by Pompeo Cesura, an important Aquilan painter of the 16th century, a disciple of the great master Raphael (Room II); Giulio Cesare Bedeschini, the most significant Aquilan artist of the 1600s (Room IV). There is an extraordinary fossil display of *Archidiskodon Meridionalis Vestinus* (435cm high, 650cm long), a particularly common species in the Aquilan basin during the Pleistocene period, found in 1954 in the Madonna della Strada di Scoppito district, recomposed and consolidated by the University of Rome's Institute of Geology and Palaeontology. There is also an interesting archaeological section, whose core came from the collection of Prince Francesco Caracciolo's mansion in Barisciano, in the mid-18th century Other precious relics came from excavations undertaken by Antonio De Nino and Nicolò Persichetti during the 1800s, in the area of ancient *Amiternum*. Some of the pieces present are extremely interesting, for instance the so-called "Calendario Amiternino" (c. 20 AD); the stone reliefs depicting a funeral ceremony and a gladiator battle; the lid of a cremation urn with serpent, of the Augustan age or slightly later, as well as a collection of celebratory or funeral epigraphs.

Pending the reconstruction of the fortress following earthquake damage, the new **MUNDA** museum has been set up in L'Aquila's former slaughterhouse, a fascinating industrial archaeology complex near the Fontana delle 99 Cannelle fountain, although the Mammoth has remained in the castle. This temporary home hosts a selection of about 60 archaeological finds and about 120 works of art from the Middle Ages to Modern, which had been on display in the castle before the 2009 earthquake.

56. Above: detail of the tempera on panel painting by the Maestro del Trittico di Beffi.
57. Below: Roman stone bas-relief depicting a funeral ceremony, Amiternum.
58. Facing page: interior of the Auditorium del Parco.

a new gateway to the old town. The stunning **Auditorium del Parco** is a short distance away, inside the park around the Forte Spagnolo fort. This wooden auditorium was designed by architect Renzo Piano after the mass destruction left by the 6 April earthquake and inaugurated in 2012. The architecture comprises three blocks, their surfaces textured by the horizontal cadence of coloured wooden slats. The central block is the largest of the three and houses the auditorium itself, with a strong colour impact, and is tilted with respect to the ground line, an inclination that corresponds to that of the steps of the stalls inside. The other two blocks, connected with the central building by iron, glass and wooden walkways, are service premises for public and performers.

The **Madonna del Soccorso church**, built in 1469–72 near the Castello gate, is interesting as is the adjacent Olivetan convent and its lovely cloister.

The handsome Renaissance façade, attributed to Silvestro dell'Aquila and erected in about 1496, pays homage to the more famous Santa Chiara church in Assisi, with the two orders surmounted by a gable and unusual Tuscan-style two-tone horizontal bands in white and pink stone. The lunette above the portal, similar to the smaller Collemaggio lunettes, was frescoed by Paolo da Montereale with a *Madonna and Child with Saints*; on the architrave, the crest of the Olivetan Order, which officiated the church until the late 1700s. There was a precious carved wooden tabernacle, but it has been stolen. The same chapel contains the tomb of Jacopo di Notar Nanni (1504) who the most important banker in L'Aquila along with his brother Nicola, and two of its greatest patrons. The church was restored following the damage caused by the 2009 earthquake.

Piazza **San Silvestro** is home to the eponymous church, with its spectacular façade, and other important buildings, like **Palazzo Branconio** and **Palazzo dei Rustici**. The church was built in the 13th–14th century and was rebuilt in stages during the following century. It was given a nave-and-two-aisle layout, separated by columns, with three polygonal apses and no transept. The ample prospect with horizontal coping and the grand, recently modified belfry on the right, were part of the 14th-century interventions. There are some significant works of art in this building. The current configuration of the church is the result of a restoration undertaken in 1967–9 which brought to light its ancient structure when the 1700s finishes were removed. There are some splendid surviving fresco cycles in the great apse bowl, brought to light back in 1946, dated late–1300s–early–1400s, painted by a prestigious painter, known as the San Silvestro or Beffi Triptych Maestro, from his fundamental opus, now in the MUNDA in L'Aquila and now attributed to Teramo artist Leonardo Di Sabino. Apart from frescoes by Paolo da Montereale and his son Francesco, there

59. Above: detail of the frescoes in the main apsidal basin in the church of San Silvestro.
60. Facing page: *Fontana delle 99 Cannelle* fountain.

is a significant *Baptism of Constantine* (dated c. 1617), by the painter Baccio Ciarpi (1574–1644), a pupil of Caravaggio, and master to Pietro da Cortona. There is also the commendable Branconio chapel, erected in the 16th century, located at the bottom of the left aisle, enhanced in 1625 by Giulio Cesare Bedeschini's frescoes; the chapel once housed the precious *Visitation* that Raphael painted in 1520 for Marino Branconio (the canvas on the altar is a copy), but it was soon removed and is now an exhibit in the Prado Museum, Madrid. During recent restorations to repair damage caused by the 2009 earthquake, the removal of the plasterwork brought to light fragments of frescoes on the side walls and 13th-century paintings came to light in the sacristy.

Continuing along Viale Giovanni XXIII and turning towards Porta Rivera, there is one of the city's most famous monuments, and certainly the oldest: the **99 Cannelle fountain**. It was built in 1272, near the River Aterno, by Tancredi da Pentima, as indicated by the plaque walled into the central section, although today's appearance is the result of various interventions. The original façade had 15 spouts and white stone grotesque masks, alternating with red tiles sculpted with a central rosette; several decades later the white and pink chequerboard wall was added (a similar finish was also being used at that time for the Collemaggio basilica). In 1578 the second bowl was added, and in 1582–5 the main façade and two bowls were extended, applying a medieval parapet to the lower bowl, with small, octagonal semi pilasters; then the left prospect was added, and another set against the walls; more grotesques and spouts were also installed, configuring the small piazza into a trapezoid form (the creator of the elaborate new mascarons was Alessandro Ciccarone, of Poggio Picenze). The fountain was damaged during the 1703 earthquake and was restored, repairing decorations, coats of arms and inscriptions that form the central plaque. Other interventions came about in 1744 (the square was paved) and in 1871, when a six more spouts were added bottom right, to reach the legendary 99, commemorating the fortified villages that were said to have founded the city together. In 1975 the Italian Postal Service dedicated a 70 Lire stamp to the fountain. In 1991-4, essential restoration reconditioned the original hydraulics and identified the springs. It was restored after the 2009 earthquake.

Returning towards the city centre and taking Via XX Settembre, beyond the Villa Comunale park, we find the city's most iconic monument: the **basilica of Santa Maria di Collemaggio** (*see box p. 44*). The basilica was consecrated in 1288, although it was incomplete and was still being built in 1294, at the time of the coronation of Pope Celestine V, with whom the magnificent place of worship is closely linked.

As part of the restoration of the church of Santa Maria di Collemaggio, after the 2009 earthquake, the important green lung, the nearby Parco del Sole, was redeveloped. The park's pride is the *Amphisculpture*, a natural amphitheatre landscaped by US artist Beverly Pepper and located on a hill slope. A work of land art fusing art, architecture and design. Accessing the park from the north entrance, the top of the auditorium cavea is marked by the *Narni Columns*, two monolithic obelisks in COR-TEN weathering steel that enhance the entrance to the amphitheatre.

Returning towards the city centre we find the **Cristo Re church**, in Viale Crispi, designed by Alberto Riccoboni (1933–5). Just behind Corso Federico II, opposite the church of Santa Giusta, we find **Palazzo Centi**, erected in 1752–66 by Donato Rocco Cicchi, of Pescocostanzo, for Gian Lorenzo Centi. The palazzo is one of L'Aquila's loveliest examples Baroque civil architecture, with a characteristic prothyrum supporting the intricate balcony.

In Piazza **Santa Giusta** we find the church of the same name, with a 1300s façade vaunting an elegant portal, its lunette frescoed in the mid-1500s by Giovanni Antonio of Lucoli, surmounted by a refined rose window, the largest in the region. Today the interior of this church, founded in the late–13th century, is dated 1620s and overall, the building was not subject to any radical changes after the 1703 earthquake, so only the presbytery roof was rebuilt. The counterfaçade chancel – installed with a priceless 17th-century organ – was built in 1617. Inside we find a precious wooden choir, the sumptuous gilt carved wood high altar by Giovanni Carinola of Guardiagrele, and several marvellous canvases by Baccio

Ciarpi and Giuseppe Cesari, also known as Cavalier d'Arpino (1568-1640). During the restoration after the 2009 earthquake, fragments of ancient frescoes and the remains of the original façade's rose window (where the Palazzo della Prefettura or del Governostands). The images of the building sadly became the iconic symbol of that tragic event.

Returning to Corso Federico II it is easy to reach Piazza della Prefettura. There are some impressive paintings by Teofilo Patini (1840–1906) – *Bestie da Soma* (1886), and *Pulsazioni e Palpiti* (1888) – in the council chamber at Palazzo della Prefettura, originally the Augustine convent founded in 1282, restructured in the 1700s then converted and adapted to use as a theatre in the 1800s.

On the same square we find the **church di Sant'Agostino**, seen in its 1700s reconstruction over the site of an older complex. It is a splendid example of L'Aquila Baroque architecture and one of the most significant central-plan buildings, rebuilt to a design by Giovan Battista Contini after the 1703 earthquake. Begun in 1710 on the site of an older complex, was completed in 1725 and improved in later years with several refinements. The striking building comprises a central oval chamber, with a tall cupola, the straight axes marked by the entrance, the deep choir and the major chapels; the diagonal axes are marked in the smaller chapels. The two-order façade has a striking and original design, with the lower front framed by the order and ending in a flattened tympanum, whereas the upper section is set back with a surface supporting an octagonal counterfort block that encloses the cupola, surmounted by the clerestory. There are several valuable paintings by Vincenzo Damini here. The 2009 earthquake caused considerable damage and the rebuilding plans with convert the entire complex into a major library project.

In nearby Piazza del Duomo we find the **Santa Maria del Suffragio** or Anime Sante church (1713–1872), built to a design by the Roman architect Carlo Buratti, a pupil of Carlo Fontana. The dramatic, Borromini-inspired prospect was designed by Giovan Francesco Leomporri, built between 1770 and 1775, and the agile cupola designed by Valadier in about 1810. The church is home to several noteworthy works like the impressive 17th-century polyptych by Francesco Bedeschini, located in the apse, and Teofilo Patini's *St Anthony of Padua* (1897), in the first chapel on the left. A priceless organ was made in 1897 by Pacifico

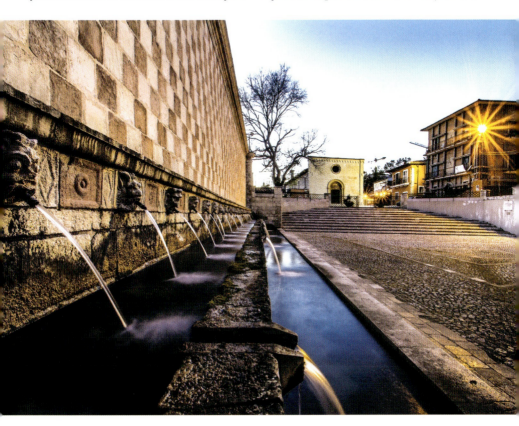

# Basilica of Santa Maria di Collemaggio, L'Aquila

The basilica of Santa Maria di Collemaggio is set on the hill which was the starting point for the *Tratturo Magno*, the principal sheep track that went from L'Aquila to Foggia. The presbytery was rebuilt a first time in 1315, following its collapse, then again in 1353 following the damage suffered during the 1349 earthquake. The striking façade with horizontal coping was probably begun in the early 1300s, enhanced by the geometric red-and-white stone pattern that creates the lovely two-tone effect, was completed by the mid–15th century. The lower part, which is particularly elaborate, includes a splendid central portal, framed by majestic piers, elegantly sculpted into orders of niches, housing six mutilated statues of saints, with cuspidate tympanums. A Cosmatesque moulding in geometrical motifs, isolating the smaller rosettes surmounting the side portals, curves to shadow the archivolt of the central portal and divides the lower section into another two parts. The central rose window is extremely sophisticated, commanding the upper part of the façade. The Holy Door or "Porta Santa", on the left-hand side, was named in the 1400s by analogy with the holy Roman doors linked to Holy Year rites. This door also opens for the city's annual jubilee, from the evening of 28 to the evening of 29 August. The door is said to be slightly older than the lunette fresco, by Antonio di Atri, dated 1397, depicting the *Virgin and Child between St John the Baptist and St Celestine*, who holds the Pardon Bull. At the top of the archivolt there is one of the city's oldest coats of arms, featuring a stylized eagle. Santa Maria di Collemaggio has a nave and two aisles separated by lancet arches set on octagonal pillars and delimited by three arches towards the transept; the latter is also divided into three bays, with a deep polygonal choir and two side chapels. Although the basilica has been transformed and restored, and undergone complete stylistic and spatial reinterpretation (beginning in the mid–1600s and completed following the earthquake in 1703), it has retained its Medieval plan, restored in the controversial 1970s intervention, when the Baroque finish was dismantled. The restoration brought to light some precious frescoes on the Gothic altars, carved out of the thick side walls, and which include a *Crucifixion* and a splendid head of a *Blessed Nun*, painted in the late 1300s or early 1400s by Antonio di Atri. The priceless canvases shown on the walls include some by Carlo Ruther (c. 1603–1703), of the Life of Celestine V, whose tomb is a Renaissance masterpiece installed in the basilica, made by Girolamo da Vicenza in 1517 to a commission by the Woolmakers Guild, the city's most important corporation for the sheep-farming trade. The adjacent monastery of Celestine monks was built at the

same time as the basilica and has been refurbished many times over the centuries. There is an admirable 16th-century cloister, with its historic well, and a 15th-century refectory, called the Sala Celestiniana, now used for conventions and conferences, decorated with a vast 1500s fresco by Saturnino Gatti.

Each year, on 29 August, the basilica celebrates the **Perdonanza Celestiniana**, commemorating the special indulgence instituted by Celestine V. A procession starts from the city hall and continues as far as the Holy Door, where the Mayor hands the Bull of Foundation to the Bishop. After the collapse of the transept vaults and parts of the roof, the arches and the dome following the 2009 earthquake, the basilica was restored and is now open to the public.

61. Facing page: the interior of Santa Maria di Collemaggio basilica.
62. Above: the façade.
63. Left: the opening of the Holy Door during the *Perdonanza Celestiniana* pageant.

64. Above: the interior of SS Massimo e Giorgio cathedral.
65. Facing page: Piazza Duomo with the church of Santa Maria del Suffragio (left) and the cathedral (right).

Inzoli, a descendent of one of the most famous families if organ makers from Northern Italyi.

Behind the Santa Maria del Suffragio church we find the **Cancelle**, an interesting example of typical simple Aquilan home–workshops, built in the early 1400s, now transferred to Via Simeonibus, but originally on the site now occupied by Palazzo delle Poste.

The **SS Massimo e Giorgio cathedral** was originally built in the 13th century, in Piazza del Duomo, although its current appearance is the result of a reconstruction following the 1703 earthquake. The original layout was a nave and two aisles, supported by octagonal supports, and a surviving section can be seen in the boundary wall on the right, finished in ashlar and with trefoil single-lancet windows. In 1711 Sebastiano Cipriani designed a majestic new church whose interior was completed in 1780. The vault was painted in tempera (1886–7) depicting the figures of the city's four protectors: St Maximus, St Bernardino of Siena, St Pietro Celestino and St Equitius. The vast rectangular space, with a barrel vault ceiling, is cadenced by very long, connecting side chapels, closed by small round rooms, next to the choir. The Neoclassical façade, with two corner belfries, was completed in 1928, to a design by Giovan Battista Benedetti. Inside there are some remarkable works, including Silvestro dell'Aquila's sepulchre for Cardinal Agnifili (1476–80), rebuilt after the 1703 earthquake, and priceless 1700s paintings by Girolamo Cenatiempo and Donato Teodoro. The altar left of the transept has a canvas by Teofilo Patini depicting *St Carlo Borromeo and the Milan Plague* (1888). There is also an exceptional 1700s wooden choir carved by Ferdinando Mosca of Pescocostanzo (1685–1773).

Along the lanes that lead off from the cathedral, we find the **church of Santa Maria di Roio**, with a striking 1300s rose window. Inside, a striking 1600s high altar in polychrome marble, by Ercole Ferrata of Como (1610–86), and the Francesco da Montereale's *Deposition*. The church was damaged by the 2009 earthquake.

The **church of SS. Marciano e Nicandro**, which already existed in 1276, is now seen in the guise of the rebuilding that followed the 1703 earthquake of some of the oldest buildings, dating to the mid-13th century. The lunette above St Marcian in the secondary portal to the right is decorated with a bas relief depicting the *Madonna with Blessing Child and two Seraphim*, attributed to Silvestro dell'Aquila. The church was seriously damaged by the 2009 earthquake.

The **church of Sant'Antonio di Padova** (1646), located near San Marciano, is certainly worthy of note, with its Baroque interior and truly priceless works, including the ceiling (1726–8) in gilt carved wood by Ferdinando Mosca of Pescocostanzo, with a canvas by Vincenzo Damini in the centre. The splendid high altar (1736) is made from 27 Castelli ceramic tiles decorated by Carlantonio Grue. The altar image of *St Anthony* was painted in 1643 by Francesco Bedeschini. The church was seriously damaged by the 2009 earthquake, especially the interior decoration.

Also nearby, the ancient Via Sassa building that was the home of the Poor Clares, founded by Blessed Antonia, since 1447, and is home to the Museo del Monastero della Beata Antonia. The **Beata Antonia church** has some excellent frescoes, including two fragments of murals that Andrea De Litio painted here, set into the walls on either side of the altar: a *Madonna and Child* and an *Adoration of the Child*. There is also a *Crucifixion* attributed to Paolo da Montereale, and another by Francesco da Montereale. The church was seriously damaged by the 2009 earthquake.

Along Via Sassa we find the square that is home to the **church of San Biagio di Amiternum**, built in the 13th century although its current appearance reflects the 1700s. Inside, Lalle II Camponeschi's precious funeral monument, made in 1432 by Gualtiero de Alemanna, who also made the sepulchre of

Restaino Caldora in Sulmona, at the Badia Morronese. In the same square we also find the **church of Santa Caterina Martire**, rebuilt in the 18th century to a design by Florentine Ferdinando Fuga (1699–1782), with an intriguing but incomplete façade. Both churches were seriously damaged by the 2009 earthquake.

In Via Patini we can see the noteworthy **Signorini Corsi house–museum**, which was the home of the family of Aquilan merchants who came here from Como in about the mid–1700s. Apart from some priceless 16th- and 17th-century furnishings, there are many other rare objects, including a collection of priceless Italian paintings dated 14th–15th century, including a 15th-century *Nativity* by the Botticelli school, the *Nativity of the Virgin* (16th century) by Baccio Bandinelli, a *Martyrdom of St Lawrence* (17th century) by Giovanni Battista Caracciolo, known as Battistello, and paintings of the Neapolitan school. The building was seriously damaged by the 2009 earthquake.

From Corso Vittorio Emanuele it is easy to reach the **basilica of San Bernardino** and its wonderful interiors (*see box p. 48*), turning onto the eponymous street at the junction called the "Quattro Cantoni".

Near San Bernardino we find the **Teatro Comunale** (1854–72). If we return to the Quattro Cantoni and continue along Corso Vittorio Emanuele as far as Piazza Santa Maria di Paganica, we find the church of the same name as well as **Palazzo Ardinghelli**. Despite a series of transformations, this mansion is one of the most impressive examples of 1700s Aquilan civil architecture, which developed thanks to the influence of a great Roman tradition. The palazzo was commissioned by the last members of the Florentine Ardinghelli family, to a design by Roman architect Francesco Fontana in the square opposite Santa Maria Paganica, and built between 1732 and 1742. It then became the property of the Marquis Giovanni Cappelli and following a 1928 design was completed in 1955, with the addition of the projecting staircase, unique to L'Aquila. The monumental façade has a dual order, and the piano nobile windows have elegant curved gables surmounted by the mezzanine lights connected to the elaborate cornice with brackets. The ashlared portal leads to an unusual exedra courtyard, and although it is small, it is the most striking element in the entire building. The reception salon staircase is especially striking, with the ceiling frescoed by Venetian artist Vincenzo Damini, painted in about the mid–1700s. In 2019 it became the Abruzzo branch of Rome's **MAXXI**, Museo Nazionale delle Arti del XXI secolo.

In the same square we admire the splendid façade of the **church of Santa Maria di Paganica**, one of the oldest in the city (the additional storey is dated 18th century). The church was almost totally rebuilt after the 1703 earthquake, over the remains of an older Medieval building (late–13th–early–14th century), which include two portals englobed in the side prospects, the lower section of the mighty belfry (demolished in 1557), and the façade

# The Basilica of San Bernardino, L'Aquila

This is the most important building erected in the city in the mid-15th century, although it was transformed during the 18th century, after the 1703 earthquake. It is the region's biggest church and the splendid façade designed by Cola dell'Amatrice, expresses the Renaissance style in all its splendour. It was built in honour of St Bernardino of Siena, and has a nave and two aisles, connected to an octagonal room surrounded by radial chapels, and is characterized by an unusual combination between lengthwise and central plan, applying design principles far removed from the typical mendicant friar models of building and with clear references to the Florentine cathedral of Santa Maria del Fiore. Designed in 1525 by Cola dell'Amatrice, the façade has horizontal coping and is a unique example to be dated between the 15th-century construction and the 18th-century rebuilding. It has three horizontal strips and is cadenced vertically by four groups of coupled semi columns. The side portals are gabled, probably datable to the early 1600s. The central portal, dated latter half of the 16th century, has a high relief in the lunette depicting the *Madonna and Child between St Francis and St Bernardino presenting Girolamo da Norcia*.

The cupola, devastated by the 1703 earthquake, was rebuilt in 1725 under the supervision of Giovan Battista Contini, and the nave was enriched with a lavish wooden ceiling (1724–6) by Ferdinando Mosca of Pescocostanzo, but also has canvases (1732) and vault fresco by Girolamo Cenatiempo in the chapel dedicated to the Saint. Mosca also manufactured the magnificent organ on the counterfaçade. There are some priceless works here, including those by Silvestro dell'Aquila (1450–1504): a polychrome terracotta statue of a *Madonna and Child* (c. 1494–1500); the magnificent mausoleum of St Bernardino (1490–1505), finished by pupils; the funeral monument of Maria Pereyra Camponeschi (1488–90). Then there is a noteworthy glazed terracotta altarpiece by Andrea della Robbia, depicting the *Resurrection* (early 1500s); a valuable 16th-century canvas of the *Crucifixion* by Rinaldo Fiammingo, and 17th-century paintings by Giulio Cesare Bedeschini. Also worthy of note are the excellent *Miracle of St Anthony* and the *Adoration of the Magi* by Pompeo Cesura, the most important Aquilan painter of the mid-1500s and disciple of Raphael. Now used for cultural events, the marvellous convent refectory, known as the Cattedra Bernardiniana, vaunts lavish 1600s frescoes.

After the 2009 earthquake that caused serious damage including the collapse of the bell tower and destroyed the apse and dome, as well as parts of the convent, the church was recently restored and reopened to the public.

66–68. Below: left, the basilica nave; right, the organ and the chapel of the saint.
69. Facing page: the façade of the San Bernardino basilica.

with horizontal coping in travertine ashlar, enhanced by the elegant portal. In the lunette we can admire an *Enthroned Madonna and Child*, and on the architrave, showing the date 1308, there is a bas relief of *Christ and the Apostles*. The current layout of the interior, designed in about 1715 and completed in the late 1700s, features a generous nave with a barrel vault ceiling, cadenced by deep chapels alternating with smaller niches. The ceiling was painted in the early 1900s by Carlo Patrignani, a pupil of Patini. Three significant canvases by Vincenzo Damini are set in the third chapel to the left, whilst in the fourth chapel on the right we find a *Baptism of Jesus* attributed to Rinaldo Fiammingo. The church closes with a great transept and cupola, and the semi-circular apse, paying homage to spatial solutions adopted in Roman architecture. The church was seriously damaged by the 2009 earthquake.

The **Convitto Nazionale**, built in 1880-1, on the site of the ancient convent of San Francesco a Palazzo (1255) is in Piazza Palazzo. Today's building includes the cell where St Bernardino died (1444), and that is all that remains of the convent, the High School, whose assembly hall has a frescoed ceiling with the famous illustration by Teofilo Patini, *Flock Surprised by an Eagle on Gran Sasso* (1882), and the Provincial Library, named after Salvatore Tommasi (1813–88), the Abruzzo physician and patriot. The library was set up in 1848 and grew thanks to donations of precious private collections, now boasting 250,000 volumes and countless, rare items (illustrated codices, 15th-century incunabola, 16th-century books, manuscripts), including the first Italian translation of *Plutarch's Lives*, printed in 1482, in L'Aquila, by Adam of Rottweil, a pupil of Gutemberg). The manuscripts include 56 volumes by Antonio Ludovico Antinori (L'Aquila, 1704–78), fundamental for the history of Abruzzo.

Near Piazza Palazzo we find Piazza Santa Margherita, with **Palazzo Pica-Alfieri**, and the charming but unfinished **church of Santa Margherita** (Il Gesù), begun in 1636 and built in the classic Jesuit arrangement, then refurbished following the earthquake in 1703. Only the gabled portal and the stone finish at the base were completed of the original design. The inner walls and chapel vaults have lavish 17th–18th-century moulded decoration, and there are valuable paintings by Cenatiempo and Damini. In the second chapel to the right there is a marble sarcophagus containing the remains of St Equitius, the city's second patron.

If we continue along Via Roma, we reach the square with the 13th-century **church of San Pietro di Coppito**, example of a complex historical and building past. Today's façade was rebuilt in 1969–71, using several original elements of the traditional Aquilan design. The church is laid out as a large rectangular room, with exposed roof trusses, a small aisle on the right-hand side, attributed to the original layout. Inside we will see an apse to the west, a precious cycle of 14th-century frescoes relating the *Life of St George*, and a Gothic aedicule, left of the entrance, with 16th-century frescoes attributed to Paolo da Montereale, depicting a *Madonna and Child, St Anthony of Padua and St John the Baptist*. The church was restored after being badly damaged by the 2009 earthquake.

The **church of San Domenico** is nearby. It was built by French masons from 1309, commissioned by Charles II of Anjou to be called the church of Santa Maria Maddalena. It was rebuilt in the 1700s, perhaps designed by the Milanese Piazzola, who kept the surviving Medieval structures. The church was the original home of the precious *Our Lady of the Rosary*, by Saturnino Gatti (1463–1521), then taken to the MUNDI. The annexed convent complex was grazed by the 2009 earthquake, while the church suffered serious damage.

The **Vincenzo Rivera Speleology Museum** in Via Svolte della Misericordia is interesting and has several sections, with a branch at Stiffe, the location of the famous caves.

Just 3km outside of the city we find the **San Giuliano convent**, founded in 1415 with a small church, and completely restructured in about 1958, embracing the remains of the small 15th-century convent that had been built into the rock. Several of the convent rooms host the **Museum of Life and Human Sciences**, which opened in October 1997 to house scientific and artistic collections from the old San Giuliano museum. The structure has been designed applying state-of-the-art museum criteria, with display areas dedicated to natural sciences, and has an archaeological section

70–71. Below left: the convent cloister in the monumental complex of San Domenico, home of the Accademia, designed by architect Paolo Portoghesi.

72–73. Below right: night view of the arcade and monumental stained-glass window by the artist Franco Summa, 19th-century Palazzo dell'Emiciclo.

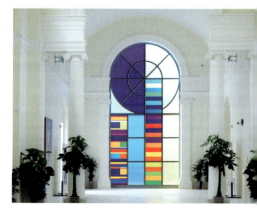

# Courtyards and Mansions

The noble residences of L'Aquila are very lavish and in particular they have splendid courtyards, elegantly enclosed by colonnaded porticoes, often with an upper loggia and monumental staircase. These are just some of the best courtyards: **Palazzo Dragonetti** (15th–16th century), in Via Santa Giusta, and **Palazzo Carli-Benedetti** (1495), in Via Accursio, both attributed to Silvestro dell'Aquila; **Palazzo Agnifili**, the only element of the ancient mansion built in 1400s–1500s, in Via del Cardinale; **Palazzo Franchi**, remains of the 16th-century dwelling in Via Sassa; Palazzo Alfieri (15th century), now the Istituto Santa Maria degli Angeli or delle Micarelli, in Via Fortebraccio; and the **Casa di Nicola di Notar Nanni** (15th century) in Via Bominaco. Opposite the Nicola di Notar Nanni house, there is **Palazzo Baroncelli-Cappa di Tussio** (16th century). The premises that surrounded its late–15th-century courtyard (entrance in Via Bominaco no. 21 or in Via Paganica no. 17–21) were the temporary home to **MUSPAC the Experimental Museum of Contemporary Art**, exhibiting a permanent collection of works by internationally-famous artists but moved to the new headquarters in Via Pasquale Ficara – Piazza D'Arti after the 2009 earthquake.

There are fine examples of civil architecture found throughout the city, like the sumptuous 18th-century prospects of Palazzo Quinzi (1725–30) in Via Bafile, designed by the architect Sebastiano Cipriani and completed by

74. Above: the courtyard of Palazzo Carli Benedetti, Via Accursio.
75. Below: the façade of Palazzo Ardinghelli, Piazza Santa Maria di Paganica.

Carlo Waldis in 1888; **Palazzo Pica-Alfieri** (1712–15), in Piazza Santa Margherita, with a monumental façade added in 1727 to a design, again by Cipriani; **Palazzo Benedetti** (1725–30), whose singular corner location connects Piazza San Biagio and Via Sassa; **Palazzo Rivera**, with its 1770 façade, and **Palazzo Persichetti** formerly Franchi with an impressive façade made in the late–1700s–early–1800s to a design by Ferdinando Fuga (1699–1782), both in Piazza Santa Maria di Roio; **Palazzo Antonelli-de Torres-Dragonetti** (1710–12), in Via Roio, whose striking façade was designed by the Roman Sebastiano Cipriani. 1800s buildings include Palazzo **dell'Emiciclo** or **dell'Esposizione** in the Villa Comunale park, whose elegant exedra was created in 1888 by the architect Carlo Waldis, now home to the regional government. Along Corso Vittorio Emanuele II we find the **Palazzo della Cassa di Risparmio** (1888). An interesting 1900s construction is **Palazzo di Giustizia** (1960–70), in Via XX Settembre.

with important prehistoric material, with a significant reconstruction of two tombs, one a chamber, explored in the extraordinary Fossa necropolis (7th century BC) and complete funeral furnishings. The location was seriously damaged by the 2009 earthquake. The atrium of the church, built between the 1400s and 1500s, renewed to its current Baroque forms in the mid–17th century (with paintings by Vincenzo Damini and Saturnino Gatti), leads into a library with over 45,000 volumes, including 15th-century incunabola, 16th-century publications, manuscripts and codices, with an important section on Abruzzo history and art.

Above the San Giuliano convent, up into the steep valley of the same name, we reach the tiny **sanctuary of Madonna Fore** (or Madonna di Cascio), once the home of the Our Lady of Seven Sorrows Congregation, now under the wing of today's church of Santa Maria dei Sette Dolori or the Addolorata (15th century), inside the city. The isolated church still has a lovely canvas of *Our Lady of Sorrows*, by Vincenzo Damini (1749).

L'Aquila is a university city and vaunts numerous faculties with a strong international vocation with ten degree courses. There are seven departments, five research centres and two service centres with cutting-edge research equipment, a museum complex and the mountain botanical garden.

L'Aquila, a city of knowledge, hosts the prestigious **Gran Sasso Science Institute – GSSI** in the heart of the city, opposite Palazzo dell'Emiciclo, home to the regional government, a research centre and an international PhD school. Founded in 2013 and recognized in 2016 as a school of advanced studies, known worldwide as a scientific centre of excellence.

L'Aquila, beating heart of regional culture, is home to numerous respected cultural institutions. The prestigious **Accademia di Belle Arti** opened its doors in 1969 in the building designed by architect Paolo Portoghesi, in the western suburbs of the city, where the School of Restoration is now located. Since the 1970s, the city opened the **Teatro Stabile** dell'Aquila, now elevated to Teatro Stabile d'Abruzzo, and is also home to the Istituzione Sinfonica, also active since 1970 and one of the 13 orchestral institutions recognized by the Italian state. Nor should we overlook the Conservatorio Alfredo Casella and the Abruzzo branch of the Centro Sperimentale di Cinematografia.

From 2015, from August to September, the historic centre of L'Aquila resounds with jazz music, offering a splendid setting for **Jazz Italiano per L'Aquila**, one of the most important Italian jazz events, with the artistic direction of Paolo Fresu, with concerts held all around the city to offer moral support to the population affected by the earthquake.

The great Perdonanza Celestiniana historic pageant is held every August, and in 2019 it was officially recognized by UNESCO as intangible cultural heritage. The very moving procession of the Dead Christ is held on Good Friday.

76. Below: a concert at the *Fontana delle 99 Cannelle* fountain for the 2018 "Jazz Italian per L'Aquila" event.

# Upper Aterno Valley

From L'Aquila we reach the nearby hamlet of Poggio di Roio, with the **Madonna di Roio sanctuary**, object of particular devotion by shepherding communities and one of Abruzzo's most important places of Marian worship, set along the sheep track. The 17th-century sanctuary building, with its richly decorated interior, was built over the 13th-century church of San Leonardo. Local legend says that in the last quarter of the 1500s, this was where the mule carrying the wooden statue of the Roio Madonna stopped. The statue was found in Puglia by transhumant shepherds from Lucoli who took it to Abruzzo. In the place chosen by the sacred effigy the **church of Santa Maria della Croce** was built from 1625 onwards. There are wonderful high altar frescoes, painted in 1676 by Giacomo Farelli (c. 1624–1709). Not far from the sanctuary there is the Pineta di Roio, a pine grove with a lovely view of the city of L'Aquila.

The small town of **LUCOLI** comprises several hamlets (the municipal offices are in Collimento) and is located in the Rio torrent valley. Between Collimento and Spogna we find the **church of San Giovanni Battista** is part of the ancient Benedictine abbey and was probably re-founded in 1077. After radical changes in the late–1300s–early–1400s, repairs and improvements that are still visible today were carried out during the latter half of the 1500s.

Poggio di Roio, Lucoli, Tornimparte, Coppito, Scoppito, Preturo, San Vittorino, Cavallari, Pizzoli, Barete, Cagnano Amiterno, Montereale, Capitignano, Campotosto.

Abruzzo's most important river, the Aterno, flows where the Laga Mountains meet the Gran Sasso massif. The peaks shimmer in the fish-rich Lake Campotosto, the largest in the Region, and the river flows along a spectacular gorge dug out in the course of time after having forged the Aquila basin. The fascinating villages we meet along the route, whose history entwines with that of L'Aquila, the regional capital, with numerous testimonies of art and history, are the theme of an itinerary that skirts along the course of the Aterno. It is not just the natural attractions that make this corner of Abruzzo unique, immersed in vegetation and part of Gran Sasso – Monti della Laga National Park: it is also the appeal of the archaeological sites, like Amiternum, and the priceless artworks found throughout the district, for a fascinating journey of discovery.

77. Below: the upper Aterno valley and Lake Campotosto.

In the 1640s–70s the church was renovated by the same craftsmen who worked in L'Aquila's most prestigious sites. Before recent interventions, the interior, with a nave and two aisles, had a simple barrel vault on octagonal pillars, later replaced by a wooden roof. The 17th-century high altar by Giuliano and Pietro Pedetti, and the 18th-century marble balustrade by Bernardo Ferradini, are particularly admirable. Restoration work brought to light priceless 15th-century frescoes of *St Laurence and St George*, seen on the pillars of the triumphal arch, a *St Francis* on a nave pillar, and a portrait of an old man on the left pillar, by Andrea De Litio, commissioned in 1461.

The **Beata Cristina church**, near the hamlet of Colle, is particularly noteworthy. Built in 1596 on the site where Blessed Cristina – born in the area in 1480 – went pray. Apart from the Baroque façade we should take note of the aisleless interior and a segmental arch barrel vault that is completely frescoed.

Taking the left of the Rio we see the **church of Santa Menna**, documented as early as the 1200s and perhaps enlarged in the first half of the 1400s. The noteworthy interior has a dual nave embellished with valuable 16th-century frescoes including the precious *Crucifixion* attributed to the school of Saturnino Gatti of San Vittorino, the most important painter and sculptor active in Abruzzo in the 1400–1500s.

From Collimento the road takes up to Casamaina and from here we reach Piano di Campo Felice, a well-known winter resort. Then there is **Villagrande**, home of the municipal offices of **TORNIMPARTE**, which comprises 18 hamlets scattered around the green surroundings. In Villagrande the **church of San Panfilo** was built in the late–12th–early–13th century and altered in the 15th then in the 18th century. The interior, with four aisles, preserves the splendid cycle of frescoes that Saturnino Gatti (1463–1521) painted in the apse, depicting the *Glory of God*, and on the arch intrados that separates the central aisle. On the left pillar of the apsidal arch there is a fresco of St Lucia by Francesco da Montereale (1466–1541). Other paintings by the same artist can be found in an aedicule in the right aisle, with the *Nativity* and above it the *Deposition*, and in the sacristy the *Entombed Christ*.

On the night between 30 April and 1 May in Villagrande and in the nearby hamlets, a rare tree ritual takes place, celebrating fertility and return of spring, known as *Ju calenne* (the May Day tree). The men of the village go to the woods where they cut down a large tree which they strip of its branches, and painstakingly carry to the churchyard where it is erected. The ritual must be completed before sunrise.

In Coppito there is the important **church of San Pietro**, one of the oldest examples of pre-Romanesque architecture although remodelled on various occasions.

Passing **SCOPPITO**, where ancient Foruli (a district of Civitatomassa) stood, we reach Preturo, where the interesting **church of San Pietro** was founded in the 12th century and restored

78. Above: *Ju calenne* at Villagrande, Tornimparte.
79–81. Below, left to right: the church of Beata Cristina, Colle di Lucoli, the church of San Pietro in Coppito, the church of San Giovanni Battista di Lucoli.
82. Facing page: detail of Saturnino Gatti's frescoes in the church of San Panfilo, Villagrande di Tornimparte.

in the early 1700s. Now appearing in the guise of subsequent reconstructions, presents an attractive stone façade, with recovered stone fragments, a Romanesque portal and a small bell gable dating back to 1495.

Recent restoration work inside has brought to light important frescoes (13th-16th century). A painting with the *Coronation of the Virgin*, with Figures of Saints and Frescoes from the school of Gian Paolo Cardone (1557).

The small village of **San Vittorino**, a short distance from L'Aquila, grew in the 12th century around the **church of San Michele Arcangelo** (*see box p. 59*) over Christian catacombs, which developed around the tomb of the martyr St Vittorino.

Ancient **Amiternum** stood at the foot of the San Vittorino hill. It was inhabited by the Sabines in the pre-Roman age, in the upper Aterno river valley, from which it supposedly takes its name. It was also the Sallustius in 86 BC.

Conquered by the Romans at the beginning of the 3rd century BC, it became a prefecture until the Augustan age, and by the 1st century BC, it was a flourishing municipium. Of the ancient town we can admire the charming traces of the **theatre**, in *opus reticulatum*, dating back to the Augustan age, with about 2,000 seats arranged on two orders of terraces, and traces of the **amphitheatre**, dating back to the 1st century AD, which is particularly well-preserved and had 48 arches on two levels, although no traces remain of the terraces, which could hold about 6,000 spectators.

Down on the valley line, Cavallari has the ancient **church of SS Proto e Giacinto**, with its 12th-century façade, rich in classical and Dark Age traces, is particularly noteworthy.

**PIZZOLI**, lying at the foot of Mount Marine, is dominated by the imposing **Palazzo Dragonetti–de Torres** (1562), which incorporates an older, pentagonal lookout tower. Nearby there is the small municipality of **BARETE**, with the **church of San Paolo**, built in the 13th century over the ruins of the *Lavaretum* Roman baths, whose remains have come to light.

Some traces can still be seen of the ancient wall structures of the fortress, which is set at about 1,220 metres asl. The garrison entrusted its effective defence almost exclusively to the treacherous lie of the land; a gap in the surviving stone curtains suggests the position of the gate hinges, but no traces of defence towers have come to light. Worth visiting, the **museo of rural culture and traditions.**

The Aterno valley narrows to the north and reaches the wide Montereale bowl, wedged into the province of Rieti. Montereale, Capitignano, Cagnano Amiterno, Barete and Scoppito territory is immersed in woodlands and dotted with numerous villages and pleasant resort locations.

83. Facing page: Roman amphitheatre, Amiternum.
84. Above: the Dragonetti–de Torres castle, Pizzoli.
85. Below: Amiternum Roman theatre, San Vittorino.

# The Church of San Michele Arcangelo, San Vittorino

Built on the site of an older church, this place of worship was re-consecrated in 1170, as indicated by the plaque set in the right nave wall. Only the apse and the left wing of the transept remain of the old building, where architectural fragments of Amiternum are walled.
The structure has an unusual Latin cross plan, with a long nave; the semi-circular apse is preceded by a transept, which is as long as the nave. The chamber is divided by a modern wall, which has separated the so-called "old church" (which retains Roman and Romanesque fragments), from the area of worship where mass is still celebrated.
The valuable sculptural fragments walled here, with episodes of the martyrdom of Bishop Vittorino, for many years were thought to be from a pulpit made in 1197 by the sculptor interesting bas relief showing various characters and an inscription that recalls the patron of the tomb.
The area with the Roman columns cannibalized to support the vault, shows a fresco dating 14th–15th–century, depicting a *Madonna and Child between St John the Baptist and a Saint*.

86. Facing page: the large catacomb room.
87. Above: exterior the church.
88. Left: the tomb of St Vittorino.
89. Below: detail of the frescoes inside the church.

Petrus Amabilis, whose name was cited in an inscription that is now lost. Recent studies believe that the stone fragments are more likely to be from the altar made by a local sculptor for the consecration of the church. The precious frescoes of the apse basin may be attributed to one of the painters of the circle of the Maestro of San Silvestro, working in L'Aquila in the late–14th–early–15th century. A legend tells that the body of the martyred saint was laid in the main **catacomb** chamber, most of which is beneath the church and reutilizes the old Roman wall structures.
Bishop *Quodvultdeus* commissioned a **monumental aedicule** (5th century AD) to honour the martyr. The front of the monument, now appearing in a restored version, is divided by four pillars supporting the top slab, with composite capitals alternating with decorated blocks.
On the marble slab there is an

In the **CAGNANO AMITERNO** district of San Cosimo (home to the municipal offices), the beautiful parish church is of particular interest, with its late Renaissance portal. in the Termine district there is characteristic **Palazzotto Ludovisi** (later Mancini).

Overlooking the great basin, charming **MONTEREALE** vaunts the **church of Santa Maria Assunta** (1745–50), with a nave and two aisles, transept and dome, as well as the 1777 organ by Adriano Fedri; nearby there is **Santa Maria in Pantanis**, once home to the priceless 13th-century *Maria Lactans* fresco as well as a 1400s canvas by Matteo da Campli, both works now in the MUNDI. The **Beato Andrea church** (1726), formerly of the Augustinians, is particularly interesting: aisleless with the entrance on the larger side, with the large domed Beato Andrea chapel on the opposite side, boasting a lavish, polychrome marble sacellum.

In a pleasant spot, in the small centre of **CAPITIGNANO**, there is the interesting **church of San Flaviano**, built in 1500, reproducing the original plan of San Bernardino in L'Aquila. The church has a nave and two aisles that meet in an octagonal chamber with a dome and radial chapels. The form of the pillars and the symmetry of the chapels were altered by subsequent neo-classical restoration work. Striking **Palazzo Ricci**, restored in Neoclassical style by Giovanni Stern around 1783, is worth visiting in the nearby district of Mopolino. Annexed to the building is the **chapel of San Domenico**, which was founded in the 16th century and transformed with Valadier's project in c. 1839.

**CAMPOTOSTO**'s greatest attraction is its artificial lake, the largest in Abruzzo, at 1,420m in altitude in Gran Sasso – Monti della Laga National Park\. The term "Castello" refers to the upper part of the town and suggests the existence of ancient castle defence structures there. Most of the inhabited area has the 17th–19th-century appearance left by reconstruction after the 1703 earthquake. The **church of Santa Maria Apparente** or **Santa Maria Assunta**, with a 16th-century façade, is very striking. The whole district, which is particularly interesting for its landscapes and nature, is protected by the nature reserve set up in 1984, which takes its name from the lake, one of the rare aquatic surfaces in the centre of the Apennines where ducks, herons and other birds typical of these habitats make their homes.

90. Above: Lake Campotosto.
91. Left: the church of San Flaviano, Capitignano.

# Rocche Plateau

**Civita di Bagno** is a hamlet close to L'Aquila, on the Aterno valley slopes, where it is still possible to identify the remains of ancient Forcona, part of the *praefectura* of Amiterno, and important bishopric after the 6th century. The imposing ruins can still be seen of the old **San Massimo cathedral**, built with material salvaged from Roman buildings. The original cathedral was mentioned for the first time in a 7th-century document and fell into ruin in the 13th century, with the transfer of the diocese to the new city of L'Aquila. After numerous changes and refurbishments, it was finally abandoned in the mid–18th century. In 1971, the remains were uncovered and restored, bringing to light late–Medieval parts incorporated in a building erected later, presumably between the 11th and 12th centuries, with a nave and two aisles, cadenced by columns and three semi-circular apses. The ruins of the old church uncovered and consolidated included apse curtain walls, crowned externally by semi-circular arches and – still visible in parts – the large, formerly vaulted crypt, and the

Civita di Bagno, Ocre, Rocca di Cambio, Rocca di Mezzo, Ovindoli, Secinaro, Gagliano Aterno.

The area explored is home to two of the highest Apennine peaks, Mount Sirente and Mount Velino, separated by the Rocche Plateau, and crossed by the River Aterno. Its cultural heritage is one of the most important in the area, and it boasts a magnificent landscape thanks to the fact that it is almost entirely within the confines of Velino–Sirente Regional Nature Park. The presence of fortified villages, sheer mountains, castles, watchtowers and fortifications, together with a vast number of important, well-preserved civil and religious architectural buildings, and modern winter sports facilities, make exploring this unspoiled area a delight. Magnificent Gagliano Aterno castle is one of the rare examples of a fortified residence now restored and put to use by the Region. The exceptional position of the fortified hilltop village of Ocre, overlooking the valley below, makes it exceptionally interesting.

92. Below: aerial view of the Altopiano delle Rocche plateau.

mutilated tower whose façade was lost. Sadly, the 2009 earthquake led to the collapse of the apse curtain walls and the tower. There were also interesting late–Medieval fragments.

Recent excavations uncovered a monumental building overlooking the entire valley, probably an important sanctuary from Roman times and closely linked to water cults. The site has mighty opus reticulatum terracing all across the northwest hill slope, below Civita di Bagno, not far from the **Feronia temple**, dating back to the Republican era. Excavations have uncovered cisterns, water channels and mosaics under the structures. The imposing works are a significant pointer to the former splendour of Roman Forcona.

The **OCRE** district comprises five "ville", the small villages of San Felice d'Ocre, San Martino d'Ocre, Valle, Cavalletto, and San Panfilo d'Ocre, which is the municipal authority. Here we find the striking **church of San Panfilo**, whose 13th-century lines were changed to some extent by 1500s changes, which came to light only recently, but which include stunning frescoes. Next is the magnificent **Ocre castle** (*see box p. 63*), built on a hilltop overlooking the Aterno valley, to ensure strategic control of access across the Rocche plateau.

The **convent of Sant'Angelo d'Ocre** is also easy to reach. An original church is documented from the 12th century, which seems to have been an annex to the convent building. The conversion of the first religious settlement into the church and convent annex complex for Benedictine nuns, is said to date to 1409 but its present appearance is the result of radical renovation work carried out by the Order of Friars Minor, who arrived in 1480, and stayed in the convent until 1593, when the Reformists took over. After 1600s work that included the addition of frescoes that can still be seen on the cloister walls today (*Life of St Anthony of Padua* painted by P. Borani in 1660), the Franciscan church of a nave and square choir, was enhanced in the 18th century with late–Baroque decorations

## Ocre Castle

This fortified village is an interesting example of its kind thanks to its exceptional landscape location and the presence, within the village walls, of a well-defined though scarce street plan, still completely visible inside the perimeter. The urban walls are roughly triangular in shape, perfectly aligned with the site, with limestone walls interspersed with quadrilateral towers. On the south-west side, near the corner tower, we find the only entrance with its austere ogival doorway, dating back to the 13th century, opening in a short perpendicular curtain wall and protected by a crossfire defence system; the tower shows, on the frontage next to the entrance, an interesting circular arquebusier at street entry level. The northwest curtain, already naturally defended by the rocky cliff, is interrupted by a section-breaker tower set about halfway along the wall and ends at northern corner with a square corner tower. The more vulnerable wall front to the north-west, with high curtain walls, is shut off by two corner towers and split by an intermediate support tower. Inside the now-derelict fortifications a street plan is easy to see, with fabric streets converging to southeast tip of the area; here there are the remains of a small church, with a nave and two aisles, cadenced by visible octagonal-base pillars and a semi-circular apse. This is the church of San Salvatore, now in ruins, documented from the 15th century up to 1581. Near the church's southern curtain wall, traces were found of important frescoes of an *Enthroned Madonna with Child between two figures* (12th century), later removed and transferred to L'Aquila's MUNDA.

93-95. Facing page: top left, the ruins of San Massimo cathedral; top right, the Roman sanctuary, Civita di Bagno; below, aerial view of Ocre castle.
96. Above: the convent of Sant'Angelo d'Ocre with Gran Sasso in the background.

and a new frontage with portico, preserving the 15th-century portal. The square layout is arranged around the cloister with porticos on all sides, the church to the north, the refectory to the south, the library to the east, and the cells to the south and west on the upper floor. On the back wall of the refectory, a precious early–16th-century fresco of the *Last Supper* is attributed to a follower of the latter Saturnino Gatti period.

The convent complex lies in a magical setting, controlling the Aterno valley, and appears to have preserved its layout and walls despite the controversial restoration by the Civil Engineering Authority between 1958 and 1972. It is currently home to a small group of Franciscans. A scenic road leads to the vast Rocca di Mezzo or Rocche Plateau, an extended karst upland between Velino's spurs and the slopes of Mount Sirente. **ROCCA DI CAMBIO** (1,433m asl) overlooks the plateau from its ridge on the slopes of Mount Cagno, and is the highest municipality in the Apennine range. In addition to the **church of San Pietro**, at the highest point of the town, and the **Annunziata mother church**, there is the important **church of Santa Lucia**, founded between the late–13th–early–14th century, with later refurbishments. The nave-and-two-aisle interior and wide presbytery without apse, vaunts lovely 14th-century paintings across the presbytery walls reminiscent of the ancient pictorial cycles of Fossa and of San Pellegrino, in Bominaco. There is a striking *Last Supper* with Christ seated at the top of the table as he blesses the Apostles who are turned towards him. The crypt can be reached via a small stairway in the nave, where there are traces of late–14th–early–15th-century frescoes, and a rustic worship aedicule. There is a 15th-century-style portal on what remains of the façade, with a small rose window above it. The portal was placed there during restoration work in 1968–70, when reinforcement and cleaning work was carried out and access to the crypt was reopened. The frontage has a small bell gable of a later period.

The Campo Felice plateau, a famous ski resort, lies between Lucoli and Rocca di Cambio.

**ROCCA DI MEZZO**, the most important centre on the Rocche plateau is a popular summer and winter resort on the other side of the valley. It is a start point for hikes and the headquarters of the **Sirente–Velino Regional Park**. Remains of the old fortified town walls include the **Porta della Morge** gate, and the town's Medieval traits are still discernible, rendered even more magnificent by the views. The town is home to the **parish church of Santa Maria ad Nives**, restored in the 1700s, now with the **Cardinale Agnifili sacred art museum** installed in the adjoining rooms of the old Confraternita del Sacramento confraternity, with valuable works that include furniture dating back to 1492, a silver processional cross by Giovanni di Meo of Sulmona (1386), and illuminated antiphonaries.

In the charming fortified village of **Rovere**, there is an **archaeological museum**, installed in several rooms under the **church of San Pietro**, of ancient origins but remodelled over time. The museum narrative documents the various stages in the development of the village and castle, whose remains can still be seen on the summit of the hill.

97. Above: the interior of the church of Santa Lucia, Rocca di Cambio.
98. Below: the fortified village of Rovere.

The itinerary continues to **OVINDOLI**, a popular summer and winter holiday resort, on the edge of the plateau. The surviving 12th-century keep overlooks the village and there are the scant remains of an early 18th-century tower. The elegant **Porta Mutiati** gate and traces of boundary walls are all that remain of this old fortified village. Some of the imposing homes are an indication of the wealth that families acquired in the past, thanks to the flourishing sheep-rearing industry. The old villages of **Santa Iona**, with its old round tower and pretty **Madonna delle Grazie parish church** with attractive stone Renaissance aedicule, and **San Potito** with the interesting remains of a castle, are worth a visit.

Next there is **SECINARO**, located on a magnificent panoramic hillside on the Subequano Valley; the **church of the Consolazione**, founded in the Middle Ages, with important frescoes, and the **parish church of San Nicola**, are worth visiting.

We now reach **GAGLIANO ATERNO**, overlooking the magnificent castle of the Marquises Lazzeroni, rebuilt by Countess Isabella di Celano in 1328, on the ruins of a previous fort, as explained on a plaque. The **castle** is built around an elegant courtyard with loggia. The irregularity of the plan, conditioned by the need to adapt to the site's unusual orography, also shows the sequence of additions that converted it from a mainly military structure to its present status of residential castle.

The northeast entrance is preceded by a sizeable bulwark tower (strengthening element) that can be reached from the yard next to it by a drawbridge, which is one of the few remaining in the region and crosses the moat, which is still recognizable today and once defended the most vulnerable parts of the building. The bulwark tower accesses the mighty battlements, protected by an embattled wall, and enclose the building on the longer sides, taking the shape of round crenellated towers at the north, east and west corners, creating a kind of strut on the last edge. The large, open stairway is magnificent and spectacular, sited in the courtyard along the northwest side leading to the first floor, which was fairly common in Lazio and Tuscany but quite unusual in Abruzzo. The main building to the southeast has a magnificent two-order portico, four outer ogival arches at the height of the courtyard, and four round arches on the upper floor. There is also an

99. Above: Santa Iona tower.
100. Below: Ovindoli town centre.

interesting square well. Following its destruction in 1462 by Braccio di Montone, it passed from the Piccolomini, feudal lords in 1463, to the Barberini family, who held the property until 1806. Downhill of the town there is a solitary but beautiful watchtower.

The **convent of Santa Chiara** is also noteworthy; one of the most important Poor Clare convents, founded between the 13th and 14th centuries, built before 1286 and inhabited until quite recently.

The church, initially consisting of a single roofed chamber with vaulted choir, underwent radical renovation work in around 1685, carried out by the Lombard, Giovan Battista Gianni, who focused his design on the monumental main altar, surmounted by the newly-stuccoed and frescoed Medieval crossing. The nave was covered with barrel vaults, creating a triple span loggia with oval calottes at the entrance. The so-called nuns' choir, at the back of the main altar, was created in 1748 by an unknown architect who laid it out on two levels. The ground floor has nine cross-vaulted bays, and is lit by a single oval opening, created above the central span, communicating with at the upper, choir level, covered with a hemispherical cupola on pendentives.

The **church of San Martino** was built during the first half of the 13th century by order of Isabella d'Acquaviva, Countess of Celano, and rebuilt after the earthquake in 1706, is in the centre of the village. The parish church has a nave and two aisles, and a small cupola, with flush transept and polygonal apse, probably left from the original building.

A scheme-arch oval cupola is installed at the chevet, closed on the outside by an octagonal tiburium. An important 14th-century style portal opens in the centre of the façade, with horizontal coping, which was given its present form before 1614, the date carved on the front coping. The portal is completed by external tortile columns, with supporting lion bases, and a slender gable with a bas-relief of *St Martin Gives His Cloak to the Beggar*; the coats of arms of the Acquaviva family (lion rampant) and of Counts Berardi of Celano (escutcheon and bend) are on the lateral cusps. In the upper order of the façade, there is a rose window dated late 1500s. Famous 16th-century frescoes depict the *Life of St Martin*.

101. Above: Gagliano Aterno castle.

# Subequana Valley

The charming village of **FOSSA**, which the Vestino tribe called Aveia, is well-known today for the small church of **Santa Maria ad Cryptas** (also Santa Maria delle Grotte), restored after the 2009 earthquake, just outside the built-up area. Founded in the latter half of the 1200s, it was originally a chapel and part of the Santo Spirito d'Ocre monastery. The building has a three-span nave, with a square choir and an asymmetrical cross-ribbed vault. In front of the presbytery, a small flight of stairs descends to the crypt – which gave the church its name – where the ancient altar can be found. Some of its features are reminiscent of Gothic–Cistercian style, like the contoured ribs and the floral motifs decorating the capitals of the choir's four corner columns. The interior is embellished with one of Medieval Abruzzo's most distinguished pictorial cycles, by a school that also embraces the murals in the San Pellegrino oratory at Bominaco, San Tommaso at Caramanico, and some of the paintings in the church of Santa Maria in Ronzano. Some of the scenes in the older pictorial cycle are attributed to Gentile da Rocca who signed and dated (1283)

Fossa, Sant'Eusanio Forconese, Villa Sant'Angelo, San Demetrio ne' Vestini, Stiffe, Fagnano Alto, Fontecchio, Tione degli Abruzzi, Acciano, Goriano Valli, Roccapreturo, Molina Aterno, Castelvecchio Subequo, Castel di Ieri, Goriano Sicoli.

The itinerary offers charming views in the stretch along the Aterno valley, in a marvellous landscape almost all within Velino–Sirente Regional Park. A treasure of interesting things to see, not only from an environmental aspect, but also intact towns and villages, and above all the large number of artworks to be found. Cultural and historical expectations are met to the full, along with excursions to natural sites and for observing wildlife. Beautiful churches, castles, archaeological traces of the past, including the sensational Fossa necropolis, which is the most important and best-conserved archaeological site in the region. Dozens of lesser-known marvels are scattered across the entire area, so the tour suggested here is particularly engaging.

102. Below: the pilgrimage from Beffi to the church of Sant'Erasmo in Acciano, with the Subequana valley in the background.

103. Above: Fossa castle.
104. Below: *Last Supper,* detail of the cycle of frescoes that decorate the church of Santa Maria ad Cryptas, Fossa.
105. Facing page: San Spirito d'Ocre monastery.

the panel painting of *Maria Lactans,* today in L'Aquila's MUNDI but originally from Santa Maria ad Cryptas. In addition to the series of late–13th-century paintings, there is a noteworthy cycle of 14th-century works, while interventions dated late–15th–early–16th century have come to light. The right-hand altar vaunts the 1583 *Our Lady of the Rosary and Mystery Tales* ancona, by Giovan Paolo Cardone.

In the village centre, the **Assunta parish church** is well worth seeing, rebuilt almost entirely in the 18th century. The fine wooden coffered ceiling has two outstanding 17th-century paintings in Greek cross frames: the *Assumption of the Virgin* (anonymous) and *Immaculate Mary* dated (1739), signed by L'Aquila's own artist, Bernardino Ciferri. The fresco showing the *Mystical Wedding of St Catherine,* by Francesco da Montereale (1502–49), is also outstanding. The third altar to the left has a wooden tabernacle with a polychrome, gilt wooden statue depicting a Madonna and Child, and called the *Loreto.* The unusual features of the old **castle** perched at the highest part of the settlement can still be clearly seen. The wall around the village gives an almost trapezoid shape to the layout, with three square towers and a sturdy, round tower that probably predates the complex, situated on the highest ground. A Gothic stone ashlar arch marks the main entrance into the wall at the northwest, while a secondary entrance opens up near the southwest corner tower. A crossbow loophole and traces of an arrow loophole can be recognised as belonging to the original defensive apparatus in the upper part of the south wall near the round tower, while in the southeast tower and the in eastern curtain wall, single-hole harquebusiers and arrow loophole-surmounted harquebusiers can be discerned.

A stone's throw from the built-up area of Fossa, within the municipal boundaries of Ocre, the imposing walls of the **Santo Spirito d'Ocre monastery** can still be seen. It is one of the most interesting examples of fortified Cistercian monastery, perfectly suited to the inaccessible nature of the site. The abbey complex was founded by the hermit Placido, around 1222, at the request of Count Berardo of Ocre. In 1248 the monastery was acquired by the Cistercian abbey of Santa Maria di Casanova.

The nucleus of the monastery has recently

## Fossa Necropolis

Almost certainly connected to the Mount Cerro protohistoric settlement, the large Fossa necropolis has been the subject of many excavations by the Archaeological Superintendency. To-date around 500 burials have come to light in an area of over 2,000 sqm: the different types of tombs and characteristics of the burial objects document different stages in the use of the necropolis. In the first stage (9th–8th century BC), identifiable with the early Iron Age, a highly monumental tumulus was preferred: enormous tumuli delimited by stone circles, in sizes varying from 8 to 15m are found in the area. These were for men or for women. What makes the burial area exceptional is the presence in male burials of alignments of 6–8 stone stele driven vertically into the ground, arranged in decreasing height, starting from the base of the tumulus. They are a sort of small menhir, a feature that has led the necropolis to be defined as a "small Stonehenge". Starting from the biggest, which corresponds to the radius of the circle, to the smallest, they form a straight line, whose significance has not yet been fully understood. With the late Hellenistic age (2nd–1st century BC), a return to monumental forms is documented, well-represented by tombs with underground stone chambers – of which only the entrance closed by one or two vertical stone slabs was once visible – and destined for the burial of several individuals. Among the items found in the chamber tombs are fantastic wood and leather funeral beds, decorated with exquisitely worked bone lamina with intricate illustrations.

106. Left: a carved bone mask found during excavations at Fossa necropolis.
107. Large image: a zenith view of the necropolis.

been restored and is now a guest facility. It consisted of a majestic square cloister around which the church was arranged, along an axis running from east to west; the various areas of the monastery adopted the Cistercian layout. Some adaptation to the traditional arrangement is to be seen in the monastic church, with no prospect, a side entrance and a nave, without transepts or apse. The choir still has an original barrel vault, while the ogival vault has been restored over the nave to replace the trusses that connected the truncated buttresses of the old vaults. The west front of the main entrance to the complex is particularly interesting, with an ogival portal of Burgundian tradition, surmounted by a two-light mullioned window, partly hidden by a typical machicolation, a basic defensive feature.

Inside the church, to the right of the entrance, there is the outstanding counterfaçade fresco, dated late 13th-century, showing a *Madonna and Child Enthroned Between Saints Peter and Paul and the Two Patrons*. The interior has a 16th-century frieze frescoed along the walls with yellow, green, white and red vertical bands, while the presbytery is embellished with late–16th-century frescoes, inspired by the life of Blessed Placido, painted by Paolo Mausonio, who also produced the *Immaculate Conception* on the back wall. In the chapel-sacristy on the left, the layers of 13th and 14th-century frescoes are particularly interesting.

Visiting the **Fossa necropolis** is a memorable experience (*see box p. 70*). It is located in Casale, where it was established in the 9th century BC on the northern bank of the River Aterno and was used for around a thousand years. Fossa is the best-preserved and most important proto-historical site in the region.

Casentino, a hamlet in the municipal district of Sant'Eusanio Forconese, is home to the **church of San Giovanni Evangelista**. Well worth visiting, it was rebuilt in the 18th century over the remains of a 15th-century building. A polychrome, gilt terracotta *Madonna and Child* (16th century) adorns the high altar. A painting of St Brigid by Vincenzo Damini, the 18th-century Veneto painter active in L'Aquila, can be seen on the altar at the end of the left-hand aisle, while there is a painting of St Charles Borromeo (17th century) on the first altar in the right-hand aisle, by Giovanni Paolo Mausonio, and a *Purgatory* (1756) by Bernardino Ciferri, over the second.

We continue to **SANT'EUSANIO FORCONESE**, dominated by the castle on the top of Mount Cerro that controlled the River Aterno valley, towards San Demetrio and Poggio Picenze. The fortified wall is rather uneven, broken by semi-circular towers and with a square layout with the function of a line break, probably dating back to the 12th–13th century. A lancet arch gateway opens to the south, near the **Madonna del Castello church**, which rises among the remains of the fortifications. The fortified wall has recently been restored, with the recovery of long stretches as well as some of the towers.

The square at the centre of village, with an elegant 18th-century fountain, is overlooked by 17th-century **Palazzo Barberini** and the **parish church of Sant'Eusanio**, rebuilt in 1198 on the site of a more ancient basilica, using some surviving fragments. The building was then rebuilt in several stages in the 15th, 17th and 18th centuries. Some restoration involved above all the façade and can be dated early–14th century, while the portal was refurbished in the 15th century although the archivolt is 13th century. Beneath is the large crypt, with its seven aisles and three apses. There are 15th and 16th-century frescoes that are particularly worthy of note. In 1970 the church underwent restoration that saw the dismantling of the Baroque furnishings on the inside while, outside, a construction that had been built onto the left-hand side of the church was removed. Now the church's original position within fortified walls can be discerned, with two surviving corner towers on splayed plinths. The church was seriously affected by the 2009 earthquake.

Outside the village we meet the austere **Angeli (or sotterra) church**, with a beautiful 18th-century portal and a canvas of a *Madonna*

108. The fountain and 19th-century façade, parish church of Sant'Eusanio Forconese.

*and child with Saints* attributed to Bedeschini. Close to the centre we find the **Madonna della Pietà church** with a frescoed *Pietà* by Paolo Mausonio.

The lovely centre of **VILLA SANT'ANGELO** is situated on a knoll at the southern end of the Aquila basin. Piazza Grande is dominated by the **San Michele parish church**, built in the 18th century, confirmed by dates on the altars (1755–79). In the built-up area behind the building, a soaring stone sculpture by local artist, Pasquale Liberatore, who also made several noteworthy fountains in Tussillo and Stiffe.

The **church of San Michele Arcangelo**, that from various sources indicate was already in existence in the early 13th century, has a façade with a flat end, the result of 18th-century restoration. Above the portal, and slightly off-centre, stands a widow with a split gable and central shell above that. The Villa Sant'Angelo coat-of-arms tops the imposing bell gable. Inside is the chapel of San Michele Arcangelo embellished by a 17th-century altar housing the statue of the saint.

Worthy of note among Villa Sant'Angelo's residential buildings are **Palazzo Colonna, Palazzo Colletti, Palazzo Andreassi, Palazzo De Matteis, Palazzo Nardis**, and **Palazzo Franci**.

Along the road to Tussillo we find the little **church of Madonna delle Grazie** (or delle Prate), linked to the fascinating Lumetta celebration, with an ancient tradition of lanterns made of hollowed-out pumpkins that takes place on the Sunday nearest 8 September. The high altar is adorned with trompe-l'oeil frescoes and a faux altar cloth depicting a *Madonna with Child between St Anthony Abbot and St John*, and two side aedicules, with the *Annunciation* to the left and the *Visitation* to the right.

In the ancient fortified village of **Tussillo**, there is the outstanding 13th century **church of Sant'Agata** with a stone churchyard famous for the so-called "Orsini column". Inside, the most precious work is the fresco painted on the right-hand side of the counterfaçade, showing the *Madonna of Loreto between two Franciscan Saints*, which recent studies suggest comes from the School of Saturnino Gatti (1463–1518 or 1521), L'Aquila's leading painter of the late–15th–early–16th century.

Once past Villa Sant'Angelo, set in the beautiful Aterno district, we reach **SAN DEMETRIO NE' VESTINI** where features of interest include the 18th-century **parish church of San Demetrio**, with an old tower that has been converted to a belfry, and interesting frescoes and furnishings, and the 1820 **church of Santa Maria dei Raccomandati**, in Malte Baroque style with beautiful paintings by Teofilo Patini (1840–1906). The particularly striking **Palazzo Cappelli** – now the Collegio dei Padri Rogazionisti boarding school – in Torano donated its Cappelli Dragonetti art collection of the MUNDI. The municipal area includes seven outlying administrative districts ("ville") with excellent examples of architecture and art: Cardabello, Cardamone, San Giovanni Battista, Collarano, Villa Grande, Cavantoni, Colle. The karst Lake Sinizzo is a local beauty spot.

The **Stiffe caves** are an impressive underground karst phenomenon and one of the most important natural monuments the area.

109. Facing page: Lake Sinizzo, San Demetrio ne 'Vestini.
110. Above: the "Roman bridge" over the Aterno, Campana.
111. Below: the fortified village of Castello di Fagnano Alto.

Visitors are taken along a 650m metal walkway around the wonderful spectacle of a series of uniquely beautiful grottoes. The Sala della Cascata is a stunning sight with the waterfall created by the mountain stream plunging spectacularly down about 30 metres. One of the most amazing caves is the Sala delle Concrezioni, where slow dripping over the millennia has formed stalactites, stalagmites and other calcareous formations.

Be sure to visit the **Vincenzo Rivera speleology museum** and the Grotte di Stiffe caves.

**Ripa** is just one of the hamlets that make up **FAGNANO ALTO**, built on a knoll and worth visiting to see the interesting rock **church of San Rocco**. There is also **Castello**, an old fortified village whose well-preserved layout is a striking example among the region's fortifications. The almost-oval fortified walls occupy the summit of the hill in a strategic position and it is still possible to discern long stretches of courtines to the east and north. At the entrance to the village we meet the church of Santa Maria, with a nave and two aisles, and an elegant stone portal dated 1568. Two recently restored polygonal section-breaker towers are visible along the more vulnerable curtain wall in the northwest and two round towers, presumably of a later date, are situated in the northeast, one of which acts as a belfry. A fifth, recently restored square tower, the most imposing, is to the northwest, where it defended the main entrance to the castle, called Porta Palazzo. The Gothic gateway has a now-illegible coat of arms above it, while it is interesting to note both the slits that controlled the drawbridge and the machicolations on corbels. The road through the gate meets the main street of Via San Pietro at right angles. The street is closed off with a smaller, surviving gate, and is protected by the building behind it, installed with harquebusiers; a second passage with a stone ashlar lancet arch faces eastward.

In the hamlet of Campana

The **parish church of San Giovanni Evangelista** in the hamlet of Campana is worth a visit. Here in the 1790s a new building fused with the Medieval structure and gave life to a very singular central space, rich in Baroque-style decorations, whose design is attributed to the Lombard architect Giovan Battista Leomporri. Outside Campana there is an enchanting walk along the Aterno, which reaches the so-called Roman bridge, with its traces of ancient structures.

The layout of the charming Medieval village of **FONTECCHIO** has not changed very much, with narrow alleys and flights of cobbled steps

lined with doorways. Entering the village, on the right there is the **Porta Piazza** or the Castello gate with its scheme arch, and from the first belt of urban fortifications a ramp ascends to the **Porta dei Santi** lancet gateway, surmounted by an impressive clock tower, which has recently been restored and has elegant machicolations on triple-course corbels . The tower clock is considered one of the oldest in Italy. The **Museo della Cultura della Memoria** is has been set up in the fortifications with a permanent exhibition of vintage and contemporary images of L'Aquila by Roberto Grillo. In Piazza del Popolo there are still some Medieval shops and the façade of the **parish church of Santa Maria della Pace**, of ancient origins it has been remodelled several times. Then we reach the splendid 14th-century fountain, the icon of the village, located at a lower level than the square. It has a 14-side basin, separated by half-columns, and with a central plinth decorated with masks, which supports a graceful six-arch shrine surmounted by a spire. Around the fountain there are drinking troughs set against the wall of the house that closes off the square. There is a striking votive shrine with traces of a fresco depicting the *Madonna and Child with Angels*. The painting, according to recent studies bf Ferdinando Bologna, could be one of the first works of the enigmatic Master, who produced the wonderful *Last Judgment* in the church of Santa Maria in Piano in Loreto Aprutino (1429–30). The **Porta dell'Orso** gate survives as does the **Porta da Piedi**, with the engraved monogram of Christ and the date 1591. The imposing fortified **baronial Palazzo Corvi** (15th–16th century), in the north east of the village, is of considerable interest.

The **San Francesco monastery** is an accommodation facility near San Pio di Fontecchio. The church was built over a previous place of worship dedicated to St Agnes, was modified several times and inside there are 15th–16th-century frescoes. The complex has one of the most interesting cloisters in the region, with a remarkable upper loggia: an inscription is dated 1488 and bears the signature of the probable architect: Maffeo de Calderonibus.

In addition to Santa Maria a Graiano, also nearby but now abandoned, it is worth stopping at the church of **Santa Maria della Vittoria** (formerly San Pietro), between the town and the River Aterno, built on the podium of an ancient Roman temple.

In the heart of Sirente–Velino Regional Park it is worth stopping to visit the enchanting **Oasi di Fontecchio** and Visitor Centre in the historic centre, inside the former tannery, with wildlife areas for observing the roe deer and learning sections.

The Medieval village of **TIONE DEGLI ABRUZZI** stands a short distance from the River Aterno. The square, 18m-high tower soaring over the ruins is all the remains of the old castle. The **parish church of San Nicola di Bari**, with its 1400s frescoes, is at the foot of the tower. The centre faces the **fortified village of Santa Maria del Ponte**, nestling in the hills,

112. 113. Below: Fontecchio clock tower and the cloister of the convent of San Francesco, San Pio di Fontecchio.
114. Facing page: Fontecchio's 14th-century fountain.

115. Above, left: the large well at Pagliare di Tione.
116. Above, right: the pentagonal tower at Beffi di Acciano.
117. 118. Facing page, below: the façade and interior of the church of San Francesco, Castelvecchio Subequo.

on the opposite side of the River Aterno. The attractive village, mentioned in King Charles II's 1294 diploma, is still characterize by two lancet gateways that open in the partially conserved defensive walls, and crossbow housings and the old drawbridge can still visible.

Just outside the Santa Maria del Ponte area there is a church of the same name, once part of a more extensive monastic complex, and probably dating back to the 12th century, but the present layout is the result of changes made in various periods, including the most recent restorations in 1967–8. Some of the most precious artworks found in the MUNDI come from this church, including the Maestro di Beffi triptych and the fine polychrome terracotta *crib figures* made by Saturnino Gatti (1463–1521). The 14th-century high altar and its *Crucifixion* are by the school of Francesco da Montereale (1466–1541).

Up in the mountains, **Tione's pagliare** are of significant interest. They make up a traditional a sheep-farming village with simple stone construction, a large drinking trough and a church. On a rock spur that rolls towards the River Aterno we can still see the ancient fortified village of **Beffi**, at 640m asl. This is a district of **ACCIANO**, with a soaring pentagonal stone tower that is still well preserved and datable to the 12th century. Together with **GORIANO VALLI**'s round tower, on the other side of the river, it was used for strategic control over access to the Subequana valley. It is probable that Beffi's recently restored walls were not used only when danger loomed, but were permanent dwellings, given the number of rooms inside the fortified walls, presumably occupied by the feudal lord and his bodyguard. The church of San Michele is found near the tower.

The village comes to life with a series of particularly evocative historical pageants held in the summer.

Also of great interest is **Roccapreturo**, an outlying district of Acciano, and a typical example of a triangular castle compound perfectly suited to the remote rocky terrain. Its location indicates that it was to defend the small Roccapreturo village below it, and the fortified compound , which must have been a key part of a more extensive defensive system in the area, does share many building and architectural features with other fortifications in the Aquilan area, including San Pio delle Camere and Bominaco. The deteriorated construction is dominated by bulwark tower, with five irregular sides, set at the highest apex of the triangle.

At the entrance to the wild San Venanzio gorges we find **MOLINA ATERNO**, on the right bank of the Aterno. Noteworthy features include the **parish church of San Nicola di Bari** and the **Pietropaoli baronial mansion,** built on the site of the ancient castle and the family crest placed on the portal.

Rising from a rocky spur, the Medieval village of **CASTELVECCHIO SUBEQUO** stands not far from the Ancient Roman Superaequum. The village's older nucleus can still be seen, marked by elegant buildings that include **Palazzo Giorgi**, with elegant two-light mullioned windows, **Palazzo Lucchini-Ginnetti**, **Palazzo Valeri**, **Palazzo Angelone** which is home to the Museo delle Tradizioni Popolari, **Palazzo Pietropaoli-Colabattista**, which houses a permanent gallery of Peligno district painters.

The **church of San Giovanni Battista** is worthy of note are a chapel of the nearby residential castle. As well as the 15th-century **church of Santa Elisabetta**, with its unusual doorway, there is the **church of San Francesco**, founded with the adjacent monastery in 1288, and modified into a large building with nave and two aisles in 1647. Inside, there is a magnificent altar in engraved wood and a cycle of frescoes, partly attributable to a first stage dated 13th century and a second stage dated 14th century, which decorate the nave and the chapel of San Francesco, by the hand of an unknown but skilled artist, depicting the Life of St Francis and paying homage to Giotto's works. The monastery houses a **museum of religious art**, with a very fine reliquary altar cross (1403) and the so-called "Pasquarella", a silver-plated sculpture of the *Virgin with Child and Two Angels*, donated by the Counts of Celano, in addition to beautiful reliquaries. The complex is still a destination for 28 August pilgrimages in memory of a journey by Pietro da Morrone. The neighbouring **archaeological museum** is particularly interesting, with finds from the site of the ancient Roman town and the catacombs situated at Colle Moro, from the end of the 4th century AD, which are some of the oldest testimonies of Christianity in Abruzzo.

The fortified village of **CASTEL DI IERI**, perching on a small plateau, is still characterize by the imposing square tower. This is of special interest because it is one of the region's rarest examples of a surviving square tower without a splayed plinth base, the origins of which can be traced back to the building of the Norman castle. The **church of Santa Maria Assunta**, with a beautiful Renaissance doorway, is also remarkable. In Piazza della Chiesa, **MAAG – Abruzzo museum of graphic arts**, is housed in an early–1900s building, exhibiting over 200 works including drawings, screen prints and lithographs, with various rooms dedicated to 19th-century masters, Abruzzo engravers, contemporary and foreign artists.

On the vast plateau separating Castel di Ieri from Goriano Sicoli there is an interesting **pre-Christian sanctuary**, still being explored and probably dedicated to a fertility god or goddess. Tucked away in a small gorge of the Subequana valley is the **sanctuary of Madonna di Pietrabona**, built into the rock face, and retaining the solitude and peace of a bygone era.

The village of **GORIANO SICOLI**, at the southern end of the Subequana valley, stands on the ancient settlement of Statulae, along the road that connected Tivoli with the Adriatic coast via Forca Caruso in the Italic era. Standing at the entrance of the town is the 15th-century **church of Santa Gemma**, patron saint of the village, whose feast day is still celebrated on May 11 every year. Inside we find excellent works by Teofilo Patini and the remains of the patron saint. Another striking church is that of San Francesco, formerly called the San Donato, of 13th-century origins but remodelled several times, with the statue of St Donatus inside. The **parish church of Santa Maria Nuova**, with its 17th-century interior, has a beautiful Renaissance portal (1553).

Inside there is a 15th-century polychrome wooden crucifix from the Abruzzo school and a 14th-century silver reliquary.

119. 120. Above: the pre–Christian sanctuary of Castel di Ieri and Goriano Sicoli.
121. Below: aerial view of the fortified village of Castel di Ieri.

# Gran Sasso and the Navelli Plain

Bazzano and the **church of Santa Giusta** (*see box p. 80*), one of the region's most important monuments, are near L'Aquila.

The itinerary then proceeds towards **Paganica**, a town at the edge of the Aterno valley. On the outskirts of the village, near the cemetery, it is worth visiting the **church of San Giustino**. This is a charming structure whose current layout may be referred to the 12th century and is built on the site of an older building, dated 9th century, of which several fragments were reused. The nave-and-two-aisle interior, restored in 1948 after removal of the Baroque finishes, is cadenced by pillars alternating with ancient reclaimed columns, and a semi-circular apse with 1300s frescoes. Another unusual feature is the position of the belfry, set in the first bay of the right-hand aisle. A simple portal opens on the façade, decorated with an intricately carved architrave. The internal portal lunette is decorated with a beautiful *Madonna and Child between Two Angels*, a fresco dated 12th century. Set against the belfry we see an altar surmounted by a niche recomposed in the 17th century, with reclaimed 1300s elements and the same period of the *Trinity* fresco. The aisles lead into the apsed cross-vaulted crypt with three bays. A precious Lombard presbytery screen, now in L'Aquila's MUNDI – Abruzzo National Museum, was brought from this church.

The original **Immacolata Concezione oratory**

Bazzano, Paganica, Tempera, Pescomaggiore, Filetto, Camarda, Assergi, Poggio Picenze, Barisciano, Santo Stefano di Sessanio, Calascio, Rocca Calascio, Castel del Monte, Villa Santa Lucia, Ofena, Castelvecchio Calvisio, Carapelle Calvisio, San Pio delle Camere, Castelnuovo, Prata d'Ansidonia, San Nicandro, Caporciano, Bominaco, Civitaretenga, Navelli, Capestrano, Collepietro, San Benedetto in Perillis.

Covering the Gran Sasso – Monti della Laga National Park area, these itineraries guide visitors to exploration of extremely significant history and art. The unique traits of the entire region are condensed into a single area, against a backdrop of rugged mountains. This is a karst landscape, reaching high altitude, where there are many well-preserved Medieval villages, including impressive Calascio, Santo Stefano di Sessanio, Castel del Monte, Castelvecchio Calvisio and on the Navelli plain, Barisciano and San Pio delle Camere. The Navelli plain is crossed by the Tratturo Magno, a lengthy sheep track, and is famous for its production of saffron, one of the main resources of L'Aquila economy. The sheep track that connected L'Aquila to Foggia was the most important transhumance route of the centre-south and overlapped precisely with the historic Via Claudia Nova almost as far as Navelli. The L'Aquila route winds its way through geographically rocky territory, characterized by a complex settlement system, which was brought about not only by a need for defence, but also by the unique conditions imposed for the rearing of sheep, which could not be practised in built-up areas. In point of fact, most of the settlements encountered en route are compact and cling to high slopes, are built completely in stone and the houses huddle together like fortifications, actually called wall-houses, as they provide an extremely efficient barrier. For transhumant shepherds, churches have always been structures offering welcome and spiritual support, and many of them are found along the route.

122. Left: the church of San Giustino, Paganica.

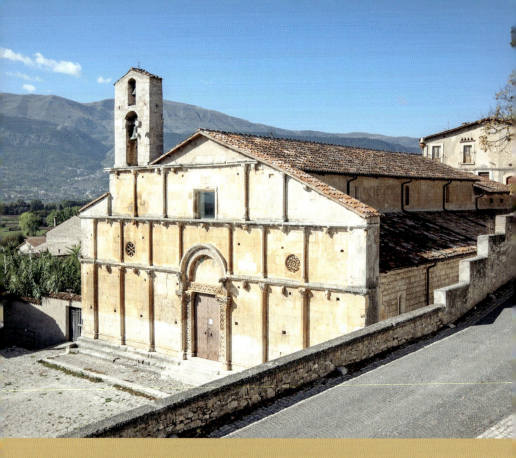

# The Church of Santa Giusta, Bazzano

The church was built on the site believed to be where St Giusta was martyred in 286 AD, tortured in a raging furnace, and although spared by the flames, she was stabbed with a lance. The current place of worship was rebuilt in the early–13th century, over an older building, over stratified Roman remains, and now appears with a quite atypical configuration. In point of fact, the original nave and two aisles were modified to two irregular aisles after refurbishment.

Of the original nave and two aisles, the nave and right aisle remain, rebuilt in 1930. In the 16th century, the central altar and its aedicule with frescoes depicting an *Enthroned Madonna and Child with Saints* were added.

The date 1238, legible on the portal architrave, would seem to refer to the architrave, the two jambs and the columns outside, while the rest of the church dates back to a phase of a few decades earlier.

The stone façade was badly damaged in the 2009 earthquake. It is divided horizontally into three orders with cornices on slim octagonal pillars below, and small columns in the two upper orders. The arched portal,

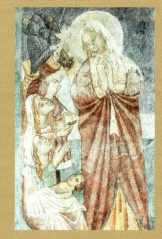

with meticulously carved jamb and architrave, dominates the centre of the façade, whose original composition makes it one of the most unique in the region. There are numerous frescoes in the interior, but the 13th-century *Redeemer and Two Saints* are the most interesting, set the upper right of the nave and in the inside portal lunette.

Inside, the date of 1218, engraved on the first right arch of the church, would seem to indicate the conclusion of the construction of this part of the building. It is therefore plausible that already in the early–13th century the works were at such an advanced stage as to be able to add an ambo, which still stands as one of the most items of most extraordinary workmanship.

The church crypt, which can be accessed through a tunnel dug into the rock beneath the ambo, retains architectural elements that were certainly salvaged from the extant Roman buildings, including columns and inscribed plaques. To the left we find the access to St Giusta's cave, where the furnace is still visible, and the entrance to the catacomb where the saint was buried.

(1771), with a late–Baroque oval interior surmounted by a pseudo dome, is found in Piazza della Concezione. Opposite, the side of the **Santa Maria Assunta parish church** (1648–55) featured a façade with horizontal coping and wrought iron railings along the entire length, where the relics are displayed. The parapet of an ambo (12th century), from the older church, is set into the wall to the right of the portal.

The **church of Santa Maria al Presepe**, with late–Renaissance lines, is found in the higher part of the town. A short distance from the town centre, in the direction of Gran Sasso and just a few kilometres from 18th-century **Palazzo Dragonetti**, we find the **sanctuary of Madonna d'Appari**, in part dug from the rock and stretching along a narrow ridge between the Raiale torrent and the crag. This is a simple aisleless layout, with an irregular presbytery area, presumed to have been the heart of the original sanctuary, which may have been built in the 15th century. The entire presbytery and part of the interior are decorated with precious frescoes dated 15th–17th century. There is a remarkable *Our Lady of the Rosary* canvas, painted in 1596 by Paolo Mausonio of L'Aquila. The rectangular façade, with bell gable, has a frescoed lunette over the portal.

Very close to Paganica there is the charming village of Tempera, where it is worth visiting the Sorgenti del Vera territorial theme park.

Continuing uphill from Paganica towards Filetto, we reach Pescomaggiore, one of the area's tiniest villages, dominated by the remains of the ancient castle-compound, whose main construction phases have been dated 12th–16th century. The shape is basically a triangle, fortified by mighty round towers of which only a few sections remain. The location of the castle influenced the lengthwise development of the village in a north–south direction. The Santa Maria "ecclesia castri", of Romanesque origin but extensively remodelled, is next to the urban gate. The 2009 earthquake damaged most of the houses and cultural heritage.

Filetto, a hamlet in the municipality of L'Aquila, is the highest settlement on Gran Sasso's Aquilan slope. From here we penetrate a quite inaccessible area to discover the fascinating **Santi Crisante e Daria abbey**, on the slopes of Gran Sasso, bordering on the vast pasturelands the Piano di Fugno and Campo Imperatore plateaux. The abbey is dated mid–12th century and its foundation was due not only to the expansion of its patrons, the Norman lords of Poppleto, but also to the revival of transhumance. Sometime in the 13th century the abbey was annexed to the more important Santa Maria di Bominaco, and it was not long before an inexorable decline began, linked to the fate of the Poppleto lords. Today's church, once flanked by a cloister, has a nave ending in the semi-circular apse while the interesting frescoes, mainly votive, which once covered all the inner walls, are now on show in the MUNDI – Abruzzo National Museum in L'Aquila.

123. 124. Facing page: top, view of the exterior of the church and, below, detail of the cycle of frescoes decorating the interior of the church of San Giusta, Bazzano.
125. 126. Below: the Madonna d'Appari sanctuary near Paganica and the SS Crisante and Daria abbey, Filetto.

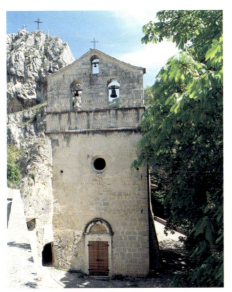

At this point we encounter the ancient fortified village of Camarda, a hamlet in the municipality of L'Aquila whose main tower survives, but sadly seriously damaged by the 2009 earthquake.

**Assergi**, a famous tourist resort is home to the Gran Sasso-Laga Mountains National Park and is traditionally identified as the ancient Vestino settlement of Prifernum. The fortified village is set on the Aquilan slope of Gran Sasso, occupying a spur at the confluence of two valleys, and at one time boasted a quite unique defence potential because of its naturally strategic site, also protected by mighty boundary walls of which significant remains can still be seen. Originally there were 12 flanking towers, some of which are englobed in private buildings, whereas the tower next to the **Porta Carbonera** gate retains its full original characteristics. The fortifications are well preserved to the southeast, and in part to the northwest, and to the south appear to be integrated in the presbytery walls of the **Santa Maria Assunta church**, which is a fascinating stratification of significant historical and architectural interest.

The church, founded in 12th century, was converted and has been integrated countless times over the years, so the current building shows evidence of this. From the late–13th century to the early–14th century, the church was enlarged with a nave-and-two-aisle interior, semi-circular apse and basement crypt, which was part of the old church of San Franco, while the current façade is thought to be mid–1400s. It was renovated during the 16th century, during the 17th century, and during the mid–18th century, with the addition of the lavish decorative device and a vaulted roof, englobing the columns in stronger supports. From the 1960s to the 1970s, a controversial restoration of the church was undertaken, and the Baroque installations were removed to reveal the original columns; it was at then that interesting frescoes datable 15th–16th century were discovered, and the paintings that came to light were attributed to famous masters like Saturnino Gatti and Francesco da Montereale. Among the other works, the so-called *Reclining Madonna* decorates a painted wooden chest dated 1636. The unusual 14th-century statue depicts the *Virgin Mary in the act of contemplating her new-born baby*. The façade has a beautiful portal and above it a rose window.

The interesting Grotta a Male, a cave discovered in 1573, is located near Assergi, and some truly important archaeological elements were found there, used to piece together the history of this territory from the Eneolithic to the Roman era. Also nearby are the **National Institute of Nuclear Physics Gran Sasso laboratories**, built in the heart of the Gran Sasso massif and considered one of Italy's key research centres.

From Fonte Cerreto, above Assergi, the 1934 cableway connects with Selva di Pratoriscio, on the western edge of the vast **Campo Imperatore** plateau, stretching from northwest to southeast for 27km, for an average width of 6km, at an altitude of approximately 1,800m, offering an immense pasture for thousands of sheep, surrounded by karst pools.

Near the small Madonna della Neve church (1935–6), there is one of Southern Europe's most important **astronomical observatories**, as well as the **Giardino Alpino d'Altitudine**, which opened in 1952, a rare mountain botanical garden which is home to various Alpine and Apennine species.

There are also the charming San Franco al Cefalone and San Franco di Peschioli hermitages, the latter on a steep crag along the path to Passo della Portella. To the southeast of Campo Imperatore, on the slopes of Mount Camicia, the hamlet of Fonte Vetica and eponymous refuge, are surrounded by the only wooded area of the plateau. Here we find Vicentino Michetti's lovely Monument to the Shepherd, in memory of the 1919 tragedy when an entire shepherd family was wiped out in a terrible snowstorm.

On the road that connects Assergi to Castel del Monte, crossing the Campo Imperatore

plateau, we find the lovely remains of the **Santa Maria del Monte monastery**, part of the Santo Spirito d'Ocre abbey, presumably built between 1222 (the year Santo Spirito d'Ocre was founded) and 1303 (the year the grange is recorded in existence). Its position at the edge of the great Campo Imperatore pastures, and between the Racollo and Passaneta lakes, must have made it a focal point for monastic sheep-rearing industry since the monks also had other rural annexes on the Le Locce plain and in Le Condole district.

On the way back to L'Aquila to take the SS17 state road, after Bazzano we pass San Gregorio, with its remarkable 1500s octagonal **Madonna della Consolazione church** and from here we proceed to **POGGIO PICENZE**, with its lovely **parish church of San Felice Martire** (16th century). For centuries the Poggio Picenze quarries were mined for a fine white stone, easy to work yet resistant. Not only is Poggio stone used for much local architecture, it is also found in the most elegant buildings of nearby L'Aquila, including the mausoleum dedicated to Pope Celestine V, in the church of Santa Maria di Collemaggio, and the Camponeschi family chapel. Over the centuries, artistic creations, restorations and precious decorations have alternated with the production of tools for daily farm and sheep-rearing tasks.

Next on the route is **BARISCIANO**, with the remains of its mighty **castle** on a hilltop to the east of the centre. This was a crest installation of the castle–compound type, straddling the mountain and controlling the Navelli plain roads to the east and Gran Sasso to the west. The compound is square-plan with traces of several internal structures and its surviving sections of boundary walls still loom on the skyline, its silhouette still discernible with four flanking towers, the two lower an L shape. Set against the southern corner tower and outside

127. 128. Facing page: the façade and the "reclining Madonna" of Santa Maria Assunta church, Assergi.
129. 130. Above: left, Campo Imperatore astronomical observatory, the hotel and the cable car station; right, the ruins of Santa Maria del Monte monastery.
131. Below: Campo Imperatore plateau.

the walls, the San Rocco chapel was built to commemorate the 1526 plague and retains traces of 16th-century frescoes. Worth visiting in the village are the **parish church of San Flaviano** (1733), with a 1500s baptismal stoup and a fine 1759 organ by Domenico A. Fedeli, as well as the **church of Santa Maria di Capodiserra** (or Buon Cosiglio), built in the 14th century, and split in half in about 1850 to include two dwellings. The church still has a handsome el 1372 portal and inside, the traces of 1300s frescoes. The **SS Trinità church**, originally known as the Immacolata Concezione, is on Piazza Trieste and was built in about the mid–17th century by the Marquis Giulio Cesare Caracciolo. In 1703, a papal bull issued by Pope Clement XI ordered the aggregation of the old church to the Roman SS Trinità dei Pellegrini e dei Convalescenti confraternity. The refined wooden choir, dating back to the mid-1800s and the organ built by the Roman Tommaso Vajola, in 1866, are especially significant. As part of the general plan to promote the nature and culture resources of the sheep-track stretches, the church has been converted into a **transhumance documentation centre**.
In the neighbouring area, on the left side of the cemetery, the Renaissance **sanctuary of Santa Maria di Valleverde** (1580) is worth visiting, with a priceless 1700s organ. Higher up, the **convent of San Colombo** with the church of Santa Maria d'Asprino was founded by the Observants in 1515, near a church that already existed, and is now the research centre into Apennine flora.
A solitary round watchtower stands between Petogna and Picenze, between the Aquila valley and the Barisciano plateau.

Continuing towards the lovely village of **SANTO STEFANO DI SESSANIO**, set on a steep slope, straddling two closed valleys, we meet one of the most prestigious and loveliest settlements on Abruzzo territory, both architecturally and environmentally. The urban fabric of the ancient fortified village – whose original oval configuration is still quite obvious – is substantially untouched, with some charming arcaded lanes, external staircases, characteristic tower-houses and perimeter wall-houses.
Hints of sheer elegance are visible in the stone portals and windows, and charming loggias. The **Casa del Capitano** and **Palazzo delle Logge** reveal the wealth enjoyed by the families involved in the sheep farming and wool trade. **Palazzo Comunale**, **Palazzo Jannarelli**, **Palazzetto Leone** and the **Ciarrocca tower–house** are enchanting.
In the upper part of the village, along the southeast side, we enter by the **Porta Medicea** gate while at the opposite end we find the so-called **Porta Lorda** along the southeast side.
The Medieval village's iconic feature is the massive embattled round tower, which collapsed after the 2009 earthquake. It is known as the "medicea" for the coat of arms of the great Florentine Medici family, who replaced the Piccolomini family as feudal lords here in the 16th century. This tower is about 18m in height and stands out from the urban skyline in an evident declaration of power over the territory. It is characterized by sophisticated building techniques including overhanging parapets with machicolations and corbels, closed by roof embattlements for overhead defence. The original parts of these elements are presumed to have been added subsequently.

132, 133. Above: the remains of the castle and the chapel of San Rocco, Barisciano.
134. Below: Casa del Capitano, San Stefano di Sessanio.
135. Facing page: aerial view of San Stefano di Sessanio.

Apart from the lovely **Santa Maria di Ruvo church**, it is worth visiting the **parish church of Santo Stefano**, with a stone Renaissance portal and, inside, a lovely 1500s statue of the Virgin Mary. The charming 17th-century **Madonna delle Grazie (or del Lago) church** is found near a small lake just outside the built-up centre. Here, the San Giovanni Battista altar along the church's right wall was decorated with a valuable 1720 canvas depicting *St John the Baptist*, by the master Domenico Gizzonio of Roccacasale. The painting has been moved to the Curia.

The lovely village of **CALASCIO** is built on the mountainside and proof of its historic prosperity thanks to shepherding activities is quite evident in the interesting civil and religious architecture, datable 14th–19th century, characterizing the entire urban fabric. The **parish church of San Nicola di Bari** (16th century) vaunts a exquisite interior, lavish chapels and beautiful canvases, including *St Nicholas* by Giulio Cesare Bedeschini and an *Annunciation* by Teofilo Patini.

The magnificent main portal with refined carvings of *The Life of the Saint* leads to the exquisite interior, in its 18th-century guise. The **church of Sant'Antonio Abate**, built in 1645, still has stuccowork by the Feneziani family and a copy of the Patini canvas of the *Temptations of St Anthony in the Desert*. The original artwork is now the large Frasca Collection set up in **Palazzo Frasca**, owned by the well-known Calascio family.

The **church of Santa Maria delle Grazie**, annexed to the Franciscan complex founded at the end of the 1500s, is also noteworthy. Passing through a stunning portico and a beautiful carved portal, we find some splendid wooden altars, a lovely 1515 terracotta of a *Madonna and Child*, a 1600s ciborium with wooden candelabra, and Giulio Cesare Bedeschini's painting of *St Francis Giving the Monastic Girdle to Louis of France*.

Sheer above the village is the ancient **Calascio keep** (*see box p. 87*), dominating the Tirino valley and the Navelli plain, set against the most breath-taking landscape, which has often been chosen as a film set.

Just outside of the ancient village of Rocca Calascio, and a short walk from the keep, we find the memorable **church of Santa Maria della Pietà**, looing above the Navelli plain below. The elegant octagonal tempietto, traditionally said to have been erected over an extant votive aedicule, was built in the late–16th–early–17th century.

The handsome central-plan layout, reminiscent of similar structures in Abruzzo, is further enhanced by the splendid landscape that is the backdrop to the site; the interior is organized as a system of Tuscan-style responds with an eight-segment cupola, configured in austere 1500s forms. A simple building, used as a sacristy, abuts one of the outer façades. The oratory is a station in an ancient devotional route.

136. 137. This double page: aerial view of Rocca Calascio village and the façade of the church of Santa Maria della Pietà.

## Calascio Keep

The fortress is a square-plan building with sloping round corner towers and a square central keep. The structure is considered one of the most significant obsidional installations on national territory for its unique layout rationality, rare building precision, and exceptional construction complexity to offset the impervious lie of the land where it is located. Built at about 1,500m in altitude and restored a few years ago, this is one of Italy's highest fortifications.

The fortification was built completely in stone and used only for military purposes, located in a point that was extremely favourable for defence. The entrance was set into the central, square tower at a height of about 5m above the inner court floor; the two stone brackets that just from the walls at the same height suggest that there may have been a wooden pull-up ladder for access purposes in the past. The fundamental strategic role played by the central square tower, originally isolated, was reinforced sometime in the mid–1400s, when the fortification – the property of the ancient Carapelle Barony for many years – was acquired by the Piccolomini family, who strengthened the structure to turn it into the mighty keep we see today. The round towers have unusual loophole-type embrasures, with underlying round arquebusiers.

The ruins of the village of Rocca Calascio, lower down the slope, are quite lovely and today partly recovered for use as guest quarters, separated from the fortress by a moat; the ancient urban walls with towers are still recognizable.

The splendid village of **CASTEL DEL MONTE**, hugging the mountain slopes and once a transhumance cultural capital, is one of the most interesting and well-preserved examples of urban fortification in Abruzzo. The outer buildings constitute a continuous terrace, and the narrow streets and compact layout generated a perfectly defendable settlement. Castel del Monte retains this plan, especially in the upper part, called the "**Ricetto**", presumed to be the original nucleus where the ancient castle was located. This area clusters around the square lookout tower, now the belfry of the **San Marco church** whose current configuration has been dated 14th–15th century. The rich interior vaults a 16th-century baptismal font with the Medici coat of arms, as well as a refined wood pulpit.
**Porta Ricetto** was one of two gates into the district of that name, which is reached by a narrow, terraced lane. Along the eastern side it is still possible to identify the walls of the ancient fortified village, thanks to the

138. 139. This page: above, the tower above the door of San Rocco church; below, aerial view of Castel del Monte.

remaining structures of a round flanking tower. **Porta di San Rocco**, with a mighty square tower above it leading into the ancient village, is still well-preserved, as are the other gates of **Porta di Santa Maria** and **Porta Sant'Ubaldo**; the latter, with a lancet arch, guards the northern slope, which must have been the most vulnerable part of the settlement.
The **Madonna del Suffragio church**, which dates back to the early–15th century, with Baroque modifications including a belfry added in 1834, is noteworthy. Inside there is a single bay with an impressive high altar in gilt carved wood, a statue of the Madonna originally dressed in ancient local costume. To the right of the altar the statue of *Our Lady of the Seven Sorrows*, dressed in a black costume interwoven with gold, follows the statue of the *Dead Christ* during the Good Friday procession. At the back there is a large organ, dated 1508. The church, which is the historic home of the Pastori confraternity, is where the *Quarant'ore* or Forty-Hour rite was held by shepherds about to undertake the long journey

down to Puglia, who went to pray before the holy effigy in the church, which was left open for 40 hours.

Those houses and stores that had fallen into disuse have now been transformed into a complex and intelligent **public museum** (Circuito Culturale-Centri Espositivi della Cultura Materiale), animated by reconstructions of traditional environments. Living conditions at the time of transhumant sheep-farming are illustrated using objects of daily life exhibited, along an itinerary that includes six stops: the mill; the municipal oven; the art of woolmaking; the home of a bygone era; shepherding; popular religious culture.

Nearby there is a wide valley, called Piano di San Marco, where it is possible to identify the remains of the Medieval village and a huge Italic necropolis has been brought to light in this area. Francesco Giuliani (1890–1970), one of Abruzzo's most evocative poets, a shepherd and talented woodcarver, was born in Castel del Monte.

Close by, **VILLA SANTA LUCIA DEGLI ABRUZZI** stands in a mountain amphitheatre, near a fortified area southeast of the town, called Il Castelluccio and thought to have originated in the Dark Ages. Also worth mentioning is the **rural church of Santa Maria delle Vicenne**, also dated to the Early Medieval period, with its interesting hexagonal floor and the splendid 1492 fresco depicting the Virgin Mary, St Christopher and St Blaise. From Villa Santa Lucia we reach the remains of the **Forca di Penne tower**, in a particularly lovely scenario. The pass, set midway on the slope, marks the southeast border of the *Comitatus* of L'Aquila, and was an important passage on the sheep track. Indeed, together with neighbouring Popoli, it was an obligatory path for shepherds and their sheep. This is the location of the Forca di Penne WWF Oasis, an ideal place for birdwatching, covered by the municipalities of Capestrano (AQ), Brittoli and Corvara (PE).

Opposite Villa Santa Lucia we see **OFENA**, the ancient Italic town of Aufinum. The fortified Medieval village still has some of its ancient walls, absorbed by the characteristic tall, compact dwellings, which also had a defensive purpose. The urban layout rarely takes into account land contours and is true to the cruciform Roman arrangement. One of the most striking noble residences is three-storey **Palazzo Cataldi-Madonna**, with an impressive stone portal. Just outside of the built-up centre there is the **convent of Santa Maria de Fantucio** (dei Cappuccini), modernized in the 1930s and later restored. The **convent of San Francesco** or San Giacomo was also restored in recent times after many remodelling episodes in the Renaissance and Baroque periods. The church portal and small right-hand loggia, with round arches and narrow stone columns, belong to the 1400s phase. The elegant rectangular cloister has a central well; the church was noteworthy but much of its priceless Baroque decoration has been lost. The aisleless interior with lunette barrel vaults has a high altar surmounted by a small oval cupola that underscores visual and symbolic significance. The small church of San Pietro in Criptys is just outside the village, with a handsome sculpted portal bearing the date 1196 and some interesting 15th-century frescoes.

140. 141. Above: left, the church of San Rocco, Castel del Monte; right, the rural church of Santa Maria delle Vicenne, Villa San Lucia degli Abruzzi.
142. Below: Ofena village.

The territories in the municipalities of Ofena and Villa Santa Lucia are part of the Voltigno and Valle d'Angri nature reserve, the biggest in Abruzzo.

On the way back to Calascio, a detour takes to a village just off the L'Aquila–Foggia sheep track, **CASTELVECCHIO CALVISIO**, of great environmental and urban significance. It is one of the most charming and the best-preserved of the Region's fortified villages. The ancient layout is still perfectly visible, with the straight streets of Roman design and an urban fabric compact behind the perimeter wall-houses that stand as an impenetrable boundary with watchtowers installed set against dwellings, and the natural defence offered by steep slopes. The round watchtower on the outer boundary, to the south, is a surviving element of the fortified walls. There were three gates into the ancient village: **Porta di Torre Maggiore** to the west, which led to Via Archi and Borghi Romani, the main streets; **Porta Ponte Levatoio** to the northeast, surmounted by a now-illegible noble coat of arms; and **Porta di San Martino** to the south. The narrow lanes, with their typical vaulted passageways and steep stone outer staircases, set mainly on rampant arches, leading to the other storeys, make the centre of Castelvecchio quite distinctive. Piazza di Torre Maggiore with its **Palazzo del Capitano** is a striking part of the village.

Medieval buildings include the noteworthy **San Giovanni Battista church** with two asymmetrical aisles and a surviving refined Baroque-style high altar, with exquisite carving. The church originally had a carved wood

143. Below: aerial view of Castelvecchio Calvisio.
144–146. Facing page: top left, the church of San Francesco, Carapelle Calvisio; top right, San Pio delle Camere; below, the church of San Cipriano, Castelvecchio Calvisio.

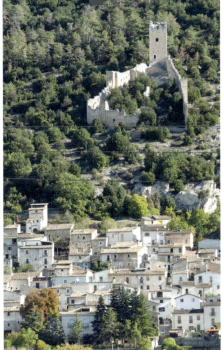

*Enthroned Virgin with Child*, dated 1400s, and now owned by the MUNDI – Museo Nazionale d'Abruzzo. Not far away there is the interesting historic **church of San Cipriano**, on the site of the San Lorenzo castle, documented as early as the 8th century. There are spectacular views over the villages of Calascio, Carapelle, and of the Ofena Basin.

The village of **CARAPELLE CALVISIO**, which is mentioned as early as the Dark Ages (779) and gave its name to the Barony of Carapelle, is one of the most interesting in Abruzzo for the uniform nature of its minor architecture. The older section, at the top of the hill, has retained in full the layout of its original fortified wall circuit; one of the ramparts was subsequently used in the building of the parish church. Ancient noble residences emerge in the urban fabric and testify to a period of great wealth brought by sheep-rearing activities. The **church of San Francesco**, part of the former Franciscan convent, is significant for its 15th–16th-century frescoes and for the striking stucco high altar, as well as interesting frescoes attributed to Francesco da Montereale: an *Adoration of the Magi* (1502–49) and a cycle inspired by the *Life of St Peter*.

The villagers are particularly devoted to St Pancras and in a sanctuary dedicated to him they still perform an anointing rite using the miraculous "oil of St Pancras".

Down towards the SS17 state road there is a particularly charming village, **SAN PIO DELLE CAMERE**, named for a system of refuges, often underground, called "camere" (chambers), used to shelter flocks from nearby Peltuinum. On the slope above the village there is its **castle**, one of the best examples of Abruzzo and Italian fortification–compounds. Presumed to have been built originally in the 12th century, it was part of an extensive fortification phenomenon undertaken then and constructed as an isosceles triangle similar to that of Roccasale. It is dominated by a pentagonal bulwark tower set at the vertex, and with other smaller four-sided half-towers.

The **parish church of San Pio**, dating back to the 16th century, with frescoes and fine sacred furnishings, and the 1500s church of San Pietro Celestino, but of more ancient foundation, with 17th-century paintings and interesting pieces of sacred jewellery are worthy of note.

We reach the state road then continue towards **PRATA D'ANSIDONIA** and after passing the fork for Castelnuovo, a singular fortified village sadly damaged by the

2009 earthquake, we encounter the magical ruins of **Peltuinum** (*see box p. 92*), an ancient town built on the sheep track.

Near to the ruins of this Vestino–Roman town, there is the **church of San Paolo di Peltuinum**, built in the first half of the 12th century, and subsequently modified. It is interesting for the extensive use of materials recovered from the neighbouring town, as well as use of fragments from the Dark Ages, possibly taken from an extant church. The church has a nave with a large transept and no apse; the façade, of which the upper part has been modified, has a slightly protruding central section, which includes a simple portal surmounted by a small wheel window. The exquisite pulpit in this church dates back to 1240 and was brought here in 1796 from the nearby Prata D'Ansidonia **parish church of San Nicola**, of 13th-century origin, but rebuilt in a Baroque style. Opposite, Prata D'Ansidonia, in attractive hillside position, there is **Castelcamponeschi**, a fortified village built mainly in the 14th–15th centuries, abandoned in the 1950s, and now under restoration. The old village is a unique example not only in L'Aquila but throughout the region, of striking defence installations and a splendid landscape setting, as well as making extensive use of stone elements taken from nearby Peltuinum. Its layout is still discernible, with boundary walls, half-towers and ogival gates; the western gate is flanked by a sturdy tower. Recent work and excavations revealed that inside the

## Peltuinum, Ancient Town on the Sheep Track

This monumental archaeological site is located on a tableland dominating the Navelli plain. The building of the Roman town began in the mid-1st century BC, which completed the central area, where excavations have identified structures connected to the town's public and cultural life, including the remains of the **temple of Apollo**, pillaged in the Middle Ages. The monumental **theatre** belongs to the Augustan era, as do several private buildings, surviving sections of the boundary walls, and, above all, the **western gate**, which comprises a double arch defended by mighty towers. The gate marked the entrance to the sheep track, which crossed the town from gate to gate, along its main axis, mimicking the Via Claudia Nova, crossed by streets at right angles, as can still be seen in the subdivision of the fields. The town's economic system was completely bound to transhumance, levying taxes for those using the *calles* and *viae publicae*.

walls, turreted near the village gates, there was a built-up area with two significant buildings: the church of San Paolo, with portals dated 1313 and 1614, and the building opposite. Leporanica "castle", whose boundary walls can still be seen clinging to a high slope, looms over the settlement of San Nicandro to the southeast. Leporanica's fortifications, strengthened by two half-towers, have a single arch positioned at the southern corner. As early as the 15th century the population began to desert the village.

On the SS17 state road, before reaching Caporciano, on the left there is the pastoral **church of Santa Maria dei Cintorelli**, set where the sheep track from L'Aquila forks into two branches after crossing the Peltuinum area: the first curves down towards the Adriatic; the second, called the Centurelle–Montesecco, continues towards Navelli and Collepietro, then down to the coast. The church, finished in 1561, was a stopover for flocks during the long transhumance journey, and has an impressive Renaissance-type façade with the date 1558 inscribed on the portal architrave frieze. In the interior the nave ends in a polygonal apse, with two side chapels, also polygonal, forming the transept wings. A triumphal arch frames the Baroque-style altar. A vaulted portico block, set against the outer right wall, was used as a refuge by shepherds.

The church was abandoned at the end of the 1800s and damaged during World War II, but was restored in the 1960s–1970s. A recent restoration and functional recovery project of the religious complex planned to install a documentation centre for local traditions and religious aspects of the main sheep track.

Turning right we come to the ancient village of **CAPORCIANO**, whose original fortified structure was subsequently absorbed by urban expansion and only the main northern tower has survived, now the church belfry, and once the foremost bastion of the ancient walls that

147–149. Facing page: views of the ruins of Peltuinum.
150. Above: the church of Santa Maria dei Cintorelli.
151. Below: the fortified village of Castelcamponeschi.

stretched southward; the irregular rectangular building has a mighty scarp and it is still possible to see the embrasures and loopholes of a later date inserted in the curtain walls.

To northwest the apse of the **San Benedetto Abate mother church** incorporates parts of the outer fortifications and the old arrow slits are still discernible, some modified to accommodate cannon embrasures. Three other half-towers are also identifiable, although they are now dwellings. The gates are virtually untouched, and the portion added in the 16th century appears well-preserved.

The **church of San Pietro in Valle**, near the Parco della Rimembranza, can be dated 9th–10th century and was built on the site of ancient burials that came to light here. The fresco depicting the *Deposition with the Virgin Safeguarding the Ampoule with the Blood of Christ, the Pious Women, Two Devotees, St Benedict Showing the Rule* was part of the church but is now kept in L'Aquila's MUNDI – National Museum of Abruzzo, while 15th-century frescoes are still visible.

In nearby **Bominaco** there are two very interesting churches: **Santa Maria Assunta** and **San Pellegrino** (*see box p. 95*), all that remains of an ancient convent complex. At the top of the mount that dominates the two churches, there is the **castle**, a quadrilateral compound cadenced by square towers, and an impressive round tower with scarp and overhanging coping. The castle was part of the extensive visual communications system that connected with other fortresses throughout the territory.

The community buzzes with activity for the feast day of St Michael the Archangel on 8 May. Following a mass in the church of Santa Maria Assunta, worshippers form a procession to the **sanctuary of San Michele**, where the signs they see etched into the rock are believed to be the imprint left by the saint as he passed.

From the Navelli plain, near the fork in the L'Aquila–Foggia sheep track, we see the village of **Civitaretenga**, which developed around a square tower, destroyed after the 2009 earthquake and now one of the most interesting villages in Abruzzo for urban

152. Above: Bominaco castle.
153. Below: the interior of the oratory of San Pellegrino.
154. 155. Facing page: above, detail of the fresco cycle in the oratory of San Pellegrino; below, the interior of the church of Santa Maria Assunta.

# Santa Maria Assunta and San Pellegrino, Bominaco

In its current layout, the splendid Romanesque **church of Santa Maria Assunta** dates back to no earlier than the turn of the 12th century: it has been nave and two aisles with round arches on columns, and three apses. The façade, austere and understated, has a single portal that imitates the motifs used for the secondary portals at San Liberatore a Majella, surmounted by a round arch window installed at a later date. The façade has a cuspidate Puglia-style coping in the centre, and horizontal over the side aisles. The lovely interior still has masterpieces like the 1180 ambo and the abbey throne (1184), recomposed in the late–1800s, both commissioned by Abbott Giovanni, who is depicted on one side of the throne with the bishop's insignia. The Paschal candle, the 1223 ciborium and the altar, and made at the behest of Abbot Berardo according to the inscription on the altar itself. The exquisite ciborium was recomposed in 1934 recovering parts removed during the 18th century. It is still possible to discern fragments of the 1300–1400s frescoes.

The **San Pellegrino oratory** was founded by Charlemagne, but rebuilt as we see it today in 1263, as indicated by the inscription above the rosette on the rear façade, as well as by a second inscription legible on the upper part of the two exquisite pluteuses that divide the oratory into two sections, separating the space reserved for the faithful from that reserved for the catechumens. The church has a clear Cistercian imprint, with a single Gothic vault interior cadenced by four bays with reinforcing arches. The small porch in front of the main entrance was added in the 18th century with the use of Roman column drums. A marvellous cycle of frescoes covers the walls and vault, standing as the apex of pictorial decoration in Abruzzo in the second half of the 13th century. *Episodes from the Life of Christ*, and scenes dedicated to the *Life of St Peregrine*, and the figures of prophets and saints were painted in three registers. The cycle in the upper section is dedicated to *describing the childhood,*

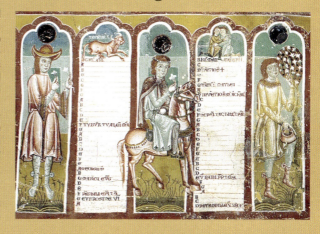

beginning with the *Annunciation* and closing with the *Presentation of Jesus in the Temple*. The lower sections illustrate the *Passion of Christ*, beginning with the *Arrival in Jerusalem*, followed by the *Last Supper*, and closing with the *Burial*. The third bay, although damaged, is a unique and extremely interesting document, being a *liturgical calendar*, which not only includes signs of the zodiac and the symbolic depiction of the months, but also lists the days of the month and the liturgical instructions. The style of three separate artists has been identified: the "Maestro della Passione", who seems to have painted all the wall frescoes as well as those in the entrance and at the back, including the *Last Supper* over the vault springer in the first bay on the left; the "Maestro dell'Infanzia", who worked in the first two bays; lastly the "Maestro Miniaturista" who painted the vault of the third bay, with the two semesters of the *Bominaco monastic calendar*, reproducing in miniature the decoration rendered on a monumental scale.

morphology and well-preserved monuments. The typical Via Giudea winds its way through the oldest district, an arcaded path that leads us to the heart of the ancient Jewish quarter. In addition to the interesting **Palazzo Cortelli** and **Palazzo Perelli**, it is worth visiting the beautiful **church of San Salvatore**, embellished with refined stuccos and the **church of Sant'Egidio** with remarkable frescoes.

Just outside the built-up area, there is the **convent of Sant'Antonio**, which was recently restored and is characterized by an elegant cloister; the portico dates back to the mid-13th century and has columns and polygonal pillars with fantastic capitals.

Slightly lower down in the village it is possible to visit the **sheep-track church of Santa Maria delle Grazie**, built in the second half of the 1500s, and with the neighbouring church of Santa Maria dei Cintorelli, near Caporciano, offered spiritual comfort and a safe refuge for shepherds and flocks. The nave interior is closed by a polygonal apse; the Renaissance-style façade is framed by corner pilaster strips and has traditional L'Aquila horizontal coping. A huge rose window in the upper part is the result of recent restoration.

On the left of the main road, next to the cemetery, just before Navelli, there is the **church of Santa Maria in Cerulis**, built in ancient times, whose name comes from the Vestino village of *Incerulae*. The current entrance on the right, moved with respect to the original access, accesses a nave-and-two-aisle with two apses, of which the left shows traces of 14th-century frescoes. Taking the fork for Navelli, along a secondary road we find the **Madonna delle Grazie church** with a portico leaning against the façade. Continuing from Navelli towards Popoli, we find the **Madonna del Campo church** on the right, also with a typical portico, and once a stopover for shepherds and flocks.

**NAVELLI**, which developed as a Medieval village over a settlement that was probably of pre-Roman origin, has the typical compact layout of many inland Abruzzo towns.

Immediately above **Piazza San Pelino**, at the foot of the town, we find the **Madonna del Rosario church**, whose austere façade is embellished with a beautiful stone portal finished by a gable and Navelli's opulent coat of arms of a ship with full-blown sails.

In the village, the presence of refined mansions is striking and suggests the historic wealth produced by the thriving saffron and sheep-farming trades. Just after Piazza Piccioli in the heart of the village, with its imposing eponymous residence and adjoining **San Gennaro and Rosario chapel**, we happen upon **Palazzo Francesconi** where the splendid loggia with round arches on columns, forward of the main building. The palazzo has its own 17th-century **San Pasquale chapel** with exquisite decoration.

The houses climb the gentle slope and gather in the highest part, around the striking bulk of late–Renaissance **Palazzo Santucci**. It replaces an older construction and despite the residential aspects dominant in this building, it is still possible to identify several typical defence elements, including exterior corner towers, supported by triple-element brackets projecting from the compact palazzo. The blocks are arranged around a courtyard dominated by a monumental well and a dual-ramp staircase leading up to the elegant loggia set on the side opposite the entrance. There has been some significant restoration work recently, converting the complex to a documentation centre for sheep-track economy.

In the Medieval part of the "Spiagge Grandi" district we find **Palazzo Onofri**, attached to one of the five access gates to the village, **Porta Villotta** also known as Porta Sud. Dating back to the end of the 15th century, it was completely renovated after the 1703 earthquake. Immediately below Palazzo Santucci we find the 17th-century **San Sebastiano church**. The

156. Facing page: the sheep-track church of Santa Maria delle Grazie with Civitaretenga.
157. 158. This page: above, the emblem on the portal of the church of the Madonna del Rosario, Navelli; below, view of Navelli.

monumental carved wooden portal leads to the interior with its nave and two aisles, embellished with sumptuous Baroque altars. In addition to a beautiful processional cross, there are two canvases ascribed to the greatest painter active in L'Aquila in the early decades of the 17th century, Giulio Cesare Bedeschini. The first is a *Madonna and Child with Saints Stephen and Nicholas*, recently restored, and a canvas with *St Charles Borromeo and a Saint Bishop adoring the Crucified Christ*.

From Navelli the itinerary continues towards **CAPESTRANO**, an ancient fortified village overlooking the Tirino valley, and with an interesting overlap of Medieval and Renaissance architectures, with a series of well-made buildings. The castle and the entire village were protected by a walled enclosure, with five urban gates: Porta Parete, Porta del Sacco, Porta del Lago, Porta la Palma, and Porta Castello also called Porta la Macchia.

The presence of the impressive **Piccolomini (or Mediceo) castle** is the main feature of the built-up centre. The history of the castle

is tied to the various important families who lived on the territory, from the Acquaviva dukes of San Valentino to the Piccolominis, then the Medicis, to whom the fiefdom belonged until the abolition of feudalism.

Despite numerous changes, the castle still represents one of the most inspiring fortified complexes in the region, with the triangular parade ground, the rooms for the garrison, and the two ravelins defending the southeast and northwest entrances. The first was strengthened by a drawbridge subsequently replaced by a stone bridge. The building is currently used as the town hall and has a 1400s layout that has embraced the remains of an extant fortification, of which the mighty prismatic tower has survived, offset from the castle layout, and subsequently integrated with an overhanging coping. The façade, with windows, faces the square and is flanked by two round, scarped towers. It was originally a blind curtain wall but was totally transformed by 1924 interventions that also made significant interior alterations. The courtyard, where a staircase accessed the upper floors, has a refined polygonal well, attributed to the 15th century.

A lovely and very ancient **parish church, Santa Maria della Pace**, was rebuilt in 1643 over an existing chapel, and consecrated in 1768. The soaring belfry with onion dome is dated 1841–57. In the area of the nearby Tirino springs, more historic events are suggested by the discovery of an Italic statue, known as the Warrior of Capestrano, now in Chieti National Archaeological Museum, emblem of a powerful class of shepherd–warriors who established themselves in Abruzzo during the Iron Age.

Nearby it is worth visiting the **San Francesco or San Giovanni convent**, founded in the 15th century, by order of Giovanni da Capestrano, and progressively modified and extended until the mid–19th century. The annexed church was extended by the addition of a large apsed presbytery (1735) with two square chapels on the right-hand side, and in in 1647 a cupola with clerestory was added to the structure dedicated to St John. In 1709, the charming frescoed cloister was added to the left side of the church and in 1742 the dormitory and the library were enlarged. The unusual staircase, added in 1750 to connect the cloister to the upper floor, is striking. Today's façade was added in 1925. This convent is home to the **San Giovanni da Capestrano convent museum**, and exhibits some priceless ancient texts, as well as numerous mementos of the life of the saint who was born and lived here from 1386 to 1456.

Near Capestrano, in the splendid scenario of the Tirino valley, it is possible to visit the **church of San Pietro ad Oratorium**, all that remains of the ancient monastery traditionally said to have been founded between the 8th and 9th centuries, by order of the Lombard King Desiderius. It was rebuilt in 1100, as indicated by the inscription on the main portal architrave, with its sumptuous foliage motif sculptures. The floorplan follows the layout of all early Romanesque churches, so it

159 Facing page: Capestrano castle.
160, 161. This page: ciborium in the church of San Pietro ad Oratorium; right, the stone ashlar walled outside the façade, left facing the main portal, with a Latin epigraph of five simple but enigmatic engraved words:
 SATOR AREPO TENET OPERA ROTAS.
In this order the inscription forms a palindrome, so it reads the same whichever way we look at it: from left to right or top to bottom, and vice versa, or alternating the direction of reading at each line it will be like entering a fascinating, symbolic maze. Of the numerous interpretations seeking to explain the meaning of the so-called "magic square", dated Late Antiquity, one associates the epigraph to the cryptographic palindrome of the anagram of the words "Pater Noster".
It seems to seek to imitate with letters the way opened by numerical magic squares, probing the infinite potentialities of language seeking to merge them with a depiction of the world.

has a nave and two aisles, cadenced by seven round arches and three apses. The 13th-century ciborium is extremely exquisite, set on its four columns with architraves, which supports 16 slim pillars surmounted by a truncated pyramid and canopy with small cupola. What makes this ciborium unique in Abruzzo is the use of majolica elements inserted in the triangles placed at the intersections of the arches. These 16 majolica tiles are decorated with geometric designs and colours that range from green to manganese brown and yellow on a white background. Seven tiles are intact while only a few fragments remain of the others.

In the apse bowl we find a striking cycle of frescoes that depict scenes from the Old and New Testaments, which are the Region's most ancient and important pictorial expressions of the 12th century.

The façade includes fragments brought from the original church and a singular ashlar has been walled back-to-front, interesting for an enigmatic word composition, which can be read in every direction. Among the numerous interpretations of the wording, one associates the epigraph with a cryptographic palindrome, an anagram of the words "Pater Noster" (*see box p. 99*).

From Navelli we can continue towards Popoli, passing through hilltop **COLLEPIETRO**, with its evident original Medieval fortified village layout and still has its tall tower from the ancient fortified wall. Nearby, the parish **church of San Giovanni Battista** has an interesting Renaissance-style portal and in the surrounding area we will find the rural **chapel of Madonna del Buon Consiglio**, set along the sheep track and now abandoned, but once a stopover for shepherds and their flocks.

**SAN BENEDETTO IN PERILLIS** was built in a dominant position over the Peligno basin and is an admirable walled village, with traces of ancient walls and towers, developing around an ancient monastic community that had settled in the "Perello" district to found the **abbey of San Benedetto**. The church inside the fortified village, on the upper part of the slope, is the only surviving testimony of the ancient abbey structure that played such a significant role in spreading monasticism in the Tritana valley and throughout the territory of L'Aquila. The building was founded in ancient times and we now see the results if many refurbishments. The façade with an exceptional hanging loggia device that is unique in Abruzzo but can be found in historic churches in the Lombard Duchy of Spoleto, in Umbria. Recent restoration dismantled Baroque additions and brought to light the original Early Medieval structures. The nave-and-two-aisle interior has a wooden ceiling and there are still traces of exquisite frescoes. Apart from the **Madonna delle Grazie church**, we recommend a visit to the **museum of material culture**. There are two sections: the first deals with prehistory and the other with anthropology; on display there are material testimonies of life and work in the local community, characterized in the past by a combination of farming and pastoral economy.

## Valle Peligna and the Cinque Miglia Plateau

The itinerary begins in the centre of **CORFINIO**, built on the site of ancient *Corfinium*, blessed with an excellent geographical position on the right bank of the River Aterno. *Corfinium* was set strategically at the confluence of important roads and was the nerve centre for the Peligno area, to the point that it became the capital of the Italic League during the Social Wars and, immediately afterwards, a Roman *municipium*. Traces of the ancient layout and remains of architectural structures can still be identified in today's urban layout. An early nucleus, which coincides with the Medieval *castrum* of Pentima, set to the north, must have extended south until it became an entire urban layout, arranged on two main axes, connected by a series of parallel streets: Via Valeria, which in the urban section coincides with today's Via Poppedio, and the route corresponding to Via di Pratola, coming from the southeast. The most significant building in this layout was the **theatre**, whose presence is also confirmed by epigraphical documents, pinpointed as being in what is now Piazza Corfinio, datable to the early–1st century BC; the layout of later dwellings, set over the ancient cavea, respected its configuration, still easy to discern in some of the structures. The invaluable relics brought to light by excavations conducted from 1989 to 1994 by the Archaeological Superintendency,

Corfinio, Raiano, Vittorito, Prezza, Pratola Peligna, Roccacasale, Sulmona, Badia Morronese, Introdacqua, Bugnara, Pettorano sul Gizio, Rocca Pia, Rivisondoli, Roccaraso, Pietransieri, Ateleta, Castel di Sangro, Pescocostanzo, Cansano, Campo di Giove, Pacentro

The suggested itinerary includes strongholds of the defensive system that dominated the natural gateways in the Peligna valley, set at the confluence of the Aterno, Sagittario, Gizio and Giardino rivers; moreover, it is marked by the passage of the most important ancient routes, the first of which is the sheep track that went from Celano, coasting the northern slope of the Fucino basin, hugging the Tiburtina Valeria road beyond Collarmele, reaching Corfinio and then turning up towards the plateaux to reach Castel di Sangro, at the centre of what is perhaps most important trade and communications crossroads in the entire Abruzzo region. From Celano onwards, the first section of the Marsican sheep track is characterized by a military element, and after Collarmele, leaves to its left the 1300s Aielli tower, reaching Pettorano sul Gizio, on the southern side of the Peligno basin, the meeting point of the sheep track after it passes Raiano, the Prezza and Introdacqua countryside, and centres around Pettorano's historic fort, before facing the assent to the Cinque Miglia plain, as far as the Altipiani Maggiori, the historic and obligatory passing on the way to Naples, which is now home to the most complete ski resort in the Centre-South of Italy. The territory lies in one of the most challenging areas of the Abruzzo mountains, famous for the artistic heritage of the Peligno towns, and immersed in the green vegetation of Majella National Park and several nature reserves, an enchanting scenario that offers visitors a truly unique experience. Of the many towns that have been linked to sheep farming over the centuries, the most significant are Sulmona and Pescocostanzo; the latter, with its compact urban fabric and buildings of great artistic value, can be called the authentic cultural "capital" of this territory.

162. 163. Facing page: left, the Medieval tower of Collepietro; right, the abbey of San Benedetto in Perillis.
164. Left: the church of the Madonna del Soccorso, Corfinio.

in the Piano San Giacomo, Sant'Ippolito, and Impianata sites, and along Via di Pratola Peligna, confirmed that this was indeed a prestigious town. A significant part of the numerous inscriptions found by the scholar Antonio De Nino on the territory of ancient Corfinium, have been taken to the **Lapidarium** of the **Museo Civico Archeologico "A. De Nino"** in Piazza Corfinio, which has the largest number of funerary and celebratory epigraphs, covering a lengthy span of time, from the 1st century BC to the 2nd century AD. The **church of San Martino** with a beautiful 15th-century portal is near the remains of the Roman theatre. Also in the heart of the village there is the church of **Santa Maria del Soccorso**, with a surviving 16th-century portal.

**San Pelino basilica** is the cathedral of Valva diocese and one of the greatest Medieval monuments in Abruzzo, found on the edge of the old town. The cathedral complex comprises two separate blocks: the Sant'Alessandro oratory, a rectangular interior with centre apse, dated 1180–90, and independent of the cathedral; and the basilica, completed in the 1130s and modified in about 1235. The basilica has a nave and two aisles, with square pilasters, and a round triumphal arch that leads into the raised transept, with barrel and cross vaults. The nave ends in the single apse, cadenced outside by four horizontal decorative strips comprising slim columns, sculpted slabs, and windows. The interior, which was given a Baroque refurbishment from 1682 to 1704, was restored in 1960–71, which gave the nave a wooden ceiling and eliminated the cupola with external lantern tower. The church furnishings are of artistic interest, including the splendid 12th-century ambo, which became an outright prototype.

Particularly precious are the frescoes, painted in several campaigns between the 13th and 16th centuries, including the *Ecstasy of Saint Francis* in the late–1200s, and a *Crucifixion* from the first decades of the 1400s. The full-height figure of *St Anthony of Padua* is outstanding and is attributed to style of a skilled late–15th-century Abruzzo painter, the so-called Maestro di Caramanico. Also interesting is a 12th-century bas-relief *Madonna and Child*. The Sant'Alessandro oratory vaunts some interesting 14th-century frescoes.

In the surrounding area the abandoned hermit's refuge of San Terenziano is interesting.

**RAIANO**, a farming town famous for its abundant cherry crops, is on the edge of the Peligno valley, to the right of the River Aterno valley, where the Celano–Foggia sheep track turns towards Sulmona. The old town was abandoned in the late–1400s and relocated downhill at the top of the slope near the Via Valeria. This new settlement takes a trapezoidal form north of Via Sansonesco between Via Rainaldi and Via San Nicola, where more buildings were subsequently constructed on the edge of the sloping area, with the fortified village with wall-houses and sloping walls pinpointed here. A surviving round tower has been englobed in the urban fabric.

One of the most important buildings is the parish **church of Santa Maria Maggiore**, with precious statue of *St Venanzio* in silver lamina, by an 18th-century Abruzzo artist, a late–1400s wooden statue of *Our Lady of the Snow*, and a *Dead Christ* of the 18th century. The slab used as the altar antependium, brought from the Madonna de Contra church and datable to the 8th century, is worthy of note. Also of interest are the **church of Madonna delle Grazie** and, in particular, the **church and convent of Sant'Onofrio**, founded in 1611 by the Reformed Franciscans. A remarkable cloister has frescoes and a wooden Baroque altar, by the Bencivenga brothers (all 18th century). Elegant noble mansions like **Palazzo Muzi**, **Palazzo Lepore** and 18th-century **Palazzo Sagaria-Rossi**, where Benedetto Croce was a frequent guest, are all very interesting.

Outside the built-up centre we find the spectacular San Venanzio gullies, which part of a nature reserve, straddling the River Aterno. The sheer rock face is the site of the enchanting ancient **San Venanzio hermitage**, popular with pilgrims, with its precious 16th-century terracotta group of the *Mourning of Christ* as well as 15th–16th-century frescoes. Also nearby there is the charming rural chapel of Madonna de Contra, the oldest place of worship in the village alongside the **church of**

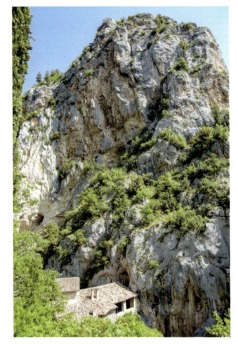

165–167. Facing page: exterior and interior of the basilica of San Pelino, Corfinio.
168. 169. This page: above, the exterior of the hermitage of San Venanzio, Raiano, and the *Lamentation of Christ* in polychrome terracotta.
170. Right: the hermitage of San Venanzio amid the River Aterno gorges near Raiano.

**Sant'Antonio**, with an inscription on the architrave that dates the building to the 11th century.
Nearby **VITTORITO** has a very characteristic upper section, with its stone houses, including one with an interesting two-light lancet window, and remains of a Medieval castle. In the lower part of Vittorito there is an attractive 1400s **church**: **Santa Maria del Borgo** or Madonna della Neve.

The nave-and-two-aisle interior includes excellent frescoes and stuccoes, as well as a magnificent wooden statue of the *Madonna of the Village*. Over the side door, dated 1513, there is a fresco of the *Enthroned Madonna with Child and two Saints*.
The **church of San Michele Arcangelo**, of ancient origins, but renovated in the 14th century (although a portal inscription indicates 1404), is very interesting. The squarish interior has no apse, with a nave and two aisles, divided by rectangular pillars, with ogival arches to the right and, on the left, a round arch. An outstanding ciborium supported by two columns on the front and two octagonal pillars on the back is set at rear of the nave, above the altar. The church has cross vaults and a tabernacle decorated with 1400s frescoes. A later belfry is set to the left of the bare curtain of the main prospect and in the centre there are the fragments of an entrance portal, produced with pillaged materials. The charm of the church lies in its religious furnishings and these pillaged architectural fragments.
The itinerary doubles back to Raiano and then moves on to Medieval **PREZZA**, built on the slopes of the mountain of the same name, set on a bastion looking out over the River Sagittario, a perfect belvedere over the valley. The original nucleus can be pinpointed in the upper part of the built-up area, clustered around the church, and buildings sloping down the incline. The **Palazzo Baronale** and the ancient **parish church of Santa Lucia** are worthy of note. A portico is set on the façade, with an ogival portal showing a lunette fresco of *Our Lady of the Rosary*. Inside, on a pillar, there is a fresco of a *Madonna and Child* attributed to the Maestro di Caramanico. In the Colle di Prezza district we find the **Santa Maria di Loreto church** with its original façade.
From Prezza the route turns back to the densely-populated town of **PRATOLA PELIGNA**,

171. Above: the frescoes on the side door of the church of Santa Maria del Borgo, Vittorito.
172–174. Below: left, the façade of the Madonna della Libera sanctuary; right, the "seven Marys" in terracotta and the frescoes in the Madonna delle Grazie oratory, in Pratola Peligna.
175. Facing page: Roccacasale.

located in the heart of the Peligno valley, to the left of the River Sagittario. This was the hometown of the illustrious archaeologist and folklorist, Antonio De Nino (1833–1907), to whom a research centre is dedicated. The original nucleus is still discernible, retaining the fortified village configuration cluster layout ("dentro la Terra" district). Ancient **Palazzo De Petris**, with a remarkable rusticated portal and an inscription above that states it was built in the 16th-century is in Piazza San Pietro Celestino. Pratola's oldest church, **San Pietro Celestino**, is also here, as well as the **Madonna della Pietà church**, with Renaissance frescoes. The **Madonna delle Grazie oratory**, built in 1540, with its terracotta *Lamentation of Christ*, known to locals as the "sette Marie", can be dated late–1400s–early–1500s.

Also worthy of note is the elegant **Palazzo Santoro**, with a beautiful portal and the inscribed date 1649, but there are several other examples of noble mansions in town, including **Palazzo Santoro-Colella**, **Palazzo Tedeschi**, **Palazzo Colella**, and **Palazzo De Prospero**, with a plaque commemorating Antonio De Nino.

The **Teatro d'Andrea** is also very interesting, built between in 1925–30.

Another monument is the majestic **Madonna della Libera sanctuary**, destination of a devout pilgrimage on the first Sunday in May. The façade of the Marian sanctuary shows two belfries and four aedicules with statues of the apostles, and was built from 1851 to a design by Eusebio Tedeschi, a Pratola engineer, on the site of an existing 1500s chapel, where a miracle was said to have occurred. The miraculous image of the Virgin Mary which inspired the construction of the original chapel in 1540, as stated by the inscription below the fresco, is found in the Madonna chapel to the right of the presbytery. The majestic layout features a nave and two aisles ending in semi-circular apses with small side chapels. The façade with its two towers has a forward central section, cadenced in two orders. The interior decoration was completed in the 1920s; the stuccoes were produced by the workshops of the Feneziani and Pavoni families of L'Aquila, with sculptures by Nazareno Di Rienzo and paintings by artists including Teofilo Patini and Amedeo Tedeschi.

In the left aisle we can admire a beautiful canvas painted in 1720 by Roccacasale painter Domenico Gizzonio, depicting a *St John the Evangelist on Patmos*. The work is signed and dated, and is a replica of a 17th-century painting by Giacomo Farelli, displayed in the church of San Giovanni Evangelista in Sulmona. Just inside the side entrance to the SS Trinità chapel, the eponymous painting by Guardiagrele painting Ferdinando Palmerio, a canvas signed and dated 1872. Palmerio also signed the altarpiece depicting the *Last Supper* painted in 1869 and found in the chapel of San Giuseppe. Leaving the town and leaving behind the SS17 state road, just after the railway bridge, it is worth visiting the **Museo della Civiltà Contadina**, dedicated to rural life and housed in the premises of the ancient **Molino dei Celestini**, a mill of uncertain foundation but probably enlarged in the 17th century to facilitate its use by local inhabitants.

The charming village di **ROCCACASALE** is near the main road, on the lower slopes of the Rocca Mountains. Above it lie the remains of the **De Sanctis castle**, part of the Peligno chequerboard defence system, built on an inaccessible site to control the underlying village. The ruins show a typical triangular layout resembling that of San Pio delle Camere, although far nearer to the village and characterized in the upper part by a soaring watchtower, of which the southeast flank and several attached structures to the south survive.

On the downstream side we see the remains of a baronial building and within the boundaries a modern construction has been added for use as a museum space.

The village has the noteworthy **San Michele Arcangelo parish church**, with a nave and two aisles, dating back to the 16th century, but remodelled in the 1700s. On the Colle delle Fate large sections of walls are still visible relating to a pre-Roman settlement.

**SULMONA** lies deep in the heart of the Peligno valley, installed in a splendid basin at the front of the Morrone massif, looking out over breathtaking mountain scenarios that are a backdrop to the remarkable monumental historic centre. The fortunate geographical location of this town, the birthplace of Ovid, was instrumental in its story, for it is at the confluence of two important communication routes: one on the Adriatic coast and one to Naples. The main trade and culture route between Florence and Naples, called Via degli Abruzzi, passed through Sulmona.

176. Facing page: Piazza XX Settembre, Sulmona.
177. Above: Porta Napoli, Sulmona.
178. Below: Medieval aqueduct.

The massive fortifications, although only partially preserved, are still evident in the sequence of historic town gates, each of which gives its name to one of the six districts that make up the town. The most monumental of the surviving gates is certainly **Porta Napoli**, the old Porta Nova, set southeast of the town in the early–14th century; the front facing today's Piazza Vittorio Veneto has an unusual rusticated ashlar finish, with less projection in the upper section, characterized by bosses sculpted with precious rosettes in the centre.

The High Medieval nucleus comes together along today's Corso Ovidio, the ancient north–south axis around which all the town's major monuments have been built.

Piazza Garibaldi, once Piazza Maggiore, is quite striking, with one side bordered by the theory of arches that were once part of the 1256 **Medieval aqueduct**, while the nearby **Fonte del Vecchio** is of obvious Renaissance stamp. The piazza is the traditional marketplace and the so-called "fontanone" in the centre is a fountain produced by Pescocostanzo craftsmen. Elegant 16th–18th-century noble mansions are built on this square, as is the **church of San Filippo Neri**, where a Medieval façade and portal (1315) were recovered from the demolished church of Sant'Agostino to be installed here. We also find the **Santa Chiara monastery** with its lovely church, with a typically Baroque interior following the 1700s reconstruction by Pietro Fantoni, striking paintings by Alessandro Salini (16$^{th}$ century) of the *Marriage of the Virgin Mary*, as well as a *Glory of St Claire* by Sebastiano Conca Salini (18th century), alongside some excellent Pescocostanzo school marble marquetry altars and paliottos. A remarkable cycle of paintings datable late–1200s–early–1300s is found in the old monastery, which is now the public diocesan cultural centre and houses the **Museo Diocesano di Arte Sacra** andthe **Pinacoteca comunale d'arte moderna e contemporanea**, a gallery connected to the "Premio Sulmona", an annual award for contemporary art.

The fascinating remains of the late–1200s **church of San Francesco della Scarpa** include the apse and highly splayed monumental side portal. The church was originally dedicated to Mary Magdalene and is said to have been extended by Charles of Anjou in about 1290. Following the ruinous earthquake of 1706, the church was rebuilt without aisles and detached from the remains of the older building. The late–1300s ogival façade portal survives, attributed to the stonemason, Nicola Salvitti. The interior is decorated with stuccoes by Pietro Piazzoli

# SS Annunziata Complex, Sulmona

Destroyed and rebuilt many times over, the complex was originally founded in 1320 as a hospital for the infirm and an orphanage. It is undoubtedly the most important monument in the city, both architecturally and for its role in the urban fabric. The building has been a hospital since the 1960s, but it developed progressively from the early–15th century. The **monumental front** is a 1400s expression, with echoes of previous styles and the new nuances of the trends brought by the 1500s. The initial building phase, which installed the left-hand portal in 1415, but in a 1300s style, and the splendid triple-lancet window above it, some decades later, was followed by a second phase, in about 1483, which added a further portion to the façade, with the 1400s gabled portal and a two-light window retaining Gothic traits. From 1519 to 1522 the monumental frontage was completed with a round arch portal and the two-light window above, which by now was a Renaissance expression. The complex has a central court and the hospital was subsequently extended up until the late 1500s. The structure was then partially transformed by a long series of interventions in the 1960s. The **church** is unusual for its innovative use of interior space with the essential feature being the vertical development of the tambour–cupola–clerestory elements. The layout includes a nave and two aisles, four bays with cupolas, flush transept and three apses, true to the structure put in place in the 16th-century reconstruction, of which the side portal dated 1590 is a part. The striking dome with clerestory is set on a drum in the chevet. The vibrant façade, designed and built in 1710, following destruction by the 1706 earthquake, is significant. It was made by Norberto Cicco, a stonemason from Pescocostanzo, and is a rare example of the use of the freestanding column, as can also be seen on the Badia Morronese prospect. The magnificent interior is further enhanced by a sumptuous Baroque decoration, with lavish wood and marble furnishings, and lovely 1600s–1700s canvases, with the outstanding *Nativity of Mary* and *Presentation in the Temple* by Giuseppe Simonelli, a pupil of Luca Giordano. The Annunziata complex is home to a remarkable museum complex, the **Museo Civico**, including a large archaeological section and an interesting Medieval and modern section on the upper floor of the main block which also houses the **Pinacoteca** or art gallery. Archaeological excavations conducted in the rear wing brought to light the remains of a **Roman domus**, with black and white mosaic floor, and remains of wall paintings attributable to the so-called 3rd Pompeian style. The relics are exhibited in the *in situ* **archaeological museum**, which was created by implementing a walkway for visitors, with entrance and exit platforms, and viewing stations for fixed relics. The **Museo del Costume Abruzzese-Molisano e della Transumanza** has been set up in the Sala del Campanile and displays prints and watercolours of costumes, as well as items from the pastoral world, used in Abruzzo and Molise from 1790 until the Unification of Italy.

179. Above: the 14th-century crozier hook, Museo Civico.
180. Below: canvas by Giuseppe Simonelli, a pupil of Luca Giordano.
181. 182. Facing page: above, the Palazzo dell'Annunziata façade; below, Museo del Costume.

and other Lombard masters, and also boasts a precious 1700s organ by Domenico Antonio Fedeli of Camerino; a 15th-century wooden crucifix and remains of late–1300s frescoes.
In nearby Piazza Plebiscito, near the 1300s **Santa Maria della Tomba gate** we find the **church** of the same name, whose origins date back to the 12th century, but which now show subsequent modifications, some as late are 1970-2. The façade has a horizontal coping that survived the 1706 earthquake and a magnificent late–1300s portal surmounted by a sumptuous 1400s rose window. The ancient hospital, erected in 1424 next to the church, survives in a façade with a double lancet window; the belfry was probably restored in 1579 and rebuilt during the most recent renovations. On the central Piazza XX Settembre we see the monument to Ovid by sculptor Ettore Ferrari (1925) and also **Palazzo Giovanni dalle Palle**, one of the town's major buildings. It was built in 1484 by the Venetian merchant Giovanni dalle Palle to designs by Venetian architect Simone, although its current appearance shows extensive modifications. Its monumental 1600s portal, facing onto the main street, bears the coats of arms of the Trasmondi–Scala families. Nearby Piazzetta Salvatore Tommasi is the home of the **Centro Studi Ovidiani** and the impressive **municipal library**. On the other side of Corso Ovidio, along the characteristic Vico dei Sardi, there is a typical example of late–Gothic civil architecture: the **Giovanni Sardi house**, built by the wealthy Pisan family, with a Durazzesque scheme-arch portal and cornice with dog-tooth moulding, surmounted by a lovely cross window. There are countless examples of civil buildings worth noting, for instance: 1400s **Palazzo Tabassi**, with an interesting Durazzesque scheme-arch portal by Pietro da Como, surmounted by a splendid Gothic-style double mullioned window; 1500s **Palazzo Sardi**, built by the Pisan family, whose portal features the family coat of arms in the keystone. The palazzo is the home of the **environmental museum of natural history** and offices of the Comunità Montana Peligna. **Palazzo Mazara** is one of the most prestigious buildings of the 18th century.
Of the many excellent monumental buildings that enrich the centre, one memorable example is the **monumental SS. Annunziata complex** (*see box p. 108*), in Piazza dell'Annunziata, comprising the building and the attached church, symbol of the town of Sulmona, and now dedicated to museum activities, with the exception of the first floor

of the northwest wing, which houses a fully-equipped auditorium.
The fascinating **San Panfilo cathedral** marks the start of the Romanesque period in Medieval Abruzzo, alongside San Pelino, in Corfinio and the abbey of San Liberatore a Majella. The basilica, built in the Dark Ages, was renovated from 1075 by Bishop Trasmondo and, following several restorations, was given a Baroque appearance in the wake of damage by the 1706 earthquake, retaining only the older surviving structures. The left-hand portal, with architrave inscriptions, and three apses, with a horizontal cornice decoration of hanging arches set on corbels, are attributable to the early construction. Today's layout shows a nave and two aisles, divided into eight pairs of columns, no transept, three apses, and a raised presbytery. The façade with horizontal coping still has its ogival portal by Nicola Salvitti (1391), although the rose window was lost. A 15th-century *Deposition* fresco, attributed to the Maestro della Cappella Caldora, decorates the lunette. The interior retains some excellent items,

183. Above: Good Friday procession, Sulmona.
184. 185. Below: left, the cathedral of San Panfilo; right: the church of Santa Maria della Tomba, Sulmona.

including the 1700s wooden choir carved by Ferdinando Mosca of Pescocostanzo and the polychrome marble high altar; in the smaller bays we find a 14th-century wooden crucifix and a 1757 baptismal font, also in polychrome marble. The crypt, which is the oldest part of this church, has an excellent 12th-century *Madonna with Child* in polychrome stone as well as the Bishop's cathedra in the centre of the crypt's main apse. The **Museo della Cattedrale di San Panfilo** exhibits part of the cathedral treasure, as well as having an extensive archive of 9th–19th-century 12,000 documents and 3,000 parchments.

The **church of San Gaetano** is also quite important, now seen in its 1700–1800s restructured guise, but retaining interesting floor mosaics that have been dated as 1st century AD, as well as the relics of an apse from a Christian church, with traces of frescoes dated 8th–9th century.

Some of the most interesting spots include the

186. Above: the Giostra Cavalleresca pageant.
187. Below: the Madonna escaping to the square in Sulmona.

**Museo Pelino dell'Arte e della Tecnologia Confettiera**, a museum dedicated to sugared almond production, installed in the building next to the internationally famous Fabbrica di Confetti Pelino in its Art Nouveau building by the Introdacqua railway station; the **Museo dell'Immagine e delle Tecniche Fotografiche**, which exhibits not only countless images relative to Italy but also has a prestigious "Fratelli Alinari" collection of photographs.

The town's public events calendar includes the religious celebrations at Easter, with the Good Friday **procession of the Dead Christ**, and the famous **Madonna che Scappa** Easter Sunday pageant, when the statue of the grieving Virgin Many is carried shoulder high from the church of San Filippo when St John and St Peter announce the resurrection of Christ, and upon seeing the figure of the Resurrected Christ under a canopy at the bottom of Piazza Garibaldi, the cortège dashes towards it, and the statue loses its black cloak revealing a festive green

gown. Another fascinating event is the famous **Giostra Cavalleresca**, a joust held on the Piazza Maggiore "field".

The marvellous **abbey of Santo Spirito al Morrone**, a rectangular-plan complex with square corner towers, is located near Sulmona, at **Badia**.

The Celestinian abbey of Santo Spirito al Morrone was founded in the 13th century by Pietro Angeleri, the future Pope Celestine V, and after numerous interventions in various periods, it was used as a jail until quite recently. The complex comprises various buildings set around a number of courts. A monumental 1700s portal leads into a central courtyard known as the "Cortile dei Nobili", dominated by the 1700s façade of the abbey church, which paid homage to Borromini's San Carlino alle Quattro Fontane frontage and is one of Abruzzo's major Baroque items. The church interior, one of the earliest Abruzzo experiments with central plan, is a Greek cross, with a deep choir that reaches the Caldora chapel. Here we see a remarkable cycle of frescoes with a marvellous *Deposition* by the so-called Maestro della Cappella Caldora, set in the same niche as an interesting sarcophagus sculpted by Gualtiero d'Alemagna (1412).

A narrow opening leads us into the small underground space with an irregular plan covered with a ribbed cross vault; here, on the perimeter wall we recognize the imaginary depiction of Pietro Celestino with the palm of martyrdom in the act of offering a book.

188. Facing page: aerial view of Badia Morronese; left, the rocky crags of Mount Morrone with the Sant'Onofrio hermitage and the sanctuary of Hercules Curinus.
189. Above: the Caldora chapel.
190. Below: the sanctuary of Hercules Curinus.

The charming **refuge of Sant'Onofrio**, where the hermit Pietro Angeleri often stayed, is set into the rock slopes behind the abbey, and there are some excellent 13th–14th-century frescoes. Beneath Sant'Onofrio there are the monumental ruins of the **Hercules Curinus sanctuary**, where the Italic population worshipped this divinity, protector of shepherds and flocks. Located on the Celano–Foggia sheep track, it was the centre for economic, religious and political activities for the entire community, and was also an overnight shelter for flocks. The Italic temple complex was radically modified by the Romans in the early–1st century BC and was brought to light in the 1950s. It comprises two Italic terraces, one over the other, and is dominated by a small square sacellum, with bare brick walls; here the inner walls are decorated with polychrome stuccowork panels whereas the floor is a black and white mosaic with red strips. One relic, now on show in the Abruzzo National Archaeological Museum in Chieti, is the precious *Hercules in Repose*. The two refuges of Santa Croce and Santa Maria de Cryptis are above Sant'Onofrio, on the Morrone pastures, in a rock strip that conceals numerous shepherd grottoes.

Between Sulmona and Pacentro we find the charming remains of the rock **chapel of Sant'Angelo in Vetuli**, where many of the architectural and decorative elements were evidently pillaged from the neighbouring area, rich in Roman remains. Several ashlars

bear Christian fish and clepsydra symbols.
The village of **INTRODACQUA**, just a few kilometres from Sulmona, lies on the slopes of Mount Plaia, at the confluence of the Sant'Antonio and Contra valleys. Introdacqua dates back to the Dark Ages (10th century), and the particularly charming older nucleus, in the higher part, is almost completely abandoned. It is dominated by a square tower that is a rare and excellent example of a Medieval tower, where the village fortifications began. Civil architecture is prevalently 18th century, enhanced by elegant carved stone windows and portals, and balconies with wrought iron railings. On Piazza Cavour we see the impressive **Palazzo dei Marchesi Trasmondi**, built in ancient times but largely remodelled in the 18th–19th centuries by the last feudal lords of Introdacqua, who had

191. Above: Medieval village of Bugnara.
192. Below: aerial view of Introdacqua.

acquired the fief from the d'Avalos family in the mid–1600s. The **Pascal D'Angelo regional museum of emigration,** dedicated to a poet born in Introdacqua in 1894 who emigrated to the United States, has been installed on the top floor. Through the experiences of Pascal D'Angelo, the museum illustrates the story of Italian emigration in the early 1900s.
Close to the palazzo we see the **Porte della Terra** gates, on one of which bears the Trasmondi family coat of arms. One of the most noteworthy religious buildings is the **SS Annunziata parish church**, with a Medieval nave-and-two-aisle layout, restructured in the Baroque period, and with a stone belfry with spire, similar to those found in other bell towers in the Peligno basin. The church houses the remains of patron saint and martyr, Feliciano. At Piano della Civitella, not far from the built-up area, there are the remains of a fortified Italic settlement.
Past Introdacqua there is the distinctive Medieval village of **BUGNARA**, built on the hill slopes of Colle Rotondo, southwest of the Peligno basin, near the River Sagittario. The presence of megalithic walls and numerous archaeological findings point to the site being settled even in ancient times. The fortified village's older sector has a cluster layout around the **Palazzo Ducal** or castle, erected by the powerful Di Sangro family who live here until the 1500s. It stands in the San Nicola district, at the edge of the inhabited area, and has lost all its ancient defence features through the countless modifications implemented over the years. The building's current configuration makes it impossible to understand the original construction features; the corner towers are still recognizable, despite being damaged, with blocks set around a large court.
In the old centre, it is worth noting the **Madonna del Rosario church** with 1500s frescoes and stuccowork inside; the Madonna della Neve church (whose cupola collapsed in 1915) and the church of Santa Maria degli Angeli (the vault and apse collapsed in 1915).
As we continue towards Sulmona, along the SS 17 state road, we encounter the captivating **PETTORANO SUL GIZIO**, nestling on the Colle della Guardiola hillside, overlooking the River Gizio.
Before venturing into its narrow streets, it is worth stopping at the **San Nicola di Bari church** outside the walls and near the gate of the same name, dedicated to the saint invoked in the prayers of shepherds headed for Puglia. On the stark 18th-century façade we admire the austere portal, the only testimony of the original Medieval structure: here a Gothic

inscription invites shepherds and pilgrims to enter the church set on the Regio Tratturo sheep track that led to Foggia.

The urban fabric was conditioned extensively by site morphology, and the fortified village layout survives, today retaining five of the six original gates. Several sections of the ancient town fortifications are still visible, cadenced by watchtowers, some still identifiable. From Porta San Nicola, a gate flanked by a round turret, we enter the village. There is a striking 17th-century fresco of St Margaret above this first threshold. The saint is the patron of Pettorano and in the artwork she holds the village in her hand.

The restored **Cantelmo castle** stands at the edge of the little town, in a dominant position. It was one of the Peligno valley's most strategically important bulwarks and played a leading role in history of the Hohenstaufen family. Certainly, this is one of the most interesting fortresses, not only in this territory but also beyond regional boundaries. The impressive pentagonal bulwark tower rises out of the castle's irregular layout, and was probably the fortification's original nucleus. This keep was subsequently encircled by sturdy boundary walls making it suitable to deal with modern attacking systems. The round towers at the northwest and southwest compound corners allowed efficient flanking defence in support of the front. Inside there are some interesting exhibition spaces displaying various archaeological finds from the pre-Roman and Roman eras, acquired from private collections. On the ground floor of the central tower an installation documents the traditional trade of the charcoal burners of Pettorano.

193. 194. This page: above, the fountain in Piazza Rosario Zannelli; below, the centre of Pettorano sul Gizio.

The magnificent **Palazzo Ducale** is in the centre of the village, flanked by the **San Dionisio mother church**, said to have been founded in the 15th century, completely destroyed following a fire in 1694, then rebuilt at the end of the 18th century in late–Baroque forms. Inside, the canvas of the *Ecstasy of St Francis* by the late–18th-century Neapolitan painter Vincenzo Figliolino, in the first side chapel to the right of the entrance, is of considerable interest, as is the contemporary statue of St Benignus, depicted holding a palm tree. **Piazza Rosario Zannelli** enchants with splendid views and was once the courtyard of the Palazzo, with the late–Renaissance fountain commissioned by Fabrizio VI Cantelmo in the mid-1600s, a date engraved on the base. The fountain is set against the backdrop of the inner

prospect with the elegant Renaissance portal at the top of the left staircase, decorated with the Cantelmo coat of arms. There are some particularly interesting examples of noble buildings and one of the best is **Palazzo De Stephanis**, the so-called *Castaldina*, with a splendid Baroque façade but now abandoned. Next to it is the **church of San Giovanni Battista** with the ancient portal and dated 1536.

Returning south and taking Via Sant'Antonio, we meet the vast bulk of **Palazzo Vitto-Massei** and the imposing **Palazzo Croce**, the latter a surprising surviving fragment in the atrium of the so-called Edict of Diocletian, issued in 301 AD, unique in Europe as the only known copy of the Edict in the West. Just outside the town it is worth visiting the 17th-century **Santi Sebastiano e Lorenzo church**, with a rich carved portal, reached along the path that connects the church of San Nicola to the River Gizio.

The Riserva Naturale Guidata Monte Genzana e Alto Gizio is a unique nature reserve in this municipality because it is the only one of its kind to encompass an entire historic centre. The ancient village of Roccavallescura, known as **ROCCA PIA** until 1865, stands on a knoll over the Peligno valley, set in a lovely scenario, in the heart of the Cinque Miglia plateau. Roccavallescura preserves much of its historic layout, which evolved along an important route, and adapted perfectly to the lie of the land. The ancient Medieval keep with what remains of a square watchtower in direct visual connection with the castle of Roccacasale is set in a prominent position, straddling a rocky promontory. The inhabited area is downstream and is set on a steeply sloping main street where the priceless buildings are mainly 1600s–1700s in appearance. Outstanding are 1500s **Palazzo Fidei**, near the Torre dell'orologio, an ancient watchtower; 1700s **Palazzo De Meis**, with a monumental portal, and 1600s **Palazzo Severo**, which, despite damage during World War II, has retained its original features and details of excellent quality. The so-called house–tower has been turned into the **Museo Civico di Documentazione Storico-Ambientale**, a museum dedicated to the rural traditions of this area.

Noteworthy frescoes are to be seen in the SS Sacramento chapel, annexed to the **church of Santa Maria Maggiore**, rebuilt in the 1950s after the fire a few years earlier had damaged the older church, which sources document to the 1300s. Of the ancient building a terracotta survives depicting a *Madonna and Child*, originally from the nearby church of Madonna del Casale. The **church of San Rocco**, completed and opened for worship in 1783 by the SS Rosario confraternity, had been commissioned after the 1656 plague, and was dedicated to St Roche, the patron protector against plagues and epidemics. The small pretty **Madonna Delle Grazie church** is just outside the town, along Via Napoleonica, and built in traditional 16th-century style. The two wooden statues of *Maria Lactans* and *St Vincent Ferrer*, now in the parish church, were originally part of its decorations.

Outside the centre, in the Colleguidone district, one of the most important monuments is the **sheep-track church of Madonna del Casale**, with a handsome 1300s stone portal. It appears as an early–14th-century building but was presumably founded earlier, set on the Piano delle Cinquemiglia and linked to the histories of the ancient settlements of Casalguidoni, Roccaduno and Casale San Nicola. It has close ties to the sheep track, used as a sanctuary by travellers and shepherds. The aisleless interior is accessed from the left through a striking portal resembling that of the church of Sant'Agostino, in Sulmona, imitating its Gothic lines. Next to the portal and set into the curtain wall, there is a truncated tower with a coat of arms suggesting the Angevin fleur-de-lis. The interior was modified extensively since the first bay to the west was used as accommodation. The apse bowl frescoes may be early–16th century and depict scenes from the *Lives of Christ* and the *Virgin Mary*.

Resuming our itinerary, we can stop at the Fonti del Casale, with visitor facilities.

Ancient **RIVISONDOLI**, once encircled by fortified walls, is set at the foot of Mount Calvario, between the upper Cinque Miglia plateau and the Roccaraso highland. Its historic and artistic heritage dates mainly to the 1800s after the old centre was almost totally destroyed by a fire in 1792. Rivisondoli's development was due chiefly to its strategic position near the junctions with important trade and military routes, mainly the Celano–Foggia sheep track. Remains of ancient fortifications, with characteristic machicolations, are visible near **Porta Antonetta**. In the modern parish **church of San Nicola di Bari**, rebuilt on the same site in the early–20th century, there is a handsome Baroque-style wooden altar by Palmerio Grasso. The charming **church of Sant'Anna** was a chapel annexed to Palazzo Baronale, and built in the late–17th century, with an interior remodelled probably on the latter 1700s, and a façade with horizontal coping. Also of interest is the **church of Santa Maria del Suffragio**, whose portal has Baroque volutes and is surmounted by the insignia of the Sardi family. Nearby is the **church of Santa Maria della Portella**, first documented in the 16th century, built on the upper Cinque Miglia plateau, near the Portella pass. This is a religious building and is linked to the neighbouring pass crossed by populations and flocks on their way to the Peligno and Sangro valleys. The marble altar is inscribed with the date 1611.

Rivisondoli is a famous summer and winter resort, a starting point for ski excursions (near to the Mount Pratello resort), and known for its charming religious *nativity tableau*, held each year on 5 January. The **Museo del Presepe** is an interesting museum with a collection of artistic nativity scenes and works by various artists. Also worth seeing is the **Museo Civico**, inaugurated in 2011.

The leading winter resort of **ROCCARASO** is very close to Rivisondoli. The extensive winter sports facilities and ski territory are located at the end of the Prato plateau, between Mount Majella and the Marsican Mountains, on the slopes of Mount Roccalta. The original settlement was almost completely destroyed during World War II. Historic sources and images depict a large fortified village (Terra Vecchia), with boundary walls, around which quarters were built in the 16th–18th century. The remains of a round bastion can be seen at the end of Terra Vecchia, to the southeast.

Worthy of note are the churches of Santa Maria Assunta, rebuilt in 1954 on the same site as the historic building and also rebuilt that year, the nearby San Bernardino. The church of San Rocco, built in the 1600s, is the only important building to have survived the war.

Moving towards Ateleta we will meet the charming little **Pietransieri**, set compact around its original nucleus, built at the foot of the Anserio castle. Sadly remembered for the 1943 Limmari massacre, one of the most brutal of World War II, with 128 victims. On the site of the massacre stands a small monument where the names of the fallen are engraved on plaques.

195. 196. Facing page: Roccapia and the Madonna del Casale church on the Cinquemiglia plateau.
197. Below: aerial view of Rivisondoli.

**ATELETA** lies on the slopes of Colle Sisto, in the centre of a wide bowl between Mount Secine and Mount Capraro, to the left of the Lavino torrent, in an area steeped in beech and oak woods, and it is also on the edge of the Abruzzo National Park, as well as being part of the Majella National Park. The urban layout was designed from scratch in 1811 (with a Royal Decree signed by Joachim Murat), and was rebuilt following World War II, when it was heavily damaged due to its position on the *Gustav Line*. Today's **church of San Gioacchino** was rebuilt in a new location, which is closer to the centre than its predecessor, which was designed by the architects Pennisi and Savelli, in the early–1800s, and destroyed during the last war. The church has a rectangular floorplan with marble altars and decorations as well as lavish mosaics, which are the work of contemporary Tuscan artists. It is worth paying a visit to the **Museum of Rural Culture**, located in the town hall.

The remains of the **Carceri keep** are very interesting, set sheer over the Sangro valley, with surviving traces of defence walls and access gates, with a path dug from the rock to reach the peak. It does not long to reach **CASTEL DI SANGRO** from Ateleta. This little town stretches down the hill slope as far as the confluence of the River Sangro with the Zittola, where the bridge and ancient tavern mark the junction of the Celano-Foggia and Pescasseroli-Candela sheep tracks. The fortunate location of the trade and communications crossroads for the entire Abruzzo Region, fostered the growth of Castel di Sangro and underscored its role as "gateway to Abruzzo". A flourishing sheep-rearing economy, in particular after legislation ordered by Alfonso of Aragon furthered growth throughout the upper Sangro territory, brought advance of a wealthy shepherd class and the fortune of several confraternities, including the San-tissimo Sacramento brotherhood, who achieved sufficient economic solidity to allow them to undertake particularly significant social and artistic works, including rebuilding of the **Santa Maria Assunta collegiate church**. The basilica was rebuilt between 1695 and 1725, over the remains of an older church (a nave and two aisles with external portico), to a design by Francesco Ferradini of Como, who was then replaced by Giovan Battista Gianni, presumably in about 1706. The current layout comprises a central eight-sided chamber, with a stilted arch cupola and no tambour, around which four other rectangular chambers have been installed. This very explicit definition of the inner space is offset by a complex exterior volume, defined by a pleasing loggia built at the sides of the two-order façade, finished with a triangular gable and two belfries, an early and rare example in Abruzzo, of the dual-tower prospect that became widespread in European Baroque. The church survived the devastation of World War II but the archives and numerous wooden furnishings were lost, although the marble altars and the splendid baptistery were saved, as were precious paintings found inside, some painted by several well-known Neapolitan masters including Francesco De Mura and Domenico Antonio Vaccaro, in addition to those by De Matteis and Sante Cirillo. A number of 18th-century painted wooden statues by the master Paolo Saverio di Zinno can still be seen inside.

The high altar in polychrome marble is a stunning 1738 opus by Aniello Gentile, one of the leading marble workers of the Neapolitan 1700s, with sculptures by the equally talented Matteo Bottigliero. The inlaid marble stoup (with a bas-relief of the Evangelists on each of the four sides – three in white marble and the fourth wooden to form the door – and a surrounding balustrade) has also been provisionally attributed to the same artists.

Particularly interesting for the 18th-century decorations is the **SS Rosario** oratory, rebuilt in the 1700s inside the **Annunziata church**, founded in ancient times but rebuilt in the late–1940s with a faithful reproduction of the façade.

Only a few fragments and the lower part of a watchtower remain of the ancient **castle**, near Piazza Castello, documented latter 9th century and indicated as a fortified location in the mid–12th century.

Part of the venerable **Museo Aufidenate**, set up at the end of the 1800s by historians De Nino and Balzano, then closed during World War II, has now been reopened in the renovated cloisters of the 16th-century **Maddalena convent complex**, the old Osservanti church.

Castel di Sangro was the birthplace of the 1840 artist, Teofilo Patini, to whom a plaque with a bronze bas-relief bust of the painter has been dedicated on the porticoed façade of the town hall in Piazza Plebiscito. The exquisite **Palazzetto del Leone**, also known as "Casa del Leone", was recently restored and is home to

198. Facing page: aerial view of Castel di Sangro.
199. Below: marble detail of the high altar in the Assunta church, Castel di Sangro.

the **Pinacoteca Teofilo Patini art gallery**. Turning back towards Sulmona, just after Roccaraso and Rivisondoli, there is a detour that takes to **PESCOCOSTANZO**, an art town located on the slopes of Mount Calvario, on the upper Cinque Miglia plateau. The intact old centre is stunning, with numerous examples of civil and religious architecture, installed in an urban fabric that is truly unique. From the original fortified village, comprising wall-houses clustered around a rock spur, the "Peschio" or urban nucleus developed through Medieval and Renaissance expansion, converging towards the Santa Maria del Colle Collegiate, a transition point between the early extensions and the definitive development of the town during the 1700s.

The numerous stately buildings, many vaunting lavish Baroque-style portals, and splendid churches with stunning decorations, document a passion for art fired by the flourishing sheep-farming economy, that also contributed to the specific development of the decorative arts.

Some of the most traditional expressions of the decorative arts survive, like goldsmithing, wrought iron, wood carving, bobbin lace, and others. The town was the home of talented architects, sculptors, marble workers and from the early–1600s documented the arrival artists from outside the region such as the architect Cosimo Fanzago, born in Bergamo and relocated to Naples, a genius of Southern Baroque. On Viale Fanzago there is the **Gesù e Maria church and convent complex**, designed by Cosimo Fanzago in the early decades of the 17th century, as a home for the Franciscan Order. The church plan is spare, but the decorations are lavish: a single barrel-vaulted bay is cadenced by pairs of pilaster strips and shallow niches, three per side, which hold sumptuous altars. The counterfaçade is installed with a balcony supported by squared pillars, that is a typical feature of Pescocostanzo churches. The prospect is the result of an 1800s reconstruction and singular for the horizontal divisions, with a triangular split gable and richly-patterned mixtilinear cornice, echoed by the three window frames. The splendid high altar, from a design by Cosimo Fanzago, was built in 1626–30 and the precious structure occupies the entire apse. Its breath-taking energy comes from its sophisticated and dramatic impact as Fanzago opened up the altar in the centre of an arch supported by cherub–brackets, exploiting the effect of the indirect light arriving from the apse window, which focuses the attention of worshippers on the tabernacle.

Continuing towards the old centre we

encounter striking **Palazzo Sabatini**, with the prospect on Via Colecchi and Via Colle dei Corvi; the structure is the result of the unification of four existing buildings that was undertaken in the 19th and 20th centuries. The palazzo housed some splendid 1700s furnishings and the great library of Gaetano Sabatini (1868-1964), Pescocostanzo's illustrious physician and historian, who reconstructed the town's historical and cultural events through extensive research.

The **Collegiate of Santa Maria del Colle** (*see box p. 122*) contains splendid Renaissance and Baroque furnishings. This building of ancient origins was modified extensively in the 15th and 16th centuries, with the addition of handsome stone portals. The 1500s **church of Santa Maria del Suffragio dei Morti**, on the same access staircase as the Collegiate, has a horizontal-coping façade of the type used quite frequently in Abruzzo. There is an eye-catching 1600s portal, with a mock-classical porch, and a triangular tympanum on Corinthian columns with tall plinths. The interior has a striking, lavish altar in wood sculpted by Palmerio Grasso between 1647 and 1649, then completed by Ferdinando Mosca in 1716, as well as a wooden caisson ceiling, with the wood section provided by Pescocostanzo's Bernardino D'Alessandro (1637-9), with the canvases painted by Falconio Falconio, between 1640 and 1657. The two torch-holders ("splendori") on the sides of the altar are quite lovely, in carved gilt wood, made in 1693 by Rocco Falconio.

The so-called "Pietra del vituperio", or stone of shame, where delinquent debtors were mocked, is set at the foot of the stairs that lead to Santa Maria del Colle.

If we turn towards **Fontana Maggiore**, a unique 1700s fountain (recomposed in its current

200. Facing page: aerial view of Pescocostanzo.
201. Above: Gesù e Maria church.
202. Below: the staircase with the portals of the Santa Maria del Colle collegiate church; the church of Santa Maria del Suffragio.

# The Collegiate of Santa Maria del Colle, Pescocostanzo

The ancient mother church, rebuilt in 1466 following the terrible 1456 earthquake, was also subjected to interventions in the 16th and 17th century, involving not only the main façade, rebuilt in 1558 on the eastern side, but also the large Sacramento chapel, built on the southern side in 1691, comprising a square chamber with a cupola roof and three windows set at a height. The large square room, which is quite unique in Abruzzo, has a nave and four aisles divided by square pillars that support round arches, no transept and a rectangular choir. The side entrance, which became the main access, was installed in the new 1580 façade, with a massive late Romanesque-style portal at the top of a striking staircase. The austerity of the layout is offset by sumptuous interior decorations, which include some splendid **wooden caisson ceilings** in the nave, the central section made in the 1680s by Carlo Sabatini. There are two intermediate gilt sections (1742), which frame some priceless artwork. The lovely high altar is also very interesting, as are the wrought iron gates installed in the **Sacramento chapel**, designed by Norberto Cicco and made by in 1699–1705 by Master Santo di Rocco, completed by his grandson Ilario (1717). The Collegiate could quite justifiably be defined an authentic museum of Pescocostanzo artistic craftsmanship for the **baptismal font** and sumptuous sculpted and inlaid **marble altars**, the wooden furnishings, and the wrought iron gates. The church also has other works of art including the impressive 1200s wooden *Madonna and Child*, known as del Colle, the church's oldest work; Baroque stuccoes by Giambattista Gianni and Francesco Ferradini; the Santa Caterina paliotto by Tanzio da Varallo (1617), one of the most illustrious Italian painters of the 17th century, depicting the *Madonna of Constantinople and Saints*; as well as ancient silver. Also interesting is a *Madonna del Rosario* signed and dated 1580 by the painter Giovan Paolo Cardone, the most important Aquila painter of the latter 16th century. The **basilica museum** has been set up nearby and exhibits collections of religious art, silver, historic vestments, sculptures and architectural elements from the Collegiate.

203. 204. Above: the nave and the Sacramento chapel gate in the collegiate church of Santa Maria del Colle.
205. Left: Tanzio da Varallo's canvas.
206. Facing page: the high altar inside the Gesù e Maria church.

appearance in 1960), decorated with tritons and horses' heads, on the corner between Via della Fontana and Via Diomede Falconio, we find elegant **Palazzo Mosca**, owned by the local family of able woodcarvers. From the 16th century until 1860, it was the home to a school of philosophy, theology, and canon law, founded by the family's learned canons. The date 1564 is carved into a window architrave, together with an inscription.

In the Varrata quarter, which emerged following 1600–1700s expansion, there is noteworthy 18th–19th-century **Palazzo Ricciardelli** (owned by the patriot Nicola Ricciardelli of the noble Pescocostanzo family), which once had corner bartizans (it also had wonderful furnishings until World War II). **Palazzo Colecchi** is in refined Baroque, rebuilt in 1771; the elegant façade is eye-catching for its attractive lines and the finely-decorated portal and windows. Opposite we see **Palazzo Cocco** (18th century), whose elegant portal is decorated with a mascaron and side volutes.

Continuing towards Strada di San Francesco, which takes its name from the deconsecrated San Francesco church, in the quarter that developed in the 16th–17th centuries in the old market area. Here there is an eye-catching monumental rusticated portal on **Casa del Sole** while on Corso Roma the intricate **Palazzo Mansi** (17th–18th century), property of a wealthy family of sheep farmers, has a handsome portal on the square of the same name. 1800s **Palazzo de Capite**, with prospects on Via Campo dei Fiori and Via Valle Gelata, stands out for its refined stonework (1850) and antique furniture found inside. At the end of Corso Roma, we find the **church of Santa Maria delle Grazie**, on the belvedere, which once was the location of the cattle market. The 1500s layout has a 1700s portal and an interior featuring a wooden balcony set into the counterfaçade (a typical element in the churches of Pescocostanzo), supported by two columns on tall plinths. In Largo del Macello, site of the ancient abattoir, there is the handsome façade of **Palazzo Grilli**, of 1600s layout, outstanding with its four corner towers.

The **church of San Giovanni Battista** has an elegant façade with horizontal coping, original portal and rose window (16th century). The portal has a triangular gable, intricate pilaster strips decorated with foliage motifs, and architrave broken by a small bas-relief depicting the *martyrdom of St John the Baptist*. The two side wings reflect typical elements in the houses of Pescocostanzo. The church is now home to the **Museum of Origins**, illustrating the history of the town through the transition from sheep-farming activities, tied to transhumance, to farming of the land.

The 1600s **church of Santa Maria del Carmine**, contained by two narrow converging streets, Via del Vallone and Via di Capo Croce, is a truly charming nook of elegant simplicity, whose impact is enhanced by the dramatic staircase. Inside it is worth noting the important Baroque altar. Late–1500s **Casa D'Amata**,

207. Above: Piazza del Municipio, Pescocostanzo. Left, Palazzo del Comune and, right, Palazzo Fanzago.
208. Facing page: *Ocriticum* archaeological area.

in Via D'Amata, presents all the typical features of a Pescocostanzo house, like the "vignale" (an external staircase with an access terrace), and develops them all thanks to especially refined construction and decoration techniques, indication both of the patron's wealth and of the skill of local stonemasons. There are some very characteristic houses built near **Isolato dell'Oca**, the compact quarter that links the 15-1600s district and the Collegiate.

The **Piazza del Municipio** is the heart of the town and node for the main streets, with Palazzo Comunale and Palazzo del Governatore, Palazzo Fanzago, the former monastery of Santa Scolastica and adjacent façade (rebuilt after the 1706 earthquake) of the old San Nicola di Bari church, one of the oldest in Pescocostanzo, now a conference centre.

One of the most famous monuments in Pescocostanzo is the former Santa Scolastica nunnery, called **Palazzo Fanzago**, begun in 1626 by Cosimo Fanzago, a Neapolitan architect and sculptor, but not completed by 1642. The dramatic façade of this nunnery, intended for cloistered Benedictine nuns, is cadenced by six great blank niches, which replace the windows, with elaborate stone frames and a gable alternatively closed and split with an intrados conch and side volutes. Fantastic carved wooden brackets support the overhanging roof, finely sculpted with dragon heads: this dragon motif was the invention of Norberto Cicco, whereas they were probably made by Palmerio Grasso. The **Museo del Merletto a Tombolo**, in the rooms of Palazzo Fanzago, displays the supreme results of Pescocostanzo lace.

**Palazzo del Comune**, dominated by a clock tower in Piazza Municipio, was built in the 1700s, and restructured several times during the 20th century, recovering the volumes, design, and decorative detail of the town hall. In 1935, the stone architrave over the entrance was sculpted with a motto, SUI DOMINA, commemorating the liberation of the small community of feudal vassals in 1774, three decades before the promulgation of the revolutionary feudality law (1806), in which King Ferdinand IV of Bourbon played a part. The eastern wall of the palazzo holds the plaques etched with 16th-century administrative articles. Opposite we find **Palazzo del Governatore**, which now shares some of its space with the library dedicated to the Pescocostanzo scholar, Gaetano Sabatini. On the corner there is the 16th-century coat of arms of the Spanish royal family. The round stone fountain with bronze sculpture is the focal point of the square.

Towards the Peschio we see a Durazzesque portal (16th century) on **Casa Schieda**, in Via Porta di Berardo. The church of Sant'Antonio Abate sul Peschio, remodelled several times, dominates the district in isolation, and is all that remains of the old quarter that once surrounded it. Near the original fortification, where several typical defensive dwellings are visible, clustered around the Peschio. Here it is worth looking at **Palazzo Cocco** (17th century), in Via delle Preci, abutting the rock, and also the elegant 1700s **Palazzo Cocco Palmeri**, on the corner of Via San Rocco and Via Delle Dee, featuring a fine portal on Via San Rocco, offset from the façade, with windows decorated with Baroque-style central conch gables. In Via delle Pigne, massive **Palazzo Colecchi** (17th–18th century) occupies an entire block.

The nearby historic **Eremo di San Michele**

hermitage is in the district of the same name, off the sheep track that rises up from the Peligno valley and crosses Cansano and Campo di Giove. The sanctuary is dug completely from the rock and is part of that system of sheep-track places of worship that brought the Gargano cult of St Michael as far as Abruzzo, linked to the presence of water and natural caves. Sources document the refuge even in the 12th century although it is presumed to be older. The rock complex was restored in 1598, an indication found on the portal inscription, and comprises the grotto and the dwelling. The interior is paved with large stone slabs and the arched niche between the doors on the main frontage has painted plasterwork. The combination of safe refuge and water made it an important stopover point for transhumant flocks and a shelter for shepherds.

At Primo Campo, a locality on the edge of the **Bosco di Sant'Antonio**, a shady and ancient beech wood that is protected by a Guided Nature Reserve, we find the rock church of Sant'Antonio, part of that system of sheep-track and traveller places of worship that crossed the upper Cinque Miglia plateau. The date etched into the portal (1577) documents the church restoration undertaken by the rural community of Pescocostanzo.

The territory includes the Quarto di Santa Chiara Theme Nature Reserve.

Returning towards Sulmona we approach evocative hilltop **CANSANO**, on the road that connects Sulmona to Campo di Giove. The original nucleus clustered around the castle, of which some traces remain. Of the ancient boundary walls and access gates, only toponym indications survive (Via Sotto le Mura, Via Due Porte).

The parish **church of SS Salvatore**, with a nave and two aisles, vaults a precious 15th-century baptistery as well as two wooden statues of *St Peter* and *St Paul*, dated 17th century.

In the main square there is a noteworthy documentation and **visitor centre**, which houses finds from the **Ocriticum** archaeological complex as well as permanent exhibition dedicated to emigration. In the surrounding area, on Colle Mitra, there are the remains of an important fortified village that are worth visiting.

Ancient fortified **CAMPO DI GIOVE** rises on the Mount Tavola Rotonda buttress, on the southern face of Majella. The municipality is home to one of the offices of Majella National Park. The old centre retains some excellent examples of civil architecture, significant for the extreme sophistication of the detail and finish, above all **Palazzo Nanni**, built in the 1600s, then 1400s **Casa Quaranta** and **Palazzo Ricciardi** (18th century), with a singular lookout tower, now used as a town hall. Palazzo del Castello and **Palazzo delle Logge** (16th century), with unique loggias on the top floor, are also worth noting. The **church of Sant'Eustachio** is also worth visiting, said to have been founded over the remains of a temple dedicated to Jove, but with the current configuration dating mid-16th century There is a prized 1600s wooden choir. The **San Paolo church** is dated 14th century, with a lovely paliotto, and the **church of San Rocco**, with fine Renaissance façade, are both worthy of note. The Oasi di San Francesco d'Assisi, recently instituted by the Franciscan order, has an interesting **ethnography museum**.

Not far away, the remains of a small mountain church, Madonna di Coccia, at 1,400 metres asl, used to be a point of reference for travellers who crossed the Guado di Coccia ford, and for transhumant shepherds coming from the Peligno valley.

The itinerary turns back towards Sulmona and a detour leads to the ancient fortified village of **PACENTRO**, set on a hill overlooking the Peligno valley, on the foothills of Mount Morrone. There is a well-preserved historic centre, dominated by the great towers of the recently-restored mighty **Cantelmo castle**, one of the most interesting fortified structures in the Region. The complex siege structure, which must have played a strategic frontline role in territorial control, has three, tall four-sided  towers and another three round towers, with the prominent remains of the curtain walls mapping out a more or less rectangular plan. The tower presumed to be the oldest, belonging to an early compound, is to the northeast, its great squared blocks dated 11th–13th century. A later intervention, perhaps at the time the Cantelmo family arrived, probably modified the early layout, with the construction of the other two square towers to the northwest and southeast, whose origins are thought to be late–14th–early–15th century, given the age of the machicolation termination. Other structures were later added at various levels, as accommodation. The round towers must be integrations to strengthen the site, presumably after the arrival of the Orsini family. Next to the castle, we see the remains of the **SS Annunziata church**, of which the Gothic portal and fragments of frescoes are visible. At the foot of the fortress, in Piazza del Popolo, with a beautiful 17th-century fountain, we find the distinctive facade of the **Santa Maria Maggiore parish church**, from the 1400s to the 1500s (the façade is dated latter 16th century), with a 1603 portal and, inside, a lavish 1653 wooden pulpit.

Nearby stands the 16th-century **Palazzo Pitassi** with the adjacent church of Santa Maria della Misericordia, with an important rusticated portal on the facade.

The **Immacolata church** of the Minor Observants convent (1589), is stunning, with its frescoed 1600s cloister, as is the **San Marcello church**, founded in the 11th century and rebuilt in the 12th century, now with a 1600s portal in carved wood.

The calendar of religious events is famous for "Corsa degli Zingari", a race held each year on the first Sunday in September, when a group of barefoot youths run down the mountainside as far as the Madonna di Loreto sanctuary, built in the late 1500s.

209. Above: Pacentro's "Corsa degli Zingari" event.
210. Below: Pacentro dominated by Cantelmo castle's tall towers.

# Fucino Basin and Marsican Abruzzo

Arriving from L'Aquila on the A25 motorway, the town of **MAGLIANO DEI MARSI** is located near the Salto River, at the foot of Mount Lo Pago, on the southern face of Velino.
The original centre was once surrounded by defence walls and towers (one still existed in the early 20th century) but today's old town was seriously damaged by the 1915 earthquake and comprises mainly replacement buildings, aligned along the original routes.
The **church of Santa Lucia**, in the centre, is particularly noteworthy; traditionally said to have been built in the 13th century, it has three portals on the lavish façade, which was altered several times and restored after the 1915 earthquake inspired by the original structure. The finely-carved panels now walled into the upper order of the façade are the pluteuses of the ancient presbytery gate, which separated it from the area where the worshippers gathered. Inside there is a Roman funeral cippus, a 15th-century baptistery, a pulpit, and interesting high reliefs. The **church of San Domenico** with its 16th-century portal is also worth visiting.
At the foot of Mount Lo Pago, the centre of Magliano dei Marsi is the home of the **Riserva Naturale Orientata Monte Velino** nature reserve visitor centre, which also covers the municipality of Massa d'Albe, as well as the

Magliano dei Marsi, Massa d'Albe, Scurcola Marsicana, Avezzano, Luco dei Marsi, Trasacco, Collelongo, Villavalelonga, Ortucchio, San Benedetto dei Marsi, Pescina, Collarmele, Cerchio, Aielli, Celano.

The area explored centres around the Fucino basin, a great ancient lake, drained at the end of 19th century at the request of the Torlonia family, to make way for today's immense, fertile plain, and giving rise to one of the area's most important works of hydraulic engineering. The itinerary skirts the towns that once stood on the lake shores and skims the slopes of massive Mount Velino. The municipalities of Magliano dei Marsi, Massa d'Albe, Pescina, Collarmele, Cerchio and Celano lie within the Velino-Sirente Regional Park. The area is extremely rich in archaeological remains and works of art, although it was seriously hit by the 1915 earthquake, which wiped out many instances. The remains of Alba Fucens constitute one of the greatest surviving expressions. There is also a significant amount of fortified architecture, some of which is particularly important, for example Celano and Scurcola Marsicana, which are among the most important in the region and testify to the area's strategic importance.

211. The illustration of Lake Fucino in the map of the "Marsorum Dioecesim" of 1735.

Museo dell'Uomo e della Natura (**MUN**), dedicated to the theme of biodiversity, and a knowledge and experimentation centre thanks to state-of-the-art interactive technologies with access for the disabled.

Near the hamlet of **Rosciolo**, we find the **church of Santa Maria delle Grazie** has interesting frescoes inside, as well as 13th- and 15th-century portals. The 1200s portal to the right of the 1400s façade is all that remains of the older church. Sources date the striking nearby **church of Santa Maria in Valle Porclaneta** in connection with the existence of a monastic foundation as early as the first half of the 11th century, but the church appears today in the guise of a subsequent rebuilding

and no trace remains of the monastery. Unlike the rich interior, the structure outside is particularly austere. A simple porch in front of the façade connects the church with the lost cloister. On the rear, the single polygonal apse is marked by a triple order of columns, a work dating back to the early–13th century and suggesting that the building was given a Gothic refurbishment.

The interior furnishings are particularly noteworthy, with the valuable wooden **iconostasis**, and the 1150 **ciborium** and **ambo** made by Nicodemo and Roberto. The two pluteuses that support the base of the iconostasis and are datable to the 1140s–1150s are of particular interest. The church has a nave and two aisles separated by quadrangular pillars, some of which retain traces of interesting frescoes also seen on the transept and presbytery walls. Although the church was remodelled with some additions and later damaged by the 1915 earthquake, it is still one of Abruzzo's most significant Medieval monuments, chiefly for the wealth of interior decorative features.

Rosciolo castle is also interesting, retaining one of its round corner towers and part of the curtain walls overlooking the southern and eastern sides. The village spreads north of this and preserves a round tower and some parts of its surrounding boundary walls, near the castle tower. The history of the village and the castle are linked to the monastery of Santa Maria in Valle Porclaneta, north of the castle, for which it must have constituted a point of control and defence along the route that led there.

The village of **Marano** is particularly distinctive. It developed around a castle whose floorplan can still be identified despite numerous alterations. The village, which extends east along the slope, is still characterized by defence elements, such as the entrance gate situated to the west, dated late–13th century, with a lancet arch flanked by two quadrangular towers, of which the south-facing construction was incorporated into a 19th-century building. To the north of the gate we see part of the walls, which connected to the castle structure.

**MASSA D'ALBE** lies a few kilometres from Magliano, on the slopes of Mount Velino and along with Corona (the municipal capital) assumed importance in the 15th–19th century. After the 1915 earthquake, they grew and merged. The spectacular San Benedetto cave, also known as the "Grotta del Cristiano", opens on the slopes of Mount Cafornia, near

212. 213. Facing page: external and internal view of the church of Santa Maria in Valle Porclaneta.
214. Above: Marano.
215. Below: view of the area of Orsini castle Albe vecchio.

Corona, offering a magnificent view over the Fucino basin and Marsica mountains.

The nearby fortified village of **Albe Vecchio**, which was almost completely destroyed by the 1915 earthquake, is set on a relief close to the ancient settlement of **Alba Fucens** (*see box p. 131*). It developed around the **Orsini castle** which, despite its current dereliction, can still be identified as a classic square plan, with round, battered corner towers and an interesting, partially-preserved gallery, with corbels in three successive overhangs that must

# The Ancient Roman Town of Alba Fucens

Alba Fucens is one of the most important and evocative archaeological sites in Abruzzo. The settlement, of great strategic importance as it is situated at a point where important routes like the Via Valeria, a continuation of Via Tiburtina, converge, became the centre of an important Latin colony after the consul P. Sempronius Sophus conquered the town, defeating the Aequi in 304 BC. Post–1949 excavations defined the ruins of the ancient colony, which spread over Piano della Civita, between the Pettorino hills to the east and San Pietro to the south. The general road plan seems to belong to the period when the colony was founded: late–4th century–early 3rd century BC; the route plan is regular with parallel roads, (facing northwest and southeast), which cross the town lengthwise (the *decumans*) perpendicular streets (the *cardines*), forming regular blocks; the *cardus maximus* and *decumanus maximus* can be identified respectively in **Via dell'Elefante**, so-called because slabs of stone were found decorated with elephant protomes, and in **Via del Miliario**, so-called because of the interesting Magnentius milestone dated 350–1 AD (the imprint of the original is kept in Chieti Archaeological Museum), showing the distance from Rome on Via Valeria, equal to 68 Roman miles (about 100km). The urban fabric's more monumental aspect seems to correspond to a general reconstruction initiated at the end of the 2nd century BC and completed during the 1st century BC, when the most important public buildings were erected, including the **basilica**, the *macellum*, the so-called **sanctuary of Hercules** and the **theatre**. The amphitheatre and porticoes in **Via dei Pilastri** date back to the Imperial Age.

216. Facing page: aerial view of Alba Fucens archaeological site.
217. Above: the amphitheatre.
218. Left: Magnentius' *Miliarum*.
219. Below: Via dei Pilastri.

have extended around the entire perimeter. The height difference between the towers and curtain walls led some scholars to suggest the castle was built in the 14th century, though with some reservations.

The little **church of San Pietro**, set up on a hill close to the site of *Alba Fucens*, is worth visiting as it is one of Abruzzo's best examples of Romanesque architecture. The current layout is the result of reconstruction work carried out between 1955 and 1967, using the original elements that survived the 1915 earthquake. Starting with modern restoration methodology, a survey was carried out, the ruins were catalogued *in situ* and the building was strengthened with an internal reinforced concrete structure.

The 12th-century church may have been built over a previous Italic temple, dating back to the 3rd century BC, and probably dedicated to Apollo and Diana. On the site, two of the Tuscan columns of the pronaos and the perimeter walls of the ancient cell survive. Remains of the temple walls can also still be seen in the crypt beneath the apse, where an early Medieval sarcophagus with a bas-relief is also found. The church has a nave and two aisles separated by recovered fluted Corinthian columns, a semi-circular apse, and a crypt. A square block abuts the façade, which acted as the base of the belfry, and the architrave of the portal opening there is etched with the date 1526 and the symbol of St Peter. Sources suggest that the work was undertaken during restorations put in place in the 16th–late–17th centuries, which also involved completion of the façade, the addition of a wooden false ceiling, new frescoes, and stone paving, as indicated by the inscription on a stone floor slab. The 13th-century **ambo** and the Cosmatesque **iconostasis** are splendid, made in 1225–50 by the Roman marble sculptor, Giovanni di Guittone, together with Master Andrea, as recalled by the inscription on the pulpit, whose design bears a close resemblance to Roman models, which was unusual for Abruzzo. The innermost portal, which testifies to the importation of Abruzzo motifs from the Campania region at the beginning of the 12th century, is also precious.

Almost all the frescoes that decorated the church were lost following the 1915 earthquake but a series of panels from a larger cycle, dated latter–14th–early–15th century, was detached and installed on the left wall of the church; seven are now found in the Museo Nazionale dell'Aquila – MUNDA.

220. 221. This page: the façade and interior of the Romanesque church of San Pietro, Alba Fucens.
222. Facing page: the Orsini fortress, Scurcola Marsicana.

Before heading to Avezzano, it is worth stopping at **SCURCOLA MARSICANA**, set strategically on the San Nicola hill slopes, between the Imele and Salto valleys, to the north of the Campi Palentini, which were the scene of the famous 1268 battle between Conradin of Swabia and Charles of Anjou for the conquest of Southern Italy. That celebrated clash, even remembered in Dante's Inferno, ended with the dramatic defeat of Conradin. The first documented information on the Scurcola fiefdom, a name that seems to derive from the Lombard "skulk", meaning "sentry post", dates back to the latter half of the 12th century, when it was a Norman estate.

The urban fabric was set on the southern side of the relief, under the imposing **Orsini fortress**, today seen in its late–15th-century transformation, commissioned by Gentile Virginio Orsini, Count of Tagliacozzo and Lord of Bracciano. It is one of the most significant and evolved siege structures, even outside of the region. The unique, triangular floorplan, with two round towers at the south and east tips, and a high scarp, shows an imposing semi-elliptical rampart in the most vulnerable part: clearly the traditional square keep was abandoned to reduce the sides at risk from besieging artillery. Hence an effective application of the principle whereby the defence potential of a fortress was based on the stratagem of its floor plan rather than on the thickness of its walls. The current layout is clearly the result of different building phases stages, still recognizable in part despite the serious state of decline caused by the long period of abandon. Indeed, the remains of a Medieval castle–enclosure were discovered, with a pentagonal bulwark tower in the highest point, subsequently incorporated into a Renaissance fortress. The Orsini family's late–15th-century transformation is the most unique and advanced in the field of fortified architecture in Abruzzo: the grazing defence system adopted was particularly advanced for its time. It is still possible to see the towers and rampart, casemates with ventilation chimneys to disperse fumes, covering both the southwest and northwest downscaled, raised entrances, whilst only the stone brackets and traces of the unusual brick corbels are left of the machicolation, which crowned the curtain walls and rampart to achieve traditional plunging defence. Some experts have observed the masterful influence of Francesco di Giorgio Martini in the Orsini project, his presence as a military architect requested in 1490 by Virginio Orsini.

There are some excellent buildings to visit in the centre: from the **church of Sant'Egidio**, with its 14th-century portal; the small **Santissimo Sacramento church** with remarkable frescoes on the vault, as well as an 18th-century chalice and monstrance of the Neapolitan school. The **SS Trinità church**, downstream of the village has a late–16th-century plan and beautiful Baroque staircase presents, and the monumental stone façade portal bears the date 1584, perhaps the year it was completed, with the exception of the staircase added later. The adjoining Concezione chapel has a

beautiful oil on canvas, dated 1641, depicting the *Guardian Angel*.

Also noteworthy is the **church of Santa Maria della Vittoria**, built from the 16th century onwards. Inside today's church there is a superb 14th-century wooden statue of the *Madonna and Child* donated, which tradition says was donated by Charles I of Anjou to the monks of the older, 13th-century abbey of Santa Maria della Vittoria, of which a few ruins survive on the plain on the Imele's left bank. The Cistercian church and monastery (built in 1274 by order of that same ruler in memory of the victory over the Swabians) were gradually abandoned, from the end of the 15th century to the turn of the next.

About a kilometre from the town, heading west, the **Franciscan church of Sant'Antonio di Padova** is worth a visit. It may already have existed in the early–16th century, a time when the convent must have been built, but restored in the 18th century. A portal from the abbey of **Santa Maria della Vittoria** was reassembled on the façade and embellished with a fine decorated wooden door.

Close by is the densely-populated ancient city of **AVEZZANO**, on the slopes of Mount Velino, at the edge of the great basin that was once Lake Fucino. The 1915 earthquake razed the built-up area to the ground and little of its past survived the earthquake and World War II. The **Orsini castle** here is surely one of the most representative in the whole region, despite various modifications. The typical square-plan fortress preserves its four round, corner towers with canons. The fort was erected in 1490 by Gentile Virginio Orsini, indicated by the inscription on the plaque above the housings of the ancient drawbridge chains, and incorporated an older lookout tower, which is traditionally dated back to Gentile de Paleria, lord of the Avezzano district in 1182. The Gothic arch ashlars in the castle gate show intricate arrangement, and next to it there is the elegant portal dating back to 1565, reconstructed after the first restoration work. The abutments are made with truncated pyramid ashlar and support a trapezoidal arch, with the Colonna coat of arms in the keystone. The garrison was transformed into a splendid fortified residence by Marcantonio Colonna from 1520 to the late–1500s, but the 1915 earthquake and 1944 bombings radically changed the castle's elaborate structure. It underwent some restoration in the 1960s, followed by 1970s excavations, and more recent restoration installed an auditorium and an area for the **Pinacoteca d'Arte**

223. Above: the Orsini fortress, Avezzano.
224. Below: San Bartolomeo cathedral, Avezzano.
225. Facing page: Luco dei Marsi.

Moderna, a gallery containing works by Schifano, Bragaglia, Brindisi, and others. The portal of the Capuchin church of Santa Maria a Vico, destroyed by the 1915 earthquake, reassembled on the side of the San Francesco church, is also of particular interest. As part of the larger "**L'Aia dei Musei**" project, the new Le parole della pietra Lapidarium and the Il Filo dell'Acqua Museo del Prosciugamento del Fucino can now be visited in the Mattatoio Comunale (former municipal slaughterhouse). The modern, multimedia layout illustrates the major works undertaken to drain the third largest lake in Italy. A second building is dedicated to contemporary art exhibitions and events.

Inside **Villa Torlonia** park we find the Museo di Arte Pastorale Abruzzese, located in the Padiglione Torlonia and known as the Chalet, a wooden Art Nouveau structure dating back to the end of the 19th century, which survived the 1915 earthquake. This park was once owned by the Torlonia family and is where we also find Palazzo Torlonia, the romantic gardens, and the icehouse, as well as the stores and barns now used for exhibitions and cultural events. In the recently redeveloped adjacent Piazza Torlonia which constitutes an extraordinary city park of about five hectares with Villa Torlonia, the 19th-century Torlonia fountain, the bronze bust of Alessandro Torlonia and Ermenegildo Luppi's Gloria del Fante monument to the fallen, dated late–1920s and moved here after World War II from Piazza Risorgimento (the central space of the new city). Here we find the mighty **San Bartolomeo cathedral**, built from 1930 to a project by the engineer Sebastiano Bultrini, consecrated in 1942 and subsequently modified after suffering war damage. All that survives of the ancient church of San Bartolomeo, formerly the collegiate, located in the old centre and rebuilt several times after various earthquakes until its destruction in 1915, is the base of the bell tower, today part of the memorial monument built in 1965.

The Riserva Naturale Guidata Monte Salviano is located on municipal territory and visitors will see wall structures built by the Romans for reclamation of the Fucino, now in an archaeological park. The **Fucino inlet** and other drainage works, carried out in the 19th century by the Duke of Torlonia, are also interesting.

A path through a thick pine wood leads to the **Madonna di Pietracquaria sanctuary**, of ancient origins but rebuilt several times, also after the 1915 earthquake, known for the miraculous image venerated there. On the Mount Salviano pass there is a sculpture by

Pietro Cascella, called *Teatro della germinazione*. Continuing along the edge of the plain southward there is the town of **LUCO DEI MARSI**, on the slopes of Mount La Ciocca, dividing the Fucino basin from the Liri valley. Luco dei Marsi acquired its present configuration in the Middle Ages, developing lengthwise as was usual with lake shore towns. There was considerable expansion when the lake was reclaimed but the town was seriously damaged by the 1915 earthquake. Despite numerous reconstructions, it retains its traditional urban fabric in the upper part, with features dating back to the 17th–19th centuries The 18th-century **parish church of San Giovanni Battista** has a striking elegant façade, but the most eye-catching building is the **church of Santa Maria delle Grazie**, just outside the inhabited centre. The church, known since the 10th century as a donation made by Doda, Countess of the Marsi to the Benedictines, was presumably rebuilt in the 13th century. Its present plan, with a nave and two aisles, separated by pillars with a cross-vaulted square choir, four chapels along the left side and two along the right, is the result of subsequent interventions. It was restored in 1565 and enlarged with four additional chapels on each side and two apses at the back of the aisles; a lunette barrel vault was installed over the nave and two aisles. The 1915 earthquake seriously damaged the structure of the church, which was restored by dismantling the falling vaults and replacing them with wooden trusses. The first two chapels on the right were also demolished, as were the small side apses. During work, the derelict belfry was rebuilt, as was the upper part of the façade, which was embellished by elegant architrave portals, with lavish decoration on the central structure. The presbytery has a precious 13th-century ambo with a pulpit showing the *Last Judgment*. The *Lucus Angitiae* town–sanctuary archaeological site dedicated to the goddess Angitia is near the centre. The remains of an Italic temple in the Il Tesoro district and a temple from the Augustan age are recognizable.

135

The interesting village of **TRASACCO** lies on the slopes of Mount Alto, on the southern edge of the Fucino basin. The town originated on the lake shore, at the outlet of Collelongo valley, , and assumed an important role in controlling the territory, which is seen in the existence of the square-based Febonio defence and lookout **tower**, whose considerable mass looms over Trasacco. From an architectural point of view, the tower is particularly interesting because of the unique combination of the lower, perhaps older, square-plan portion, with the circular upper storey.

The striking **Santi Cesidio e Rufino church** was noticeably altered in 1618 by Abbot Cicerone de Blasis, who transformed the presbytery and transept, adding a third aisle. The building has a basilica layout with a nave and three aisles, and a rectangular apse, a frescoed barrel-vault sacristy, a massive bell tower and a block extending to the east, called the "Oratorio della Confraternita della Concezione". On the gabled façade, partially hidden by the oratory, there is a small Renaissance portico preceding the older, "women's" portal, leading to the nave, which consists of a rectangular space with piers and architraves finely decorated with the traditional interwoven acanthus branches and animal and human figures within the volutes. The right side features the next, larger "men's" portal, dated mid–15th century, where elements already tending to Renaissance mingle with those borrow from the Romanesque of the previous portal. Inside we find lovely frescoes dated 1300s and 1400s, as well as a semi-circular relief, probably coming from an ancient podium is used as a pulpit and resembling the pulpit in the church of Santa Maria delle Grazie, in Luco dei Marsi.

**Santa Maria del Perpetuo Soccorso church** and the nearby sanctuary of **Madonna di Candelecchia** are good examples of Renaissance architecture, the latter with a precious painting depicting the *Virgin Mary*, dated 16th century.

The old town was destroyed by the 1915 earthquake and part of the centre was rebuilt. The **Centro di documentazione A. Radmilli** documents the excavations and studies undertaken at the Continenza cave and is particularly interesting for finds displayed, dated from the Neolithic to the Roman age.

A detour to the south leads to the village of **COLLELONGO**, on the slopes Mount Malpasso, at the centre of Vallelonga and on the boundary of Abruzzo – Lazio – Molise National Park. Traces of defence systems from the ancient fortified village can be seen on tower-type buildings on the west side. More complex, noble buildings replaced the modest Medieval structures. The 1915 earthquake seriously damaged the built-up area. The **church of Santa Maria delle Grazie**, with its 16th-century portal, the **church of Santa Maria la Nova**, with an 18th-century organ and priceless modern paintings (including Mario Ceroli's *St Michael the Archangel* and Piero Guccione's *The Gaze of St Roche*) are worth seeing. **Palazzo Botticelli** (17th century) houses the remarkable **Museo Civico Archeologico** with its important Italic–Roman finds dating from the 6th century BC

226. Facing page: Trasacco defence tower.
227. 228. Below: the bell tower and the men's portal of the church of SS Cesidio e Rufino, Trasacco.

to the 1st century AD, brought to light by excavation campaigns conducted since the 1960s, in the Amplero valley, on the boundary of Abruzzo – Lazio – Molise National Park.
The Museo della Civiltà Contadina e del Lavoro delle Montagne abruzzesi is an interesting multisite museum that starts from Palazzo Botticelli and ends at the Casa del Tempo, guiding visitors in a discovery of ancient traditions linked to the objects exhibited in old houses or in external display cases along the streets.
There is a fascinating celebration of St Anthony Abbot held on the night between 16 and 17 January, with the traditional opening to the public of the *cottore* – houses with large fireplaces where *cicerocchi* (corn cobs) are cooked and distributed.
Neighbouring **VILLAVALLELONGA** hugs a hillock on the Colle dei Cerri slopes, in Abruzzo – Lazio – Molise National Park, set in a splendid natural scenario. The fortified village did not extend beyond the perimeter wall until after the 17th century. The types of buildings in the historic centre are hard to classify because of the damage caused by the 1915 earthquake and because of the alterations made to the original features. Incorporated in the building fabric, the ancient defence wall is partially preserved. In addition

to the **San Leucio e San Nicola parish church**, there is the **Madonna delle Grazie church** with a late–15th-century terracotta statue depicting *St Bartholomew*; the church houses the remains of local priest Gaetano Tantalo, considered one of the *Righteous Among the Nations* for saving the lives of two Jewish families during World War II.
The celebration of the feast of St Anthony Abbot here is fascinating, with its traditional *Panarda* dinner held on the night between 16 and 17 January. On the afternoon of 17 January, a cortège of masks sets off, opening Carnival.
The **Museo dell'Orso** is worth a visit, in the Park Visitor Center, with an interesting wildlife area. Past the town there is the Madonna della Lanna sanctuary and Abruzzo – Lazio – Molise National Park starts just beyond this.
Turing back to Trasacco we find the ancient village of **ORTUCCHIO**, which was also affected by the 1915 earthquake. Set on a hillock at the southeast edge of the Fucino plain, it was one of the strongholds on the area's defence system. The imposing **castle** was built by Antonio Piccolomini in the latter half of the 15th century but was damaged by the 1915 earthquake, then restored in the 1970s. It was a rare example of a fortified complex that could only be accessed by water although this characteristic was lost with the draining of the lake. When the extant fort was destroyed, by Napoleone Orsini, following orders from Pope Pius II, in

229. 230. Below: left, "cottore" at Collelongo; right, the feast of St Anthony Abbot, Villavallelonga.

about 1465, Antonio Piccolomini, the new feudal lord, had it completely rebuilt, except for the dungeon, as described by the inscription on the main portal. The outer trapezoidal wall, with round corner towers, surrounded by a wide moat, incorporates the higher square keep with machicolations and remains of battlements. Only a trace is left of the base of the northwest tower.

The **Sant'Orante sanctuary** stands in the upper part of the town and is of ancient origins, although it was rebuilt at the end of the 1960s, after being destroyed by the 1915 earthquake, which had spared the precious portal. Inside, fragments of the ancient frescoes are still visible. The grotte di Ortucchio are a well-known group of karst caves called La Punta, Maritza, Ortucchio, and La Cava, in the areas around the village, inhabited from the Palaeolithic through to the Roman age. To the northwest of the town we find the Centro Spaziale Piero Fanti, known as **Telespazio del Fucino**, one of the largest telecommunication centres in the world and the largest teleport for civilian use.

Moving onward we come to the hamlet of **Venere**, which is part of Pescina, where it is worth paying a visit to the round Medieval lookout **tower**. Also on the eastern edge of the Fucino plain there is the modern town of **SAN BENEDETTO DEI MARSI**, built over the ruins of *Marruvium*, a Marsi tribal capital, once on the lake shore. The built-up area, which was semi-destroyed by the 1915 earthquake, has a regular, orthogonal plan. A complete urban layout of the Roman town is documented for the period between the end of the Republic and the beginning of the Empire, when the town was forced to erect monumental buildings indispensable for its new functions, after becoming a *municipium*. Of these, the area of the ancient forum with the *capitolium* has been identified as being near the **cathedral of Santa Sabina**, part of whose stone façade embellished with a wonderful 14th-century portal, is preserved, despite being partly destroyed by the 1915 earthquake. The ruins of the imposing **"morroni"** are preserved along Via Marruvio: these funeral monuments were made of cement but now lack the upper surface, which was subsequently removed. Some parts of the boundary wall, in a technique resembling *reticulatum*, and the ruins of

231. Above: the portal of San Sabina cathedral, San Benedetto dei Marsi.
232. Below: Ortucchio castle.

baths, northeast of the present centre, can still be seen in the town today and are believed to date back to the foundation of the *municipium*. The site where the **amphitheatre** once stood has been identified to the north of the built-up area and can be dated to the Augustan period because of the building technique used. Today it is possible to see the *opus reticulatum* walls on the southeast entrance, where the vaulted corridor slopes gently towards the arena.

**PESCINA**, a few kilometres from San Benedetto dei Marsi, is set partly in the Fucino plain and partly on a rocky ridge, on the left bank of the River Giovenco. The **Piccolomini tower** and ruins of the ancient fortification overlook the ancient village, which developed on the hillside, privileging strategic aspects rather that a favourable north-facing direction for the urban fabric. As a result of the 1915 earthquake, the old town, in the upper part of the site, was abandoned, which encouraged subsequent development on the opposite riverbank. The **cathedral of Santa Maria delle Grazie**, which was finished in the late–16th century and restored in the 20th century, is remarkable for its beautiful façade-pronaos and the *Madonna and Child* wooden sculpture found insied, brought from the church of San Berardo, now derelict. The **church of Sant'Antonio da Padova** has an elegant 14th-century portal surmounted by the coat of arms of the Counts of Celano and was partly damaged by the 1915 earthquake.

The church and the upper part of the façade were modified in 1640–8 by Giovanni Artusi Canale, known as "il Piscina", a pupil of Bernini. Inside, the decorative scheme is mostly 18th-century, with traces of a 16th-century fresco depicting the *Presentation of Jesus in the Temple*, by Michele da Tione, visible on the counter-façade. The convent, a square block with a central courtyard, has been completely converted and currently houses the **Centro Studi Ignazio Silone**, in honour of the writer born in Pescina, which organizes the Premio Internazionale Ignazio Silone international award each year. Inside we find the **Museo Silone** with a precious library, personal objects and the writer's awards. In 1978 Silone's wishes were fulfilled when his ashes were placed under the bell tower of the church of San Berardo, rebuilt in the 1700s over the remains of the older church of Santa Maria del Popolo or Porta. In the original aisleless church with a choir with horizontal termination, the round-arch portal is surmounted by the coat of arms of the Counts of Celano. A lunette contains a 16th-century fresco depicting the *Madonna and Child between St Francis and St Bernardino*. The town was also the birthplace of the famous cardinal Giulio Raimondo

233. Below: Pescina.
234–236. Facing page, left to right: the round tower and façade of the church of Santa Maria delle Grazie, Collarmele; Porta Nuova gate, Aielli.

Mazzarino (1602–61), to whom the main square and the **Casa-Museo G.R. Mazzarino** (opened in 1971–2) are dedicated. The house-museum is next to the remains of his birthplace and stores documentation relating to the political and private life of "Cardinal Mazarin", as well as having a small specialist library.

Pescina spinnery, near the River Giovenco, is a venerable point of reference for local sheep farmers, who brought their wool here to make yarn.

Continuing north we reach the **COLLARMELE**, overlooking the Fucino basin. The built-up area is eye-catching for its handsome **round Medieval tower**, which drove development of the ancient village. After surviving the 1915 earthquake it suffered serious damage in the 2009 earthquake. The tower's outer face presents a striking structure of various types of ashlar, which suggests the use of cannibalized materials. The raised entrance, with protruding brackets, is surmounted by the coat of arms of the Berardi family, who were the Counts of Celano. Inside, the tower has an octagonal plan in the upper part, and it is thought a cistern may have been installed below.

The nearby **church of Santa Maria delle Grazie** was built by the Piccolomini family in the second half of the 16th century on the old Regio Tratturo sheep track. The isolated chapel is worth visiting, one of last important expressions of the Abruzzo 1500s. The simple, rectangular chamber has wooden trusses and a square, raised choir, with a ribbed cross vault; a monumental stone altar, embellished with a lavish bas-relief decoration, dominates the presbytery. The façade, which is particularly interesting because of a polychrome majolica cladding characterizing the upper part, is sliced by a protruding cornice; beneath it the portal is surmounted by a triangular gable and flanked by two small side windows. The decorated upper part is cadenced with two niches with statues of *St Peter* and *St Paul*, and ends in a tympanum with a central round window. Inside we find an impressive late-1500s altar from the parish church destroyed in the 1915 earthquake. The church was seriously damaged by the 2009 earthquake.

**CERCHIO** is close by, on the slopes of Mount Corbarolo, in the northern foothills of the Fucino basin. After the 1915 earthquake, all that remains of the original fortified village, clustered around the castle, are traces of its layout and a few buildings. There are some 16th-century terracotta statues worth seeing in the **church of San Bartolomeo** (formerly Sant'Antonio), with its Renaissance portal, and the **parish church of Santa Maria delle Grazie** has a silver cross of the Sulmona school. The **Museo Civico** in the nearby Augustinian convent is particularly interesting, with sections on religious art, ethnography, and farming culture.

**AIELLI** appears grouped on a hilltop just above Cerchio, with a panorama of the Fucino plain, in the perfect position to defend the western access and signal to the ancient garrisons of Collarmele, Pescina and Ortucchio. It is still possible to see the ancient plan of the fortified hillside village, with flanking towers incorporated into more modern buildings. The two parts of the settlement are particularly fascinating, with two surviving gates: monumental **Porta Nuova** to the south, dated latter half of the 15th century but seen in its 1900s restoration alongside the Torre dell'Orologio clock tower, and **Porta Montanara** in the north closing off Via Montanara, an older gate with a Gothic arch near where the castle once stood. The third existing gate, **Porta Iannetella** or Porta della Terra, was probably built in 1594 as indicated in an inscription and reassembled in 2008. The ruins of fortifications built by Ruggero, Count of Celano, in 1356, are preserved in the upper part, called Castello. A stone tower, round outside and octagonal inside is still visible, developing over three levels above a base with a simple stone cornice. On the east side of the tower we see the moat pillar that allowed access to the upper level via a drawbridge. The roof of the ground floor section is particularly refined, with an elaborate eight-gore umbrella vault, divided by ribs on small brackets, part of the works commissioned by the Piccolomini family from the 15th to the 16th centuries. The engraving on the window architrave is of considerable interest, documenting the date 1356 and the name of the Count, Ruggero of Celano, referable to a second construction phase of the tower. Now called **Torre delle Stelle**, the tower has been recovered and is in use as an astronomical observatory with an adjoining **Museo del Cielo** and a specialized scientific library. Silone's famous novel, *Fontamara*, has been transcribed onto a wall of the building at the foot of the Torre delle Stelle.

Among the most interesting religious buildings is the **SS Trinità church**, founded by Count Ruggero II in 1362. The façade was completed in 1479, as inscribed in the arch of the entrance portal, and then rebuilt after the earthquake of 1915. The 1479 portal and the coat of arms of the Piccolomini family have survived from the original building. The **church of San Rocco**, at the entrance to the village, was founded in 1546, with an interesting 16th-century fresco of the *Madonna del Buonconsiglio* as well as an 18th-century wooden sculptural group of *St Anthony of Padua with Child Jesus*. In **Aielli Stazione**, a neighbourhood that emerged after 1915, the church of **San Giuseppe**, formerly the Sant'Adolfo, is of interest, built in the first three decades of the 20th century, and restored in 2012, whose decoration included contributions from Manifattura Chini of Borgo San Lorenzo in Mugello for the windows, while sculptor Arturo Dazzi made the two marble statues of St Guido and St Adolph, seen inside, and Emilio Musso produced the carved wooden main entrance door.

Finally, we reach **CELANO**, where the Marsica sheep track originates. The track starts downhill from the village and continues towards the Fucino basin, hugging the route of the Tiburtina Valeria until past Collarmele, running parallel to a stretch of the ancient Roman road.

Despite being compromised by the 1915 earthquake, it is still possible to see Celiano's original layout, compact around the imposing castle. The **church of Sant'Angelo**, with its refined

237. Below: aerial view of Celano.
238–240. Facing page: external view of the castle, inner courtyard and a room in the Museo Nazionale d'Arte Sacra della Marsica.

# Celano Castle

The complex, external fortified wall of Celano castle encompasses a perfectly symmetrical, rectangular central body, with four corner towers, an elegant inner courtyard, a well and an open gallery with two overlapping orders. The fortified residence appears as a compact, rectangular block, with the long sides facing north and south respectively, and the short sides facing east and west. The corners are accentuated by four square towers, which protrude slightly, with overhang and battlements. The buildings are arranged around the courtyard with an upper open gallery and loggia, accessed by a monumental archway entrance. The building is also surrounded by an irregular boundary wall, which follows the lay of the land, strengthened by small, square-plan towers and more effective truncated conical base towers for flanking fire. On the southeast, protected by a dry moat, the outer wall opens up through a first entrance with a drawbridge, followed by a second, older entrance, with an ogival arch surmounted by a slit. The entrance portal to the castle, along the southeast façade is particularly striking. It has two striking arches, one is segmental and is outlined by a second, a lancet arch. The foundation of the modern castle is traditionally attributed to Count Pietro De' Berardi, who presumably completed the boundary wall and first two levels of the castle up to the string-course cornice around 1392. The building was continued by Lionello Acclozamora, in 1451, who added the piano nobile, the machicolations, parapet walks above, and the four corner towers, giving the building its current unified structure. After being invested as Earl of Celano, Antonio Piccolomini certainly contributed to transforming the castle from an essentially military building to a comfortable noble residence. He completed the second floor of the courtyard loggia with round arches on capitals bearing the family's symbols, a cross and a crescent moon. Then he added several small vaulted loggias on the overhangs, supported by stone corbels, as well as opening several windows, including the rectangular window in the main façade, to give the castle all the air of a residence.

Piccolomini significantly reinforced the outer fortifications by strengthening the more vulnerable corners and incorporating the extant U-towers with mighty, escarped round towers; the southeast pedestrian entrance had a triangular ravelin with a round tower in the corner.

Through history the castle was home to different families, such as the Sforza-Cesarinis and the Dragonettis, who made no significant alterations to the structure. The 1915 earthquake seriously damaged the building, which was left in a state of complete abandon until 1940, when meticulous restoration work was started and completed in 1960. although interrupted by World War II. The restoration work involved the scientific reconstruction of the missing parts using substantial photographic documentation.

It has been home to the **Museo Nazionale d'Arte Sacra della Marsica** since 1992, installed on the first floor of the castle, enriched ten years later by the archaeological collection purchased by the Torlonia descendants with finds discovered during the draining of the Fucino plain. After the 2009 earthquake, the museum installations were renovated and reopened to the public.

241. Above: frescoes in the church of Santa Maria in Valleverde, near Celano.
242. Below: the modern MUSÈ structure in Paludi di Celano.

18th-century stucco work is particularly noteworthy, as is the **church of San Francesco**, with beautiful portal and painted lunette. The **church of San Giovanni Battista**, founded in the latter half of the 13th century and completed in the 15th century, was renewed in a Baroque key and restored after 1915. It preserves important 15th-century frescoes inside that reveal the hand of the Maestro della Cappella Caldora and contributions from the workshop of the Maestro di Beffi. The beautiful splayed portal stands out against the stone façade.

The mighty **castle** (*see box p. 143*), which towers above the town centre, against some stunning natural settings, overlooking the Fucino basin, constituted one of the main military strongholds, fundamental for protecting the sheep track, especially during the bloody 13th-century power struggles between the feudal and imperial forces, which took place in Marsica.

The nearby **church of Santa Maria di Valleverde**, annexed to the Riformati di San Giovanni di Capestrano convent, with some of the region's most important 16th-century paintings, is worth visiting. The convent was founded in the 15th century, whilst the building of the church was completed in 1509, which can be seen from the date on the portal with its lunette fresco of the *Madonna and Child between Saints and Francis and Bernardino*. The aisleless layout has three square cross-vaulted bays on corbels. A segmental lancet arch leads into the presbytery, which ends in a polygonal apse. Three small chapels open on the left and are also cross-vaulted. In the first and third chapels we can admire a large cycle of frescoes completed in 1559 by the Venetian Paolo Zoppare, also active in Abruzzo in the 16th century.

The noble Piccolomini family vast chapel, known as the Paradiso, is an extraordinary and unusual area beneath, entirely frescoed and accessed by a stairway with a balustrade in the centre of the third bay. Alfonso II Piccolomini commissioned the walls to be decorated between the 1530s and 1540s.

Here we find the sepulchre of Berardino Silveri Piccolomini, Bishop of Teramo, dated 1553. Also worth seeing is the cloister with late–17th-century frescoes and the refectory with the episodes of the *Last Supper*.

The **MUSÈ – Paludi Celano museum** has been built on the shores of ancient Lake Fucino, dedicated to Prehistory, designed to integrate perfectly with the important Paludi prehistoric archaeological site, a Bronze Age pile-dwelling village and the coeval necropolis with tumulus tombs. The modern architectural structure is inspired by the typical shape of these burials, almost camouflaged by the green areas that cover the roofs.

The lovely hermitage of San Marco alla Foce is said to be the site of the ancient monastery of San Marco. The complex stands on a narrow balcony of the impassable Celano gorges, closed upriver by another rock face and towards the valley by the La Foce torrent precipice.

# Piana del Cavaliere and the River Liri Valley

The road from the motorway exit of Carsoli-Oricola leads to **ORICOLA**, located on an isolated hill between Mount Amone and Colle della Capretta, straddling the Aniene river basin and Piana del Cavaliere. The original settlement, an ancient fortified town, arose around the castle-residence. Though the castle was restructured extensively, its layout is still visible in the forms dating back to the 15th century The **church of Santa Restituta**, with its 13th-century fresco, and the **parish church of Santissimo Salvatore**, which has an excellent 19th-century organ, are noteworthy. The stately **Palazzo De Vecchi** stands out among the examples of civil architecture. In the surrounding area, the Bosco di Sesera woods are a Site of Community Interest.

Our itinerary takes us towards **ROCCA DI BOTTE**. This town, founded in the early Middle Ages, is on the slopes of Colle della Civitella, the hill marking the southern boundary of Piana del Cavaliere. The old town layout can be noted in the upper part of the site and there are still vestiges of its fortification. In the 19th century the town developed down the valley. The **church of Santa Maria del Pianto** (also known as Santa Maria della Febbre) has lovely frescoes, probably 15th-century. The 13th-century ambo and ciborium in the old **church of San Pietro Apostolo**, which was later remodelled, are noteworthy examples of Cosmati-style work. The ambo in particular was recently damaged when several sections were stolen, including the spiral colonettes. The precious organ made by the famous Catarinozzi workshop in Affile is of particular importance. Also of note, located next to the birthplace of St Pietro, the

Oricola, Rocca di Botte, Pereto, Carsoli, Pietrasecca, Tagliacozzo, Cappadocia, Castellafiume, Capistrello, Canistro, Civitella Roveto, Civita D'Antino, Morino, San Vincenzo Valle Roveto, Balsorano.

This itinerary winds its way through the very edge of the region, between the picturesque upper valley of the River Liri and the plain extending from Carsoli through the valleys of the Simbruini Mountains. Countless examples of artwork can be seen along this delightful route, which passes some of the region's most important examples of military architecture, due to the fact that the area was near the border between the Papal States and the Bourbon Kingdom. The towns delimiting Piana del Cavaliere are the picturesque resort of Rocca di Botte, Oricola and Pereto, with its hilltop castle and tall towers, and the sanctuary of Madonna dei Bisognosi. As we head towards Balsorano, we come across the Liri valley's most important castle, which paints a striking picture in this setting. However, there is also the beauty of a natural environment with countless waterways that form breath-taking waterfalls, like Zompo lo Schioppo near Morino, a splendid area protected as a Nature Reserve.

243. Below: Cavaliere plain seen from Rocca di Botte.

145

church of San Pietro Eremita, rebuilt in 1777 as declared by the portal inscription.

On the Serrasecca hill, between Pereto and Rocca di Botte, the **sanctuary of Madonna del Monte** (or Santa Maria dei Bisognosi) is one of the most important Marian sanctuaries in the province of L'Aquila. The original church is traditionally dated 7th century and built to keep safe a venerated image of the Virgin Mary. It was restructured for the first time in the 16th century, then the convent and the aisleless church were added, the latter consecrated in 1781. Changes over time and the 1915 earthquake have not affected the integrity of the older interiors, which are home to precious 1400s frescoes. Older frescoes were produced by Jacopo di Arsoli, active in the first half of the 15th century, as indicated by an inscription still found in the church. Repair work was conducted in 1979 and again in 1982, and the complex is currently run by the Friars Minor. An interesting wooden *Madonna and Child* and a priceless wooden crucifix was donated by the Chapter of St Peter's at the Vatican in 1724 is found here, with a priceless wooden *crucifix*, both datable to the 12th–13th centuries.

The nearby town of **PERETO** is located on the eastern edge of Piano del Cavaliere, along the rocky spur that extends between Fosso Pachetto and Fosso San Mauro, starting from Colle della Difesa. The intriguing **castle**, composed of an enceinte that incorporates an imposing donjon – probably the original heart of the stronghold – and two tall quadrilateral towers around an internal courtyard, can be considered one of Abruzzo's most highly developed examples of its kind to monitor Piana del Cavaliere and the Via Valeria, at the border between Abruzzo and Latium, the layout we see today dates back to the 14th century and has features that are quite unusual in this region. The stout rectangular tower on the south side rises over the settlement. Once an isolated structure, it has a typical elevated access and has traditionally been dated back to the 12th century. The striking complex, which has undergone restoration work that has also

244. Above: frescoes in the sanctuary of Santa Maria dei Bisognosi.
245. 246. Below: left, Pereto; right, the church of Santa Maria in Cellis, Carsoli.

recreated the battlemented parapet, has an irregular trapezoidal layout. The entrance is on the widest side, to the north, and was monitored by tall quadrilateral towers. The northeast tower is rotated with respect to the contour of the tall curtain walls forming the courtyard. A stairway created on the east curtain wall leads from the courtyard to the chemin de ronde between the towers. Once the property of the Orsini and Colonna families, it was later owned by the Maccafanis and then the Arenas. The **Porta Nord** or Castello, **Porta Sottoponte** and the west **Porta Matticca** gates have survived of the ancient enceinte. The interesting **church of San Giovanni Battista** is of ancient origins, remodelled in around 1524, with 16th-century frescoes on the choir walls and a 17th-century mural painting of the *Madonna and Child*.

Located nearby is the **church of San Silvestro**, with frescoes and a wooden statue of the *Virgin Mary*.

Taking the state road, we now head to the historic town of **CARSOLI**, on the eastern edge of Piana del Cavaliere, where the plain opens into Valle del Fucino. The original settlement was built on a hilltop around the castle, whose ruins are still visible. Its construction can be attributed to the Angevin decision to reorganize the strongholds along territorial borders during the late 13th century. Characterized by four-sided towers, it has an inverted L shape. The cropped tower, located in the corner between the two curtain walls, was probably older and constituted the fulcrum for the subsequent fort. Once a section of the southeast curtain wall was lost, the southwest section of the walls, flanked by the access ramp, was also considerably reduced. Various stages of renovation works are recognizable, including one undertaken in the 1910s by the owner of the time, Giovanni Battista De Leoni, stated on a plaque on one of the entrances.

Medieval constructions can be seen in the older settlement on the hilltop, while the buildings near the enceinte are in the Renaissance style (16th–17th century). The 1500s **church of Santa Vittoria** is exceptional, with its 16th-century stone altars and outstanding 17th-century paintings. On the façade the two portals were brought from the **church of Santa**

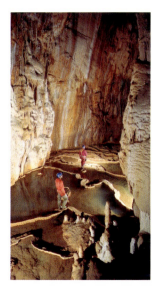

247. Grotta del Cervo, Pietrasecca.

**Maria in Cellis**, which is a short distance from the centre, by the cemetery.

This church is all that remains of the ancient monastery founded in the 11th century at the behest of Rainaldo Conte dei Marsi, today seen in its guise of a later reconstruction using salvaged elements including the portal at the centre of the façade, remodelled in a late–Renaissance style, and an imposing bell tower with double- and triple-lancet windows, the foundation elements from the Roman era. The aisleless church is split into two bays by a pillared arch set against the walls. The portal, clearly influenced by Benedictine architecture, is composed of two jambs and an architrave, and Abruzzo's first example of an outright "decorative device", with five square tiles decorated with the symbols of the Evangelists and the cross-bearing Lamb. The architrave ends in an archivolt decorated with a garland of leaves and palmettes that appear to come from another portal. The famous 1132 wooden doors are carved with episodes from the *New Testament* and are now displayed in Celano's Museo Nazionale d'Arte Sacra. The oldest pulpit in Abruzzo, dated early–12th century, presumably by the same hand that sculpted the portal, is still found inside, although it was reassembled at a later dated with some additions.

There are numerous hamlets nearby, notably **Colli di Montebove**, with its Medieval castle ruins, and the **church of San Nicola** with its 16th-century frescoes and, above all, the 1579 *Our Lady of the Rosary*. There is charming **Poggio Cinolfo**, with the ruins of the old urban walls dominated by the mighty **Palazzo Coletti** and the nearby parish church of Santa Maria Assunta. One hamlet is the ancient fortified **Pietrasecca**, whose oldest section, built around the Palazzetto to the west, and the area outside the urban gate, were built between the 15th and 19th century. The interesting **Santa Maria delle Grazie parish church**, vaunts marvellous paintings in the interior. The village enjoys a splendid position on a rugged cliff and is surrounded by the Riserva Naturale Speciale Grotte di Pietrasecca, established in 1992 to protect the unique karst environment around Pietrasecca. The reserve has spectacular natural formations, such as the **Ovito Sinkhole**, with rapids, lakes and waterfalls, and the **Grotta del Cervo**, a cave with striking concretions and important archaeological findings.

A few steps from the road that connects Pietrasecca to **Tufo Basso**, near the cemetery, we find the solitary **church of Santa Maria delle Grazie**, with the ruins of the small hermitage of the Benedictine monks. If there are not many remains of the medieval church, the beautiful tuff portal, dated 1581, belongs to the sixteenth-century renovations. Inside there is a beautiful high altar in carved tuff and popular seventeenth-century frescoes.

At **SANTE MARIE**, set in an extraordinary natural landscape, the 16th-century **church of Santa Maria delle Grazie** merits a visit, remodeled in the 18th and after the earthquake of 1915. Inside there is a polychrome terracotta depicting the Madonna dated to the 16th century. **Palazzo Colelli** is worth a visit and houses the Brigade exhibition-museum as well as the Multimedia Museum of Astrophysics (Mu.M.A.). It is worth visiting the Riserva Naturale Grotta della Luppa.

From here, our itinerary takes us to **TAGLIACOZZO**, set on a steep slope along a fissure framed by tall limestone cliffs between Colle dei Tufi and the mountain of La Difesa. The original town, built on the slope beneath a fortified settlement that monitored Via Tiburtina-Valeria, follows the contours of the mountain. Its 15th-century expansion centred around the monastic complexes, the Palazzo Ducale and Piazza dell'Obelisco (formerly Piazza da Piedi), extended southward to a less rugged area. It thus developed based on a more open layout with the noble architecture distinctive of the Renaissance.

The remains of the old **stronghold** which was to consist of a quadrangular layout with corner towers, scarp walls and internal courtyard, to guard the Tiburtina Valeria still dominate the town of Tagliacozzo. The fortress, with a west facing quadrangular layout, is composed of corner towers, a scarp wall and internal courtyard, next to which there was a wide low construction that may have been used as a residence. **Tremonti castle**, a fortified structure not documented by sources until the 12th century, is clearly visible to the west of the fortress, whereas the ruins of the fortified enclosure of Castiglione di San Donato, cited as a castellum in the second half of the 11th century can be seen to the northeast. The three structures formed an effective defensive network to monitor the border between the Kingdom of Naples and the Papal States.

A system of walls and towers, little of which remain, extended down the rocky cliffs towards Porta Romana and the **church of Santa Maria del Soccorso** with its handsome portal dated 1495, for a rapid connection between the castle and the settlement below. A wall to the northeast extended downstream. Starting from Piazza Duca degli Abruzzi we meet the **Annunziata church**, next to Palazzo del Municipio, with a beautiful portal dating back to 1475 from the

248. Below: Piazza dell'Obelisco, Tagliacozzo.
249. Facing page: the façade of the San Francesco church, Tagliacozzo.

lost church of San Giovanni Battista, founded by Roberto Orsini in the open countryside towards Colle San Giacomo. On the left capital we note the Orsini coat of arms. Turning to the right, we reach the striking **Porta dei Marsi** with a Gothic arch and then the delightful Piazza Argoli where the handsome **Palazzo Rota** and **Palazzo Mastroddi** stand. Turning right again we arrive in the charming Piazza dell'Obelisco, the heart of the village, its name inspired by the obelisk fountain that stands in its centre. The steep slope of Monte La Difesa soars in the background, while elegant buildings with loggias, mullions and windows with finely carved cornices form the backdrop.

The magnificent former **convent of San Francesco**, with its charming courtyard, was founded in the first two decades of the 13th century and reconstruction work on the church began in the mid-13th century, continuing until about 1270, although some of the later changes and additions are undated. It seems that the complex was enlarged in the 16th–17th century, and decorations were added to it during the first half of the 19th century, only to be removed in 1960. The aisleless church has three bays with ribbed vaults. The elevated presbytery is composed of an unusual series of rooms that are probably the result of several different refurbishments. The façade, which originally had a horizontal termination, is now embellished by a pointed-arch portal, probably from the 15th century, and an elegant rose window.

Inside the church, where the remains of Blessed Tommaso da Celano are kept, we can admire an interesting painting depicting the *Madonna and Child with saints Anne, Magdalen, and a Young St John the Baptist*, and a 15th-century polychrome wooden crucifix on the altar. To the left of the church, Via del Teatro leads towards the square of the same name where we find the **Teatro Talia**.

The majestic **Palazzo Ducale** was built in the tradition of Simone Architetto and when the Orsini family was in power. The irregular plan building already existed at the beginning of the 14th century, but it was in the latter half of the 1400s, with the enlightened Roberto Orsini, that the palazzo acquired its stately appearance that has not changed, even today. On the second floor we find the family chapel, with a painted coffered ceiling, and the loggia once decorated with striking frescoes, later detached and taken to Celano's Museo d'Arte Sacra della Marsica. From a stylistic standpoint, the entrance evokes Urbino's Palazzo Ducale. The mansion is set around two courtyards: the first, with a trapezoidal plan, is paved with cobblestones and delimited by three prospects and the outside wall, which has a beautiful decorated entrance. Two sides of the palace and the outside wall border the other courtyard, which is irregular in shape.

We reach the mighty bulk of the **monastic complex of Santi Cosma e Damiano**, an ancient property of the Abbey of Montecassino. It was one of the most important and ancient monasteries of Marsica and a cloistered life is still practiced there. The entrance to the monastery is marked by a beautiful portal built in 1452 by the Lombard Martino De Biasca. From here we enter the courtyard where the church is set, with a charming 15th-century facade embellished with a rose window and a Renaissance portal that leads into the aisleless interior with three bays and two round arches. Next to the church we find the bell tower built in 1564.

Located near Tagliacozzo, the **sanctuary of Madonna dell'Oriente**, with its panel painting of the *Madonna and Child*, typical of Byzantine art. According to tradition, it arrived in Italy after having miraculously escaped the iconoclastic fury of the 7th century. The **Museo Orientale** is installed in the sanctuary and houses a fascinating collection of votive offerings and archaeological finds, as well as Byzantine icons, coins and liturgical furnishings from the Middle East.

The River Liri, which forms a waterfall near **CAPPADOCIA**, the ancient fortified town damaged by the 1915 earthquake, nearby, the **Grotte di Beatrice Cenci** caves are worth a visit, interesting from an archaeological as well as speleological point of view. The river continues through an enchanting, picturesque valley,

250. Above: aerial view of Civitella Roveto.
251. 252. Facing page: above, the ambo of the church of San Nicola, Corcumello and a view of Civita d'Antino.

passing **CASTELLAFIUME**, a village whose original settlement, with remains of the **castle**, can still be seen alongside its 18th–19th-century expansion.
From here we come to **CAPISTRELLO**, the mining town at the entrance to the Roveto valley, with a new section built after the 1915 earthquake, along state road to the Liri valley. The old part is located under Punta del Ferro at the southwest end of Mount Arezzo. One of the most significant examples of civil architecture is **Palazzo Lusi** with a characteristic corner turret. A section of the Cunicoli di Claudio tunnels, built by Emperor Claudius, is visible below the town, with the outlet of the Emissario di Claudio emissary. The tunnel, constructed by the Romans to drain Lake Fucino, leads to the River Liri. The Madonna del Monte sanctuary stands on the crest of Mount Arezzo, site of a unique cult.

The hamlet of **Corcumello** is also fascinating. This ancient fortified village still has portions of its defensive walls, but it also boasts 15th- and 16th-century structures, as well as **Palazzo Vetoli** and **Palazzo De Pontibus**. The 13th-century ambo in the **church of San Nicola** is stunning.

The today's **CANISTRO**, a village in the Liri valley, developed after the 1915 earthquake, when the residents of the old town of Canistro Superiore, on a hilltop at the northern end of the Roveto valley, were forced to move to Case Santacroce, in the valley. The Medieval layout of the old fortified village, whose expansion was limited, can still be seen, but the urban fabric was irreparably compromised, mostly by the reconstruction work that followed World War II. The remains of the parish church of San Giovanni Battista and the 18th-century Palazzo Vecchiarelli, on the street by the same name, are noteworthy. The **Parco La Sponga** with its natural cascades and artificial pools is worth visiting.

Canistro boasts a wealth of natural springs and even has its own hot spa. It is surrounded by chestnut groves, source of the famous Roscetta chestnut, and which extend towards nearby **CIVITELLA ROVETO**. The village is located in the heart of the Roveto valley, against the backdrop of Serra Sant'Antonio. The eastern end of town, near the walls, has maintained its Medieval character with traces of the old defensive walls. The **church of San Giovanni Battista** is striking. The **Museo Pinacoteca Enrico Mattei** is worth visiting. The founder of museum–art gallery was from Civitella Roveto and it regularly organizes the "Valle Roveto" painting and sculpture prize. Not to be forgotten is the **Museo Etnografico De' Colucci** and the interesting feast of St John the Baptist, with the ritual bathing in the Liri waters, celebrated on 24 June.

Nearby are the remains of the old fortified village of Meta, set on a hill at the foot of Mount

Viglio, where it stood guard over the Liri valley. The village below it has been completely abandoned, but the ruins of the churches of San Savino and Santissima Trinità can still be seen. Following the 1915 earthquake, the population moved downstream and built a new town.

Modern **CIVITA D'ANTINO**, which is just off the state road, has maintained not only the name but also the location of the Roman town of *Antinum*, one of the most important of the Marsi population and the only Roman *municipium* in the Roveto valley. It became a *municipium* in the 1st century AD, at the end of the Social War. It maintained the elevated position of the previous fortified town whose vestiges are evident in the ruins of the polygonal wall that dates to about the first half of the 5th century BC. The wall had three gates, the most important of which, located on the north side, connected the town to the valley, where places of worship were located and trade was conducted. This portion of the wall can still be seen from the road that leads into town. On the south side, where **Porta Campanile** is now located, there was an opening leading towards Sora, crossed by the main access road that ran through the middle of town. The road from **Porta Flora**, to the west, led to the acropolis and thus to the temple area, corresponding to the area that was occupied by the **Torre Colonna** (which is still visible) starting in the 13th–14th century.

In Civita d'Antino, Piazza del Banco marks the centre of town. Its most distinctive architecture is the **parish church of Santo Stefano Protomartire**, where the *forum* of the old Roman *municipium* has been identified. Here a precious inscription from the Condotto district – with a spring still in use – can be found. The church, built in the 18th century, was seriously damaged during the 1915 earthquake and the work conducted to restore its original appearance was completed in 1951. It has an interesting octagonal layout with a segmented dome. Notably, its façade is reminiscent of more famous models, with a tripartite lower portion with diagonal wings, an octagonal dome lantern at the back, and two curved walls that connect it to the body of the edifice. Inside the church is the miraculous image known as "Madonna della Ritornata", which is carried in a procession every year to the Madonna del Monte sanctuary. Near the church we see the house traditionally indicated as the birthplace of Benedictine St Lidano Abbot (1026–1118), pioneer of the reclamation of part of the Pontine Marshes.

From Piazza del Banco, we go to Piazzetta del Colle, where two honorary epigraphs can

be seen opposite **Palazzo Ferrante** (with the annexed Santissima Concezione family chapel). In an epigraph carved in rock near the **Fonte Vecchia**, towards the edge of town, a mother commemorated the untimely death of her daughter, Varia Montana. Civita D'Antino, between the late–19th early–20th centuries, became a popular place of inspiration and residence for a large community of Danish artists, including Joakim Frederik Skovgaard and Peder Severin Krøyer, who portrayed local landscapes and customs. The key figure who led this discovery of Civita D'Antino with its breath-taking landscapes was above all the master Kristian Zahrtmann (1843–1917), considered one of the most representative Danish painters of the latter half of the 19th century, who arrived in Italy after embarking on the Grand Tour, in 1883. He even set up a "school" for young painters who also brought other artists like architects and sculptors into contact with village, who all lived in the old **Casa Cerroni**, where the so-called "sala degli stemmi" ("salon of insignia") still displays a collection of symbols, signed by each artist who came to the centre. It is thanks to this lively circle that today Abruzzo landscapes can be admired in numerous Scandinavian museums. Zahrtmann became an honorary citizen of Civita d'Antino in 1902 and he is commemorated by a plaque affixed on the "casa dei pittori" – "house of painters", and a square is name after him. The **Museo di storia e civiltà contadina** is an interesting museum of history and rural culture, with many period photos, tools used by the ancient farming community, and artworks by Danish painters.

In the nearby woodlands we find the **sanctuary of Santa Maria del Monte** (Madonna della Ritornata), which is the destination of a popular traditional procession. Precious frescoes decorate the apse of the church and are dated late–12th–early–13th century.

Historic **MORINO** stands opposite Civita d'Antino on a hill between Fosso di Rio and the Schioppo stream, which flows through the Roveto valley. The town was destroyed by the 1915 earthquake, and only a few ruins remain, including the church belfry. The new town is located in the valley, southeast of the abandoned town, near the state road and the Romito torrent. Its territory includes the Riserva Naturale Zompo lo Schioppo with its spectacular eponymous **waterfall** which gives the reserve its named, and with its drop of about 80 metres is the highest natural waterfall in the Apennines. The visitor centre is by the river and is home to the small but important **Zompo lo Schioppo ecomuseum**, which documents the habitats of the reserve. The museum uses an innovative exhibition approach and multisensory language. The little mountain **church of Madonna del Cauto** (Madonna del Pertuso), located in the beech forest on the reserve, welcomes a traditional pilgrimage every May.

Before reaching San Vincenzo Valle Roveto visitors can head to **Morrea**, perched on a rocky overhang. The Medieval hamlet, with its typical

253. Above: the abandoned village of Morino.
254. Facing page: aerial view of Balsorano castle.

## Piccolomini Castle, Balsorano

Piccolomini castle, built in 1470 over a previous defensive structure, had two towers along the River Liri, allowing it to monitor the valley below. This impressive construction seems to fit in perfectly with its surroundings. It has an uneven plan, with round corner towers whose batters probably date back to the Angevin period, and an L-shaped courtyard with an elegant well. The castle is surrounded by a lush park through which a long pedestrian path leads to the main entrance. The interior is characterized by its dramatic décor, recreated in a period style during 1930s restoration work although the project did not envisage the reconstruction of the ancient central tower. Though the castle's current configuration is that of a noble residence, its original military function is evoked by the corner towers and the recessed battlements, which play a purely decorative role here.

The name of the site comes from the ancient place-name "Vallis Sorana", transformed into the modern name Balsorano. Owned by the County of Albe until the 13th century, in the 14th century Balsorano became part of the County of Celano, which was ruled by the Orsini family. The Piccolominis took over in 1463 and held it until feudal rights were abolished. The Testa family of Rome then took possession of the castle, followed by the Lefevres in the early 19th century. In 1915, the earthquake damaged the castle badly. In 1930 it was purchased by the Fiastri Zanelli family, who commenced restoration work and today is used as accommodation.

elongated configuration, was one of the oldest and most important fortified villages in the valley and retains its appearance. It was part of the Piccolomini Colonna fortified village and still shows the walls, towers and (perhaps 14th-century) gateway, on the southeastern side. In the **church of Santa Restituta**, rebuilt in the 1950s, an ancient fresco dedicated to the saint is found in one of the side chapels

**SAN VINCENZO VALLE ROVETO** was built after the 1915 earthquake, when the town of San Vincenzo Valle Roveto Vecchio was abandoned. The old town, located on the right bank of the Liri, was uphill from the modern town. Here we find the **San Diodato sanctuary** with the remains of St Deodatus and nearby the Madonna del Romitorio sanctuary. The nearby hamlet of Roccavivi was also rebuilt after the old town of Rocca Vecchia was swept away by a landslide in 1616. Ruins are all that remain of the old town, located high under the mountain crest. The disaster is commemorated by the Madonna delle Grazie chapel.

We now come to the new town of **BALSORANO**, which was built after the 1915 earthquake, when the ancient fortified town of Balsorano Vecchio was abandoned. The ruins of the old town are visible on a hillside by the slopes of Mount Cornacchia, at the southern end of the Roveto valley, not far from the right bank of the Liri. The Medieval town developed on the west side of the mountain dominated by the majestic **Piccolomini castle** (*see box p. 152*), which long served as the stronghold controlling the southern access to the Roveto valley and Marsica area.

In the **church of San Francesco**, in the convent complex rebuilt after the earthquake of 1915, there is a high altar with an early–1700s paliotto, as well as an 18th-century *crucifix*, and a 1400s wooden statue of *St Paschal*.

The southwest border of Abruzzo was protected by Balsorano, with Roccavivi to the west, and the two towers in Le Starze along the Liri. The northern tower, four-sided with battered base, is surrounded by vegetation, while the southern building, barely 50 metres away, incorporates the remains of the church of Santa Maria delle Grazie, surrounded by a lovely poplar grove on the riverbank.

In the area, the **Sant'Angelo cave sanctuary** has an interesting 16th-century fresco and is worth visiting. On the weekend closest to 8 May it is the destination of a popular spiritual retreat.

255. Below: the sanctuary of Sant'Angelo near Balsorano.

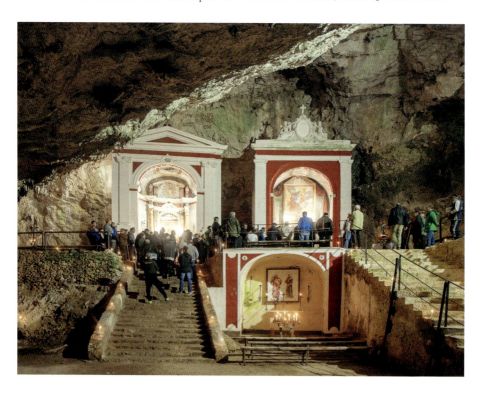

# Sagittario Valley and ALM National Park

The village of **COCULLO**, located just beyond the motorway exit of the same name, overlooks the valley of the Rio Pezzana, a tributary of the River Sagittario. Its minor architecture makes it one of the most interesting villages in the region, the old fortified centre still dominated by its ancient urban gates. At the highest point, incorporating the San Nicola neighbourhood, the houses cluster around the sparse remains of the castle. Traces also survive of a square tower at **Porta Ruggeri**, datable 12th century, later serving as a bell tower for the now-derelict church of San Nicola di Bari and then as a clock tower. Interesting to see **Porta di Manno** and the recently restored **Porta Renovata**, the latter overlooking the valley to the south. The **church of Santa Maria delle Grazie** is of some interest, built in the latter half of the 13th century, with a 1300s façade restored in the 1500s, the addition of two striking Renaissance stone aedicules, with statues enhancing the main and side portals. The aisleless interior vaunts lovely 16th-century frescoes.

The famous **San Domenico sanctuary**, built in the late–19th–early–20th century on the site of an older church, dominates the lower part of the village. On the morning of 1 May, the

Cocullo, Anversa degli Abruzzi, Castrovalva, Villalago, Scanno, Villetta Barrea, Civitella Alfedena, Barrea, Alfedena, Scontrone, Opi, Pescasseroli, Bisegna, Ortona dei Marsi, Gioia dei Marsi, Lecce dei Marsi.

In a magnificent natural context, the suggested itinerary winds its way from the Sagittario Valley whose rugged but spectacular gorges conceal ancient settlements, with a lavish history and marvellous works of art, surrounded by some splendid scenery, to continue as far as the adjacent upper Sangro valley, in the heart of the historical Abruzzo – Lazio – Molise National Park, dotted with numerous old mountain settlements, with as precious artistic heritage and surviving folklore traditions, that make this itinerary a must for the curious and enthusiastic visitor.

256. Cocullo with the narrow Sagittario valley in the background.

church of **Santa Maria delle Grazie** (after the 2009 earthquake rendered the sanctuary unsafe) is visited by thousands of pilgrims for the feast of St Dominic Abbot and the **snake-catcher rite**. From here the statue of the saint, covered with live, non-poisonous snakes, captured by the village snake catchers. After the celebrations the snakes are set free). The **Museo delle Tradizioni Popolari** is located in the municipal building and is named after anthropologist Alfonso M. Di Nola. The museum revolves around the multimedia exhibition illustrating the various stages of the ritual and there is also a documentation centre about popular traditions that is a reference point for studies on the topic, as well as a specialist library, a newspaper reading room, and a large archive. West of the town, along Via della Fonte, we fins a typical **Medieval stone fountain** with three Gothic arches.

The nearby village of **ANVERSA DEGLI ABRUZZI**, on a spur overlooking the stunning River Sagittario gorges, an outright canyon dug out by thousands of years of river water erosion. The centre is dominated by the remains of the Conti di Sangro castle and its square stone bulwark tower, with the striking scarp. The structure seen now is the result of restoration and extension work carried out in the 15th century by Antonio di Sangro, on the original fortification with its uneven pentagonal plan, whose tall derelict tower, dating 12th–13th centuries, is still standing. Gabriele D'Annunzio, who visited Anversa castle with the scholar Antonio De Nino, set his tragedy *La Fiaccola sotto il moggio* here, with outstanding descriptions of the natural elements in the Sagittario valley, especially in the passages dedicated to the castle remains.

In the excavations of the Coccitelle necropolis about 50 slab tombs dated 4th century BC have come to light, complete with grave goods. The finds are now visible at the **Centro di Documentazione Archeologica di Anversa** documentation centre.

A compact wall of houses still delimits the old village, reminding us of its ancient origins as a fortified centre guarding the valley, with two surviving gateways: **Porta Pazziana** door and **Porta San Nicola**. Interesting examples of civil architecture overlook Largo Porta Pazziana.

In Piazza Roma we meet the striking **Santa Maria delle Grazie church**, built at the behest of the Belprato feudal lords of Anversa. The façade with horizontal coping features a lavish Renaissance portal dated 1540. The rare iconographic repertoire

257. Above: the snake-catcher rite in Cocullo.
258. Below: the church of Santa Maria delle Grazie, Anversa degli Abruzzi.
259. Facing page: the hermitage of San Domenico, Villalago.

is striking, with fluted columns and pilasters decorated with pagan motifs, even a relief over the *Deposition of Christ*, the statues of *St Onuphrius* and *St Jerome*. High up we see a beautiful rose window dated 1585, in addition to Anversa's traditional coat of arms with snakes entwined around the needles of a compass. The nave-and-two-aisle interior has a lovely polychrome terracotta statue of St Roche, made in 1530 by local potters and a 16th-century carved wooden tabernacle. At the moment the high altar displays a reproduction of the 16th-century Anversa triptych, depicting the *Coronation of the Virgin with St Thomas receiving the girdle and the Apostles at the Sepulchre, St Michael Archangel and St Francis of Assisi*, replacing the original stolen in 1981.

The **church of San Marcello** according to tradition was founded in the 11th century, in honour of the patron saint and subsequently modified. The elegant late–Gothic portal is embellished with a rich figurative repertoire, with a lovely 1472 fresco depicting a *Madonna and Child, and Saints Marcellus and Vincent* in the ogival lunette.

The town of Anversa degli Abruzzi is home to the **Parco Letterario Gabriele D'Annunzio**, of which the towns of Cocullo, Bugnara and Villalago are also members. The association intends to protect places that inspired great artists and poets.

The municipal boundaries include the magnificent **Riserva Naturale delle Gole del Sagittario** with its vast heritage of flora and fauna. Outside the village we can go as far as the nearby Cavuto springs, the centre of the protected area. Here an interesting museum housed in an old mill is dedicated to the description of reserve habitats. It is also worth visiting the regional botanical garden, with about 380 different species of plants, many of which are species of conservation interest.

The fortified village of **Castrovalva**, a district of Anversa, is set to the right of the Sagittario gorges, on the crest of Mount Sant'Angelo. It dominates the deep River Sagittario valley and was a strategic control point for one of the southern access routes to the Peligna valley. It was the visionary Dutch artist, Maurits Cornelis Escher (1898–1972), the visionary Dutch artist, who discovered the village during one of his trips to Abruzzo and it inspired his famous 1930 lithograph, now exhibited at the Washington Museum of Art, casting an unexpected fame spotlight on the district. Castrovalva has named the so-called "girone" – the last bend in the road into the small town – to the Dutch artist. In the main square we find the 16th-century local parish **church of Santa Maria della Neve**, with a beautiful facade and a snug interior. We pass a beautiful Medieval gate to reach the **church of Santa Maria delle Grazie**, also 16th century, and going downhill we reach the discreet old **church of San Michele Arcangelo**. Before reaching Villalago, we can visit the old **hermitage of San Domenico**, on the shores of Lake San Domenico, created with a dam on the River Sagittario. Restored several times, the hermitage includes the cave where St Dominic lived, with the neighbouring church and small portico.

Picturesque **VILLALAGO** sits on the summit of Mount Argatone, in a splendid location between the charming Lake San Domenico and natural Lake Scanno, the two main basins that define the valley. The ancient centre retains the characteristics of a fortified village, with buildings set sheer on the rocky peak, perching on the site of the ancient fortress, around the **Palazzo Baronale**, to which the Addolorata oratory was once annexed. A beautiful round tower, part of the ancient fortifications, stands next to the mansion, while inside we find the **Museo delle Arti e Tradizioni Popolari di Villalago**.

The old parish **church of Santa Maria di Loreto** is interesting and was restored following destruction caused by the Second World War. A splendid 15th-century round arch portal is set into the façade, while one of several works of art inside includes the remarkable 1500s painting of *Our Lady of the Rosary*. The **church of San Michele Arcangelo**, in the upper part of town, is also charming.

The picturesque town of **SCANNO**, overlooking the upper Sagittario valley is part of Abruzzo – Lazio – Molise National Park. The most photographed village in Abruzzo has enchanted some of the best artists and master photographers, who captured its most striking views, preserving them for history. Scanno is famous all over the world thank to visitors of the past, like Edward Lear, and his memorable romantic landscapes of the village, Dutch genius Maurits Cornelius Escher who produced the most imaginative image of Scanno, Henri Cartier-Bresson and Mario Giacomelli, who were able to capture the soul of the area with their camera lenses.

The old town centre is remarkable for the quality of its architecture, with its narrow lanes often with steps, small squares, gateways and underpasses, monumental fountains, compact houses, elegant buildings in carved stone with a rich production of artistic portals and evidence of its wealth, earned thanks to the flourishing sheep farming industry that lasted until the 19th century. This industry fostered successful trading of wool and dairy products, but also prestigious craft production, especially lace and gold jewellery.

There are a significant number of excellent religious buildings in the small town, including the **church of Santa Maria della Valle** (*see box p. 159*), down in the Carapale valley. The original church, already in existence in the 12th century, was converted in the latter half of the 16th century and today's layout reflects that project, although later stucco refurbishment was added in the 17th and 18th centuries

The **church of Santa Maria delle Grazie** and the annexed convent, on Via Roselli, were built in 1733-60, the site managed by Panfilo Rainaldi of Pescocostanzo. The octagonal church has a cupola and harmonious 18th-century stucco décor, the work of Pietro Piazzoli of Como; the side altar to the right, possibly also the work of Piazzoli, has an important canvas by Domenico Raimondi (1767), depicting *St Giuseppe Colasanzio*, founder of the Piarist Congregation.

Along Via Abrami we find the former **church of Anime Sante del Purgatorio**, built on this spot in the 17th century then rebuilt in 1716. It underwent considerable restoration work and now houses the Guido Calogero auditorium. In Piazza San Rocco, we find the **church of Santa Maria di Costantinopoli**, with a standard rectangular façade in two overlying sections, while inside there is an excellent fresco of the *Enthroned Madonna and Child*, dated 1418 and attributed to the so-called Maestro di Caramanico, pointing to the existence of the church as early as the beginning of the 15th century. As well as the **church of San Rocco** (Madonna del Carmine), with an attractive 16th-century-style portal, made famous by one of Cartier-Bresson's photographs, the **church of Sant'Eustachio e Santa Maria** is also worth a visit. It dates back to the 12th century but was restored at the end of 1600s by Lombard architect Giovan Battista Gianni, a leading figure in 1700s Abruzzo. Outside the walls we find the **church of Sant'Antonio di Padova** with the adjoining convent of the Reformed Friars Minor, finished at the close of the 1500s, as the portal indicates, and with a Baroque interior frescoed on the vault in the early 18th century by Giambattista Gamba.

The interesting **Museo della Lana**, set up in 1993 in the old town abattoir, exhibits tools and documents that illustrate sheep-farming culture from 1850 to 1930, as well as the daily work and life of Scanno residents.

The **church of San Giovanni Battista** in Via Silla, probably dating back to the first half of the 16th century, has an original collection of statues of saints made by shepherds in the period 1600s–1900s.

One of the numerous eye-catching buildings in the town is **Palazzo Mosca**, with a splendid stucco cornice and lavish 18th-century portal; **Palazzo di Rienzo**, restored in the 1900s, is also worth a mention, as are **Palazzo Serafini Ciancarelli, Palazzo Colarossi** and **Palazzo De Angelis** with its sumptuous portal. **Palazzo**

## The Church of Santa Maria della Valle, Scanno

The interior of Santa Maria della Valle has a nave and two aisles and segmental barrel vaults, separated by two 12th-century columns and four square stone pillars. Recent restoration work eliminated the Baroque finishes and brought to light old Renaissance frescoes on the first two entrance pillars. Some of the valuable surviving interiors include the magnificent central altar in polychrome marble (1732), designed by Pescocostanzo's Panfilo Rainaldi, and four finely-carved 1766 confessionals, with a decorative pulpit by Ferdinando Mosca, also from Pescocostanzo. Worthy of note are the San Costanzo chapel with the magnificent altar with marble niche (1765–6), containing remains of St Constantius, designed by Ferdinando Mosca and carved by Nicodemo Mancini and Loreto Cicco of Pescocostanzo, who also crafted refined marble baptismal fonts.

The pictorial device with remarkable 17th-century paintings is also precious and includes a Roman school painting depicting the *Virgin and Child Giving the Crown to St Domenic and St Catherine*, and 15 tondos depicting the *Mysteries of the Rosary*, dated 1604. The 16th-century restoration transformed the original Medieval church, preserving the central portal of Burgundian forms on the façade, the latter remodelled several times, surmounted by an elegant rose window, restored after the damage suffered in the 1915 and 1917 earthquakes. The square bell tower with pyramid-shaped cusp dates to the 16th century.

260. Facing page: night view of Scanno with a *Gloria*.
261. 262. Below: the façade and the chapel of San Costanzo, Santa Maria della Valle church, Scanno.

**Nardillo**, in Via Porta Sant'Antonio, vaunts a quite remarkable Baroque portal.

Along the SS479 Sannitica state road, on the southern shores of Lake Scanno, we find the charming **church of Santa Maria dell'Annunziata** or Madonna del Lago, consecrated in 1702. English artist Edward Lear left a view painted in 1843 showing the original entrance on the western façade with a small five-arch porch, demolished in 1870 to lay the carriageable road. Work undertaken on the church at the beginning of the 20th century includes replacement of the old altar with current marble Gothic Revival version. There is a small old hermitage next to the church.

The enchanting Sant'Egidio hermitage can be found nearby, at the top of a hill, dedicated to the saint who protects against the plague. There is a magnificent view of the lake and surrounding mountains from here.

One traditional event worth seeing is the "Glorie", when large wooden towers are erected and set alight on the afternoon of 10 November, on the ever of St Martin's Day.

Prominent cultural events include the "Scanno dei fotografi" international photography prize.

Leaving Scanno and the Sagittario valley in the direction of **VILLETTA BARREA** and the upper Sangro valley, we reach the western tip of Lake Barrea, in Abruzzo – Lazio – Molise National Park. The remains of a round defence tower can be made out in the old Castello district, in the upper part of the residential area. After its restoration, the tower became the home of the Santa Maria Assunta parish church museum, with the Abruzzo – Lazio – Molise National Park environmental documentation centre.

The striking 1700s and 1800s mansions reveal a solid local economy of a bygone era brought by a thriving livestock trade and expert use of wood resources. **Palazzo Fontana** and **Palazzo D'Orazio** (now the town hall) are both noteworthy. The parish **church of Santa Maria Assunta** was found in the upper part of the town but only a few fragments survived the 1925 earthquake. Rebuilt on another spot, the finely worked stone portal, dating back to 1720, was preserved but without the section above the architrave. The elaborate altar designed by Bernini and part of the wooden choir also survive, while part of the furnishings and works of art of the ancient church are on display in the modern museum in the tower.

Some scholar believe today's San Michele church, restored in the 20th century, retains architectural and pictorial fragments from the old abbey of Sant'Angelo di Barreggio, dated 8th century, now no longer visible but previously located near Villetta Barrea cemetery.

The **church of San Rocco**, also known as the Purgatorio, dates to the 15th–16th centuries

and what we see is the result of more recent work and refurbishment, which changed the previous structures and horizontal coping façade, especially after the 1915 earthquake.

Inside the church we find the 1525 wooden sculpture of St Michael the Archangel, an 1834 organ, and an 18th-century canvas depicting the *Souls of Purgatory*, by Filippo Canciano, a painter of the Neapolitan school (1752).

The landscape is the most attractive feature and the village has become a tourist resort and reference point for visitors to the park, whose visitor centre hosts permanent nature exhibitions. The **Museo della Transumanza** and **Bottega del Buon Gusto** in the Baraccone – a 19th-century rural building – are worth seeing, the former with its display of typical tools used in the production of wool and cheese, and organization of shelters, not to mention the chance to taste local products. The **Museo dell'Acqua**, dedicated to water, is set up in the old mill, near the hydroelectric plant.

Close to Lake Barrea is the village of **CIVITELLA ALFEDENA** on the Meta mountain range, in Abruzzo – Lazio – Molise National Park. Its appearance is that of the fortified village clustered around a castle, whose presence is remembered in the Via Castello street name. A round Medieval tower survives. The beautiful **parish church of San Nicola** has a wooden Baroque choir and paintings. The **Santa Maria del Carmelo church** has a handsome 1542 pipe-organ with a 1700s cantoria. The village is a leading tourist destination in the park, mainly thanks to the **Area Faunistica del Lupo** (wolf wildlife area) and the **Area Faunistica della Lince** (lynx wildlife area), alongside the interesting museum dedicated to the rare Apennine wolf.

In the surrounding territory we find the Riserve naturali Orientate di Colle Licco e Feudo Intramonti, nature reserves of natural and environmental importance, part of Abruzzo – Lazio – Molise National Park's protected reserve zone.

263. Above: Medieval tower of Civitella Alfedena.
264. Below: view of Lake Barrea with Barrea village in the foreground.

The ancient village of **BARREA** is historically linked to the famous but now lost Sant'Angelo monastery. It is part of Abruzzo – Lazio – Molise National Park, built on a rocky spur for strategic control of the Sangro gorges and in a picturesque position, overlooking Lake Barrea and the sheep track coming from Pescasseroli. It has always been a wealthy sheep-farming centre and the municipality and its lords could count on vast pastures, especially those on the Feudo di Chiarano plateau. Originally the village clustered around the Studio, an ancient convent–fortress of which scant remains survice. In ancient time it was protected by its compact construction whose perimeter comprised typical wall–houses that opened only in two gateways: the so-called "Porta di Sopra" and "Porta di Sotto". The remains of the ancient castle can still be seen in the old centre and are now being recovered. The building was perfectly adapted to the irregular morphology of the site. Worthy of note are the churches of **San Tommaso Apostolo**, with its Baroque interior, and **Madonna delle Grazie**, rebuilt in the 1950s, cannibalizing elements of the ancient church. The **Centro Visita del Pipistrello** is a fascinating bat wildlife centre with a colony of these mammals.

The municipal area includes the Lago Pantaniello nature reserve, set up to protect the eponymous lake, located at the foot of Mount Greco, a natural basin of glacial origin.

Just a few kilometres from Barrea we find **ALFEDENA,** famous for its stone-cutters. The village is in Abruzzo – Lazio – Molise National Park, straddling Rio Torto, upstream from the confluence with the River Sangro. We find a tiny hamlet with iconic gateways and remains of its castle, and a layout still showing some of its Medieval plan. The oldest part ended its winding streets in the fortified area at the pinnacle of the landscape, but there are few remains: the polygonal tower, despite having been cropped, appears well-preserved after its restoration and is probably the only example of this shape found in Abruzzo military architecture, although possible comparisons can be made with bordering Marche and Lazio structures. Some of the public and private buildings like **Palazzo De Amicis** (in Via Pescara, close to the Pescara and Principe gates, leading into the Medieval village) are interesting, as is the old town hall with plaques on its external wall commemorating or bearing witness to Vittorio Emanuele II's sojourns in Alfedena.

One church worth seeing is Santi Pietro e Paolo, founded in the 13th century, destroyed during World War II, then rebuilt in 1954. The only original element is the portal with its spiral colonettes.

The **Museo Civico Archeologico Antonio De Nino** is most interesting. Inaugurated in 1897 but ransacked during World War II, it reopened in 1997, in a new building thanks to the Archaeological Superintendency. It brings together the most important exhibits from the imposing Samnite necropolis at Alfedena–Campo Consolino.

The nearby village of **SCONTRONE** clusters around a spur of Mount Tre Confini, on the left bank of the Sangro, at the edge of the Abruzzo – Lazio – Molise National Park. It preserves its fortified village layout and we can still see the arch of the San Rocco gate and remains

265. Above: the ruins of Alfedena castle.
266. Below: Scontrone
267. Facing page: aerial view of Opi.

of the towers that defended it, even if clearly modified. In the old part, from Piazza Sangro, as far as the **church of Santa Maria Assunta** (founded before 1356) with precious marble statues and frescoes, there are 24 murals painted from 1988 onwards by Italian and foreign artists.

The **church of Sant'Antonio** is worth visiting for its lively Baroque frontage and stone decorations from the late–18th century. The church was founded in ancient times but was rebuilt in 1759 after a partial collapse and has belonged to the Costantinian Order since 1791. The façade has a curvilinear coping with a round window above a slightly projecting cornice. The small portal, preceded by a few steps, is framed by a pleasant beaded cornice and overlapped by a dedicatory gable.

Of particular note is the **Centro di Documentazione Paleontologico**, dedicated to the fossil site located north of the town on the slopes of Mount Greco. It can be reached from the museum along a signposted learning path. The site is unique for a surprising presence of terrestrial vertebrate bones and teeth. Inside Palazzo Municipale, it is worth visiting the **MIDA, International Museum of Women in Art**, the first dedicated to contemporary female art, but also the Museo della Radio and the Museo della Montagna, with paintings, sculptures and photographs.

Remains of the monastery of San Giovanni d'Acquasanta, founded in the 13th century by Pope Celestine V, still visible, located near the **Villa Scontrone** sulphur springs.

To visit the pretty village of **OPI**, one of the highest in Abruzzo – Lazio – Molise National Park, stretching across a rocky crest between the Sangro, Fondillo and Fredda valleys, we have to turn back towards Villetta Barrea. In ancient times this was the border between the Marsi and Caraceni Samnite tribes, and the site of Ope, a settlement dedicated to the goddess of abundance. The Medieval structure can still be discerned, with houses grouped together and narrow streets with steps and buildings set on the edge of the rocky peak. There are lovely lavish views of the surrounding mountains, cloaked in luxuriant beech woods. One of its most important buildings is the old parish **church of Santa Maria Assunta**, presently under complete restoration, and the **chapel of San Giovanni Battista**, formerly the Rossi family chapel, with a splendid marble altar in the Baroque interior. The town hall is housed in elegant 17th-century **Palazzo Rossi**.

The interesting Abruzzo chamois wildlife area is annexed to the **Museo del Camoscio**, housed in the 17th–18th-century **Palazzo Bevilacqua**, in the centre of the village, where the **Museo dello Sci e della Montagna** is worth a visit, in the town hall. The **Museo della Foresta e dell'Uomo** has been reopened in the premises of the old sawmill in Val Fondillo. In Opi territory we find the Val Fondillo necropolis, dated 6th century BC, which constitutes one

## The Church of Santi Pietro e Paolo, Pescasseroli

The church has been modified several times and restored in 1747, as indicated by the inscription under the bell tower cornice. The interior, after restoration work in the 1900s, still has its 15th-century layout with a nave and two aisles. The horizontal coping façade has an attractive Gothic portal and marries Aquila and Chieti styles nicely. One of the right-hand portals is presumed to be original, with its Romanesque imprint, now shoring the bell tower. The late–16th-century window above the portal has a simple, moulded frame and appears closed by a dual rosette ornamentation, surmounted by an open triangular gable. The *oculum* opening on the left, near the bell tower, can also be dated to the same era. All worthy of note are the precious wooden choir and ambo, and the magnificent astylar cross in the sacristy, a marvellous piece of Sulmona silversmithing, dating to the 15th century. The altar in the left aisle has the extremely old *Enthroned Black Madonna* statue, which is still greatly worshipped. Traditionally, the ancient wooden carving comes from the small church of an early Medieval settlement later abandoned. The image was donated by the Vatican Chapter on 8 September 1752, feast of the Nativity of the Virgin and the Crowned Virgin, and date of the annual fair granted by Charles of Anjou in 1283. The Virgin holds a globe with her right hand and with the other she supports the Child seated on her left knee. The stylistic features place it in the cultural period of the 12th and 13th centuries when the wooden sculpture developed in Abruzzo.

268. Above: Pescasseroli centre.
269. Left: the parish church of the SS Pietro e Paolo, Pescasseroli, lit by the traditional "Tomba" bonfire held every year on the night of 24 December.
270. 271. Facing page: above, Bisegna; below, the sanctuary of Madonna di Monte Tranquillo.

of the most significant examples identified in the Alto Sangro area relating to populations of Safino tribal origin.

Dutch artist Maurits Cornelis Escher rendered the village of Opi portrayed in one of his most striking lithographs.

**PESCASSEROLI** is very close to Opi and is the home of the **Abruzzo – Lazio – Molise National Park** head offices as well as being a tourist resort and starting point for lovely nature excursions. Pescasseroli was the home of philosopher and historian Benedetto Croce, and in the past was also the transhumance "terminus". The sheep track leading to Candela, a town just south of Foggia, started at the Santa Venere bridge. The residential area was damaged by the 1915 earthquake but preserves a few architectural vestiges of the former village with important decorative elements. The oldest district stands at the foot of the rocky spur, the so-called "pesco", where we can find remains of the trapezoid-shaped Castel Mancino (10th–12th century), a strategic fortress that dominated the entire valley. We can also see two of the five perimeter towers.

The **parish church of Santi Pietro e Paolo** (*see box p. 164*), mentioned in a papal bull of 1115, stands on the site of an old chapel.

Other interesting places of worship include the **Carmine church**, founded in 1729 by the Gentile family and restored in 1989, with an impressive late–Baroque altar, a 1600s crucifix, a 17th–18th-century image of the *Immaculate Mary* and a statue of the *Virgin* by the Puglia school; the organ built by the famous Tagliacozzo organ-makers is also of considerable interest. At present the church is only open for worship on the feast of Our Lady of Mount Carmel.

The old town centre vaunts the elegant **Palazzo Sipari**, a large 18th-century simple but

impressive noble mansion in Piazza Benedetto Croce, with the annexed Addolorata chapel. The palazzo is laid out over three floors around a central court. The rooms have barrel and cross vaults and the façade is graced by a beautiful Gothic two-light lancet window. This is the birthplace of Benedetto Croce (1866) and the house-museum with foundation named after Erminio Sipari, initiator of the national park. Visitors can view the display of documents from the historical archives of Croce and Sipari.

The interesting **Museo Civico delle Tradizioni Popolari** is another of the cultural attractions that include the **Abruzzo – Lazio – Molise National Park visitor centre**, with a nature museum, wildlife park, Apennine garden, a laboratory and an ecological research centre. There is also an archaeological section dedicated to the incredible findings in the Val Fondillo.

The **Madonna di Monte Tranquillo sanctuary** is hidden away in Abruzzo – Lazio – Molise National Park's lovely countryside. Said to have been founded in the 12th century and rebuilt in 1956. it is a destination for pilgrims on the feast of the Black Madonna, celebrated each year on the last Sunday in July, one of the most important dates of shepherd tradition dedicated to the Virgin Mary.

Heading along the Sangro valley, a turn leads to **BISEGNA** on its rocky ridge sheer above the Giovenco valley, at the foot of Spina di Cerreto and Montagna Grande, in Abruzzo – Lazio – Molise National Park. Remains of the old fortified village that controlled the valley can still be seen, with traces of boundary walls in wall-houses and a single tower, later incorporated into a 1700s noble mansion, damaged in the 1915 earthquake, with a surviving refined portal. Much of the original façade of the 1300s–1400s **Santa Maria Assunta church** remains, with a small belfry above, added in 1618. Sadly, precious 1400s Sulmona school silver has been lost.

The **Museo del Capriolo**, a museum dedicated to roe-deer, with an annexed wildlife area are interesting services offered by the park.

About two kilometres from the town, surrounded by the park's mountains, we find the **San Giovanni church** and cave, where a statue of St John can be seen. Not far off a spring collects the water from a nearby stream that flows into the River Giovenco. On the morning of 24 June, groups of pilgrims gather for the feast of the Baptist and bathe in the spring waters, believed to have healing properties.

The nearby hamlet of **San Sebastiano**, an old fortified village set strategically on a rocky spur over the Giovenco valley, is near here, with remains of the old castle. Other churches include **Santa Maria delle Grazie** or **Santa Gemma**, with an altarpiece by Giuseppe Ranucci, a pupil of Sebastiano Conca. On the afternoon of 19 January, on feast of St Sebastian Martyr, the characteristic "panette" (votive bread rolls) procession takes place. Of particular interest is the visitor centre with its **bear museum**, replacing the old insect museum, and with exhibition rooms and teaching areas.

The itinerary continues to **ORTONA DEI MARSI**, in the River Giovenco valley at the foot of Mount Parasano. Despite the numerous alterations, the layout of the old fortified village is still visible. The remains of the **castle** and round tower with scarp wall are still visible at the highest point of the hamlet, with the remains of the boundary walls that protected the tower itself. Inside the **San Giovanni**

272. 273. Above: left, the pilgrims at the San Giovanni springs, Bisegna; right, the "panette" procession for the feast of St Sebastian.
274. Below: the abandoned village of Sperone and panorama.

Battista parish church (1300s façade and 1735 portal, as indicated by the architrave inscription), enlarged between the latter half of the 1400s–early 1500s, we find a decorative 17th-century pulpit and, above all, the 1752 organ by Domenico A. Fedeli.

The hamlet of Rivoli stands in that area of the district where Milonia was once to be found: the ancient fortified Marsi settlement, of which stretches of urban walls remain.

To reach **GIOIA DEI MARSI**, on the edge of the Fucino valley, in Abruzzo – Lazio – Molise National Park, we pass through Pescina (*see p. 140*). The new Gioia dei Marsi was erected after the 1915 earthquake had destroyed ancient Gioia Vecchio, whose ruins can be seen immediately above Gioia dei Marsi, alongside the settlements of Le Grette, Le Grippe and Casali d'Aschi, located on the sides or slopes of the mountainous ridge, and built in the 17th–19th centuries as Gioia Vecchio gradually depopulated. Gioia dei Marsi is now a typical plains town built along a main road, as is standard urban planning practice. The 1950s **church of Santa Maria Nuova** retains altars and paintings from the ancient church that survived earthquake destruction.

In the neighbouring village of **Sperone**, partly damaged by the 1915 earthquake, there is well-preserved externally round watch tower but with an octagonal interior, datable to the latter half of the 13th century.

Today's **LECCE DEI MARSI**, in Abruzzo – Lazio – Molise National Park, also developed after the 1915 earthquake destroyed most of the surrounding towns, including Castelluccio, Vellemora and Taroti, which had been founded after the inhabitants of **Lecce Vecchia** gradually transferred to the plains area. Only the belfry survives of the **San Martino church**. Amidst the remains of the old village there are still parts of the fortified walls and the Trasmondi castle. The only parts remaining of the Sant'Elia church are an angle iron on the façade and part of the ashlars.

275. 276. Above: left, San Giovanni Battista parish church; right, the ruins of the castle at Ortona dei Marsi.
277. Below: the abandoned village of Lecce Vecchia.

# Chieti
## and province

# Chieti

## The City

The pre-Roman settlement was built on the Civitella on the highest part of the hill, where the city's acropolis later developed. In the 1960s, there were discoveries of terracotta fragments from buildings, statues, and bronze decorations and mosaics from the temples of the Republican acropolis of the 2nd century BC, as well as the sacred well sanctuary whose remains were yielded in Chieti city centre. These findings are now exhibited in the room dedicated to temples at the new **Museo Archeologico Nazionale La Civitella**, designed by Ettore De Lellis and inaugurated in 2000, perfectly integrated with its surrounding landscape. The museum stands in the area of the ancient Teate acropolis, built in the first half of the 1st century AD, an integral part of Civitella archaeological park but also an events and performing arts venue.

The museum narrative is dedicated to the Italic and Roman history of ancient Teate, told through the most extraordinary archaeological finds, from the city itself and the Marrucino district, supported by information systems devices and evocative backdrops.

The thoughtful installation comprises three themed pathways: the first covers the "beginning of urban history" and is dedicated to Teate in the Republican period; the second illustrates the "first city", displaying finds coming from the sacred well sanctuary; the third explores the "land of the Marrucino tribe" and is dedicated to the area covering the Aterno-Pescara valley as far as the Adriatic coast.

Chieti boasts spectacular surroundings and stands on a panoramic hilltop between the Majella mountain range and the Adriatic, which extends into the Pescara valley. Ancient Teate was built on the hill between the River Pescara to the west and the River Alento to the east, populated as far back as protohistory. Because of its strategic position overlooking part of the Aterno valley, with the port of Aternum, Chieti became the capital of the Marrucino tribe, an important Italic community that had settled on the right bank of the river. Later proclaimed a *municipium*, it developed into a vital Roman city. The city's golden age came under Angevin rule during the latter half of the 13th century, becoming the capital of Abruzzo Citra under Charles I. Following a period of decline, it flourished again in the 17th–18th-centuries as a leading cultural centre, above all for the presence of the Piarists and the Tegea Arcadians, whose founders included the Marquis of Valignani, of Chieti's old noble family. Above all, however, Chieti's cultural life was noted for the brilliant intellect of the Marquis Romualdo de Sterlich, one of the city's leading figures during the Enlightenment. Though Chieti was overwhelmed by the construction boom of the 1960s, its precious art and history have survived.

278. In the previous double page: night view of San Giustino cathedral.
279. Facing page: aerial view of Chieti with the Majella massif in the background.
280. Below: Civitella museum.

The modern museum structure, partly underground, is a multipurpose complex with gardens, pedestrian areas and a series of related services that are independent in terms of both accessibility and use. These include an auditorium, an archaeology workshop, areas given over to fun and to learning activities, and a temporary exhibition space.

The development of ancient Teate was already under way in the 2nd century BC, but it intensified after the Social War (91–88 BC), following the institution of the *Teate Marrucinorum municipium*. There followed the major Late–Republican and Imperial reconstruction and monumentalization period, when the new Roman city expanded towards the northeast, with the most important buildings concentrated in the southeast, where the city's public area was located.

Leaving the Civitella district and turning downhill towards the city, the surviving structures of the **theatre**, dating to the mid–1st century AD, can be seen at the intersection of Via di Porta Napoli and Via Generale Pianell. Though the ruins are now surrounded by modern buildings that have completely concealed the orchestra and proscenium, the northeast curtain wall of the cavea can still be seen. It was built using the *opus mixtum* technique typical of the city's other Roman monuments. Part of the cavea was built at the foot of the Civitella slope and is partly supported by barrel-vaulted voussoir rooms. The theatre was built on two levels: vault sections of the semi-circular corridor separating the upper level are still visible, as are masonry segments sections in the outside walls of adjoining houses. Modern-day Piazza dei Templi Romani, in the city centre, was once the religious and civic centre of ancient Teate. Remains are visible of three **tempietti**, rebuilt in the Imperial Age built over the *opus quadratum* structures of an older place of worship site annexed to a deep sacred well. The area remained sacred over the centuries with the consecration of the church of Santi Pietro e Paolo, documented on the site of the main temple since the end of the 8th century AD.

The three temples facing southeast towards the ancient Forum, still reveal striking wall finishes with stone and brick segments, and courses of thick bricks with stone and marble cladding. A terraced podium held twin temples, subsequently adjoined by a third smaller temple; the left-hand side of the square was closed by a fourth temple whose remains have been partially incorporated in the Post Office building. The inscription on the façade of the preserved building documents important construction work that may have been carried out on the central area by Marcus Vettius Marcellus and his wife Elvidia Priscilla, leading figures in Teate, in the second half of the 1st century AD.

The striking remains of the **baths** built in the 2nd century AD are at the eastern end of the city, at the bottom of the hill, and were supplied by water from a cistern set behind the structure itself. This cistern was actually underground, made up of nine large communicating rooms built against the hillside, and was also the source of the ancient city's water supply. The tanks were designed to withstand water and soil pressure through an ingenious system of niches at the back of each of the nine rooms. The structure was accessed down wide steps that led to a long crosswise corridor with a mosaic floor, decorated with black crosses on a white background. From here, a broad *atrium*, with a mosaic floor with a sea illustration symbolizing the god Neptune, and a colonnade entrance led to the actual baths. The *atrium* also led to other rooms: on the right there were three rectangular *calidarium* rooms with a floor raised by

# Abruzzo National Archaeological Museum, Chieti

The Abruzzo National Archaeological Museum is one of the points of excellence of the city's excellent museum network and since 2014 it has been part of the Polo Museale d'Abruzzo hub, brilliantly documenting the historic culture of the Abruzzo area, from the protohistoric period to the Late Imperial Age. The museum's remarkable narrative comes from its artefacts, and the scientific accuracy its exhibits, winning it the 1984 European Museum of the Year.

The new museum visitor path was expanded in 2014, and showcases the ethnic and topographical aspects of ancient populations. Fascinating examples of Italic sculpture on the ground floor include the impressive funerary statue of the **Capestrano Warrior**, dated mid–6th-century BC, was unearthed by chance near the village Capestrano. It now has its own room in the "Al di là del tempo" ["Beyond time"] installation curated by artist Mimmo Paladino. According to the inscription on the side, the statue portrays King Nevius Pompuledeius, and displays an extraordinary array of ancient attack and defensee weapons (a set of disc-type armour or *kardiophylakes*, a sword, a small dagger, an axe, and two long lances). The statue seems to be proof of the institution of a monarchy during the 6th century BC. An important numismatic section and the 19th-century Pansa collection are found on the same floor, while on the first floor there are exhibits from the most diverse regional archaeological contexts, especially necropolises and shrines.

As far as epigraphic evidence of Pre-Roman Abruzzo is concerned, the three funerary steles (5th century BC) from Penna Sant'Andrea are highly significant. Their inscriptions in Old Sabellian provide key information about the social organisation and political development of the local populations. One of the museum's most important artefacts is the famous bronze **Hercules at Rest**, portraying the deified hero as a middle-aged figure, found several decades ago at the sanctuary of Ercole Curino, near Sulmona. It is thought to date to the 3rd century BC and is considered a masterpiece of ancient sculpture. There is also the colossal statue of **Hercules Seated at a Banquet**, found in Alba Fucens and dated 1st century BC.

281–283. Facing page: above, remains of the spa complex; below, detail of the theatre (left) and remains of the Tempietti (right).
284. 285. This page: the bronze statue of *Hercules in Repose* (below left) and the funerary statue of the Warrior of Capestrano (right) both in the Museo Archeologico Nazionale.

*suspensurae*. Opposite the *atrium* there was a large square room with two semi-circular marble-lined tubs at the sides, with a larger tub at the back, all part of the *frigidarium*.

The **Museo Archeologico Nazionale d'Abruzzo** (*see box p. 173*) is a fascinating museum, which was opened in 1959, in Neoclassical **Villa Frigerj**, a remarkable building erected by Baron Frigerj in about 1830 and part of the magical city park, the **Villa Comunale**.

One of the most significant religious buildings is the **cathedral of San Giustino**, once dedicated to St Thomas. The building dominates Piazza Vittorio Emanuele II (*see box p. 175*) and was built in the early Middle Ages. Attone I, Bishop of Chieti, re-consecrated the church in the 11th century. The **Palazzo Comunale** is also located in Piazza Vittorio Emanuele II. Formerly known as Palazzo Valignani and once city hall, the façade has plain Neoclassical lines and courtyard with arcade. A Roman column supports the equestrian statue of Achilles, symbol of the city of Chieti. A ceramic panel painted by Tommaso Cascella is found along the staircase, commemorating Archbishop Venturi, who saved Chieti from destruction by bombings during World War II by having it declared an "open city". The building is next to "**Casa Sirolli**", which once belonged to Giovanni Battista Spinelli, the famous Caravaggesque painter active in the 17th century. In addition to the cathedral, **Palazzo di Giustizia** and **Palazzo Mezzanotte**, outstanding examples of 19th-century architecture, also face the square.

The cathedral's imposing tower is a distinctive part of the cityscape, together with the cupola of **San Francesco della Scarpa church** informally known as "al Corso", which rises above a tall double staircase along Corso Marrucino and designed in the late–19th. The cathedral was built in the 13th century, radically remodelled in the 17th century, when the vaults were added, and the presbytery was rebuilt (completed in 1689). At the end of the century the dome was erected upon a tall, airy tambour. The decoration of the interior – nave with side chapels – was completed over the following 20 years, although some of the chapels have preserved decorations from the mid–17th century. Various artists were involved in this work, notably Giovan Battista Gianni, who created the stuccowork in the chapel of Santa Caterina; Neapolitan sculptor, Giacomo Colombo, who carved the wooden bust of St Anthony (1711) in the Lombardi chapel; Michele Clerici, who completed the stuccowork in the San Ludovico chapel. The renovated part of the façade is incomplete and shows an upper portion in brick with an exquisite 14th-century rose window from the original building, and a lower stone section with the elaborate new portal, flanked by two side niches with statues from the demolished church of San Domenico. The staircase was built in 1879 to overcome the height difference that came about after the roadway was lowered to accommodate the regeneration taking place in the city. There are marvellous canvases by Giovanni Battista Spinelli (17th century), Ercole Graziani (18th century), and Donato Teodoro, as well as a richly decorated Baroque pulpit by Orsogna woodcarver Modesto Salvini.

Several lovely noble buildings can also be seen along Via Cesare De Lollis. Especially worthy of note, 18th-century **Palazzo De Lellis-Carusi**, with frescoes and stuccowork on the piano nobile; the single storey of **Palazzo De Sanctis-Ricciardone**, with its refined oval double staircase with small cupola, is reminiscent of Vanvitelli; **Palazzo Toppi**, with its 14th-century tower and battlements, as well as the inner courtyard with double stairway. Diodato and Agatopo Toppi, who founded the Tegea branch of the Accademia dell'Arcadia, together with Marquis Federico Valignani in 1720, refurbished the building to its current appearance. Next to this, we find 13th-century **Porta Pescara**, the only original gate still standing; the gate we pass further down is dated 18th century. The striking **Palazzo Zambra** is also on this street, in the old Angevin quarter of Trivigliano, restructured in the mid–18th century and since 1993 home to Abruzzo's Superintendency for Archaeology, Fine Arts and Landscape. In Via degli Agostiniani

# The Cathedral of San Giustino, Chieti

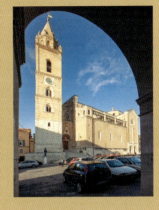

Originally dedicated to St Thomas Apostle, the cathedral has been restored several times over the centuries and the current interior layout is the result of remodelling work carried out in the second half of the 18th century, commissioned by the Archbishop Francesco Brancia. The exterior reflects the stylistic changes implemented in the 1930s by the architect Guido Cirilli. The building has with a nave and two aisles, with domed transept set above the crypt. The nave has a barrel vault with lunettes, while the aisles are surmounted by calottes.

The cathedral is home to 18th-century canvases by Neapolitan painters Saverio Persico – his is the *Incredulity of St Thomas* on the high altar – and Ludovico De Majo, who painted the beautiful altarpiece of *St Cajetan Thiene*, who founded the Theatine Order with Pope Paul IV). Stuccos are by the Piazzoli brothers and Stefano Mambrini. The exquisite wooden choir is attributed to Ferdinando Mosca (18th century). The remarkable marble frontal of the high altar is by the renowned Neapolitan sculptor, Giuseppe Sammartino. The lovely Sacramento chapel was restored in the 19th century by Bishop Luigi Ruffo Scilla. The bell tower dominates the exterior, its first three levels built in 1335 by Bartolomeo Di Giacomo, and the belfry and cusped octagonal crowning by Antonio da Lodi were added towards the end of the 15th century (1498). The cusp, which collapsed in 1706, was reconstructed during restoration work done in the 1900s. The crypt, which dates back to the 11th-century construction, is divided into bays with cross vaults supported by compound pillars, was distinguished by rich Baroque decoration, dismantled during restoration work in 1970–6.

Today, it is composed entirely of brickwork, with the exception of the capitals and polystyle pillars, and preserves fragments of frescoes dating back to the 1300s and 1400s, which came to light during 20th-century restorations, and suggest 14th-century restructuring. Inside there are the frescoes depicting a *Crucifixion* and a scene of the *Pietà*, attributed to the circle of Francesco da Montereale (documented 1502–49), as well as a fresco with the rare early–15th-century effigy of St Giustino. Adjacent to the crypt is the Arciconfraternita del Monte dei Morti chapel, a fine Baroque example with rich stuccos and an altarpiece with *Our Lady of Grace with the Purging Souls* by Paolo De Matteis, active in the Kingdom of Naples between the 1600s and 1700s.

286. 287. Facing page: above, the equestrian statue of Achilles in the Palazzo Comunale courtyard; below, the church of San Francesco della Scarpa called "al Corso".

288–290. This page: above, San Giustino cathedral; below, detail of Giuseppe Sammartino's high-relief frontal; right, the high altar.

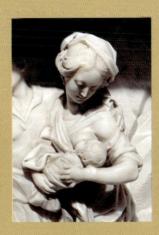

the noteworthy **San Raffaele church**, annexed to the eponymous Conservatory of Music, erected in 1625 as Santa Maria della Pietà, and with a fine stone doorway. Also worthy of note here, 18th-century **Palazzo De Pasquale**.

The striking **church of Sant'Agostino** was built in the 14th century but restructured by Lombard masters, including Michele Clerici, in the second half of the 18th century. The stunning high altarpiece is attributed to Chieti painter Donato Teodoro and his son. From here we can take Via Vicoli to reach the ancient **church of Sant'Agata**, with its surviving 1288 pointed stone portal. Nearby, the impressive brick building is the **Seminario Arcivescovile**, built in the 16th century and enlarged at the end of the 18th century with a lovely, eye-catching Neapolitan-style façade and staircase. The building also encompasses a private chapel and a small theatre dedicated to Alessandro Manzoni, entered via the portico. The quaint traditional fish market, the **Pescheria**, is a 19th-century Neoclassical exedra standing opposite, and now a charming venue for cultural events. Nearby **Palazzo Santuccione**, built in the 18th–19th centuries, is also fascinating, with a dramatic staircase on Via Arniense and a series of small courtyards visible from Via Toppi. This was the location of the finish line for the "Palio dei Barberi", a race among riderless horses held in Chieti from the mid–1600s until the 1930s. It is now a competition for runners.

291. Above: ancient Porta Pescara.
292. Below: the distinctive Pescheria.

We recommend a visit to the **SS Annunziata dei Crociferi church** (Auditorium delle Crocelle) originally annexed to the Camilliani hospital, with paintings by Ludovico de Majo and stucco decorations by Michele Clerici.

One of the most striking monuments near Piazza Matteotti is the **church of Santa Chiara**, whose sumptuous interior includes paintings by Giovanni Battista Spinelli (17th century) with the high altar ancona depicting Pentecost and in the third chapel on the right a *Madonna and Child with Saints*, and Severino Galante (18th century), who painted *St Ignatius and St Francis Xavier* in 1793. Adriano Fedri's 1778 organ is an authentic masterpiece.

The construction of largest Poor Clare church in the region began in 1644 but was completed over a century later, with magnificent decorative work that involved some of the most important Lombard stucco artists of the 18th century. The aisleless church features a barrel vault with side chapels; an area with an oval calotte leads to the deep polygonal nuns' choir, surmounted by a cloister vault.

The parish **church of Sant'Antonio Abate** is also

worth a brief visit. It was founded in the Middle Ages by the Canons Regular of St Anthony of Vienne and restructured between the 17th and 19th centuries. The Gothic portal (1375) is a remainder of its original structure, whereas the chamber is a powerful reminder of the influence of Vanvitelli. The **San Giovanni Battista church** is all that remains of the Capuchin monastery, which was completely renovated. The interior features a tall nave with a barrel vault and four square chapels on the left-hand side, with wooden altars crafted in the 18th century by Capuchin artisans. A monumental Baroque wooden tabernacle stands on the main altar. There are also several fine Veneto school paintings (16th–17th century).

**Teatro Marrucino** (1813–18), in Largo Valignani is a gem designed by Eugenio Michitelli and still a cultural point of reference for the city, offering an extensive calendar of plays, opera and concerts. The artistic curtain painted by the Neapolitan Giovanni Ponticelli in 1875 is an outstanding interior feature. The elegant soaring 15th-century brick tower, **Torre Valignani,** is notable for the battlements set on a cornice with suspended arches and decorated with polychrome majolica tiles. The tower is part of the **Palazzo Arcivescovile** complex opposite the theatre.

The **Costantino Barbella art museum** is dedicated to the famous Chieti sculptor (1852–1925) and can e found in **Palazzo Martinetti-Bianchi**, built in the 17th century as a Jesuit College, becoming a private home in the late 1700s. The largest section of the museum is dedicated to

293. 294. Above: detail of the fresco decorating the vault of the central salon and a room inf the Costantino Barbella Art Museum.
295. Below: Teatro Marrucino.

the 19th century in Abruzzo, with a conspicuous group of works by Costantino Barbella and the leading artists of the time, including Francesco Paolo Michetti, Basilio Cascella, and Filippo Palizzi. A collection of 18th-century majolica from some of Castelli's most important producers of ceramics and 14th-century frescoes recovered from the demolished church of San Domenico are also exhibited. The vault fresco of the main salon, painted by Giacinto Diano in 1796, is entitled *Jupiter Welcomes Psyche to Olympus*.

**Palazzo de' Mayo** is one of the most significant examples of Chieti's civic architecture. The building, in Corso Marrucino, is the outcome of a series of works that began with the older building after it was sold to the Costanzo family, which brought about the current complex. Taken over by the Mayo family in the early–19th century, the building was restored in 1884–6, as indicated by the panel seen in the entrance courtyard. The forepart, in Piazzetta Martiri della Libertà (formerly Piazza San Domenico) is unique, with a wide stone portal and classical marble busts. An Eastern-style pagoda can be seen on the rooftop loggia. The theatrical staircase is the building's iconic feature and snaking through two lovely courtyards it underpins the palazzo's connection with the urban setting and with the large garden, once famed for its rare plant varieties. Other architectural features suggest that the designer was connected with the Neapolitan school, inspired in particular by Fuga and Vanvitelli.

Since 2012 Palazzo de' Mayo has been home to an important museum complex. On the second floor, the **art museum** vaunts precious permanent collections and temporary exhibitions. In the building there is also a fine art library, and the Francesco Sanvitale theatre-garden for cultural events and concerts. There are also guided tours of Via Tecta available to visit the underground gallery that was an historic connection route between the monumental urban area and the Roman baths.

Overlooking the charming square behind the building is **Palazzetto del Teatro Vecchio**, which housed the Venice army offices during World War I. The façade is decorated with sgraffito work by Venetian artists. **Palazzo Durini**, in Largo Barbella, is also striking, with an 16th-century inner court and a stone well that bears witness to the historic building. A second courtyard boasts a lovely Neapolitan-style staircase and a unique puteal. The 16th-century rusticated portal is also remarkable.

The interesting 17th-century **church of San Domenico Nuovo**, formerly dedicated to St Anne and the BElssed Virgin, was consecrated in 1672 and annexed to the Convent of the Piarist Fathers, which became the Convitto Nazionale

296. Above: Largo Valignani and Corso Marrucino. Left, Palazzo Arcivescovile.
297. Below: the arcades on Corso Marrucino.
298. Facing page: Largo Gian Battista Vico with the church of San Domenico Nuovo (left) and the Palazzo della Camera di Commercio (right).

G. B. Vico boarding school in 1861. It acquired its current name in the early 1900s when the original Dominican church was demolished to make way for Palazzo della Provincia. The aisleless interior has a number of side chapels, a square presbytery and a barrel vault, embellished with stuccos by the Lombard Giovan Battista Gianni as well as a lavish high altar with 18th-century ancona. The design has been attributed to St Joseph Calasanz, founder of the Piarist order. The stone façade was completed around 1720, and the interior has valuable paintings by Giacomo Farelli (17th century) and Giacinto Diano (18th century). The **diocesan museum of sacred art** is housed in several of its rooms.

Detouring from the Corso, we reach the nearby **Mater Domini church**, with the precious 15th-century statue depicting the *Virgin Mary* but without *Child Jesus*. For years it was attributed to the sculptor Gagliardelli but recent critical investigation has now assigned to the well-known Paolo Aquilano.

The city has several interesting examples of Fascist architecture, notably the bizarrely eclectic **Palazzo della Camera di Commercio** (which once housed the Fascist corporations), and the headquarters of the Opera Nazionale Dopolavoro, which was later became the ENAL national association for worker aid. The latter is an eloquent example of the bombastic style of the regime: both buildings were by architect Camillo Guerra.

The former ENAL building is home to the **university museum**, formerly a museum of the history of biomedical sciences dedicated to biological and medical aspects that emerge from

archaeological and paleontological research. At the entrance we can admire the reconstruction of an Allosaurus skeleton.

The prestigious **A.C. De Meis Library**, prior to a partial collapse, was housed in the city centre in an elegant 1940s building. It boasts a rich collection of 16th-century editions, incunabula and manuscripts, including D'Annunzio's *The Child of Pleasure*.

Located nearby is the **church of San Gaetano di Thiene**, of the Theatine order, which was consecrated in 1655 and rebuilt between 1697 and 1701. It was one of the first buildings in Abruzzo to use the Greek-cross plan with dome. The interior boasts 17th-century Lombard stucco decorations, which have been attributed to Giambattista Gianni, and dome frescoes by Giuseppe Lamberti of Ferrara (18th century).

The stunning **church of Santa Maria della Civitella** was founded in the 13th century but was renovated between 1677 and 1684. The façade has its original 14th-century ogival portal with a faux prothyron, cusped pediment and slender carved columns, the work of Nicola Mancino of Ortona, 1739 vault frescoes by Donato Teodoro. Nearby, in Piazza Trento e Trieste, the beautiful **Santissima Trinità church**, whose interior dates from the 18th century, has a chapel built into the tower of the lost Porta Sant'Andrea gate. Inside there are the paintings by Ludovico De Majo with the *Coronation of the Virgin* on the high altar and the *Virgin and Child with St Filippo Neri* on the left altar.

Another intriguing city monument is the late–15th-century **Santa Maria del Tricalle tempietto**, with its singular octagonal plan and hemispherical dome.

A leading cultural presence in the city is its **G. D'Annunzio University**, occupying several buildings lower down and where there are also other structures including the Clinical Hospital health facilities.

Chieti's re-enactment of the Passion of Christ through the Good Friday **Procession of the Dead Christ** is worth attending. It is accompanied by clergy and confraternities, and a choir and musicians perform the heart-rending *Miserere* composed in the 18th century by Saverio Selecchy, who was the cathedral choir master.

299. Above: "G. D'Annunzio" University
300. Below: Good Friday Procession of the Dead Christ.
301. 302. Facing page: above, raw-earth houses, Casalincontrada; below, view of Bucchianico.

# The Hills Between the River Alento and Foro

**CASALINCONTRADA** is a charming village set on a hill between the Alento and Pescara rivers. Points of interest include the **Porta da Capo** town gate and the **Caracciolo-Del Giudice baronial palace**. There are also some noteworthy churches here: **Santo Stefano Protomartire** (14th century) with its large painting by Francesco Maria De Benedictis in the centre of the interior, depicting *Solomon and the Queen of Sheba* (1843). Then there are the **churche of Santa Maria della Pietà** formerly San Domenico, of 14th-century origins, now deconsecrated, and with a beautiful stone architrave carved on a side portal. Also worth mentioning is the **church of Santa Maria delle Grazie,** formerly Santa Maria della Porta, dating back to the 15th century, with an oil on canvas – again by De Benedictis – depicting *St Roche Interceding for Help Against tthe Plague* (1872). An ancient but well-preserved icehouse is still visible in the centre.

Some of the houses built in raw earth (a type of construction used in several Abruzzo areas until after World War II) are fascinating. An interesting **CeD Terra – permanent documentation centre on raw-earth houses –** has been set up in some of the rooms on the ground floor of the town hall, to preserve this art. This centre is found in **Villa De Lollis**, the birthplace of the illustrious man of letters, Cesare De Lollis, born

Casalincontrada, Bucchianico, Villamagna, Ripa Teatina, Torrevecchia Teatina, San Giovanni Teatino

The area just outside Chieti is equally striking. From the city of Chieti, this area extends in a network of rolling hills stretching towards the Adriatic coast and dominated by majestic Mount Majella, a spectacular habitat protected as a national park. All the towns we cross – Casalincontrada, Bucchianico, Villamagna, Ripa Teatina, Torrevecchia Teatina and San Giovanni Teatino – have preserved traces of the original fortified settlements in their urban fabric, with gates, wall houses and, in many cases, splendid secular and religious architecture.

in Casalincontrada in 1863.

The village of **BUCCHIANICO**, which dates back to the early Middle Ages and was a fiefdom of the Caracciolo di San Buono family for many years. It stands on a hill between the Alento and Foro rivers in a setting of spectacular gullies and ravines, as well as thriving vineyards and olive groves.

The **sanctuary dedicated to St Camillo De Lellis** (1550–1614; born in Bucchianico) was built in the 17th century in Piazza Roma. The façade dates back to the 1910s and features a lovely statue of the saint, a copy of the original found in St Peter's Basilica in Rome. Inside, the rich 17th-century high altar of gilded wood is remarkable; on the left, the statue of the saint and opposite there is the Reliquia del Piede altar, with the relic of the saint's foot, object of special veneration.

The so-called *Coverto Lungo* also overlooks the square. This is a characteristic portico of 14th-century origins, once occupied by traditional shops, and the parish **church of San Francesco**, built in the 13th century, but completely restructured in the 18th century, with work that also involved the façade. Inside the church the sequence of rectangular bays is broken up in the centre by a square cell topped by a calotte, highlighted by the decoration of the dome, frescoed with biblical scenes, depicted in perspective, and

attributed to Domiziano Vallarola, the Penna artist (1731–1811). The original characteristics of the structure are evident in the sacristy and the ancient square choir, covered with a ribbed cross vault set on slender corner pillars. The refined dual-order monumental façade is virtually concave and surmounted by a curved pediment, with the stunning carved stone portal on whose lintel we observe the coat of arms of the Franciscan Order and the date of completion of the restoration work (1770).

The adjoining convent is now the town hall. The facade once faced the lovely residence of the princes of Caracciolo di San Buono across the square, but unfortunately the latter was demolished several decades ago.

Skirting the San Silvestro portico, we reach the **chapel of San Camillo**, built in 1712 in the stable where, according to tradition, St Camillo was born in 1550. Next to the chapel, with the red cross symbol of the Camillian Order on the façade, is the birthplace of the saint, today a **house-museum**. Along Corso Pierantonj, in addition to the 18th-century Palazzo Monaco-Valletta and Palazzo Pierantonj, we find the

303. 304. This page: above, façade of the sanctuary of San Camillo De Lellis; below, St Camillo's house–museum, Bucchianico.

**Purgatorio church,** rebuilt in the 18th century. The unfinished façade is marked by pilasters of a giant order and the aisleless interior has a barrel vault with lunette and dome in the presbytery. It retains a precious wooden choir (18th century) as well as interesting paintings produced in 1846 by the Guardiagrele artist Francesco Maria De Benedictis, also active in the **church of Sant'Urbano**, rebuilt in the second half of the 18th century, which preserves the relics of the patron saint of the village. The points of interest in the village end with **Porta Grande**, still with its original features. The **nunnery of Santa Maria e Santa Chiara**, just outside town, is said to date back to the mid–1200s and was restored several times. The square cloister, with an arcade and central well, boasts 17th-century frescoes that Tommaso Cascella repainted and integrated between 1932 and 1937. The high altar is lovely, with fine canvases by the Lanciano painter Federico Spoltore (1902–88). To the right of the nave there is a rectangular chapel.

The unique **Banderesi pageant** is at its peak on 25 May each year, during the celebrations in honour of St Urban. This re-enactment celebrates the legendary victory of the town of Bucchianico over Chieti through the miraculous intervention of its patron saint and includes a spectacular "snail dance" (known as the "ciammaichella"), evoking the ruse the villagers devised to force Chieti to withdraw. The dance

305. 306. Above: San Francesco parish church and the monastery of Santa Maria e Santa Chiara, Bucchianico.
307. Below: the Banderesi festival.

takes place amidst decorated floats and votive donations.
The village of **VILLAMAGNA**, overlooking the River Foro valley, is surrounded by olive groves and vineyards, in the kingdom of good wine and age-old popular traditions. Beyond the **Porta da Capo** gate, we find ourselves in the main village square of the village and location of **Palazzo Vescovile**, the bishop's palace which is worth visiting and incorporates older structures. Also noteworthy is the 18th-century parish **church of Santa Maria Maggiore**, which existed before the 14th century but was then modified in the 18th century (1730–50) by the Lombards Giuseppe Zanolli and Giovanni Battista Bossi. The church features an ambulatory and four small domes around the central cross with the main dome. The interior is richly decorated with the valuable polychrome marble high altar of the Neapolitan school and, in addition to works by the painters Donato Teodoro and Antonio Sarnelli, there are paintings by Ludovico de Majo including in special *Our Lady of Suffrage, St Pantaleone and St Giulio*, dated 1753.

Adjacent to the church is the 16th-century **Monte dei Morti chapel**, home of the Confraternity of the same name, with a collection of statues dating back to the 17th–18th centuries. Continuing along Via del Popolo, if we detour to the left, we meet **Palazzo Battaglini**, built in the 16th century, and we reach the small **church of San Francesco**, what remains of the larger convent complex, with traces of a 16th–18th-century decorative device inside.

In July, the town re-enacts the miracle of St Margaret, the assault of the Turks and their defeat and flight thanks to the intervention of the saint.

The picturesque town of **RIPA TEATINA**, located to the right of the River Alento, has maintained its medieval town layout, with evident remains of its ancient walls. Two large round brick towers stand out, one at the ancient Porta Gabella annexed to Palazzo Garofalo.

The **convent church of Santa Maria della Pietà** (1525) is noteworthy. It features an elaborate façade with two orders connected by volutes and crowned by a broad, round multicentred pediment, executed in the late 18th C., when the church's interior decoration was also completed. The interior evokes the work of the Lombard stucco decorators who were active during this period in central-eastern Abruzzo.

The 18th-century interior of the parish **church of San Pietro** is lovely, its origins traceable to the 14th century, then modified at the end of the 17th century. Here we can enjoy an interesting *Madonna del Sudore* work, attributed to the painter Antonio Solaro (known as "Lo Zingaro"), a 16th-century polychrome wooden statue depicting a *Madonna and Child*. There are also three valuable paintings by Ludovico de Majo (1739). There are Roman ruins in the San Felice district.

**TORREVECCHIA TEATINA**, in a picturesque setting on a ridge between the Izzo and Vallepara rivers, is home to **Palazzo dei Baroni**, owned by the Marquis Federico Valignani and now university premises, with a botanical garden, and the San Rocco chapel used as a conference room.

**SAN GIOVANNI TEATINO** is made up of two centres: the historic Forcabobolina, set on a hill overlooking the Pescara valley, and the more recent Sambuceto, along the Tiburtina Valeria road, a strategic point of the Chieti–Pescara metropolitan district. In San Giovanni Alta, the parish **church of San Giovanni** was entirely restored in the 19th century. The new **San Rocco complex**, in the heart of Sambuceto, was initiated in 2011 to a project by architect Mario Botta.

308. Above: one of the towers of Ripa Teatina's ancient walls.
309. 310. Left: the feast of St Margaret and the interior of the parish church of Santa Maria Maggiore, Villamagna.

# From the Aventino to the Sangro

The charming village of **CASOLI** is set on a hill overlooking the Aventino valley, a striking natural scenario. The original settlement, perched on a hillside and dominated by the ducal castle, presents the distinctive cluster plan typical of fortified villages, perfectly adapted to the lay of the land. The contour of the town walls can be perceived from the vestiges of the towers set along them, and the urban fabric still boasts important architectural and historical structures. The most important is the **castle**, distinguished by its impressive tower. The fortified complex, recently restored, is set in the middle of town and is its most important building, defining its very appearance. The original castle, built to monitor the Aventino and Sangro river valleys, presumably coincided with the pentagonal bulwark tower that is now between the apse of the church of Santa Maria Maggiore and the castle whose entrance it overlooks. The complex is set around a central quadrilateral space and its current layout has been attributed to the Renaissance period, particularly with reference to the main building along the south side of the courtyard, which is the most significant part of the structure. The façade is characterized by a single projecting portion composed of brick brackets that sustain lancet arches. The top of the tower instead has a more developed appearance, with projecting triple corbels in stone, and murder holes. The castle was owned

Casoli, Altino, Roccascalegna, Gessopalena, Torricella Peligna, Monterodomo, Colledimacine

This area, part of which is located in Majella National Park, is crossed by the Sangro and Aventino rivers. Despite the fact that natural calamities and wars have profoundly influenced the decline and abandonment of many of its most interesting historic towns, it can rightly be considered one of the region's most interesting areas, due to its stunning natural beauty and landscapes, as well as its extraordinary cultural features. The area is distinguished by the presence of some of Abruzzo's most important fortresses, set in true symbiosis with their surroundings: the majestic castle of Roccascalegna is one of these. Once a Lombard outpost, it perfectly reflects the ruggedness and strategic location of the site. Marvellous natural balconies afford the most breath-taking views of Mount Majella, which dominates the towns built on its slopes. One of these, Iuvanum, bears witness to thousands of years of history, and is one of the most popular archaeology and nature trails.

311. Below: Casoli.

185

by the Masciantonio family until 1981, which contributed to the building appearing mainly as a stately home. From the end of the 1800s to the early 1900s, Gabriele D'Annunzio was often a guest, along with leading cultural figures of the time, who formed his famous circle, the *Cenacolo Dannunziano*. There are still several texts on some of the walls written by D'Annunzio himself.

Next to the castle, the striking parish **church of Santa Maria Maggiore**, set on the Arco del Purgatorio arcade, the ancient entrance to the castle, and the eponymous chapel intended for use as a cemetery. Built by the Orsini princes in 1455, it was enlarged in the latter half of the 18th century and modified into a church with a nave and two aisles. The work that gave it its current Neoclassical appearance began in the latter half of the 19th century. The choir, a wooden statue of St Joseph and numerous Neapolitan school furnishings and silver items were added in 1868. Irregular pieces of sculpted stone are set in the bell tower and outside walls. The interior has a canvas of *Our Lady of the Rosary* (anonymous, 1572), a painting by F.M. De Benedictis portraying the *Madonna with Child, St Hyacinth and St Dominic* (1848), and a painting of *St Gilbert* (1797) by Pasquale Bellonio of Ortona.

The **churches of San Rocco**, with a Neoclassical façade (1847), of **Sant'Agostino**, originally a Benedictine cell dependent on Santa Maria dell'Avella and previously known as San Giustino, and the **Santa Reparata church** near the Villa Comunale park, are also noteworthy. Little is left of the latter's original 15th-century structure, destroyed by bombing in 1943, but it is still a destination for worshippers and attracts numerous pilgrims, and vaunts many admirable artworks. The 1539 high altar, with its lovely Renaissance crafting, although it was rebuilt in the 1930s. There is a niche with the 18th-century statue of St Reparata, whereas the left aisle has an exceptional triptych (1506) of *St Liberata* by Antonio di Francesco di Tommaso of Fossombrone, a painter influenced by the Crivelli school.

The town also has striking examples of 18th- and 19th-century civil architecture, such as the 18th-century **Palazzo Tilli**, whose stone entrance is carved with floral motifs and a coat of arms; **Palazzo De Vincentiis** and **Palazzo Travaglini**, with frescoed rooms; **Palazzo De Cinque**; **Palazzo Ramondo**, with its

312. Above: the sale of gifts for the feast of St Reparata.
313. Below: the triptych depicting St Liberata, church of Santa Reparata, Casoli.
314. Facing page: Altino.

elegant staircase entrance; **Palazzo Ricci**, rebuilt in the 19th century, and **Palazzo Di Giorgio**. The Torretta lookout tower, near the town centre, is especially interesting. Set on a steep, wooded hill near Lake Casoli, it was a key observation point, making it strategic in defending the upper part of the valley. Located along the border with Guardiagrele, **Casina di Capoposta**, a picturesque aristocratic country estate built in the second half of the 19th century, is composed of the main residence and a church in an eclectic style, with a Romanesque-style entrance. The complex is surrounded by farmhouses, built using river stone, and ancient mulberry groves.

On the stunning nearby **Lake Sant'Angelo** visitors can enjoy marvellous views of the Majella massif while the Riserva naturale Lago di Serranella, partly within municipal boundaries, offers a pristine natural environment. In the **Piano Laroma** district, between Casoli and Palombaro, we find significant traces of *Cluviae*, an ancient fortified settlement built by the Carricini, the smallest of the Samnite tribes living on the Majella slopes, and which became a municipium in the second half of the 1st century AD.

The **feast of Santa Reparata** takes place on 8 October, which involves the sale of food products, offered by the faithful, with the use of traditional *conocchie* (wooden pyramids) to which the donations are hung; the proceeds will be used to finance the party of the following year. At the end of September, similar events are celebrated on the occasion of the feast of the Saints Medici in Altino and Roccascalegna.

**ALTINO** is perched on a hill near the confluence of the Aventino and Sangro rivers, dominating the valley that extends to the Adriatic coast, in an area dotted with small towns such as Colli, Sant'Angelo, Briccioli and Selva.

The original settlement dated back to the Middle Ages and is laid out as a typical fortified hamlet, extending across a terrace reached by a steep ascent skirting the front of the **Santa Maria del Popolo parish church**, documented as early as the 1300s and restored in later centuries. The path leads to a small square where the old fortress was probably located and is the site of the **Sirolli baronial palace**, which is considered Altino's most important architecture, together with the parish church.

In terms of religious buildings, in addition to the parish church, the **church of Madonna delle Grazie** is especially interesting. It was originally located outside the town walls, on the road to Roccascalegna, and has a precious image of *Our Lady of the Rosary*. The Neoclassical **church of San Rocco** is also outside the walls. Nearby, the interesting **monumental fountain** dates back to the 16th century, showing the year 1558 engraved on the stone ashlar closing off the arch. **Villa Di Lello**, or "La Silvestrina", is also noteworthy for architectural features reflecting a stylistic revival.

It is worth a visit to the nearby **Lake Serranella nature reserve**, bordering not only Altino but also the municipalities of Casoli and Sant'Eusanio del Sangro. The reserve is one of the rare wetlands of Abruzzo, a preferred destination for migratory birdlife en route to the Adriatic. The numerous species nest here include the Northern pintail, the reserve icon.

The town of **ROCCASCALEGNA**, dominated by its impressive **castle** (*see box p. 189*), rises on a rocky spur on the slopes of Mount Majella, overlooking the valley of the Rio Secco, a tributary of the River Aventino. The old town

extends from the ancient **church of San Pietro**, on the south side of the castle.
The modern urban area developed downhill from the old town, moulded along paths influenced by the local geography: Via Vazoli, behind the rocky terrain on which the castle was built, and Via Codacchie, on the level beneath it. The old fortified town was once encircled by walls and had two gates, Porta della Terra and Porta del Forno. In Via San Cosimo we can admire **Palazzo Mastrangelo** and near the town hall, the **church of Santi Cosma e Damiano**, whose earliest documentation dates back to the 16th century, while a dedicatory epigraph on the main portal recalls the restoration carried out two centuries later.
The lovely **church of San Pancrazio**, all that remains of the ancient abbey, lies in the direction of Collegrande, outside the urban boundaries. The outside curtain walls are made of distinctive reddish stone typical of this area, together with pale limestone. The façade is flanked by the bell tower, and its portal is decorated with a round arch and a simple frieze dating back to the 13th century, as indicated by the date – 1205 – carved on the architrave. Along the road of the nearby cemetery, there is another entrance, likewise marked by a round arch with a braided decoration. From here, the church could be accessed from the old courtyard, located on the site of what is now the cemetery. Two artefacts, parts of old columns, were unearthed near the entrance. The stark interior, with two aisles, can be visited on request or during the hours the church is open for masses and weddings. The entrance decorated with friezes, arches and the statue of St Pancras are the extant parts of this ancient building.
The atmospheric old village of **GESSOPALENA** rises on a gypsum cliff to the right of the River Aventino. Its name recalls the main resource of the area, "gesso" or gypsum,

extracted from the numerous quarries concentrated above all around the large rock called la Morgia, south of the ancient village.
The modern quarter is known as Terranova and was built further downhill after much of the ancient settlement was deserted following the destruction caused by German mines. Nonetheless, there are substantial remains of the old town, a full-fledged cluster of rock dwellings hollowed out in the soft gypsum. It is set high along the ridge in a protected position, where the old castle was probably located. Though the castle has since disappeared, its ancient presence is evident from place names such as Via Castello, Largo del Principe, and Piè di Castello. The ridge is crossed by the main street, Via Castello, lined with the most important buildings, mansions, churches, shops, stables. Secondary streets – perfectly adapted to the terrain – are connected to it, forming the town's distinctive fishbone layout. Some of the most important buildings are still evident, such as **Palazzo Persiani**, **Palazzo Pellicciotti**, the **Madonna del Rosario church** and the **Sant'Antonio church**, an 1800s chapel built by the Tozzi family, adjacent to their mansion. On Largo del Principe we see the foundations of the **Santa Annunziata church**, dug from the rock. The exquisite portal was dismantled and reassembled at the **church of Santa Maria Maggiore** in the new part of town. Of all the churches here, Sant'Egidio was the most impressive: a staircase in local limestone, river pebbles and plaster rises towards

315. Above: the church of San Pietro, Roccascalegna.
316. Below: overview of the abandoned ancient village and modern Gessopalena.
317. Facing page: Roccascalegna castle.

# Roccascalegna Castle

This majestic castle, emblematic of Abruzzo's military architecture, is set on a rocky cliff over the Rio Secco valley. Originally a Lombard outpost, it perfectly reflects the ruggedness and strategic location of the site. The complex is one of the most fascinating siege structures in Abruzzo. It is laid out in a complex and uneven plan, enclosed by fortified walls with towers and smaller semi-circular towers, and buildings erected in different eras. Emerging above it is the isolated square tower, set on top of the cliff at the end of the ramp that rises from the east walls. A long flight of steps leads from Piano di San Pietro to the entrance to the fortress, monitored by the Sentinel's Tower, which was extensively remodelled over the centuries. After years of abandonment, restoration work was recently completed making the castle available as a truly unique venue for prestigious cultural events.

the recently reconstructed portal, framed by a limestone cornice surmounted by a triangular pediment. On Easter Wednesday afternoon the re-enactment of the **Passion of Christ takes place**, ending with the Crucifixion in the magical setting of the old town. This biennial event has reached its 36th edition.

The 16th-century **church of Santa Maria dei Raccomandati**, whose Neoclassical façade overlooks Piazza Roma (the façade was modified in the 19th century) preserves significant architectural elements. The 16th-century side door, which was moved to the west side in the 19th century, leads to the interior, which has a nave and two aisles, and a truss ceiling.

The church hosts the **Madonna dei Raccomandati parish museum**. Its main collections include religious works by Neapolitan goldsmiths, dated 1700–1800s. Other works include an 1587 *Deposition*, a *Pentecost* and two panels on a gold ground with *Saints Peter and Paul*, attributed to the "painter of Dio Aiutarà" (doc. 1581-7), earning his named for his unique signature. There is also a delightful polychrome reliquary in the form of a Gothic temple, of Tuscan origins.

Some buildings in the old town have been recovered and today house the **Museo del Gesso**, a museum created for the protection and promotion of cultural heritage linked to the naturalistic capital of gypsum in the Aventino valley.

**TORRICELLA PELIGNA** is located on a hillside between the Aventino and Sangro river valleys and is dominated by a shady pine forest. Despite the destruction caused by World War II the original layout can be seen in the elongated built-up area, closed off on the east side by the recently restored parish **church of San Giacomo**, documented as early as the 12th century, and today see with its subsequent renovations. Inside, the numerous fine furnishings include a Neapolitan silver monstrance and a wooden statue of the *Madonna of the Rosary*, both 18th century. Nearby is the birthplace of Domenico D'Amico (1819–1901), a master artist whose descendants included Silvio D'Amico (1887–1955), a leading figure in the Italian theatrical scenario.

318. Above: the parish church of San Giacomo, Torricella Peligna.
319. Below: the Gessopalena Passion Play.

The interesting Museo Territoriale is in Via Michele Persichitti, inside the **church of San Rocco**, among other precious finds displays a valuable mummy that came to light during the restoration of the parish church.

The numerous fountains in this area are especially interesting, such as the Fonte di Sant'Agata and another known as Fonte Flaviana. The memorable **Madonna del Roseto sanctuary** is nearby: mentioned by D'Annunzio in his *Novelle della Pescara*, it stands on an isolated rocky hill and still attracts pilgrimages. The complex is composed of a small aisleless church and the hermit's dwelling. The entrance architrave indicates the date 1552, which may refer to the year the sanctuary was founded.

Ettore Troilo – commander of the Majella Brigade, a glorious partisan formation that fought alongside the Allies for the northbound liberation front in World War II – was born in Torricella Peligna. Two plaques, recently affixed to the town's Carabinieri barracks, commemorate the heroic commander and Torricella's Majella

## Ruins of Roman Iuvanum

Iuvanum, founded following the Social War (90–87 BC), was built over the ruins of a Samnite sanctuary. The urban area is outlined by a network of streets – Via Orientale, Via del Teatro and Via di Bacco – paved with enormous polygonal stones. The **Italic sanctuary** is on the hillside and dates back to the 2nd century BC, set within an almost square enclosure. Inside there are the remains of two temples, which can be accessed from the east side. The Santa Maria del Palazzo Benedictine abbey was built over the older of the two. The **forum**, a rectangular monumental space, dates from the mid–1st century AD. Three sides of this space are defined by the arcades that once housed *tabernae* (shops), whereas the **basilica** (the building where justice was administered, and business was conducted) dominates the north end. The apsidal room was dedicated to the Augustales imperial cult. The urban layout is composed of the artisan district, southeast of the forum, and the residential district east of the Via Orientale. The **theatre** (2nd century BC) is set against the southeast slopes of the acropolis. The remains of the cavea include the first seven rows of terraces and the orchestra (with a diameter of 17m), paved with large rectangular stones in a parallel layout. Around the town excavations have brought to light what is presumed to be the baths complex. Numerous findings – earthenware, glass and personal accoutrements – testify to the vitality of this settlement until the 4th century AD, whereas there are relatively few findings from the Late–Roman period.

320. 321. This page: Iuvanum Roman forum (above) and theatre (right).

Brigade fallen. Some years the name of Torricella Peligna came to the public eye thanks also to the literary talent of John Fante, an American cult writer whose father came from the village. Today Torricella dedicates a very popular festival, **Il Dio di Mio Padre**, inspired by the title of well-known story by Fante, *My Father's God*. John's son Dan Fante, who passed away in 2015, had frequently returned to stay in his grandfather's house. Quaint **Fallascoso**, a hamlet of Torricella, is also noteworthy. Set on a little cliff, it boasts a **baronial palace** that once belonged to the Croce family, and the **church of San Nicola**, built in the 18th century over the ruins of an older structure.

The **hermitage of San Rinaldo** and the little church across from it are located just below the village of Fallascoso, at the bottom of an enormous cliff. The chapel was built directly on the rocky base between 1838 and 1844. Inside, a niche with a small statue of the saint is set over the altar against the back wall. The bell tower exploits the crag above by adding a small arch to hold the bell. The cave is composed of a narrow passage where the saint is traditionally said to have stayed.

The town of **MONTENERODOMO** rises on a rocky crest in Majella National Park, between the courses of the San Giusto and San Leo streams. The breath-taking view from here extends from Mount Majella to the Adriatic. The ancient origins of Montenerodomo are proved by the remarkable remains of **megalithic walls** visible at the gates of the town and belonging to the defensive system of the Carecini, a Samnite tribe settled in the area. The ancient fortified village, developed around a lost defensive garrison, was a thriving centre devoted to sheep farming, but which suffered serious destruction during the last war, also leaving damaged the homes of the ancestors of Benedetto Croce and the De Thomasis family. The oldest part of town, which is still visible, is located around the parish **church of San Martino** (14th century). The **church of San Vito**, built in the 18th century, is located in Piazza De Thomasis, and it has a 1757 inscription from Pope Benedict XIV. The town was rebuilt following World War II devastation.

The ruins of **Iuvanum** (*see box p. 191*) are located in Madonna del Palazzo. Iuvanum, which has been turned into a prestigious archaeological park, was a Carricini settlement and later became a Roman *municipium*, with an acropolis, forum and theatre. Nearby there is a modern structure whose first floor is home to the Iuvanum **archaeology museum** and exhibits valuable relics found in the area.

The ground floor now houses the **Museo sulla Storia e Trasformazione del Territorio**, a narrative of the history and changes to the area between Mount Majella and the Sangro. The museum uses descriptive panels and everyday items to guide the visitor in an exploration of the interaction between people and landscape.

The town of **COLLEDIMACINE**, set on a hill between the tributaries of the Aventino Cupo and Torbido, is set in a breath-taking natural landscape, with a belvedere facing Mount Majella and the Taranta gorge. The little town clusters around lovely Piazza Barbolani, with the 18th-century **Palazzo Barbolani**, which may have been built over the castle; the parish **church of San Nicola di Bari**, the former **San Rocco church** – now the parish hall – and annexed clock tower. The monumental fountain near the square was built in the late 19th century and was recently restored.

The area's traditional watermills, with stone channels, are well worth a visit.

# Lanciano, Town and territory

LANCIANO is a must for the thoughtful visitor because of the urban fabric and wealth of artworks that make it one of the region's most dynamic, interesting towns. The town was known for its cultural investments rendered possible by the sheer economic prosperity that identified Lanciano for many years. For centuries it was one of the most important trading locations in central-southern Italy and this encouraged the development of a flourishing trade and artisanal economy. One of the most striking features of Lanciano is the clear division between its ancient part, traditionally considered as the four districts of Lancianovecchia, Civitanova, Sacca and Borgo, which are still recognizable in the original layout, and the modern part which developed rapidly along the new Corso Trento and Trieste, from the latter half of the 19th century and throughout the Fascist period.

Anxanum was originally an ancient Frentano settlement and became a Roman municipium following the Social War. Medieval sources place it on the Erminio Hill, where the ancient settlement of Lancianovecchio developed, with the so-called "Lombard Castle", whose ruins were partially reused in the 18th century to build **Palazzo Vergilj**, as we can see from the robust masonry structures on the ground floor (between Via degli Agorai, Largo C. Topia, Via dei Frentani and Largo San Giovanni). In addition to the fortified sector on Colle Erminio (**Lancianovecchio**), already protected by massive walls and sheer drops, the urban districts of Borgo on Colle Pietroso and Civitanova–Sacca were fortified during the early

Lanciano, Frisa, Castelfrentano, Sant'Eusanio del Sangro, Filetto, Vacri, Ari, Giuliano Teatino, Canosa Sannita, Crecchio, Poggiofiorito, Arielli, Orsogna, Treglio, Mozzagrogna, Santa Maria Imbaro

IThe itinerary starts in Lanciano, one of the most important and well-preserved old towns in Abruzzo, with turreted walls, picturesque narrow streets and churches that are splendid examples of devotion and religious art. Lanciano's strategic position as a junction on the sheep track not far from the Adriatic coast promoted the development of craft and trade in the town and for many centuries its fair – that reached the height of its splendour in the 16th century. – was an important periodic event for merchants. The fair also made Lanciano a trading bridge between inland Abruzzo and the markets of Venice and Dalmatia. The town is surrounded by attractive villages dotted over the vineyard-covered hills.

322. Facing page: Colledimacine with the Majella massif in the background.
323. Below: view of Lancianovecchia.

Middle Ages. In the 13th century the three settlements were enclosed by a single boundary wall with nine gates: Santa Maria la Nova, della Noce, San Nicola, Sant'Antonio, Santa Chiara, Sant'Angelo (demolished in the 19th century), Porta Diocleziana, Porta Pozzo Bagnaro and finally **Porta di San Biagio** in Lancianovecchio, which is the only Medieval gate to have survived, opening onto the Feltrino valley in the direction of the Ortona sheep track.

A well-preserved stretch of the old walls is still visible on the southern side of the old town of Civitanova, with the **Torri Montanare**, so called because they defended the settlement on the side of the mountains. The walls are interspersed with the old Medieval watchtower, closed on three sides, and the squatter corner tower later topped with machicolations on corbel supports. The masonry walls are uniform and well-preserved, the bricks laid perpendicular in the upper part and sloped in the lower part, with wide counterforts and mural towers. Beyond the corner, along the western perimeter, there is a sloping curtain wall made from stones, pebbles and brick that constitutes the oldest stretch and surrounded the parade ground currently used for outdoor events and shows. At the end of the road, we reach Via del Torrione with its distinctive 15th-century Torre Aragonese round tower on a sloping base, at the edge of the old town, built entirely in brick, including the crown with corbel support.

Abruzzo's most original Medieval building is undoubtedly the **church of Santa Maria Maggiore** (*see box p. 195*), which was rebuilt in the heart of the Civitanova quarter in the period 1250-75 and modified over time.

In Largo San Giovanni, we find the tower called **Torre della Candelora**, a surviving 14th-century belfry of the church of San Giovanni Battista, demolished after World War II bombings. A stone's-throw away we have the **church of Sant'Agostino** with its handsome 14th-century façade and fine portal and rose window. It also has a bell tower dating to the same period, whose interior is decorated with 18th-century stuccowork, in addition to the small but impressive **Santa Croce church**. Further on we find the **Botteghe Medievali,** a beautiful example of 15th-century civil architecture, better known as Casa di Nicolao from the inscription on the front along Via dei Frentani, dated 1434 and the name of the rich Lanciano merchant Nicolao De Rubeis.

324. 325. This page: above, aerial view of Lanciano; below, Porta San Biagio.
326. 327. Facing page: the portal and interior of Santa Maria Maggiore, Lanciano.

This part of the Lanciovecchio district still revolves around the **San Biagio church**, traditionally believed to be the oldest in Lanciano, founded before 1059. It is home to the Medieval reliquary statue of Blaise the bishop saint and the 18th-century *Madonna dei Raccomandati* by Neapolitan Giacomo Colombo. Beyond nearby Porta San Biagio, we can walk the along the charming Via dei Bastioni, where there are still remains of the ancient fortifications. Returning to Piazza Plebiscito, we enter the Civitanova district and walk up the fascinating Salita dei Gradoni to Via Cavour, with the monumental **Palazzo Stella**. Almost in front of Palazzo Stella is the **Madonna degli Angeli church**, decorated in the mid-18 century by Ticino artisans. At the end of Via Cavour, we see the arches of the ancient Ammazzo bridge, built to connect the districts of Civitanova–Sacca and Lancianovecchio, and continuing up Via San Rocco we find the **church of San Nicola** built on the remains of the older San Pellegrino church, destroyed in 1226, with a 14th-century bell tower and, inside, the coeval frescoes depicting the *Stories of the True Cross* taken from Jacobus da Varagine's *Golden Legend*. The church is currently home to an interesting **Centro di Documentazione Museale** with some of the church's precious furnishings.

The **church of San Francesco** is one of the town's most important monuments, also in terms of religious devotion. The high altar preserves the holy relics known as the housing the **Eucharistic Miracle.** It is said that in the 8th century the Host and Wine were transformed into flesh and blood during the celebration of mass (in the church of Santi Legonziano e Domiziano, identified in the rooms beneath today's square) by a Basilian monk who doubted the Eucharistic presence. The fruits of the prodigy are now kept in a precious 18th-century ostensory of Bernini inspiration, and in an engraved crystal chalice dated 17th century. The church was built in the mid-13th century

## Church of Santa Maria Maggiore, Lanciano

The fine church features aspects of Burgundian Cistercian architecture with an interesting combination of central and longitudinal space. The original layout comprised a cross-vaulted nave with two aisles and ended in an octagonal area with a ribbed, gored dome. The 16th-century remodelling added two more aisles and a building on the northern side. The current arrangement is the result of a controversial renovation program carried out in 1968–9, which restored the arrangement prior to the 16th-century enlargement, dismantling the 17th–19th-century decorative device. The **monumental east façade** was built in the late–1200s, early decades of the 1300s, with a splendid splayed portal featuring a lunette containing a *Crucifixion* group produced in 1317 by Lanciano sculptor Francesco Petrini. Inside the church there is a 16th-century wooden **triptych** with the *Virgin and Child between St Nicholas of Bari and St Thomas*, with an *Annunciation* in the lunette above, attributed to Venetian painter Girolamo Galizzi da Santacroce, as well as Nicola da Guardiagrele's famous 1422 silver an enamel **processional crucifix**. On the high altar we can admire Giuseppangelo Ronzi *Assumption* ancona.

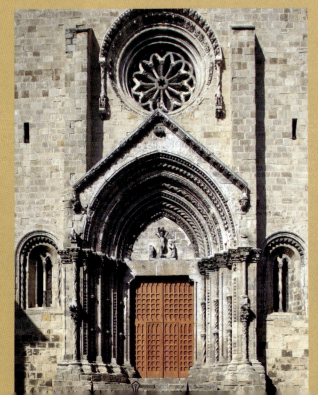

over the remains of the Santi Legonziano e Domiziano church, and was completely remodelled in around 1737, with the construction of a domed room and presbytery. An interior richly decorated with stuccowork by Michele Clerici dated to around the mid-18th century. The lower half of the façade, with a fine Burgundian-style portal with ogival arch, and the base of the bell tower, are the only parts of the original building to have survived. The end section of the bell tower, with octagonal belfry and dome, was added in the 16th century. Piazza Plebiscito is the heart of the town and is surrounded by monuments that are urban icons, such as the 17th-century bell tower and slightly detached **Madonna del Ponte cathedral**, which was remodelled from the 16th-century premises built on the remains of the **Roman-Medieval Diocleziano bridge**, to a design by Carlo Fantoni and implemented by Giovanni Antonio Fontana in 1785. A majestic Neoclassical portal graces the 19th-century façade of the cathedral, designed by Eugenio Michitelli in 1817, while the gable solution is from the 20th century. The forepart, inspired by 16th-century classical Rome and Veneto style, is accentuated by four imposing Corinthian columns. The vault of the vast aisleless interior is embellished with a cycle of 18th-century frescoes by Giacinto Diano. The Diocleziano Bridge is said to have been built by the Romans, ordered by the Emperor Diocletian, after whom it is named. From here it is possible to go follow the enchanting archaeological–monumental Ponte di Diocleziano – Santuario del Miracolo Eucaristico route, recovered in 2000 and opened to the public. The itinerary follows an ancient path used by pilgrims to reach the sanctuary after entering the town over the bridge and it winds along the important archaeological and monumental finds from the various historical periods of the town and the sanctuary. Beneath the Franciscan complex we find the fascinating San Longino chamber, a vast space with a fine cycle of frescos with scenes of the Apocalypse, dated 15th–16th century.

The numerous examples of noble buildings include **Palazzo De Crecchio** in the Lancianovecchio quarter, which dates back to the early–19th century, with a two-storey brick structure and pedimented façade whose lines recall

328. Above: the Ponte di Diocleziano bridge, Lanciano.
329. 330. Facing page: top, the Cyrene; below, Piazza del Plebiscito, Lanciano.

the designs of Vanvitelli. Until 2006 the palazzo was home to the venerable Raffaele Liberatore public library, now in the **Polo Culturale Villa Marciani**, in Via del Mancino.

The nearby **Fenaroli Theatre** is another attraction, and was built around 1840 by Taddeo Salvini, with an elevation added in the 1930s. The town and its surroundings also boast numerous examples of Art Nouveau architecture. In nearby Largo Tappia we see the Liberty façade of **Palazzo del Capitano**, built at the behest of Captain Alfonso Cotellessa in 1923 and now owned by the De Giorgio family.

The **diocesan museum** is found on the second floor of the Seminario Diocesano in Largo dell'Appello, with a noteworthy 13th-century portal recovered from the lost Annunziata church. The museum has a valuable collection of wooden statues, gold and silver, and sacred vestments, paintings and furnishings from the area. The 16th-century **church of Santa Giovina**, with relics of the saint, also overlooks the square.

Along Via Federico Spoltore we find the beautiful **Palazzo Spoltore** which became the **Casa Museo Federico Spoltore** in 2001, dedicated to the Lanciano artist (1902–88). The museum collects furnishings and art objects owned by the Spoltore family in addition to the artist's most significant works.

Modern Lanciano developed rapidly along the new Corso Trento and Trieste, an extraordinary "invention" by Filippo Sargiacomo, from the second half of the 19th century throughout the Fascist period. The town was enriched with remarkable examples of refined architecture that are striking for the marvellous combination of Renaissance-inspired revival forms and floral decorativism. Along Viale dei Cappuccini it is still possible to admire some of the most interesting suburban residences, including Villa Carabba, designed in the early 1900s by the famous Coppedè studio for publisher Rocco Carabba.

A recent restoration recovered the old **Santo Spirito monastery** and annexed church, built at the end of the 13th century on the edge of the great field used for the fair. Linked to Pietro da Morrone's Celestinian movement, the monastery (also thought to have been a pilgrim hospice) was suppressed in 1654, and the church reduced in size, although it continued to be used up until the early decades of the 20th century. During the 1830s the complex became a candle factory and a cement works in the 20th century. Following restoration, the monastery complex became a museum hub and home to the Centro di documentazione sull'economia della transumanza negli scambi del mediterraneo and the new Civico Museo di Archeologia Urbana e dei Commerci Antichi in Abruzzo museum installation.

The installation uses multimedia and a time narrative of six sections to reconstruct the history of the town and its hinterland from the Neolithic to the Middle Ages. It is home to many of the numerous precious finds uncovered by the recent excavation campaigns undertaken in the town and surrounding area. It houses the extremely interesting finds from the Neolithic settlement at Marcianese, known as **Villaggio Rossi**, which was discovered during the first scientific campaign of excavations conducted in the territory of Lanciano by Alfredo Geniola, in 1969, and the precious early Medieval ceramics found in 1993 during excavation of the Miracolo Eucaristico sanctuary.

One of Lanciano's most significant traditions is the solemn **Dono procession** in honour of the Madonna del Ponte. This is an ancient rite that takes place on 8 September when jewellery, money and grain are offered to the Virgin Mary to seek her intercession for the coming agricultural year. Another evocative moment is the **Squilla**, when the small bell in the cathedral tower chimes on the evening of 23 December and the townsfolk gather in a gesture of peace, exchanging gifts and remembering their dead. In ancient times the Bishop of Lanciano led the worshippers to the **Iconicella church** (near the fork in the L'Aquila–Foggia Regio Tratturo sheep track), thus marking the start of the Christmas celebrations. During the 17th century, Monsignor Paolo Tasso enlarged the sheep-track church erected in 1524 by a devout Lanciano citizen, ordering frescos of the *Virgin and Child with Saints Roche and Sebastian* to be painted. There is also an *Our Lady of the Rosary* here, by the Bassano school, brought from the church of San Francesco.

Lanciano's Maundy Thursday and Good Friday are truly unique, a moment of collective worship that culminates in the slow pace of the **Cireneo**, a faceless and nameless man who walks the streets barefoot under the weight of a large cross, renewing the actions of Simon the Cyrene who was chosen to help Christ in his ascent to Calvary.

Two important moments in the life of the town are the commemorative re-enactment of the

investiture of the **Mastrogiurato** – the head of the Lanciano fair – on the last Sunday in August, and the **Fair of Sant'Egidio**, also known as the Canestrelle Fair (31 August). Other recurrent cultural events are the **Estate Musicale Frentana** concerts in July and August.

The picturesque village of **FRISA** is situated on a hill ridge between the Moro and Feltrino rivers surrounded by villages like Guastameroli and Badia. In Piazza Principe di Piemonte there are noteworthy buildings including the old **Palazzo Baronal Caccianini** with an ancient tower, and the church of Santa Lucia. The **church of Santa Maria del Popolo**, built in the 17th century, along the sheep track, has a Baroque altar decorated with a *Virgin and Child* painted by Pietro Annigoni, which replaced the 16th-century painting of the same subject that was stolen a few decades earlier.

In the hamlet of Badia, the **church of Santa Maria Assunta** – part of the lost monastery – has the remains of a 13th-century painting in the attic.

Lying between the Feltrino and Sangro basins, the town of **CASTELFRENTANO** – the old

331. Above: Vacri Medieval tower.
332. Below: aerial view of Castel Frentano with Majella in the background.

Castelnuovo – was partly destroyed by a landslide but still vaunts important artistic heritage, whose highlight is the 18th-century parish **church of Santo Stefano**, in Piazza Caporali, rebuilt between 1749 and 1780 by Mario Gioffredo. The nearby **SS Rosario church** was also remodelled in the latter half of the 1700s. Other fine churches include the **Trinità** and **Santa Maria della Selva** (or Madonna dell'Assunta), which houses a 15th-century wooden statue of the *Virgin and Child*. Noteworthy examples of civil architecture include **Palazzo De Vergilij**, **Palazzo Caporali**, **Palazzo Cavacini** and **Palazzo Crognale**. In Piazza Crognale some parts of the ancient urban walls are recognizable. The interesting **Museo Civico** has been opened in the former town hall and has an archaeology section and a religious art section.

**SANT'EUSANIO DEL SANGRO**, on a hill not far from the Sangro valley and dominated by the Majella massif, has the interesting **Assunta parish church** in Gothic revival style. **Palazzo Finamore** is a notable building, with a splendid garden, in the centre of the village. A further interesting attraction is the elegant

Art Nouveau house that was the home of the famous local poet, Cesare De Titta, and which is now the **Casa Museo Cesare De Titta**. In the surrounding area, it is worth visiting the Riserva Naturale Regionale Lago di Serranella, a nature reserve around the artificial lake created at the confluence of the Sangro and the Aventino rivers, which also touches on the districts of Casoli and Altino. The visitor centre is in Brecciaio.

Filetto, Arielli, Canosa Sannita, Poggiofiorito and Giuliano Teatino are found in a large winegrowing and farming area.

Visitors to hilltop **FILETTO** overlooking the Dendolo and Venna streams, should not miss the 19th-century **Madonna della Libera sanctuary** with its façade decorated with a majolica panel by potter Fedele Cappelletti. Built over an extant chapel, the ancient *incubatio* rite is practised here.

**VACRI** has a noteworthy 18th-century parish **church of San Biagio** with a 16th-century stone portal. The Nicolini tower and castle ruins are relics of this ancient fortified village.

The highlights of the picturesque town of **ARI**, situated on a ridge amid vineyards and orchards, are its fine **baronial palace**, of ancient origins but extensively remodelled, and the wooden statue of the *Virgin and Child* in the **Madonna delle Grazie church**.

**GIULIANO TEATINO** nestles among the lush green countryside, offering splendid views over the Majella massif. The town was largely destroyed in 1843 by a devastating landslide. It is famous not only for its excellent wine production but also for the cultivation of delicious cherries and a cherry festival is held every year between May and June.

**CANOSA SANNITA** was extensively rebuilt after World War II, with the **Santi Apostoli Filippo e Giacomo parish church** reconstructed over the site of ancient Palazzo Celaya. The **Museo della Guerra per la Pace** war museum is housed in 16th-century **Palazzo Martucci**, which has always belonged to the family of the same name and is documented as far back as 1342.

The village of **CRECCHIO** stands on a hill to the right of the River Arielli. Close to **Porta da Piedi** is the late–16th-century **church of Santa Maria da Piedi**, now deconsecrated and used as an auditorium. The church is opposite Palazzo Monaco, possibly of 14th-century origins. The village is dominated by a massive **ducal castle** composed of four blocks of buildings joined by the same number of corner towers to form a quadrangle with open

333–335. Above, from right to left: the churches of Santa Maria dell'Assunta, Castel Frentano; Madonna della Libera, Filetto; parish church of San Biagio, Vacri.
336. Below: Palazzo Baronale, Ari.

## Museo dell'Abruzzo Bizantino e Altomedievale, Crecchio

The museum was founded in 1995 to house the precious exhibits – including some of exceptional workmanship – that were unearthed during a series of excavations concentrating on the Roman country villa at Casino Vezzani-Vassarella near Crecchio. The digs uncovered many extremely important objects, which are displayed in four rooms of the museum: bowls, lamps and amphorae imported from Africa, trinkets and refined bronze and painted ceramic tableware, as well as an extraordinary collection of wooden exhibits of Coptic influence, such as a chair with finely carved back, and fragments of the frame and small drawers for women's toiletries. The exceptional finds have enabled a tentative reconstruction of the historical events of an Abruzzo village that was influenced by the settlement of Lombard peoples between the 6th and 7th centuries, documenting the existence of an extensive trade network between Byzantine Abruzzo and the East, and Egypt in particular. Another extremely interesting highlight is represented by the numerous pieces of "Crecchio pottery", which was produced locally between the 6th and 7th centuries, decorated with colourful geometric and floral motifs. The Alberto Carlo Fraracci room is home to an Etruscan collection.

337. Above: Crecchio castle.
338. Left: an Egyptian statuette displayed in the museum.

galleries on two sides. It is one of numerous examples in Abruzzo of prevalently defensive buildings converted into residential architectures. In its current form, we see the castle after a series of stratifications, superimposed over the original Medieval nucleus constituted by the northeast tower known as "Torre dell'Ulivo". These works continued right up until the extensive restoration work that repaired the serious damage sustained during World War II. The two southward-facing towers, that of the outside wall and several internal rooms date to a single construction phase that commenced in the 15th century. Two successive phases have also been identified: the first of these involved the building of the southern gallery and the western block, presumably with just one storey, whilst the upper level of the gallery and the piano nobile of the adjoining block date to the second period. Finally, the battlements were demolished and replaced with a cornice when the second floor was added. The fourth tower, destroyed in 1881 by a strong earthquake, was almost completely rebuilt in 1904. Following further modifications to enhance its residential function, the castle became a famous stop for Italian royal family as they fled the country in September 1943. It was then damaged in the air raids of the following June. It has recently undergone extensive restoration and now houses the **Museo dell'Abruzzo Bizantino e Altomedievale** (*see box p. 200*).

The **SS Salvatore church** and the **Santa Elisabetta sanctuary**, with the 15th-century statue of the saint and some 19th-century ex-voto paintings, are now seen in the guise of postwar reconstructions. The municipal authorities

have recently developed the charming **Parco dei Mulini**, a park with amenities of significant naturalistic value for the protection and promotion of the numerous mills located along the 3km course of the River Arielli.

**POGGIOFIORITO** is situated in a splendid panoramic position on a rise to the left of the River Moro, while **ARIELLI**, which retains the

339. Above: historic centre of Crecchio.
340. Below: former church of Santa Maria da Piedi and Palazzo Monaco, Crecchio.

relics of a Medieval castle, is home to the **Madonna delle Grazie sanctuary**. According to tradition, the ancient chapel was built during the 14th century. The Marian shrine, which emerged near one of the transhumance routes, is an ancient site of pilgrimage and still attracts numerous believers and features a polychrome wooden statue of the *Virgin and Child*. The church was extensively restored following the damage sustained during the World War II and subsequent earthquakes.

The town of **ORSOGNA** developed along the sheep track but is largely of modern construction as it was destroyed during World War II. However, it still boasts the fine late–Baroque parish **church of San Nicola**. The building was designed by Giovanni Antonio Fontana and commenced in 1780, although it was not finished until after 1810 by Aniello Francia. The façade was completed during the second half of the same century and restored following the damage sustained in the World War II. Inside there is a precious processional cross known to come from the close circle of Nicola da Guardiagrele. A nearby attraction, in the Parco Territoriale Attrezzato dell'Annunziata, is the **Friars Minor Annunziata friary**, with a refectory vaunting 17th-century frescoes. On the Tuesday after Easter the town is the stage for the **Talami** procession of floats carrying Biblical tableaux.

Nearby, on the Reguro sheep track, we find the **Torre di Bene**, once used for levying taxes and tolls. After its restoration, it is a service centre and art gallery.

**TREGLIO**, situated in a panoramic position in the River Feltrino valley, has the fine **Santa Maria Assunta parish church** and opposite Palazzo Di Renzo, with a corner bartizan and garret. The 18th-century former **Palazzo Vescovile** has been renovated recently and is now the town hall.

The town of **MOZZAGROGNA**, which stands on a rise dominating the lower Sangro valley, is renowned for the nearby **Villa Marcantonio**, which was built in eclectic style at the turn of the 20th century, attributed to the Coppedè firm of architects.

**SANTA MARIA IMBARO**, amid lush farmland, owes its name to its location near the L'Aquila–Foggia sheep track (*Sancta Maria in viam Bari*). The aisleless **church of Santa Maria Imbaro** is interesting for its lengthwise layout and apse closure. It is documented as early as the 11th century but has been remodelled several times. Inside there is a statue of the *Madonna and Child* and a *Crucifix* of the 13th-century Abruzzo school.

341. Above: Villa Marcantonio, Mozzagrogna.
342. 343. Below: left, the Torre di Bene on the Tratturo Regio sheep track; right, one of the "Talami" carried on the shoulders of the Alpine regiment of Orsogna.
344. Facing page: aerial view of Vasto.

# Vasto and Hinterland

On the last strip of the Abruzzo coast, almost clinging to a cliff, the town of **VASTO** dominates the coast in the surprising natural scenery of the Golfo d'oro, whose beauty can be fully grasped by looking out from the **Loggia Amblingh**, a breath-taking balcony promenade reaching out to sea. It takes its name from the Austrian Guglielmo Amblingh of Graz, secretary of Cesare Michelangelo d'Avalos, and resident in Vasto in the early 18th century. Nearby is the **house of Gabriele Rossetti**, now home to one of the municipal libraries and further ahead we happen upon the only surviving Medieval urban gate, Porta Santa Maria, also called **Porta Catena**.

Ancient Histonium was the urban centre of the Frentano area, whose major monuments still survive. Although many of the original buildings were destroyed over time or cloaked in Medieval or modern refurbishments, it is still possible to admire the enchanting remains in the historical centre. The most remarkable traces still visible are mainly of the period between the 1st and 2nd century AD, when the town acquired its final urban layout. The oval outline of central Piazza Gabriele Rossetti, dedicated to Vasto's poet and patriot, reflects its former role of amphitheatre and chief monument of the Roman town, built between the late–1st–mid–2nd century AD. It is one of the most impressive in all of Central Italy and its remains of polychrome

Vasto, San Salvo, Lentella, Fresagrandinaria, Dogliola, Tufillo, Celenza sul Trigno, San Giovanni Lipioni, Castelguidone, Schiavi d'Abruzzo, Castiglione Messer Marino, Torrebruna, Carunchio, Fraine, Roccaspinalveti, Montazzoli, Liscia, Palmoli, San Buono, Guilmi, Carpineto Sinello, Furci, Gissi, Casalanguida, Cupello, Monteodorisio, Scerni, Villalfonsina

The area in question, located in the southernmost part of the province of Chieti, on the Molise border and delimited by the Sinello, Treste and Trigno rivers down as far as the coast, is dotted with small hilltop villages, dominated by massive ancient fortresses, standing guard over important routes, immersed in an unadulterated and little-known landscape. Densely wooded, water-rich mountains are a contrast to the capricious and jagged coast. The area's main attractions are the remarkable environmental value of the sites and traditional building features, still partially preserved, together with the ancient urban installations. The district offers thoroughly unexpected landscapes in a perfect combination of human milieu and natural habitat. The splendid town of Vasto is the most outstanding of all the settlements on the last strip of Abruzzi coastline: a thriving commercial centre of Italic origin, now an extremely dynamic modern town, with the development of the Punta Penna industrial estate and businesses in nearby San Salvo, but due also to a lively cultural centre, with a wealth of monuments and works of art.

opus mixtum and reticulatum alternating with brick layers are still visible, in part buried at different depths by modern paving (the northern entrance and a final segment of ellipse are englobed in the Caldora Castle cellars), and in part inserted in the walls that make up the curvilinear façade of the square's eastern side. Sections of the elliptical wall are visible next to the Bassano tower and inside a shop along the same side of the square. South of the square, continuing along Via Cavour, we reach the highest point of the ancient town, where the remains of the nine large **Santa Chiara cisterns**, fed by the ancient Luci aqueduct, are still visible. These impressive structures are made from brick and clad with *opus signinum* – a special hydraulic plaster used by the Romans – and incorporated in the foundations of the block of buildings located around Via Cavour, Piazza Marconi, Piazza Santa Chiara and Vico Moschetto; the rectangular barrel-vaulted rooms have communicating arches.

The section of the town's eastern border devastated by a disastrous landslide in 1956 begins in Piazza del Popolo. The landslide brought to light numerous remains of the ancient settlement's walls, visible today on Via Adriatica. Here we see the façade of the **medieval church of San Pietro**, its handsome portal the only element surviving of the building demolished after the landslide. In the lower section of the walls, alternating sections of polychrome reticulate and brick, attributable to an older building, were reused in the church, and can be seen in the façade. Continuing along Via Adriatica, northeast of the residential area, we reach the archaeological area of the ancient **Roman baths**, which were recovered thanks to complex archaeological excavation and restoration, and are now open for visits. The complex, which dates back to the 2nd century AD, comprised three terraced levels down the slope between the churches of Sant'Antonio and Santa Maria delle Grazie. The restoration of the spa complex began in 1994 and included *in situ* recovery and re-laying of the first important **mosaic**, discovered in 1974, featuring some splendid marine illustrations. Also extraordinary is the more recent

## Caldora Castle, Vasto

The castle's current layout comprises four blocks set around a rectangular courtyard with the longer sides facing east and west, reinforced at the corners by distinctive bulwarks. Although it was originally a keep that later developed into a fortress, the castle nevertheless preserves some archaic elements, like the machicolations overhanging the mandorla ramparts that coexist with the round, outmoded towers. The western and northern portions have successfully retained original features that are not found in the others, and whose appearance has been heavily altered by additions and replacements made around the latter half of the 19th century.

The original building, a square plan with round corner towers – only two of which have survived – incorporated another round tower that dates to somewhere between the 14th and 15th centuries. The original castle was then refurbished in about 1439by Giacomo Caldora, feudatory of Vasto, using more up-to-date fortification techniques, then converted into a fort towards the end of the 15th century, at the time of Innico d'Avalos, which incorporated the pre-existing fortification, strengthening it with new curtain walls and mandorla corner brick ramparts (one of which is missing today). The lance-shaped tower ramparts are low, without openings and on a sloping base, with middle cornice and jutting Gothic arches. The use of lance-shaped towers is a remarkable evolution in the fortification technique because it minimized the vulnerability of the corner by increasing its resistance. Possible subsequent interventions commissioned by Cesare d'Avalos may have been undertaken in the early–18th century. In abot the mid–1800s the building was partly converted for residential use, along the side facing onto the square.

discovery of a second, priceless, large black and white mosaic floor, characterized by interlacing stylized vegetable elements that create a central quatrefoil dominated by the figure of *Neptune and his trident*. Four Nereids are depicted in the other eight fields, two on horseback, one on a dragon and one on a seahorse. Later excavations brought to light four rooms with a heating system, brick floor still intact, and the complex's heating structures including the *praefurnium* (furnace). At the end of Via Adriatica we find the **church of Sant'Antonio**, with an interesting Gothic portal and a fine Baroque interior with paintings by the Palizzi brothers and a wooden crucifix attributed to the sculptor Giacomo Colombo. To the left of the church we see a long section of wall in polychrome opus mixtum and brick layers from the ancient complex (late–1st–early– 2nd century AD), incorporated into the current block's ground floor structures.

Taking Corso Palazzi, we reach Via V. Laccetti, below which we find the so-called small cisterns on the corner. One of these a barrel-vaulted brick rooms supplied by the ancient Murello aqueduct is still visible. Along Via Laccetti we can enter the 1700s **Trinità church**, whose left wall was constructed in ancient opus reticulatum masonry, of which a 2m-high section survives.

The magnificent **Caldora castle** (*see box p. 204*), with its fascinating complex stratification, is found between Piazza Rossetti, site of some of Vasto's loveliest monuments, and Piazza Barbacani.

The presence of round towers on the eastern side of the urban perimeter, which also includes the castle, is significant; they were altered in the 15th-century layout when more storeys were added. The round **Bassano tower**, with part of the ancient walls, stands near the square, and was recently restored and reinforced. This is a brick construction with machicolations on corbels supporting archlets with decorative brickwork. Now a prestigious museum hub, **Palazzo d'Avalos** (*see box p. 207*) closes Piazza Lucio Valerio Pudente, its frontage another outstanding feature of the meticulous urban planning of the old town. This richly decorated and furnished stately home was the seat of a real court in about the mid–18th century: a palace looking out to sea, erected over the layered past of Roman, early-Medieval and certainly 1400s remains but rebuilt in the classic lines preferred in the 16th–18th centuries. Piazza Lucio Valerio Pudente is also home to the **cathedral of San Giuseppe**, completely refurbished at the end of the 19th century with stylistic modifications dictated by the revival trend of the day. The ancient church annexed to the convent of the Augustinians, originally the church of Santa Margherita, was embellished by the rich portal, engraved on the lunette with the year of its construction, 1293, and the name of the architect, Ruggiero

345. Facing page: Caldora castle.
346. Above: portal of the Medieval church of San Pietro.
347. 348. Below: left, Porta Catena; right, detail of the mosaic of *Neptune with trident*.

349. 350. Above: round Bassano tower in Piazza Rossetti and the cathedral of San Giuseppe, Vasto.
351–353. Facing page, top to below: self–portrait of Filippo Palizzi, Pinacoteca Civica; Roman funerary urn, Museo Archeologico; Palazzo d'Avalos, all in Vasto.

de Fragenis, today the only trace of the Medieval church. It was burned down by the Turks in 1566 and restored in 1568, as told by the plaque placed inside the main entrance on the right. In about 1730, the bell tower was rebuilt. In 1808 the ancient Augustinian church was raised to the status of parish for all of Vasto and renamed as San Giuseppe. It was subsequently further elevated to rank of cathedral in 1853. It had been declared dangerous in 1842 and it was completely rebuilt in Gothic style to designs by the engineer Francesco Benedetti but not completed until after his demise, in the early–20th century. Striking aspects include a Tuscan- and Puglia-inspired dual colour scheme, ribbed vaults and lancet arches indicating that the architect was an expert in Medieval architectural codes. In the 1970s the surviving structures of the adjoining convent were demolished, definitively isolating the façade, which became a dramatic backdrop for the oldest square in the city. Worthy of note are the 19th-century statue of St Joseph and a triptych dated 1505, by Albanian artist Michele Greco of Valona, active in the early–16th century in Abruzzo and Molise, an exponent of Greek–Byzantine painting in the context of the artistic trend identified as the "Adriatic Renaissance" by some scholars. The opus is a cuspid tabernacle comprising a central panel depicting *Our Lady of Mercy with Child* and side panels with *Saints Catherine of Alexandria and Nicholas of Mira*.

The striking **church of Santa Maria Maggiore** was built in the distant past and acquired its current late–Baroque appearance in 1785. The internal stucco decoration, with inflexible geometric motifs, was completed in 1853. We can see the signs of the original phase in the right-hand side and in the powerful structure of the bell tower. We will find some remarkable paintings inside by Francesco Solimena. The **Sacra Spina chapel** is worth a visit, with its Holy Thorne relic, given to the town by the D'Avalos family in the 1500s. Said to be from Christ's crown of thorns, the relic is especially venerated, above all during the Good Friday religious procession.

The splendid late–Baroque stucco decoration inside the **church of Sant'Antonio** was completely renovated in the 1730s and 1740s, and there are some sumptuous side altars. Also interesting ancient is the **church of San Francesco di Paola**, renovated under Cesare Michelangelo d'Avalos (1697–1729), now with a 19th-century façade. Inside we find priceless paintings by Nicola Maria Rossi and Filippo Andreola, pupils of Solimena, and an interesting *Pietà*.

The **church of Santa Maria Del Carmine** is a noteworthy example of Abruzzo Baroque, rebuilt in 1758–61 on the site of the older San Nicola degli Schiavoni church, designed by famous Neapolitan architect Mario Gioffredo. The symmetry of the plan is offset by the greater depth of the entrance wing, flanked by two side blocks. The cupola of the central chamber, invisible externally, has neither a tambour nor clerestory. The inside space is cadenced by slightly embedded cantons and Corinthian columns, with 18th century Neapolitan fluting. The central cupola's lacunar motif is of clear classical inspiration. The façade, cadenced by two pairs of pilasters, features a stone portal by Molise mason Giovanni Crisostomo Calvitto, to a design by Gioffredo. The 1762–5 stucco decorations by Michele Saccione are interesting, and Fedele Fischetti's paintings in the side chapels are noteworthy, as is the *Presentation of Mary* canvas by Crescenzo La Gamba for the high altar.

The Baroque wooden high altar in the **church of San Michele Arcangelo** is noteworthy. This octagonal building was completed around 1675 and enlarged at the end of the 1930s.

Also in Via Luigi Marchesani, the elegant, recently restored **Teatro Rossetti**, built in 1818 over the old Santo Spirito church annexe to the Celestine convent.

ancient and contested feud of the Lupara, also site of a farmingl village that has since disappeared. During the early 16th century, the ancient chapel, already mentioned in the 14th century, was part of a more extensive convent refurbished and managed by the Minor Friars Minor Order. After an 18th-century reconstruction, the monastery declined during the 19th century and the church was destroyed during World War II, then built in its present form in 1943. The site was a strategic transit node for the sheep track and a much-used place for business dealings. A strong religious vocation is testified by the traditional **Madonna del Monte feast**, now celebrated in September, with its fair once popular in the pastoral world. The town comes alive for the famous Castiglione carnival with the popular parade of masks led by a large group of **Pulcinellas** (a mask characterized above all by the immense and imaginative conical hat).
Worth seeing is the **Museo delle Tradizioni Familiari** displaying local handicrafts. The **Oasi Naturale Abetina di Selva Grande**, managed by the WWF, with its rare silver fir wood, is worth visiting.
The ancient fortified village of **TORREBRUNA** is located on the southeast of the tall Carunchina and Civitella hills, in a position overlooking the middle Trigno valley. The village developed on the hillside, hugging its contours, in all likelihood a fortified structure that expanded on the southern side. At the apex of the village is the **Trasfigurazione church** with a portal decorated by the Caracciolo Pignatelli coat of arms and, inside, an 18th-century wooden organ All that remains of the ancient wall is the **Porta Murella** gate, the wall-houses of Via Orientale and a round tower of the urban walls. Noteworthy the quaint 18th century fountain in Piazza 4 Novembre.
The heart of village of Guardiabruna is the interesting **Piccirilli baronial mansion-castle**, built on the rock, which forms the centrepiece of the settlement, presumably the result of the conversion of an existing garrison. In Piazza Santa Vittoria there are the remains of the homonymous church.
**CARUNCHIO**, perched on a hill to the right of the River Treste, was established as a fortified village, whose nucleus was called Case Turdò and can be seen in the current site

of **Palazzo Turdò,** belonged to the Tour d'Eau family of Marseille origin, who settled in the area in the 1700s. The elegant residence with corner bartizans recalls the fortified country villa concept. Palazzo Turdò, together with **Palazzo Castelli**, is one of the most important monuments. Traces remain of the urban walls in wall-house structures and **Porta Coluccia**, the village gate. In the heart of the village there is the parish church of **San Giovanni Battista**, founded according to some sources in 1570 over an older structure and then modified several times. On the dome pendentives we see the figures of the *Four Evangelists* painted in 1857 by Guardiagrele artist Francesco Maria De Benedictis. There is also the recently restored wooden choir and the stunning organ, whose mechanical parts were repaired and modified in 1775 by Francesco d'Onofrio.
The more recent village of Sant'Antonio revolves around the square where the **church of Santa Maria del Purgatorio**, formerly of Sant'Antonio, was seriously damaged during the last war. The beautiful portal dated 1504 and the remains of frescoes inside survive. **Palazzo Grosso** and the monumental 1895 fountain are also interesting, on the site of the ancient parish church, how demolished.
**FRAINE** is set on a hill of the Costa Crognale ridge, between the River Treste and the Lama torrent. The earliest sector, established as a fortified village, is around two monuments: the parish **church of San Silvestro** and Palazzo Tilli, a fine example of 18th–19th-century noble dwellings. Traces remain of the fortifications in some wall-houses on the east side Subsequent expansions can also be identified: one section facing southwest, towards the chapel of Santa Maria and another, smaller quarter, to the north, towards the cemetery chapel of San Rocco.
Nearby, the **Sanctuary of Santa Maria in Mater Domini** stands on the site where a shepherd girl had a vision of the Virgin Mary among the trees. Documented in the 11th century, the sanctuary was modified in the 19th and 20th centuries.
The town of **ROCCASPINALVETI** rises on the Forra della Scarpa slopes, in the upper River Sinello valley. The new Roccaspinalveti is an interesting example of a 19th-century layout, dating to the period when the ancient inhabited area was permanently abandoned

because of the instability of the slope, then rebuilt lower down in the valley, on its present site. The ancient Medieval centre has a characteristic concentric structure hugging the contours and clustered around the derelict **church of Santa Vittoria e San Nicola**. The new **San Michele Arcangelo parish church**, built after 1850 is noteworthy for several artworks brough from the church of Santa Vittoria, as well as an 18th-century organ, and 19th-century papier-mâché statues by Michele Falcucci, active during the late–1800s. A stunning silver processional cross is attributed – for its "knot" style – to Nicola da Guardiagrele. In the eponymous district there are traces of the ancient **church of San Pietro**.

The picturesque village of **MONTAZZOLI** is built on the summit of a ridge that flanks the upper Sinello River course, on the left, at the centre of a district of considerable landscape value, between the woody slopes of Mount Fischietto, Lake Negro and countless springs. The district is fairly intact from an environmental viewpoint. The delay in industrial development in the River Sinello valley has contributed in part to the preservation of the of the centres and of the agricultural landscape. The Medieval quarter is to the east, on Colle Ripa, and is dominated by the massive **Franceschelli Castle**, which was used for surveillance and control of the Sinello River valley and the Roccaspinalveti and Castiglione mountains behind, as well as the nearby sheep track. This complex originated from an older square tower set on the highest point of the site, around an irregular court, with cisterns and material from the 15th century, while the residential and service areas may date back to the 17th–18th centuries. Despite natural calamities and interference over time that accelerated the structure's decline, leading to reconstruction of some parts, the building is still in authentic symbiosis with the surrounding landscape and a monument of some cultural significance. Very close to the castle stands the Baroque parish **church of San Silvestro Papa**, founded on the site of the pre-existing chapel of San Vincenzo and replacing the ancient Purgatorio parish church. Behind this stands the **church of Sant'Antonio**, perhaps rebuilt in the 1700s over an existing chapel. Some secular buildings were erected for noble families, close to the oldest nucleus in a southerly direction. The subsequent blocks originated from the suburban market area, where **Palazzo Recchia** (now the town hall) was built between the 1700s and 1800s. Some noble residences like **Palazzo Franceschelli** and **Palazzo Monaco** have elegant round portals with refined ashlars. Another unique detail is the travertine moulding, while jutting corbels made out of so-called "smooth" stone – also used at one time instead of roof tiles – are sometimes used for the trim. Outside of the inhabited area, rural residences such as the **Baronessa Bonessa farmhouse** and **Villa Franceschelli** are especially interesting for their design, as well as for the refined workmanship of some of the decorative details. Of particular importance in the surrounding area are the San Giovanni church and the recently restored **Madonna della Spogna church**, with its statue of the *Virgin Mary* the subject of special worship.

**LISCIA** is located on the southeast slopes of Colle San Giovanni, to the left of the River Treste. The original nucleus was presumably a fortified village set around the **church of San Martino**, which scholars deem to have been founded in the 1300s but modified in the mid–1700s. The precious portal survives and lovely stuccoes inside. Nearby there is also the **church of San Michele**, with an entrance to lovely San Michele Arcangelo **cave**, a destination on 8 May for a popular pilgrimage that follows ancient rituals linked to the miraculous properties of the waters.

The village of **PALMOLI** is on a hilltop to the right of the River Treste. The original nucleus, established as a fortified village, is identifiable in the characteristic fishbone layout with a central path leading to the Medieval **castle-mansion**, but with extensive subsequent changes that brought about the current configuration of the marquess's residence. The complex has an impressive tower with a polygonal sloping base, a round central core finished by embattled brick coping. Rectangular windows open on each side of the polygonal tower, except for one side on which an exposed stone building was installed as a noble residence. Attached to the castle is the 18th-century **San Carlo chapel** of Baroque form. The castle is a village landmark and now home to the town hall and the **Museo Civico della Tradizione Contadina**. In the heart of the Medieval village we find the **Santa Maria delle Grazie church** and nearby the **Madonna del Carmine sanctuary**, said to have been built in the 13th century but modified over time. On the morning of 27 July the village comes alive for the *Pacchianelle* procession of girls in traditional costume, who carry the Madonna del Carmine donations, mostly foodstuffs, which are then auctioned in the afternoon.

**SAN BUONO** is located on a hill slope to the left of the River Treste. The original layout stretched from Largo Sant'Angelo to the parish church and encircled the site now occupied by the church and by **Palazzo Caracciolo**, which we now see in its 17th–18th-century guise. The changes were ordered by the Caracciolo family, who adapted the early castle structure, transforming it into a residence, especially after it was raised to the status of principality (1590). There are some interesting examples of 18th–19th-century civil building from the Baroque **Palazzo Rosso** to other, more recent constructions like the more modest 19th-century **Palazzo Carmenini** or **Palazzo Cerella** on Largo Sant'Angelo. In the parish **church of San Lorenzo** there are some remarkable 17th-century Neapolitan school paintings and an 18th-century marble altar, which came from the nearby **convent of Sant'Antonio di Padova**, also noteworthy for its harmonious relationship with its environment. The complex was founded in the 16th-century for the Franciscan Friars Minor by the San Buono Caracciolos, but the church acquired its current appearance following renovations carried out in the 1730s. The aisleless church has four barrel-vaulted bays with lunettes, with three side chapels on the right, dedicated to St Francis, St Anthony of Padua and St Diego. The middle chapel, which houses the 1762 statue of *St Anthony*, is unique for its cupola on pendentives with external tiburium. There is a charming light stucco interior with a hint of Rococo. The slightly convex façade is lively, divided into three levels by pairs of overlapping pilasters, animated by a lively chromatic device obtained thanks to the use of different materials, unfortunately partially reduced after some restoration. The portal opens on the first level, embellished with a fastigium with a Franciscan emblem; at the top there is a large

364. 365. Facing page: left, the cave of San Michele Arcangelo, Liscia; right, the "Pacchianelle" festival, Palmoli.
366. Below: Palazzo Marchesale, Palmoli.

window surmounted in the last level by a niche with the statue of the saint.
The interesting **Museo per l'Arte e l'Archeologia Vastese** is housed inside the convent, with finds of the material and artistic culture of the Vasto district, from the Pleistocene to the Middle Ages.

**GUILMI** is located on the northwest slopes of Colle San Giovanni, which overlooks the upper Sinello valley from the right. The semi-circular layout around the **Immacolata Concezione parish church**, a striking element of the old centre. The church was remodelled in the 1700s and the 1766 Baroque portal has survived Only place names remain to sugges the presence of a castle. **Palazzo Lizzi** is interesting and in Via Torrione we can visit the **Museo degli antichi mestieri**, exhibiting ancient household objects, furnishings and more on the ground floor of an ancient building that was recently renovated. The town is famous for the production of the delicious ventricina, a typical salami from the upper Vasto area.

**CARPINETO SINELLO** sits on a steep hill, a spectacular bijou village of ancient origins, with a contour structure favoured by its aspecting. Today's village lies between the parish **church of San Michele Arcangelo** and Salita Vico Storto and Salita del Tritone. The Medieval-style portal suggests the church was built in the 13th–14th century. In the centre we find the **Bassi-D'Alanno castle**, refurbished as an elegant residence during the 18th century, a remarkable building even though today it is in decline, dominating the town and the surrounding territory. The castle, on a hilltop that overlooks the Sinello valley, is a striking part of the territory and landscape, and has definitely been a primary element in urban development. The north tower is probably original to the castle which ruled by the County of Sangro in the late–12th century. The fortress, which became the stable headquarters of the feudal lords, progressively acquired the appearance of a mansion, up to the 18th-century changes by Baron Michele Bassi. The complex includes several buildings around a small courtyard and has a typical interior with a spectacular great staircase and frescoed rooms. In the vicinity of the old slaughterhouse, the **Museo del Maiale** illustrates the customs, traditions and food culture related to pork, with five displays. There is also the opportunity to sample and purchase related products.

**FURCI**, on the slope of a hill ridge between the Sinello and Treste rivers, was founded as a fortified village whose traits are still visible today. The hilltop section clusters around the parish **church of San Sabino**, restored in the 17th century but presumably built earlier than this, and with 15th-century statues. A surviving round tower with sloping base, part of the fortifications, flanks the gate to the ancient section. In the vicinity is the modern **Beato Angelo da Furci sanctuary**, dedicated to the miracle-worker whose tomb is the object of special devotion.

The old layout of **GISSI**, located along a hill between the Ferrato and Morgitella torrents, which flow into the River Sinello, is still visible as it clusters around the **Santa Maria Assunta parish church**, with a beautiful 17th-century wooden organ wind-chest. One gate into the village survives and, in some buildings, there are still 18th–19th-century decorative details. Of interest also 19th-century **Palazzo Carunchio**, once residence of the Carunchio family, from whom it takes its name, and now the town hall.

The village of **CASALANGUIDA** stands on a spur on the Montagnola slope, between the Osento and Sinello valleys. Traces remain of the wall and towers that once surrounded the original settlement, clustered around the parish church. These include the **Palazzo Procaccini** tower, with a porch and rusticated portal on the square, and the tower englobed into **Palazzo Cauli**, to the east of the ancient sector. Also worth seeing is the **church of Santa Maria Maddalena**, documented since the 1300s but today in the guise of 19th-century changes. Nearby is the beautiful 1800s monumental stone fountain with decorative cast-iron elements.

**CUPELLO** stands to the right of the Sinello valley, its district delimited by the Trigno and Treste rivers and the Cena torrent, crossed by two sheep tracks (Centurelle–Montesecco, Lanciano–Cupello). Its present structure dates back to the early 19th century when it separated from the municipality of Monteodorisio and acquired administrative independence. The establishment of the original section most likely dates back to the early 16th century when the d'Avalos marquises of Vasto used colonies of Slavs who arrived in Abruzzo after the Turkish invasion of their homeland. They were able to settle here and develop agriculture.

The oldest nucleus develops between Piazza Garibaldi and Via Orientale, where we find the **Maria SS della Natività church**, restored and enlarged at the end of the 19th century.

The terraced configuration of the site fostered a dynamic expansion of the built-up area during the past 30 years, with regular layout and the progressive decentralization of old Cupello and its functions. An interesting stately home is **Palazzo Boschetti**. The **Travaglini-Fiori** and **Di Stefano-Muzii houses**, and the important **Del Re villa and park complex**, are built on Via XX Settembre, the road to Monteodorisio, at a tangent to the village.

**MONTEODORISIO** is a hill village of considerable interest, situated in the Sinello valley, with some extremely important architectural monuments. The first settlement, which is thought to date back to the 10th century, is located to the southeast on Colle Capo di Rocca. Strategically built at the top of the village, the **castle** overlooks the Sinello valley and despite alterations and some inexpert remodelling, it is one of the most interesting fortified complexes in the region because of the historical events surrounding it and the construction characteristics, similar in type to Ortona and Ortucchio. The building, whose original quadrangular layout with round, sloping corner towers are ascribable to the 15th century, is still visible and is strongly characterized by its original defence function. The castle acquired its present residential configuration after a series of refurbishments following its passing from the Caldora to the d'Avalos family. The curtain walls and three of the four towers are partially preserved. The west tower is embellished by a corbel coping, without machicolations, since it is purely decorative, surmounted by

367–369. Facing page, left to right: the parish church of San Lorenzo, San Buono; the round tower, Furci; the church of Santa Maria della Natività, Cupello.
370. Below: Monteodorisio castle.

a frieze. An unusual decorative motif can be seen in the north tower, with bricks set in a herringbone pattern. The walls were for the most part built using local materials, mainly pebbles and bricks. Today there is a private home in what was the fourth tower. A water tank, improperly installed against the castle, to the south has irremediably affected the context. Today the castle is home to a museum and documentation centre: Museo per l'economia tra antichità e rinascimento – Centro di Documentazione dell'Ordine francescano in Abruzzo e Molise.

Along Via Muro Rotto we find traces of the fortified urban walls with the round **Muro Rotto tower** and an escarpment flanked by ancient buildings and 19th-century mansions, coeval with the Largo Porta Carbonara tower, which is the fulcrum of the Capo di Rocca quarter, where there are traces of a square base tower called "il Castelluccio", an ancient watchtower. There are some remarkable examples of 19th-century building, including **Palazzo Suriani**, which contains wall decorations by Neapolitan artists Nicola Biondi and Gaetano D'Agostino, as well as **Palazzo Fanghella** with an elegant portal. There is also the interesting parish **church of San Giovanni Battista** with a precious carved organ dated 1757, the work of Francesco D'Onofrio.

The **Madonna delle Grazie sanctuary** is located in the vicinity, built near one of the transhumance tracks; today it is still the destination of a pilgrimage on the first Sunday in September. It was erected between 1887 and 1895, in eclectic style, to a design by an engineer from Vasto called Francesco Benedetti, and the interior was decorated between the end of the 19th century and the early 20th century by the Neapolitan painters Nicola Biondi and Gaetano d'Agostino who executed here a rare example of religious Art Nouveau painting. The numerous ex-votos in a room adjoining the church bear witness to the diffusion of this cult.

Small **SCERNI** stands on a hilly ridge, with Colle dei Sospiri rolling towards the Sinello valley, known for its numerous vineyards and olive groves as well as for the prestigious agricultural college.

This village has an older section, of Medieval origin, still clearly recognizable, around which the more modern blocks of buildings developed. Impressive **Palazzo De Riseis**, a late 19th-century construction owned by an influential local family, is set to the west of the original fortified village, on the square of the same name. The interesting parish **church of San Panfilo** is now seen in its 19th-century reconstruction guise designed by the engineer Luigi Dau.

The complex of buildings generically identified as **Castello Antenucci** is located to the east of the ancient nucleus, with substantial remains of **brick walls and two sloping towers**, modified over time, belonging to the early Medieval fortifications. It is worth mentioning some examples of late–19th-century and early–20th-century buildings, including **Casa Ciccarone**, **Casa Marollo**, **Casa De Mia**, **Casa De Risio**, **Casa Ranalli** and **Palazzo Raimondi** on Piazza De Riseis.

The early–1500s *Enthroned Madonna and Child* statue of the Aquilan school is found in the modern **Madonna della Strada church**, built over an older chapel near the Centurelle-Montesecco sheep track, which crosses municipal territory. The artwork seems to bear a resemblance to the style of the sculptor Giovanni Antonio da Lucoli. There are also two interesting wooden sculptures dated 14th-century, one of *St Pamphilus* and one of *St Donatus*. The ancient chapel of Santa Maria, at one time with a small portico to shelter pilgrims and shepherds, was built on the spot where a legend tells that an older image of the Virgin was found after it had been stolen by some inhabitants of Atessa, then abandoned as it became – miraculously – too heavy to be carried.

The **rural church of San Giacomo** is also found in the vicinity of the sheep track; erected before 1850 and then rebuilt in its present form during the 1930s.

The village of **VILLALFONSINA**, built on the crest of a hill to the right of the River Osento, near the Ripari stream, was founded towards the very end of the 16th century by Alfonso d'Avalos, housing his colony of slaves here. Originally a farming settlement, it is characterized by a linear layout on a ridge. In addition to the **Madonna della Neve parish church**, in Baroque style, there are interesting examples of stately homes such as **Palazzo Salerni Gizzi** and **Palazzo Cinosi**. The public fountain and nearby 19th-century **Villa Adami** are interesting.

# Sangro River Valley

The tiny but highly evocative stone village of **PERANO** is on the crest of a hill to the left of the River Pianello, amidst orchards and olive groves, offering splendid views over the Sangro valley. Long a fiefdom of the abbey of San Giovanni in Venere, the village is clustered around the parish **church di San Tommaso Apostolo**. Every year since 2001, the Raffaele Pellicciotta National Literary Prize has been held there, in honour of the town's humanist and scholar.

Nearby, the small old town of **ARCHI** is on a wooded hill between the Pianello and Sangro rivers. The original settlement is arranged along the crest in a typical elongated pattern, dominated by the ruins of the castle and the **church of Santa Caterina** in Piazza Castello, probably founded in the 17th-century and with an interesting statue depicting *St Catherine of Alexandria*, attributable to the circle of Giovanni Antonio da Lucoli. The town develops lengthwise along Via Palazzo, closed next to Palazzo Cieri by an ogival arch, **Porta Cieri** presumably the ancient Porta da Piedi gate, situated at the opposite end to the Porta da Capo that once stood next to **Lannutti Castle**. However, after having been used an important outpost to block the advance of the British Allied troops, the castle was destroyed by the Germans during World War II. Although the imposing castle, situated at the highest point of the site, is now in ruins, it nonetheless constitutes one of the most important architectural

Perano, Archi, Tornareccio, Atessa, Bomba, Colledimezzo, Pietraferrazzana, Monteferrante, Roio del Sangro, Rosello, Borrello, Quadri, Pizzoferrato, Gamberale, Fallo, Civitaluparella, Villa Santa Maria, Montelapiano, Montebello sul Sangro, Pennadomo

The itinerary winds along the breath-taking valley of the Sangro, Abruzzo's second most important river in terms of flow and length, which forms an enchanting artificial lake with shores dotted with pleasant tourist resorts on its shores. The delightful villages perched on the higher spots overlooking the lake and the natural havens that preserve these unique habitats make this area one of the most interesting in Abruzzo. The important archaeological ruins of Mount Pallano constitute another attraction along the route.

371. Facing page: Madonna della Neve parish church, Villalfonsina.
372. Below: aerial view of Archi.

testimonies of the fortified village. The fortress, located in a highly strategic position between the Sangro and Aventino river valleys, was one of the strongholds of the Caldora fortifications for the control of the southern entrance to the central Sangro valley. The castle, subsequently transformed into a baronial palace, had an almost square plan, with mighty cylindrical towers at the corners, which are still partially visible today. The building features traditional rough-hewn stone and mortar construction. Analysis of the curtain walls reveals the many modifications that were made over the years.

In addition to the **SS Rosario church** and the **San Rocco church**, with its lovely statue of St Roche by sculptor Gabriele Falcucci, called the "deaf mute of Atessa", and the former **church of San Giovanni Battista**, now owned by the municipality and used for meetings and conferences, it is worth visiting the parish **church of Santa Maria dell'Olmo** in Via dell'Olmo or Via della Chiesa, which a fine 15th-century panel painting of *Our Lady of the Elm*, a wooden crucifix by the sculptor Gioacchino Pelliciotti of Peran, and the 17th-century canvas depicting *St Vitalis*, by the Atessa painter Felice Ciccarelli.

In the surrounding area, the natural Oasi Vallescura lake is a lovely place to practice angling.

**TORNARECCIO**, on a spur on the Mount Pallano slopes, dominates an extensive territory that reaches from the mountains around Vasto to the Adriatic coast. It is also known as the birthplace of Pasquale Borelli (1782–1849), doctor, jurist and philosopher who was president of the Parliament of Naples in 1821.

A farming town, it is renowned for its dairy products and especially for its excellent honey. The **Porta Nuova** gate enters the Medieval village, which retains two round towers from the ancient urban walls, now englobed in the houses. The village is still characterized by its typical cluster plan around the parish **church of Santa Vittoria**, which was founded in ancient times, but extended during the 1700s and 1800a, when it assumed its current Latin-cross plan with a nave and two aisles. In addition to the **church of San Rocco**, there is the beautiful 19th-century fountain in Piazza Fontana, called "Piano la Porta", while the most interesting buildings in the historic centre include **Palazzo Daniele** and **Palazzo Melocchi**.

Nearby is the **church of Madonna del Carmine**, which was founded in the 16th century, but rebuilt between 1886 and 1897, while the bell tower dates back to the 1930s. All that remains of the old chapel are the altar, the niche and the Baroque reredos with the two statues of *St Apollonia* and *St Lucy*. The church has a rectangular plan with a nave and two aisles, and a small apse, now used as a sacristy. It has a 15th-century polychrome terracotta statue of the *Virgin and Child*, traditionally attributed to Gian Francesco Gagliardelli, but recently ascribed by Enrico Santangelo to the small circle of Paolo Aquilano. The façade was designed by Vasto engineer Francesco Benedetti and built in 1894, while the large square in front of the church, with

373. Below: the megalithic walls of Pallanum, in Tornareccio.
374. 375. Facing page: Porta San Giuseppe (above) and aerial view (below) of Atessa.

staircase and campanile, are recent additions.

The old fortified Italic town of **Pallanum** was on the imposing Mount Pallano massif, which dominates the central and lower Sangro valley, for control, defence and shelter of the population and the livestock, and now part of the Monte Pallano archaeology park. Still visible today, the extraordinary **megalithic walls** were presumably built by the Lucano people between the 5th and 4th centuries BC, and in some cases incorporate natural rocky outcrops.

Along the boundary walls, visible for about 160 metres, blocking access to the mountain from the northeast, there are still access gates: Porta del Piano and Porta del Monte, with typical mighty lintels. The presence of several stone shelters testifies to the presence of shepherds, who reached the site from the nearby sheep track. In nearby Fonte Benedetti there are still ruins of an extensive Italic–Roman settlement, which developed between the 2nd century BC and the 1st century AD.

**ATESSA** stands on two hills south of the Sangro valley, along the ridge that divides the Sangro and Osento rivers. An old legend narrates that the old town formed by fusing the two villages of Ate and Tixa, now identified in the two districts of San Michele and Santa Croce, the latter also called Castello and which has preserved its old urban structure. The gates include the imposing **Porta San Nicola** (Arco Adriano), rebuilt in the 18th century, the 13th-century **Porta San Giuseppe** and the more modest Porta Santa Giusta, while the **Porta Santa Margherita** still stands on the western side of town. The east side is clustered around the church. The point in which the two centres merge is the flat area between Piazza Benedetti and the beginning of Via Castello, and the site of the town hall and the fine **church of San Leucio** (*see box p. 222*), documented as far back as the 9th century. Examples of 16th-century buildings are rare but include **Palazzo Flocco** in the Castello district and **Palazzo Coccia-Ferri**. There are more examples of 18th–19th-century buildings like **Palazzo Codagnone** and **Palazzo Mascitelli**. In addition to the 19th-century **Palazzo Spaventa**, there is the outstanding **Palazzo Marcolongo**, built in 1724 in Neapolitan Baroque style.

The many religious buildings include the **Madonna della Cintura church**, with its sumptuous interiors, and the **church of San Domenico**, founded in the 1200s with a convent annex. There is a striking 17th-century marble portal and, inside, a terracotta statue of St Dominic. the old convent is now a theatre and municipal offices. The aisleless **church of San Rocco** has a Baroque interior with a canvas of *Our Lady*

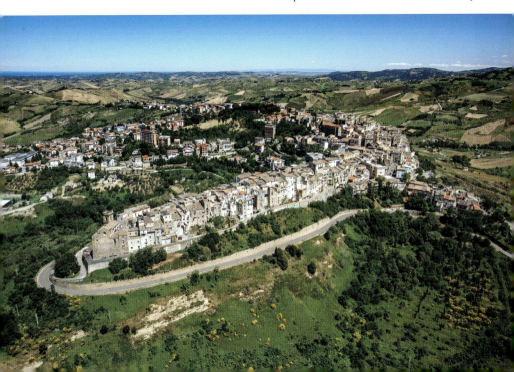

# Church of San Leucio, Atessa

The church of San Leucio is a true architectural and art masterpiece and has been mentioned in sources since the 9th century. The outstanding feature of the monumental façade, the result of a 1935 restoration, is the splendid portal, attributed to the school of Lanciano artisan Francesco Petrini. The rose window surmounted by the agnus cruciger and the symbolic representations of the four Evangelists, formerly at the sides of the rose window, are thought to be part of a 14th-century phase of the church. The interior may originally have had a nave and two aisles and acquired a further two aisles during the 18th century, when the façade was also modified with typically Baroque elements, which were subsequently removed during a 19th-century restoration. While the interpretation of the various stratifications of the monument is a stimulating exercise, the interior of the church offers furnishings of considerable artistic interest like an 18th-century wooden choir and an organ with a facing produced by the famous Mascio carvers of Atessa, to whom other splendid furnishings are attributed, including the pulpit, the wooden choir and the episcopal throne. There are also a remarkable silver crucifix of the Neapolitan school and a silver bust of St Leucius, in addition to the mythical "rib of the dragon" from the beast that according to legend the saint slaughtered to free Atessa. The greatest attraction of the church, however, is the magnificent **monstrance**, a 1418 masterpiece by Nicola da Guardiagrele, one of the greatest exponents of the goldsmith's art in the early Renaissance. The two altarpieces, *St Michael the Archangel Fighting Satan* and the *Education of the Virgin Mary*, produced in 1854 by Guardiagrele artist, Francesco Maria De Benedictis, loyal pupil of Nicola Ranieri. A recent restoration has also brought to light two frescoes datable to the 13th–14th century.

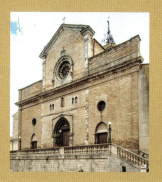

*of Mount Carmel* by Atessa painter, Felice Ciccarelli, dated 1603. Behind the church is the building that once housed the Carmelite monastery, founded at the beginning of the 17th century and later a hospital. Another interesting attraction is the **church of Santa Croce**, on the outskirts of the town and once the site of continuous pilgrimages. The interior was enlarged during the 18th century and has lavish Baroque decoration.

In May the town comes to life for the ritual *'ntorcia* di San Martino. Worshippers set off from Atessa carrying a great wax torch and the procession winds along the Sangro, Aventino and Verde valleys, as far as the Santo Spirito gorge, near Fara San Martino, the site of the monastery of San Martino in Valle. This event has its roots in an ancient farming rite.

Nearby, visitors can admire the **San Pasquale monastery** and the **church of Santa Maria degli Angeli** in the district of Vallaspra. Founded in the 15th century, the church was extended in the 17th-18th centuries with the addition of an aisle to the right of the original rectangular nave. A wide arcade leads to the convent cloister with the so-called "miracle well" in the centre. It is said that during an exceptionally dry season, the St Martin caused miraculous water to gush from the well. The church consists of a roofed nave and a presbytery with frescoed vault. The aisle features a cross vault, as does the adjoining porch that leads to the monastery and the cloister. At the end of the 18th century the third bay of the aisle was "perforated", covered with a calotte and transformed into the entrance to a new square chapel, surmounted by a cupola with pendentives, in which a marble altar was placed. The bell tower collapsed in 1925.

The picturesque village of **BOMBA** (430m) sits on the western slopes of Mount Pallano, on the right side of the central Sangro River valley, blocked by a dam in this spot, forming a lake that stretches for 7km, as far as Pietraferrazzana. Its unspoiled natural setting, traditional architecture and old town plan are the main attractions of Bomba. The settlement is arranged in concentric rings around a circular hill and focuses on the imposing parish **church of Santa Maria del Popolo**, and the site of an old castle or tower that monitored the Sangro (modern-day Largo or Piano della Torre). The parish church was rebuilt during the Baroque period in an understated, composed style. A handsome portal dated 1742 opens on Largo Chiesa, surmounted by a bas relief with the insignia of the Marquises Adimari, while the façade overlooks a panoramic parvis. The interior of the church has a Greek cross plan with elongated apse, which houses a walnut choir and confessionals by Domenico De Simone of Agnone. It is decorated with stuccowork by Carlo Piazzoli and Alessandro Terzani, and the side chapels feature splendid canvases by the Neapolitan painter Ludovico De Majo, including a 1757 *Our Lady of the Rosary*, signed by the artist.

The original settlement, showing extensive remains of wall-houses on the southern side facing the gorge below, opened eastward through Porta San Rocca, which is still in place. On Piazza Matteotti we see the 19th-century **Palazzo Comunale** which is home to an interesting Antiquarium with relics from the Monte Pallano site. The branch of the sheep track leading from the River Sangro up towards Tornareccio also passed nearby.

376. 377. Facing page: the silver monstrance by Nicola da Guardiagrele; the façade of the church of San Leucio, Atessa.
378. Below: view of Bomba.

**Palazzo Spaventa**, which belonged to Bomba's most famous brothers – Silvio Spaventa (1822–93), the eminent politician and patriot, and Bertrando Spaventa (1817–83), the philosopher – is worth noting. Next to the town hall, there is Alfonso Laurenti's 1898 monument to Silvio Spaventa. The **ethnography museum** is worth a visit, as is the nearby **sanctuary of San Mauro**. The previous 17th-century sanctuary was destroyed during World War II and was rebuilt at Vallecupa, on the bank of the River Sangro. It is home to a statue of St Maurus (17th-century polychrome terracotta), venerated throughout the valley for its miraculous healing powers, which are especially effective for bone ailments. For the feat of this patron, celebrated on the last Sunday in May, thousands of pilgrims flock to the sanctuary and rub aching parts with holy oil, kept in a hollow stone in the sanctuary.

The lovely town of **COLLEDIMEZZO**, set on three hills with a wide panorama of Lake Bomba, also presumably originated as a fortified village extensively adapted to its site. The original settlement seems to have been established behind today's 18th-century parish **church of San Giovanni Apostolo ed Evangelista**, built on a spur dominating the Molino gorge below. The church was extended in the 1700s and is decorated with stuccowork by Carlo Piazzoli, and canvases and frescoes by Chieti artist Donato Teodoro, with some handsome Baroque furnishings, a 14th-century

*Madonna del Casale* statue. The church also brought forth one of the region's most important paintings – the 17th-century *Virgin with Child, St Francis and Donor* by the Valsesia painter, Tanzio da Varallo (c. 1580–1633), a great follower of Caravaggio, who worked mainly in Lombardy and Piedmont. Along with splendid canvases in Fara San Martino and Pescocostanzo, the painting (now found in Chieti's Diocesan Museum) documents the artist's presence in Abruzzo between 1611 and 1616.

The picturesque **PIETRAFERRAZZANA** crag is on the right of the central Sangro valley, on the eastern bank of the River Sangro, known here as Lake Bomba. The settlement originally took the form of a fortified village, clustered around the 17th-century parish **church of Santa Vittoria**, already known in the 14th century but subsequently remodelled several times and with some fine Baroque stucco altars. The village is dominated by the ruins of the old castle on top of the cliff.

**MONTEFERRANTE** is situated in the surrounding hills, on an evocative spur on the right of the centre Sangro valley overlooking the Gufo Gorge to the east. It boasts excellent springs and a very evocative natural setting, amid meadows and woods. It originated as a fortified village clustered around the castle, whose ruins are still visible in the upper part of the settlement, along with traces of fortifications in the form of scattered wall houses. The characteristic centre is located on the rocky ridge with a main axis along which the parish **church of San Giovanni Battista** was built, prior to the 1300s and enlarged after 1750. On St Joseph's Day, episodes from the life of the saint are re-enacted, and families lay a table for a sumptuous meal, with his image.

The village of **ROIO DEL SANGRO** extends along a promontory delimited by two deep valleys on the slopes of Mount Lupara, in the Turcano valley. It is a hospitable summer resort in the woods, with an enchanting view over the Sangro valley. Worth visiting are both the **church of Nicola** and the towering parish **church of Santa Maria Maggiore**. The interior has a nave and two aisles, and the tomb of Giulio Caracciolo, the village's ancient feudal lord. An interesting 1864 canvas by the Guardigrele artist Ferdinando Palmerio depicts *Our Lady of the Assumption between Angels and Saint*. The portal bears an inscription stating it was built in 1832.

The village of **ROSELLO** is on the slopes of a panoramic hill between the Verde and Turcano rivers, overlooking the Sangro valley. It too originated as a fortified village and was built

379. Above: Pietraferrazzana.
380. Below: Colledimezzo.
381. Facing page: aerial view of Borrello, with the centre of Quadri on the left and the Majella massif in the background.

around a lookout tower situated in the upper part of the rocky mount that rises above the old settlement. The place name La Torre", north of the parish **church of San Nicola**, bears witness to this ancient presence. The church we see is a reconstructed version since it was destroyed, along with much of the village centre, during World War II. The quaint hill village of **Giuliopoli** features traditional stone buildings and was founded by Giulio Caracciolo in around the mid–1600s. Here the **church of San Tommaso** has an inscription on the main portal with the date 1651. In the Macchie district we find the **Sanctuary of Santa Maria delle Grazie**, with its 16th-century canvas of *Our Lady of Grace* attributed to Flemish painter Dirk Hendricsz. Nearby, visitors can enjoy the **Riserva Regionale Abetina di Rosello**, an important nature reserve protecting one of the last forest habitats with the rare silver fir. In addition to a Centro di Educazione Ambientale [environmental education centre], the structure also has a centre for study and documentation of Mediterranean firs [Centro Studi e Documentazione sugli abeti mediterranei].

**BORRELLO** is set on a promontory halfway up the hill and overlooks the Sangro valley. The original site is perched on the rock, naturally protected by the cliff, thereby adapting the manmade structures to the lay of the land. At the ends of a central axis, the old Via Marsica we find the two main buildings: the **Palazzo Baronale**, up at the top and now the town hall, perhaps the ancient site of a castle; lower down, the **church of Sant'Egidio** of ancient lines with a gabled façade and portal in Baroque forms. The old centre is bordered by the circular course of Via Sant'Egidio, which follows the old loop of wall houses. However, the old urban fabric was partially destroyed by the 1933 earthquake and World War II. The **Museo dell'Arte Contadina** is housed in two buildings adjoining the town hall. A particularly evocative spot in the surrounding countryside is the **Verde Waterfall**, the highest falls in the Apennines, now protected by a Regional Nature Reserve.

The early settlement of **QUADRI** was located among the woods of the upper Sangro valley, on a low headland upstream of the confluence of the Parello with the Sangro forming a magical waterfall. Scant traces of the village walls remain, clustered around the ruins of the old castle in Via Colle. The **San Giovanni Battista parish church** has a fine Medieval wooden statue of *Our Lady of the Thorn and Child*. The best example of civic architecture is **Palazzo D'Amico**.

On the left of the river the ruins of an **Italic temple** are still clearly visible, datable to the 2nd century BC. Over this, between the 9th and 11th centuries, the Benedictine monks founded the now-derelict **church of Santa Maria dello Spineto**, although its nave and two aisles terminating in apses, and a bell tower to the right of the façade are discernible. An inscription dating to Emperor Hadrian's time records the existence on the same site of the ancient *vicus* of Trebula that, along with Cluviae and Iuvanum, became a municipium of the Carricini Samnites following the Social War. This is also testified by the numerous

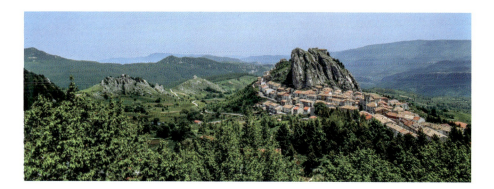

finds from monumental buildings and the discovery of a small **amphitheatre**, built between the Augustan Age and the first Imperial period, of which part of the arena has been excavated. Several excavation campaigns were conducted on the sacred site and a circumscribed surrounding area in 1990–1 and 1995, uncovering a several sections of the sacred wall of the sanctuary in polygonal masonry. The temple, which some scholars believe was dedicated to *Jupiter Trebulanus*, is orientated north–south. Today all that remains is part of the cella floor and the podium, which recalls the great Schiavi d'Abruzzo temple, and was inspired by the Hellenistic culture that swept through Samnite territory after 217 BC and through the following century. The space destined for the altar can still be seen on the polygonal flagstones of the sacred area.

**PIZZOFERRATO** is a Medieval village at the foot of a rocky cliff known as the Pizzo. It overlooks the Sangro valley from the left, in an area of alternating copses, pastures with rocky outcrops and fields that are still partially cultivated and slope down towards the river, with rural houses standing alone or in small groups. The original settlement is arranged on a rocky ridge that drops sheer on three sides, whilst the fourth side can be accessed by a path along the ridge that runs around the rock and along which the first buildings leading down to the valley are situated. The ancient castle stood in the upper part of the village, called Terra Vecchia, where today's **Palazzo Ducale** was built, with the front enclosed by two round turrets. Slightly higher up, the **church of Santa Maria del Girone**, of ancient origins but modified during the 19th century and restored after the 1984 earthquake. With a lengthwise plan, an aisleless interior and a barrel vault with a lunette, the apse roof is made up of a segmented semidome. The façade is plastered and there is a bell tower in exposed stone, with frescoes on the nave vault and a stoup in Majella stone. Moving downstream of the cliff where the first settlement stood, the more recent village then developed around the new parish **church of San Rocco**. At the church of **San Domenico in Silvis**, near the Valle del Sole, a small cave linked to the cult of St Dominic nestles among the rocks.

Picturesque **GAMBERALE** is a summer and winter mountain resort on the left of the centre Sangro valley. It is built on a rocky spur with three sheer sides, while a road leading up to the village is cut into the fourth side of the rock and ends in the square near the church. The original settlement is constituted by a ring of houses around the old castle that dominates the village and was successively transformed into a **baronial palace**. However, its appearance has been greatly modified by renovation work. The current parish **church of San Lorenzo Martire** traditionally dates back to 1709 and has been remodelled over the centuries. It is flanked by a tall bell tower with an old clock and houses works of art including an 18th-century painting of the *Virgin and Child* with a handsome inlaid wooden frame. Nearby, among beech, pine and oak woods, we find the Santissimo lake where the traditional Sagra dell'Agnello lamb festival takes place on 11 August.

Lower down, **FALLO** occupies a spectacular panoramic position on a rise on the left side of the centre Sangro valley. The oldest part of the settlement stretches out along a long hilly promontory that slopes downwards on one side, while the road leading up to the village is carved into the other side. The village itself has a tightly packed centre enclosed by wall houses. The presence of two churches – Madonna del Soccorso to the north and the parish to the south – presumably determined its successive expansion, which followed straight lines along the roads leading to the centre. The parish **church of San Giovanni** has a precious chased silver monstrance and processional cross, attributed to the 18th-century Neapolitan school. A painting of the *Enthroned*

*Madonna and Child between St John the Baptist and St Nicholas* is found on the high altar. Illustrious citizens of Fallo include the patriot and writer Alceste De Lollis, who was born here in 1820.

The characteristic village of **CIVITALUPARELLA**, is clustered on a rocky spur of the Lupari Mountains, in the central Sangro valley, with a splendid view, and is dominated by the **San Pietro mother church.** No traces survive ruins of the ancient Caldora Castle except in some of the underground areas of the Annunziata church. Although the historic centre suffered serious damage during World War II, it retains the old charm of a Medieval village. A particularly interesting place nearby is the Cese cave, where Palaeolithic remains have been found.

Although the stunning view of the village once offered by the road has been altered by the construction of the imposing viaduct, **VILLA SANTA MARIA** has lost nothing of its old charm. It is on the southern slopes of Mount Vecchio, on the left bank of the River Sangro, upstream of its confluence with the River Turcato. The typical urban fabric is composed of closely packed houses sheltered by the overhanging rock. In Piazza Marconi, we find the **church of Sant'Antonio**, and the annual festival dedicated to St Anthony is centred around the lighting of the traditional bonfires. From the square we reach the upper part of the village, set right against the cliff and once sheltered by the ancient castle, whose residual structures are now part of a larger complex which includes the recently restored **Palazzo Caracciolo**, in Largo San Francesco Caracciolo. Today the building is home to the **Museo dei Cuochi,** a singular collection of documentary evidence of the careers of Villa Santa Maria chefs in the world's top hotels and homes of nobles and aristocrats. Construction of the Palazzo ended in the 17th century with the construction of the San Francesco private chapel, where tradition has it that the saint lived when he was struck down with leprosy.

Leaving behind the bronze monument to St Francesco Caracciolo (1563–1608), patron of the chefs of Italy, we reach the parish **church of San Nicola**, the interior elegantly decorated by Terzani, and with three large canvases dated 1844, by Francesco Maria De Benedictis. On the southern side we see the ruins of a small round tower, whilst another tower can be distinguished in the structure of the steep ramp that leads up to the site of the presumed southern gate, behind the church of

382. Facing page: above, Pizzoferrato.
383. Above: Fallo.
384. Below: view of Villa Santa Maria.

San Nicola, from the bridge over the Sangro. During the 17th century the village continued to expand, skirting the crags and along Via Mercato, which achieved its current length at the end of the last century, when it reached Palazzo Castracane, built in the mid-19th century. From here we can go to the **Madonna del Rosario church**, of 17th-century origins, with valuable paintings by the artist Nicola Ranieri, executed between 1818 and 1823.

The first Villa Santa Maria settlement is believed to be linked to the arrival of a Benedictine community from the abbey of San Vicenzo al Volturno, which established itself around the **church of Santa Maria in Basilica**, in the 8th–9th centuries. The church still stands, just outside the village on the right of the River Sangro, and today the interior reflects the late–18th–early–19th-century refurbishment, with a nave and two aisles and three side chapels on the right, with the 19th-century Castracane chapel on the left. The first chapel, to the right of the main entrance, revealed the original wall structure and the space houses interesting archaeological finds that emerged during excavations for installation of a gas pipeline. There are also various elements that refer to its ancient origins of great interest for documenting the building of the church, which include the column with traces of fresco inside the left pillar, between the nave and transept. The 19th-century paintings of Guardiagrele painters Francesco Maria De Benedictis and Ferdinando Palmerio are striking, as is the priceless *Madonna and Child* wooden statue dated first half of the 15th century, an object of particular devotion for the villagers.

Villa Santa Maria is famous as the homeland of chefs and boasts a renowned hotel management and catering institute. Be sure to catch the **Rassegna dei Cuochi del Sangro** (Sangro Chef Festival), a unique chance to taste the most refined recipes of the art of cooking.

The ancient fortified village of **MONTELAPIANO** occupies a steep rock slope. Worthy of note the 17th- and 18th-century wooden statues are found in the parish **church of San Michele** and the **church of Sant'Antonio** built by the Caracciolo family in the early 1600s.

The evocative old village of **MONTEBELLO SUL SANGRO**, once known as Malanotte and successively Buonanotte, extends on a ridge, and was abandoned following destruction during World War II and a 1920s landslide. It is dominated by the ruins of the old castle and the structure of the fortified village is still visible today. The new settlement was rebuilt in a more stable area, less than a kilometre away.

The village of **PENNADOMO**, on the other side of the Gran Giara gorge, is very picturesque and set in a particularly beautiful landscape, on a hill on the left side of central Sangro valley. It originated as a fortified village and was greatly conditioned by its site, characterized by strange jagged rock formations – called "lisce" – that tower above the settlement. Attractions include the 19th-century **Palazzo Troilo**, with a watchtower at the corner, with embrasures for defensive shooting, and the parish **church of San Nicola**, which has been remodelled several times and has 16th-century wooden statues and a precious cross attributed to Nicola da Guardiagrele. The **church of Sant'Antonio Abate** is in the heart of the village, a small 17th-century chapel restored during the mid–18th century. It has two paintings by unknown artists depicting *Our Lady of the Rosary* and Brother Rosario, and a bronze bas relief by Nicola Lucci. It also has a distinctive façade with curved terminations, a central portal and window above it.

385. Above: aerial view of Pennadomo.
386. 387. Facing page: during the religious wolf miracle play; the canvas of the *Last Supper*, church of San Nicola, Pretoro.

# Guardiagrele and Mount Majella

The old village of **ROCCAMONTEPIANO** destroyed by a landslide in 1765, also comprised numerous farms scattered over the Montepiano slopes and was situated higher up than the current settlement. Nearby, visitors can admire the 18th-century. **Caracciolini Fathers monastery** and the remains of the **monastery of San Pietro a Majella,** recently recovered and enhanced. The winter sports resorts of Passo Lanciano and Majelletta are easily reached. During the traditional festival of St Roche, celebrated on 16 August, devotees of the saint drink the water of the miraculous fountain from typical Rapino pottery jugs.

The characteristic village of **PRETORO**, famous outside the region for its flourishing wooden craft industry, is perched on a hill on the slopes of the Majella massif, and still retains its air of an old Medieval town. Before going up to the village we meet the **San Nicola church** of Medieval origins but renovated in the 17th century. Inside there is a beautiful *Last Supper* canvas by the Guardiagrele painter Francesco Maria De Benedictis (1800–72). This is where the religious re-enactment "**Lu Lope**" begins on the first Sunday of May. After the procession, guided by the statue of St Dominic Abbot, accompanied by snake breeders the story of the wolf miracle is staged, narrating how the saint saves a new-born stolen by the predator. Towards the castle area, we meet the parish **church of Sant'Andrea** with a beautiful 17th-century portal on a tall staircase and the architrave bearing the date 1606. Further down, in the heart of the village, we find the

Roccamontepiano, Pretoro, Rapino, Fara Filiorum Petri, Casacanditella, San Martino sulla Marrucina, Guardiagrele, Pennapiedimonte, Palombaro, Fara San Martino, Civitella Messer Raimondo, Lama dei Peligni, Taranta Peligna, Lettopalena, Palena

In an area distinguished by the lively art scene of its most important town, Guardiagrele, with its fine secular and religious monuments, the itinerary winds along the eastern side of Majella National Park, furrowed by rugged gorges in a truly unique natural setting. Screes and ravines plunge dizzily downward, while sinkholes, sheer rock faces, needles and pinnacles give this mountainous crook a wild and spectacular appearance. Small groups of drystone huts, often in the typical tholos structure, are particularly common and were built by shepherds on their arrival at the high summer pastures to offer a more stable shelter for themselves and their flocks. Hermitages, tholos huts and a string of villages, monasteries and churches make the Majella a sacred and solemn massif.

old 17th-century **Purgatorio church**, recently restored and now home to the interesting **Centro Museale di San Domenico**, a museum that is dedicated to the culture and natural aspects of the wolf, snakes and the history of Pretoro. Visitors can explore the surrounding area and discover the charming rock mills along the course of the River Foro, in the lower part of the Valle del Foro nature reserve, which safeguards natural environments of exceptional importance. Also of great interest is the **Apennine wolf wildlife area**, located in the perfect habitat for this animal, between the Calvario and Falselongo quarry districts.
Higher up, towards Passo Lanciano, the evocative **Madonna della Mazza sanctuary** probably dates to the 13th century. The statue of the Madonna is brought to the village on the last Sunday of April and returned to the mountain sanctuary on the first Sunday of July. The striking Grotta dell'Eremita is situated in the Sant'Angelo Valley on the slopes of the hill of the same name and is famous for having housed many evacuees during World War II.
Casacanditella, San Martino sulla Marrucina, Fara Filiorum Petri and Rapino stand on the far slopes of the Majella massif, in a hilly area eroded by ravines.
**RAPINO** lies on a slope crossed by the River Arsella, in an area originally occupied by the Marrucini tribe. Its lovely old centre vaunts the 18th-century **Palazzo del Municipio**, the town hall whose council chamber is decorated with precious majolica panels by Gioacchino Cascella who lived in Rapino until his death. At the end of Via Roma, we find the elegant façade of the **church of San Giovanni** and nearby the round **Torre del Monarca** tower, the only surviving trace of the ancient urban walls. Worthy of note is the portal of the old abbey of San Salvatore a Majella, whose scant remains can be seen near the village. The portal has been moved to the porch of the **convent church of Sant'Antonio** (1645) with its singular façade and rich interior, refurbished in 1731. The convent is home to the **Museo Internazionale della**

388. Above: "Verginelle" procession, Rapino.
389. Below: historiated plate made in the early 1900s by Fedele Cappelletti.

**Ceramica**, an international museum exhibiting the works of Rapino's most famous potters alongside works by international counterparts. Rapino is a remarkable ceramic production centre and was home to the illustrious ceramist Fedele Cappelletti (1847–1920), Southern Italy's leading artisan of the genre in the late–19th century. On the morning of 8 May the town holds its typical **Verginelle Procession**, during which local children are adorned with jewellery and walk from the parish **church of San Lorenzo** to the **Madonna del Carpineto sanctuary** (in the old potters' district), to commemorate the apparition of the Virgin Mary said to have occurred in the late–18th century.
Just a few kilometres from the current settlement we find **Grotta del Colle**, a cave and natural shelter at the foot of the Majella massif's eastern slope, which was once used as a place of worship by the communities that inhabited the surrounding areas. The site is known beyond the region for the 19th-century discovery of the so-called Rapino Bronze which bears an important religious inscription in Oscan, the language of the Marrucino tribe, and which dates back to the 3rd century BC, with information about worship of a divinity. The exceptional value of this documentary source lies in the fact that the text mentions "touta Marouca", which can be identified as being the Marrucino tribe. The place name of Italic origin indicates an area in the immediate vicinity, where it is possible to see the remains of the ancient urban walls made from great dressed blocks of stone, known as polygonal masonry. It was once surrounded a settlement dating from the same period as the nearby sanctuary, as testified by the discovery of residential buildings. Subsequent excavations resulted in the discovery of a bronze statuette of a female deity – the goddess of Rapino – and a series of terracotta items connected with her worship.
The partially preserved Torre del Colle tower near the cave is all that remains of a fortified Medieval settlement.
The enchanting town of **FARA FILORIUM PETRI**, on

the edge of Majella National Park is an interesting town whose name recalls its ancient Lombard origins. Visitors should not miss the parish **church of San Salvatore**, which boasts a silver cross by Nicola da Guardiagrele. Inside, of particular interest there are paintings by Guardiagrele painter Francesco Maria De Benedictis, who executed the *Transfiguration*, the *Our Lady of the Rosary* and the *Immaculate Conception* here in 1820. The 14th-century portal of the lost church of Sant'Agata has been reassembled under the portico. A particularly evocative moment in the life of the town is the feast of St Anthony Abbot (17 January), which is celebrated with the burning of the traditional *farchie* – 12 tall bundles of dry reeds, one for each of the town's districts, which are set alight on the eve of the saint's day, before the small **Sant'Antonio Abate church** to commemorate the miracle attributed to the saint, who is said to have saved the town from the French army in 1799, transforming a neighbouring oak thicket into menacing torches. The origins of the great bonfires of Fara actually lie in ancient pagan rituals for the return of spring. The villages of Casacanditella and San Martino sulla Marrucina, on panoramic knolls over the Foro valley, were severely damaged during World War II but retain interesting examples of 19th-century buildings. **CASACANDITELLA** is home to the charming feast of Santa Maria Assunta or Madonna della Quercia, in honour of the Virgin Mary who appeared on an oak at the point where the **Madonna dell'Assunta sanctuary** was later erected. On 15 August there is a lovely procession with wagons decorated with wheat and gifts.

Nearby Semivicoli is home to the imposing **Castello Baronale**, now restored and in use as a hotel and wine cellar.

**SAN MARTINO SULLA MARRUCINA** is known as the "powder-keg town". The **church of the Madonna del Colle** on the edge of the town is worthy of note, as is the centrally located **church of San Cristinziano**, of ancient origins but modified over history. The village celebrates the feast of the "Holy Spouses" every 23 January, in honour of the marriage of the Virgin Mary to

390. Above: Feast of the Holy Spouses, San Martino sulla Marrucina.
391. Below: the "Farchie" for St Anthony Abbot, Fara Filiorum Petri.

# Cathedral of Santa Maria Maggiore, Guardiagrele

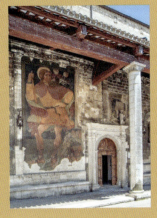

The cathedral was built around the 12th century, with modifications in the 13th and 14th centuries that can still be seen today. However, during the 1800s it underwent a complete transformation that gave it its present form, achieved by the connection of three separate parts of the building: the forepart with the bell tower and atrium; the ancient nave that originally extended from the main façade to the underpass in Via Dei Cavalieri, which was later used as a crypt; and – to the east – the Madonna del Riparo chapel, now the church of San Rocco, along which the lengthy 18th century nave was arranged. The most emblematic part of the church is the stone façade with central tower, which had the dual function of entrance and bell tower and is aligned with the building, something very rare in Italy and inspired by French Romanesque models. The original 12th-century façade was drastically changed the subsequent century when a bell tower was certainly added. A later refurbishment was undertaken in the 1300s, seen in the splayed ogival **portal** with clustered columns, which probably replaced an older portal. Another particularly noteworthy feature is the wooden doors, dated 1686. The precious sculptural group of the *Coronation of the Virgin*, attributed to the workshop of Nicola da Guardiagrele and originally found in the lunette above the portal, is now kept in the cathedral museum. The left side of the façade was successively modified and shows a striking statue of *St John the Baptist* in a 16th-century aedicule beneath the clock bearing the town's coat of arms. The 14th-century extension of the church comprises the portico with stone columns and wooden roof that runs along the southern side of the church. However, the current appearance of the **portico**, which was extended beyond the Via Dei Cavalieri vault arch in 1882, is the result of rebuilding work completed in 1954. The same portico has several important features, such as the Renaissance portal, dated 1578, and the huge fresco of *St Christopher*, which is the only dated (1473) and signed work by Andrea Delitio, a leading 15th century Abruzzo artist, who also painted a monumental fresco cycle in Atri cathedral. In 1884, the town coat of arms and three rows of insignia of Guardiagrele's leading noble families were added beneath the inscription commemorating the extension of the portico. The **northern portico** was restored in the 1950s, when the first three bays were completely rebuilt. The last bay houses the extraordinary late–16th-century aedicula with the 14th-century painting of the *Madonna Lactans* by an unknown artist, perhaps a follower of Delitio. The 18th-century church above the crypt (where the original buildings of the complex can still be discerned) is accessed by a flight of stairs that leads to the aisleless upper storey, with giant pilasters surmounted by a continuous cornice that supports a wooden truss roof. The 17th- and 18th-century paintings include the *Entombment of Christ*, by Ferrara artist Giuseppe Lamberti, above the third altar on the left. Other highlights include the 18th-century wooden pulpit with a carved central panel depicting three episodes from the life of Christ, and the carved and painted stone frontal of the last altar on the right side, put together from earlier pieces. Finally, there is an interesting 17th-century wooden tabernacle beneath the late–16th-century painting of the *Assumption*.

The three rooms of the crypt house the **Don Domenico Grossi cathedral museum**, exhibiting works dated 14th–18th centuries. These include precious sacred vestments, mainly 1700s, reliquaries of the Neapolitan school and wooden statues. The most striking exhibit is the precious fragments of Nicola da Guardiagrele's cross in gilt, embossed silver, signed and dated 1431, recovered after the theft of 1979.

392. Facing page: Santa Maria Maggiore cathedral façade.
393. 394. This page: above, the southern portico with the fresco of *St Christopher*; below, the northern portico, with the *Madonna Lactans* fresco.

St Joseph. Their statues are symbolically placed next to each other and carried in a procession through the town, as the onlookers shower them with flowers and sugared almonds.

**GUARDIAGRELE** stands on a clay ridge whose slopes are crossed by the Laio and Vesola rivers. The town is set against an extraordinary natural backdrop and is home to the headquarters of the Majella National Park. The "noble stone town" immortalized by D'Annunzio in *The Triumph of Death*, is an old settlement with an extraordinarily rich artistic heritage. The centre is characterized by the typical layout of a fortified town and was once surrounded by walls with towers and gates. The course of the walls can still be seen, although most of them have been incorporated in the buildings that subsequently developed along the perimeter, with extra storeys and transformations. Today only two of the round towers that once strengthened the defensive ring have survived. **Torre Adriana**, at the far northern point of the walls, is the most important of these and has a circular plan. Nearby is **Porta San Giovanni**, rebuilt around 1841 on the site of the Medieval Porta della Fiera. In the middle of the western side of the urban walls the surviving **Torre Stella** tower, also round, where the noble coat of arms of the Stella family is still recognizable, set in the curtain wall. The most ancient defensive perimeter is still **Porta del Vento**, formerly Porta di Grele a short distance from the suggestive **Torrione Orsini** tower, named after the powerful family who dominated the town from 1340 for many years. The massive tower, whose current appearance could be the result of work the Orsini also ordered on the walls, seems to replace a Lombard military garrison. The **San Pietro tower and gate** complex represents what remains of a 14th–15th century Celestinian convent: the square bell tower, with a single lancet window and an inscription on the outer wall, and masonry sections. A stone portal with a brick scheme-arch leads into the courtyard, where the portal opens at the base of the bell tower on the left. The belfry has clear late–Gothic features in the ogival order and column jambs. On the same side, a third arched portal leads to an inner courtyard with surviving sections of walls, where we still see the springers of two other long-lost arches.

The urban fabric vaunts handsome noble mansions dating 17th–19th century. I of the finest is **Palazzo Vitacolonna**, which is among the most representative examples of local 18th-century secular architecture. The composition of the elegant brick façade, inspired by Renaissance tenets, provides a fine contrast to the northern portico of the cathedral, contributing to the spectacular effect of the square. The band decorated with circular motifs that runs around the upper part of the façade is topped by a large cornice, while the tall windows of the piano nobile are surmounted by alternating triangular and curved tympana and rest upon a long balcony supported by brackets. A large entrance hall, with a well-preserved cobbled floor, precedes a dramatic staircase with rampant vaults on pillars made from mixed brick and stone, which follows

395. 396. Above: Torre Adriana and Torrione Orsini, Guardiagrele.
397. 398. Left: the façade of Palazzo Vitacolonna and the internal staircase of Palazzo De Lucia, Guardiagrele.

the dictates of 18th-century Neapolitan architecture. The vault of one of the rooms of the piano nobile features a mid–19th-century fresco of *Leda and the Swan* by the local painter Francesco Maria de Benedictis.

Another fine mansion is the **Palazzo Montanari-Spoltore**, with rooms decorated with tempera and oil paintings by the Lanciano artist Federico Spoltore, who stayed in Guardiagrele for an extended period, painting characteristic views of the town. The central position and unusual architecture of the splendid **Palazzo De Lucia** make it the more important of the two mansions of the De Lucia family and one of the town's most significant 17th-century civil buildings. The interior features a staircase with rampant vaults and a skylight. The current layout of the old **Palazzo Elisii** is the result of rebuilding in the 17th century. **Palazzo Liberatoscioli**, built in the 1920s according to the most classical Art Nouveau canons, is the only example of the style in Guardiagrele and one of the most interesting in the region.

The town's many fine religious buildings include the **cathedral of Santa Maria Maggiore** (*see box p. 233*), it's most famous monument, with a Majella stone façade dominated by a bell tower, where there is also a fine **museum**.

The **convent complex of San Francesco** (*see box p. 235*) is extremely interesting and second in

## Monastery of San Francesco, Guardiagrele

The Franciscans originally settled outside the town, at Campotrino, but were granted permission by Tommasa di Palearia to move to the site of the old church of San Siro in Guardiagrele in 1276. During the 14th century the monastic complex became one of the town's most important religious and secular hubs, along with Santa Maria Maggiore. In 1338 the Orsini donated the relics of St Nicola Greco – still venerated today – to the Franciscans. In 1384, Napoleone Orsini left orders to be buried in San Francesco. The church was repeatedly remodelled before the interior was rebuilt to an almost definitive result between the end of the 17th and first half of the 18th century. The lower part of the façade up to the stringcourse, and the right side up to the cornice separating it from the 18th-century upper storey (added to make the vault more spacious) are both part of the 14th-century church. The **portal** has been attributed to the school of Nicola Mancino because of various elements in the composition and decoration. The 13th-century side portal comes from the church of Santa Maria Maggiore, brought here in 1884. The interior of the church dates back to the rebuilding undertaken in the 17th and 18th centuries, which eliminated the side chapel dedicated to St Leo Pope. It consists of a nave divided into two square bays surmounted by cupolas, and a square choir. The walls are cadenced with pilasters with acanthus leaf capitals that alternate with four side altars decorated with stuccowork and niches containing painted wood statues. A high mixtilinear cornice encircles the nave and is repeated lower down to shadow the altar crowning. A masonry structure decorated with polychrome stuccowork divides the nave from the handsome 18th-century wooden choir, which features 12 stalls and is crowned with 4 busts of sibyls either side of King David, placed above the sacristy door. The fine paintings decorating the walls include a late 16th-century *Annunciation* with the Farina family coat of arms and a canvas of the *Virgin and Child with St Joseph, Evangelist, Angel and Donor*, dated 1604 and donated by the De Sorte family. The **cloister** and monastic outbuildings, which now house the town hall, are built against the left side of the church. The rectangular brick cloister features round arches with slender octagonal columns that support the cross vault. The arches of the upper loggia have recently been filled in to create an area serving the municipal council. The elegant square bell tower is partly hidden by a modern building and features a belfry with round arch, closed by a roof and spire added at a later date.

The monastery has an interesting Archaeological Museum (*see box p. 237*).

399. Left: 18th-century wooden sculpture on one of the side altars.
400. Below: view of the church façade.

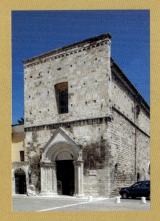

architectural importance only to the cathedral. It is believed to have been founded in the mid-13th century.

Next to the church of Santa Maria Maggiore, beyond Via Dei Cavalieri, is the **church of San Rocco**, originally the Madonna del Riparo chapel, which extends beneath the 18th-century. complex. A simple, round-arch portal leads onto the evocative interior beneath the huge vault. It is divided into a nave and two aisles with round arches that spring from pillars, and vaulted ceilings. The original layout is still clearly visible, although the sumptuous polychrome stuccowork was added when the church was restored in the 18th century. Its handsome furnishings, most of which date back to the 18th century, include the fine wooden pulpit and confessional against the wall of the left aisle, which are attributed to the Orsogna cabinet-maker Modesto Salvini. The noteworthy paintings include a *Virgin with Child* or *Madonna Lactans*, in a medallion above the altar, by Nicola Ranieri, a local painter who lived in the 18th–19th centuries. II very interesting stone arches can be found to the sides of the entrance. They are the only surviving parts of the previous church and have been recomposed on the walls of the aisles. The refined decoration, featuring climbing foliage on the archivolts and spiralling branches of oak and hops entwining the narrow supporting columns, can be ascribed to German craftsmen active in Abruzzo during the 15th century, under the master Gualtiero di Alemagna.

Traditionally, the **church of San Nicola di Bari** is said to have been built on the site of a previous place of worship during the 5th century and its current form is the result of rebuilding following the disastrous 1706 earthquake. The 16th-century main portal shows Corinthian half-columns on pedestals and jambs richly decorated with braided motifs and foliage. The two column-bearing lions either side of the entrance may have belonged to the old portal. The side portal dates more or less to the same period, but its composition is more elaborate, with classic 16th-century motifs combined with local ornamentation, which continued to be influenced by Medieval tastes. The aisleless interior, cadenced by side altars, has a handsome high altar decorated with motifs inspired by 18th-century Neapolitan art, and a precious canvas, over the first altar on the left, by Guardiagrele painter Francesco Maria de Benedictis, depicting *St Nicholas of Tolentino Interceding with the Virgin*, dated 1859.

Other notable religious buildings include the **Capuchin convent church**, with late–Baroque wooden furnishings and altars, along with the precious inlaid wood and ivory tabernacle of the high altar, crafted during the first half of the 18th century by skilled Capuchin carvers, and the **church of Santa Chiara**, with an aisleless apsed nave, that has numerous artworks, including a wooden pulpit, an elegant wooden Baroque crucifix and several canvases dating from the 18th-19th centuries. Visitors should also see the **church of San Silvestro**, with Romanesque origins but remodelled several times (currently deconsecrated and used for cultural activities); the **Madonna del Carmine church** in a conventional eclectic style, rebuilt during the early decades of the 20th century on the remains of an earlier architectural complex believed to have been a Celestine monastery; the **church of San Donato**, whose high altar features a large painting of *St Donatus* by Federico Spoltore; and finally the **church of Madonna dell'Addolorata**, situated at the end of the eponymous lane, whose striking interior is embellished with a handsome

401. Above: high altar in the Capuchin convent church, Guardiagrele.
402. 403. Below: archaeological museum and military shrine in Bocca di Valle.
404. Facing page: the parish church of San Silvestro e San Rocco; Pennapiedimonte.

coffered wooden ceiling on which local artist Ferdinando Palmerio, active between the 19th and 20th centuries, painted episodes from the life of Christ on copper sheet. Another striking feature is the antique organ by the Bologna maker Adriano Verati, still in working order.

Today Guardiagrele is still renowned for the quality of its craftwork, especially in the sector of metalworking. The art of wrought iron and copper is particularly popular. While once closely associated with the needs of the agricultural and pastoral economy, the products are now more in line with the various demands of the market. Several workshops still produce home furnishings, sculpture and ornamental embossed and chased plates depicting typical Abruzzo subjects. The goldsmith's art, which in the past produced works of notable technical and artistic value, such as the refined 15th-century religious pieces by Nicola da Guardiagrele, has also now turned its attention to new models. Last but not least, the permanent **museum of Abruzzo decorative arts** in Palazzo dell'Artigianato. Its 8 rooms and its Salone dei Concorsi salon are home to the best of Abruzzo decorative arts, which include outstanding masterpieces by the Ranieri workshop (late 1800s–early 1900s). In August each year the town hosts an important and very popular **Abruzzo decorative arts fair**.

The **Filippo Ferrari archaeological museum** in the monastery complex of San Francesco was inaugurated in 1999 as a temporary exhibit and then extended to become a permanent feature. It has 6 rooms and is very interesting for those who wish to know more about the history of the area, as it displays the most significant finds from the protohistoric necropolis of Comino, situated on a plain west of Guardiagrele, used uninterruptedly over a long period that went from the end of the 9th to the 3rd centuries BC, with various types of tombs.

Do not miss the nearby **Galleria del Gusto**, managed by the San Nicola Greco Foundation and set up to promote local food and wine specialities.

The nearby **Museo del Costume e della Tradizione** is found in the San Francesco convent cloister. Worth a visit, the museum covers a period that extends from the late–17th to the mid–20th century.

The picturesque tourist resort of Bocca di Valle is situated nearby, at the mouth of a deep gorge. It is noted for the presence of a **war memorial** in honour of Abruzzo's military fallen, while the grotto, hollowed out in 1923, houses the remains of Lieutenant Andrea Balile, who was killed in World War I. The interior is decorated with ceramic panels by Basilio and Tommaso Cascella. Bocca di Valle is the starting point for numerous excursions in the Majella National Park, including the panoramic itinerary that enables visitors to reach the spectacular waterfall of San Giovanni. The characteristic villages of Pennapiedimonte and Palombaro, in Majella National Park, are situated on a rise with a panoramic view over the Avello valley and are part of the Feudo Ugni state nature reserve.

**PENNAPIEDIMONTE**, at the mouth of the impervious Tre Grotte gorge, boasts a noteworthy cycle of paintings by the painter Nicola Ranieri (1749–1850) in the 18th-century **San Silvestro e San Rocco parish church** in local stone, in addition to the statue of the *Virgin Mary* from the abbey of Santa Maria dell'Avella, of which some remains are visible by the eponymous river in the Selvaromana valley.

Since 2003 an interesting **Museo Civico** has been housed in the so-called Torre Romana, a tower in Via Salita della Piazzetta, exhibiting the collection of precious archaeological finds from excavations in the Cavata area.

From the centre, steep stair cases lead to the highest part of the village, called "il Balzolo", with its dizzying vistas onto the Avello valley and the Ugni mountains. Some of the most eye-catching attractions in the surrounding area include Grotta Nera and Grotta

di Faggi, the first cave known for its distinctive, soft, clear concretions, also called "mountain milk", and the latter, almost inaccessible at over 1,300m, where a brown bear skull dated to about 10,000 years ago was found.

**PALOMBARO** has the handsome parish **church of San Salvatore**, reopened for worship in 1672, with 18th-century furnishings. There is also the **Santa Maria della Serra or dell'Assunta church**, said to have been rebuilt in the 16th century and restored in 1841, with the addition of a tall bell tower in Gothic revival style. Inside there is an interesting wooden statue of a *seated Madonna holding Child Jesus in her arms*. The **former church of San Rocco**, dating from the latter half of the 18th century according to some sources, currently houses a small theatre and a library. In Piazza Plebiscito we find lovely **Palazzo De Menna** (17th–19th century).

**Grotta Sant'Angelo** is a fascinating cave found nearby, which retains the apse of a small but refined Medieval chapel, traditionally said to have been founded between the end of the 11th and the beginning of the 12th century, first dedicated to St Agatha and then consecrated to the cult of St Michael Archangel. The left side of the river valley is dotted with an extraordinary and uninterrupted series of caves enclosed by drystone walls, which were used as shelters by shepherds.

**FARA SAN MARTINO** stands at the foot of the Majella massif and is known all over the world for its pasta factories. The spectacular scenery of the untamed, winding Santo Spirito valley, is the backdrop to the ancient Benedictine **monastery of San Martino in Valle**, already present in the 9th century according to some sources. Repeatedly damaged by landslides and floods now recent archaeological excavations have brought to light the remains of the church, with a front portico, a bell tower, a vast entrance courtyard, and monastic buildings set against the rock face, as well as finely decorated columns and bas-reliefs. Despite the sheer devastation left by World War II, the oldest part of the settlement – known as **Terravecchia** – still retains the layout of the ancient fortified village, with remains of walls and towers. The **Porta del Sole** gate still opens onto Piazza del Municipio, a striking gateway to the oldest quarter, then incorporated into the ancient **Annunziata church**, rebuilt in the

405. 406. Below: the Sant'Angelo di Palombaro cave (left) and the eponymous Lama dei Peligni cave.
407. 408. Facing page: above, remains of the monastery of San Martino in Valle, Fara San Martino; below, parish church of SS Nicola e Clemente, Lama dei Peligni.

18th century. In addition to the **Madonna delle Grazie** and **Suffragio churches**, it is worth stopping at the parish **church of San Remigio** with a splendid 17th-century canvas of the *Circumcision with Saints Charles Borromeo and Francis of Assisi*, by Caravaggio's great follower, Tanzio da Varallo (1575–1635). The Riserva Naturale Orientata Fara San Martino-Palombaro also lies partly on municipal territory. The reserve's visitor centre is in the main square and incudes a modern **nature museum**.

Worth visiting are the nearby River Verde Springs, where the water gushes directly from the rock and collects in an emerald-coloured pool near the **church of San Pietro**, at the edge of the village. Welcoming amenities are located along the banks of the river and a wildlife museum reproduces the various habitats of the animals living in the park.

The old fulling-mill premises on the right bank of the Verde, once used for making cloth, is now home to the **Museo delle Arti e Tradizioni faresi – Macaronium**.

Beyond the quaint village of **CIVITELLA MESSER RAIMONDO**, which faces the Majella massif and overlooks Lake Sant'Angelo – better known as Lake Casoli – with its fine stately home, **Baglioni Castle**, we find **LAMA DEI PELIGNI**, on the southwestern slopes of Mount Amaro, to the left of the upper River Aventino valley and on the edge of Majella National Park. A series of earthquakes in the 18th century destroyed the Medieval village (Castello district), which was definitively abandoned following the 1933 quake and World War II. The traditional centre was further altered when the village was rebuilt although the 16th-century **Santi Nicola e Clemente or Bambino Gesù parish church** (the right portico is 20th century) still stands in the centre. Its interior, with a nave and two aisles, features fine works of art, including a wax statue of the Christ Child in a silver urn, a wooden pulpit and a well-preserved organ, both 17th century.

Also of interest, the **Palazzo Ducale**, said to have been built in the 16th century by the

Di Capua family; **Palazzo dei Baroni Tabassi**, with a refined portal surmounted by the family coat of arms; and **Palazzo Verlengia** with the precious Verlengia Library, inaugurated in 2010 with about 1,000 volumes in addition to the Fondo Velengia donated by the heirs of Francesco Verlengia the scholar born in Lama dei Peligni.

The **Maurizio Locati Archaeological and Naturalistic Museum** and the adjoining **Michele Tenore Majella botanical gardens** are particularly interesting. The Francesco Verlengia archaeological section, dedicated to the famous local scholar, exhibits items from the surrounding area, dating from prehistory to the Middle Ages, using modern museum and display techniques to illustrate the integration and cultural development of the communities with the environment in the area of the eastern Majella massif. The naturalistic section illustrates the programme for the reintroduction of the Abruzzo chamois to the Majella massif.

The **Abruzzo chamois reserve** can be found above the town and offers visitors the chance to watch a group of these animals in a semi-wild habitat. The recently-opened **Museum of the Origins and Development of Agriculture in Abruzzo**, with the adjoining Neolithic Village, aims to document the use and knowledge of plants in popular medicine, human diet and the wool industry, as well as the historical continuity of building techniques and objects that have been made and used for thousands of years.

409. Left: Grotte del Cavallone caves.
410. 411. Facing page: above, the surviving portal of the church of San Biagio, Taranta Peligna; below, coat of arms of Abbot Vincenzo Marino, abbey of Santa Maria in Monteplanizio, Lettopalena.

The territory of Lama dei Peligni comprises part of the Oasi Naturale Majella Orientale nature reserve, where it is possible to visit the Grotta Sant'Angelo, an early Medieval rock church that was home to Blessed Roberto da Salle, who founded the underlying **monastery of Santa Maria della Misericordia**, rebuilt during the early decades of the 18th century and subsequently modified. Suspended at halfway down the left side of the Taranta valley, which outlines the southeast edge of Mount Majella, rich in karst phenomena, we find the **Grotte del Cavallone** caves, at an altitude of 1,475m, some of the most interesting in Europe. In the last 500m they reveal their breath-taking beauty, with a spectacular array of stalactites, stalagmites and cavities named after characters from D'Annunzio's tragedy *Jorio's Daughter*, since the writer chose this spot as the setting for the entire dramatic second act of the play. About 20 minutes' walk from the caves, in the heart of Majella National Park, we find the lovely Fonte Tarì refuge.

**TARANTA PELIGNA**, on the slopes of the Majella massif in the upper River Aventino valley, captures the abundant Acquevive springs in an area of huge natural interest to form the **Acquevive river park**. The original Medieval core, which was almost completely destroyed during World War II, stands around the parish **church of San Nicola di Bari** with an elegant Baroque façade and several precious paintings, as well as precious wooden *crucifix* from the SS Trinità church. The growth of the small local wool industry gave rise to subsequent development of a further nucleus around the **church of San Biagio**, dedicated to the patron saint of wool merchants, erected in the second half of the 16th century under the dominion of the Malvezzi, whose coat of arms is set on the remains of the bell tower. The remains of its stone façade with 16th-century portal and handsome carved wooden doors with the figures of St Blaise and St Roche, in the central aediculae, are still visible. In the cellars of ancient **Palazzo Malvezzi** we find a virtual museum dedicated to the Cavallone caves, with four exhibition rooms. Following the destruction caused by the earthquakes of 1915 and 1933 and by World War II, yet another nucleus formed on the other side of the River Aventino, near the **Santa Trinità church**, which was founded in the 15th century but subsequently remodelled several times. During recent restoration work, handsome frescoes of the *Evangelists* were discovered behind the altar. In the upper part of town, we find the **Madonna della Valle sanctuary**. Beneath the rocky spur that is home to the Brigata Majella and victims of World War II memorial, there are the so-called "luggette" – channels cut out of the rock and already in use during the Middle Ages to transport water needed for fulling and other mills.

The nearby pastures of the Majella massif have always been an important resource for the production of rugs, tapestries and blankets. Taranta Peligna's wool blankets, called "taranta", made the town famous as far back as the 16th century and are still woven today, using modern looms, by the renowned **Vincenzo Merlino wool mill** near the Acquevive river park. During the days leading up to the feast day of St Blaise, visitors can watch the ritual preparation of "**panicelle**", bread rolls in the shape of four fingers, stamped marked with St Blaise's seal and distributed to believers on 3 February. Since 2001, every April the charming **Sentiero della Libertà** march covers the route that crossed the Gustav Line during German occupation to reach the area liberated by the Allies.

The ancient Medieval track, known as the "Tagliata", connects Taranta Peligna and Lettopalena and was used to transport goods – chiefly wool and cloth – on donkeys.

The old village of **LETTOPALENA** has Medieval origins but was destroyed during World War II. It was rebuilt on a spur on the right bank of the Aventino, on the opposite side to the original settlement. A few ruins survive of the ancient parish church of San Nicola di Bari, of Medieval origin, rebuilt in the 19th century but damaged and abandoned, like the rest of the ancient village, after the last war. The church was the original home of the splendid carved wooden portal, now in L'Aquila's

Museo Nazionale. The interesting Benedictine **abbey of Santa Maria in Monteplanizio** was founded in the 11th century. After the 1563 earthquake, which also caused the collapse of the main façade, the complex was by partly rebuilt by order of Abbot Vincenzo Marino, whose coat of arms overhangs the entrance portal to the abbey enclosure. The numerous columns in the surrounding garden presumably come from the old building. Inside there are numerous relics of sculptures, a statue of the Virgin Mary and a canvas of Our Lady of the Rosary by an unknown author.

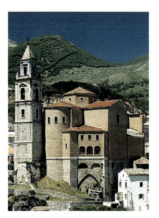

It is situated close to the **Fonte della Noce park**, which features nature trails for outdoor sports enthusiasts. **PALENA** is situated on the southern slopes of the Majella massif, on the left bank of the upper course of the River Aventino. Despite the destruction of World War II, (the Gustav Line ran through Palena), part of the original core of the settlement has survived. The old town retains noble mansions including **Palazzo Margadonna** and **Palazzo Villa**, not to mention the particularly striking municipal fountain, decorated with mascheron spouts, at the entrance to the Medieval district. The **Ducal Castle** (also known as Castel Forte) has ancient origins but was recently rebuilt following war damage. It has a handsome loggia overlooking a sheer cliff and houses the **Museo Geopaleontologico dell'Alto Aventino**, an astounding fossil collection of immense scientific value including outstanding local finds.

The **Madonna del Rosario church** (formerly the church of Santa Maria della Neve) of 15th-century origins but restored after the 1706 earthquake, then also survived World War II. We are greeted by a spectacular façade preceded by a fine double staircase, with a stone portal surmounted by a rich gable and a remarkable rose window. In the Greek cross interior, with a dome at the intersection of the two arms, there is a 15th-century wooden *Madonna and Child* group, also called the *Madonna della Neve*, on the main altar. To the left of the main altar we can admire a 19th-century painting depicting *St Andrew Apostle*, by Oreste Recchione (1841–1904), a painter originally from Palena. On the counter-façade, the ancient organ was built in 1779–87 by Antonio d'Onofrio, replaced by the Fedri di Atri workshop. It is enclosed in a precious wooden frame sculpted by the master Ferdinando Mosca of Pescocostanzo. The **church of San Francesco**, completed in the early 14th century and restored after the earthquake of 1706, is characterized by a typically Baroque decorative device. The main altar shows an altarpiece by Girolamo Cenatiempo (documented 1700–44), depicting the *Madonna and Child with St Francis*, flanked by two statues depicting King Solomon and King David. The ancient parish **church of Sant'Antonio e San Falco** today seen in its 1950s reconstruction, has retained only the beautiful bell tower. The 1800s **Teatro dell'Aventino** is interesting as it is one of the smallest Italian theatres with two tiers of boxes and a gallery. It is cultural reference point for the area and is now dedicated to Palena author and screenwriter, Ettore Maria Margadonna.

A particularly interesting and evocative site in the vicinity is the **Madonna dell'Altare sanctuary**, in the eponymous district of the same name, situated on a cliff that makes it almost inaccessible. It is believed to have been built in the 14th century on the site of a previous Celestine hermitage. The recently restored complex comprises a small convent, now used as a hostel, an aisleless church, vegetable plots and storerooms.

Other nearby attractions are the simple church of San Cataldo, set in the greenery of Majella National Park, and the Madonna del Carmine **church**, built in about 1835, which is actually a chapel carved into the rock. Piana del Casone is the site of a typical example of an isolated fortified farm, known as **La Castelletta**. It was a livestock farm that once exploited the western pastures of the Pizi Mountains and is believed to have been founded on a previous building dating back to the 10th century. This ancient property of the barons of Colledimacine was built from local white stone and was striking for its two round towers set at the corners of the main façade.

Nearby, at Villa Galardi, is the **convent of Sant'Antonio**, founded in the 16th century, destroyed by an earthquake in 1706, and subsequently rebuilt in its present form. It is made up of an aisleless church and a cloister with a rectangular two-storey arcade. It is now home to the **Marsica bear museum**.

In the Capo di Fiume district visitors can enjoy the **Palena Geosite**, one of the richest and most important deposits of fossils and archaeological artefacts in Europe and place of provenance of the Di Carlo collection, which constitutes the heart of the geo-palaeontology museum.

# The Coast from Francavilla to Casalbordino

The enchanting town of **FRANCAVILLA AL MARE** extends partly on the slope, where the oldest nucleus was built, and partly along the coast, where the popular seaside resort developed during the 19th century. The destruction wrought during World War II brought Francavilla a Gold Medal for Civic Valour but left much of the town derelict. The few surviving elements are some towers and the ancient **church of San Francesco**, formerly San Giovanni Battista, behind the Ciarrapico tower, on the highest point of the ancient "Civitella" district.

A famous circle of artists known as the "Cenacolo Michettiano" set up house in the **Santa Maria del Gesù convent**, formerly called the San Giacomo and dating from the 15th century, changing names in 1548. It was extensively restructured in the 18th century and remained in use until religious communities were suppressed, when it was taken over by the municipal authority. Abruzzo painter Francesco Paolo Michetti bought it in 1883 and welcomed one of the liveliest and most unconventional art communities of the late 1800s there. The artistic and literary circle was led by Michetti and sculptor Costantino Barbella, as well as Ortona musician Francesco Paolo Tosti, Gabriele D'Annunzio, Edoardo

Francavilla al Mare, Miglianico, Tollo, Ortona, San Vito Chietino, Fossacesia, Rocca San Giovanni, Torino di Sangro, Paglieta, Casalbordino, Pollutri

Sandy beaches and craggy reefs are the hallmarks of this jagged stretch of the Chieti coastline. Its spellbinding landscape, which inspired poets like D'Annunzio, is accentuated by the elevated structures of the trabocchi, ancient fishing platforms that reach out to the sea. There are numerous trabocchi along the stretch between Ortona and San Salvo, and they have come to symbolise the measures taken to protect this part of the coast. Plans are now in place to turn it into the Chieti National Coastal Park, with a wealth of natural and maritime assets, but also significant historical and artistic features – such as the abbey of San Giovanni in Venere, near Fossacesia, set high above the Adriatic and surrounded by olive groves.

412. Facing page: the church of San Falco, Palena.
413. Below: Francavilla al Mare pier.

Scarfoglio, Matilde Serao and later the very young Nicola D'Antino, who dedicated to Michetti the 1939 bronze statue placed in front of the portico, after the painter's death in 1929. Photographs of Michetti are found in the refectory while his equipment is on dispaly in the adjacent studio where he worked.

The **MuMi – Michetti Museum**, in Piazza San Domenico, is named after him and housed by the restored, enlarged structures of the ancient San Domenico convent, founded in the 13th century, modified in the 18th century, then destroyed by German occupying forces. The first floor of the museum hosts temporary exhibitions while the lower – partly underground – room is the space dedicated to two of Michetti's most famous paintings, *The Lame* and *The Snakes*, displayed in the town hall before the museum was built.

The modern **church of Santa Maria Maggiore** or San Franco, designed by architect Ludovico Quaroni for the 1948 competition, was completed in 1956 over the site of an existing church destroyed during World War II.

Its unique layout – an uneven octagon inspired by modern spatial concepts – has lengthwise symmetry with enormous reinforced concrete pillars that divide the interior in two: a large central space with a soaring cloister vault, and a narrow perimeter ambulatory. Pietro Cascella's polychrome ceramic *Enthroned Madonna and Child* graces the terracotta façade, and his sculptures are also inside, including the colossal piece behind the high altar to celebrate the theme of the Resurrection, and closely tied to the rebirth of Francavilla. The church also houses what is commonly referred to as the "Treasure of San Franco", which includes

an exquisite gilt silver and enamel monstrance, a striking example of late–Gothic goldsmithing from Abruzzo, dated 1413, the first known dated work by Nicola da Guardiagrele. The tall, slender reinforced concrete bell tower soars about the skyline.

In the early post-war years the town began to celebrate with its cortege of allegorical floats for the traditional **Abruzzo Carnival**. Then the three-day San Franco festival draws crowds to town from 16 to 18 August every summer, with processions, bands and spectacular fireworks at sea. The town also organizes numerous other cultural events, notably the **F.P. Michetti Premio Nazionale di Pittura** painting competition held every summer.

The scenic village of **MIGLIANICO** stands on a rise in the luxuriant countryside, near the point where the Dentolo stream flows into the River Foro. This is an important town for olive and grape farming. Dominated by the parish **church of San Michele Arcangelo**, now known as the sanctuary of San Pantaleone, with beautiful 18th-century stuccowork, and vaunting the Valignani-Tedeschi Medieval castle, which was damaged during World War II but has been completely rebuilt. The popular feast of St Pantaleon inspired Francesco Paolo Michetti's painting, *The Vow*, as well as one of Gabriele D'Annunzio's *Novelle della Pescara* short stories.

One of the major attractions here is the modern golf course designed by Ronald Kirby.

414. Above: the bas–relief of the *Enthroned Madonna and Child* on the façade of the church of San Franco, Francavilla al Mare.
415. Below: Francesco Paolo Michetti's canvas *The Snakes*, in the Michetti Museum.

Just a few kilometres away, **TOLLO** – famed for its wine production – is located between the Arielli and Venna river valleys, in an area dotted with vineyards and olive groves. The historic centre was almost completely destroyed during the last war and the parish **church of Santa Maria Assunta** was rebuilt on the site of the Nolli baronial castle. The first Sunday in August celebrates *Our Lady of the Turks* with the staging of the battle that remembers the assault suffered by the Turks in 1566: Christians were barricaded in a wood and papier-mâché tower they had built in the previous days and repelled the attack by throwing of buckets of water, pieces of watermelon and spaghetti until the Turks finally surrendered thanks to the intercession of Our Lady of the Rosary.

**ORTONA**, set on a promontory covered with flourishing vineyards, has a very old history. Although it was heavily damaged during World War II, significant examples of its art were spared. Ortona is the region's leading commercial port and marina, and its beaches – notably, Lido Riccio and the famous Ripari di Giobbe – are considered some of the most enchanting in Abruzzo.

Along the magical stretch of Ortona coast, with its trabocchi fishing platforms, there are three protected areas, reflecting the elevated natural importance of this shoreline. The Punta dell'Acquabella and Ripari di Giobbe regional nature reserves are flanked by the Parco delle Dune on the northerly coast, founded by the municipal council in 2007 and located on that section of coast that goes from the mouth of the Arielli as far as Tollo station to the north, for about 1,200 metres.

Founded by the Frentano tribe, Ortona was an important seaport and decreed a Roman *municipium* called Ortona Augusta. Conquered by the Normans in the 12th century, it was reborn under the Swabians. In the 15th century it became the fiefdom of Giacomo Caldora, who built new walls around it. The Caldora fortifications, of which traces remain along the current Via D'Annunzio, allowed the town to withstand the extended siege of Alfonso of Aragon in 1442, who is said to have ordered the construction of the recently restored majestic **castle**

416–418. Above, from left to right: Michetti Museum, Francavilla al Mare; sanctuary of San Pantaleone, Miglianico; "Madonna dei Turchi" pageant, Tollo.
419. Below: Ortona castle.

(1452). Recent theories, however, seem to prefer the idea of the reinforcement of an extant fort in the Angevin era. Ortona castle is one of the most significant examples of the transition from Medieval to Renaissance military architecture. The original structure, which was essentially trapezoidal with four round corner towers and curtain walls, was built on a battered base and outlined by a traditional stone cornice. The curtain walls were as tall as the towers, anticipating a classical element that would later be used in many central northern strongholds, making it easy to walk around the entire chemin de ronde. The castle was seriously damaged during World War II and the northern curtain wall was completely destroyed by a landslide in 1946.

A flank side of the rebuilt **cathedral** stands on Piazza San Tommaso. The place of worship dates to the 12th century and was originally dedicated to Holy May, but later renamed after the Apostle Thomas, after some of his relics were transferred there in 1258. The cathedral was modified extensively in the 16th–17th centuries, and was restructured in the 18th century by Giovan Battista Gianni, who added the dome, and then by Michele Clerici who rebuilt the façade. Heavily damaged during World War II, it was reconstructed using fragments of Ortona sculptor Nicola Mancino's 14th-century portal in the new doorway, while other salvaged parts are on show in the adjacent **diocesan museum**, alongside artworks from various urban churches. Traces of the original structure are evident in the lancet arches set on compound pillars on the right side and the ribbed vaults of the apse basin.

Inside the San Tommaso chapel two majolica compositions, painted in 1968 by Tommaso Cascella, recall the journey made by the saint's bones from Chios to Ortona. On the left side of the church a canvas by Basilio Cascella depicts the *Incredulity of St Thomas* (1944). The crypt houses the Apostle Thomas' tombstone in chalcedony marble and the gilt silver urn with his bones and an image painted in 1612 by Ortona artist Tommaso Alessandrini is set into the altar. The buildings on Piazza San Tommaso include **Palazzo De Pizzis**, **Palazzo Rosica** and **Palazzo**

420. Facing page: aerial view of Ortona.
421. Above: the portal of San Tommaso cathedral.
422. Below: the church of Santa Caterina d'Alessandria, Ortona.
423. Right: *Mater col Puer Dolorum*, 15th-century panel in Ortona Diocesan Museum.

**De Thinis**, the beautiful 16th-century **Palazzo De Sanctis** (now Mancini).

Along the picturesque Passeggiata Orientale promenade we find the majestic **Palazzo Farnese**, commissioned by Margaret of Austria, the only residence that the Duchess ordered to build anew in Abruzzo but it was never finished and later the subject of several interventions. The building currently houses the premises of the National Association of Italian Sailors ANMI and the **Emeroteca** reading room on the ground floor, with upper floors, entered from the Passeggiata Orientale, hosting the **Museo di Arte contemporanea** and the **Pinacoteca Cascella art collection**, a vast selection of the works of the famous family of artists.

A stroll down to Piazza dei Lavoratori del Mare will lead to the façade of the **Teatro Tosti** (formerly Teatro Vittoria), completed in 1930, and to the side of the **Santa Caterina d'Alessandria church**, perhaps dating back to the 12th century, modified in the 17th century. In the adjoining **Oratorio del Crocifisso Miracoloso**, the ampoule of blood of the "Miracle of the Crucifix", which tradition says flowed from the side of Christ depicted in the 15th-century fresco seen in the church before the Turks sacked Ortona in 1566, and a harbinger of the protection afforded to the town and the convent. Beneath the 15th-century Crucifix, an older version was found, also visible inside and dated post-1275. On the high altar of this church, with interiors finished with 18th-century stuccos by Giovan Battista Gianni, we admire works that include Giambattista Spinelli's canvas of *St Catherine of Alexandria*.

Another worthy building is **Palazzo Corvo** is also notable. The building houses the Istituto Nazionale Tostiano, dedicated to the famous musician Francesco Paolo Tosti (1846-1916) and home to the Francesco Paolo Tosti Archive, the Centro di Studi Musicologici Abruzzesi, the Biblioteca Musicale Abruzzese, and the Museo Musicale d'Abruzzo. There is a vast archive of manuscripts, scores, photographs, letters and approximately 1,000 compositions by Abruzzo musicians in the museum.

The **church of Santa Maria di Costantinopoli** is also worth visiting. Built in the Middle Ages, it was restored following war damage and houses lovely late–16th-century paintings.

Outside the urban walls, notable monuments include the **Trinità church** that was annexed to the old Capuchin monastery, with interesting wooden tabernacles.

In December 1943 Ortona was a theatre of battle and became known as the "Stalingrad of Italy", later awarded the Gold Medal for Civic Valour. Thousands of civilians and military died during those weeks and many soldiers are buried in the now resting in the nearby monumental military cemetery, the **Moro River Canadian War Cemetery**, in the San Donato district, visited every year by many Canadians.

## The Trabocchi Coast and the Cycle Path

The Trabocchi Coast is a 50km strip of Abruzzo's Chieti shoreline, with a high, jagged morphology, which includes the districts of Francavilla al Mare, Ortona, San Vito Chietino, Rocca San Giovanni, Fossacesia, Torino di Sangro, Casalbordino, Vasto, San Salvo, all small towns, all seaside resorts dedicated to tourism and maritime activities.

Sandy beaches and rocky cliffs alternate with rare coastal dunes and sketch this articulated stretch of coast whose landscape spell inspired Gabriele D'Annunzio and is even more accentuated by the presence of the trabocchi, ancient fishing platforms projected on the sea, icon of maritime culture but also a last gasp attempt by rural communities to conquer the water. There are several trabocchi, some still in working order or converted into lovely restaurants, dotted along the coast rolling from Ortona to San Salvo – from Punta Acquabella and Punta Mucchiola, in Ortona, to the famous structures of San Vito, then Punta Cavalluccio in Rocca San Giovanni, and those of Punta Penna and Punta Vignola in Vasto, symbols of this coastal strip to be protected by the planned Parco Nazionale della Costa Teatina. It is already possible to reach the Trabocchi on foot or by bicycle, along the **Via Verde Costa dei Trabocchi**, an amazing **cycle and pedestrian track** that will exploit the old rail tracks for the construction of further stretches to make it possible to pedal or walk the entire 40 kilometres along the coast from Francavilla to San Salvo.

The tragic event is narrated in the touching **Museo della Battaglia** (MuBa), a museum housed in the convent of Sant'Anna
One of the most fascinating religious pageants in Abruzzo is Ortona's **Festa del Perdono**, celebrated on the first Sunday of May, in memory of the 1398 Bull promulgated by Pope Boniface IX, which grants a Plenary Indulgence to those who venerate the sacred relics in the cathedral of San Tommaso. The "Procession of the Keys" takes place on the Saturday, carrying the keys that open the reliquary with the relics of St Thomas.

**SAN VITO CHIETINO**, known as "the town of genista", was immortalized by Gabriele D'Annunzio and can be found on a ridge that extends seaward between the Feltrino stream and the Rio Fontana, on the heart of trabocchi country. The town, whose original layout is still evident, boasts several interesting architectural works: the **Santissima Immacolata Concezione parish church**, with a nave and two aisles, built in the first half of the 19th century and restored in the early 1900s, with Leonzio Compassino's canvas inside depicting *St Vitus with the Evangelists Matthew and Mark*. The noble **church of San Francesco di Paola**, at the southern end of town, where Corso Trento e Trieste ends. Also of note are some fascinating examples of civil architecture built in the 1800s and 1900s. Around Piazza Garibaldi, **Palazzo Tosti**, **Palazzo Javicoli**, now the town hall, and **Palazzo Nobile**, home to the **Museo Civico**.

Going down the coast we find the modern Marina di San Vito, a resort between Ortona and Punta del Cavalluccio, where a large built-up area developed in the early 20th century, offering seasonal accommodation and some interesting Art Nouveau houses. The last weekend of July the village comes alive with the Madonna del Porto event, including the traditional Saturday afternoon procession at sea, which is worth seeing.

A lovely spot nearby is known as the **Eremo Dannunziano** with a country house overlooking a cove where Gabriele D'Annunzio set his work *The Triumph of Death*, and where he spent a short holiday with Barbara Leoni in

424. Facing page: cycle path near Ortona.
425. Above: sea procession for the "Madonna del Porto" festival, San Vito Chietino.
426. Below: Turchino trabocco.

the summer of 1899, and it is here that her remains are now buried, brough from the Verano cemetery in Rome.
The view of the coast is breath taking and this stretch is striking for several magnificent surviving trabocchi. To the left, the marvellous Capo Turchino promontory and the **Turchino trabocco** – "the great fishing machine" described so well by D'Annunzio – can still be seen here.
The town of **FOSSACESIA** has a built-up area on a scenic rise to the left of the mouth of the Sangro and another section along the coast (Fossacesia Marina).
The old town is interesting, despite the devastation left by the last war. In Piazza del Popolo we see the parish **church of San Donato**, rebuilt after World War II. Here we also find the 19th-century Cinque Cannelle Fountain, and the impressive **Palazzo Contini**, built by the Contini family at the end of the 18th century and then in part owned by the Mayer family, of Austrian origins. Nearby **Palazzo Mayer** dates back to the 1830s, enlarged in 1852 and today a house-museum that incorporates the ancient chapel of Sant'Antonio Abate. It is home to a collection of rural artefacts and a permanent **war museum**.
The **Marina del Sole** is a recent addition to Grotte, along one of the loveliest parts of the Abruzzo coast. This modern marina is a member of the Italian Association of Tourist Ports of the Adriatic. The **abbey of San Giovanni in Venere** (*see box p. 251*), surrounded by olive groves, is located nearby on a plateau overlooking the gulf. It is one of the most important abbeys in the region and is famous for its beautiful, ornately carved "portal of the moon". In the charming **Parco dei Priori**, in front of the abbey, the elegant 19th-century villa was restored and opened to the public in 2012 to host art and culture events.
Not far from here is the village of **ROCCA SAN GIOVANNI**, located on a scenic hill between the mouths of the Sangro and the Feltrino, close to the Adriatic coast. Part of the original layout is still evident in the blocks between Via dei Bastioni, the outside wall of the church, Corso Garibaldi and the Via del Portico arch. Part of the ancient fortified walls – the round **Torre dei Filippini** tower with a battered base and characteristic embrasures – can still be seen along Via Orientale. Another section of the **urban walls**, recently restored together with the allure, extends from the tower.
The town's most important buildings include the eclectic **Palazzo Municipale**, in Piazza degli

# Abbey of San Giovanni in Venere, Fossacesia

According to tradition, it was founded over the ruins of a Roman temple dedicated to Venus. The church and monastery were rebuilt in 1015 by Trasmondo II. The abbey we see today was reconstructed in 1165 by the abbot Oderisius II, and it was during this period that the western entrance was built. The decoration of the entrance, carved with exquisite reliefs, was later modernized by Abbot Rainaldo from 1225 to 1230. The church, with a nave and two aisles, has three apses and a raised presbytery over the crypt, and is one of the most important abbeys in Abruzzo, with significant Burgundian Cistercian influences. The **crypt** has two aisles with five bays covered by cross vaults and supported by columns taken from older structures. The frescoes decorating the apsidal basins are from the 12th, 13th and 14th centuries. The enchanting **cloister** is the outcome of reconstruction done during the 20th century. The splendid reliefs on the huge side pillars of the **western entrance**, executed under Oderisius and remodelled later by Rainaldo, are arranged in four large panels on two registers, and they illustrate the childhood and early years of John the Baptist, the saint to whom the church is dedicated alongside the Virgin Mary. The cycle of Stories of John the Baptist is framed by animal motifs as well as sacred and secular subjects. The reliefs of Fossacesia, the work of at least two masters, are highly significant for the sculptural art of Abruzzo, and from a stylistic standpoint, they are similar to the panels sculpted by Maestro Niccolò on the façade of San Zeno in Verona. The reliefs of the lunette over the entrance, which are stylistically related to the sculptural motifs evident at the cathedral in Termoli (Campobasso), reflect the third stage of work at Fossacesia and date back to the first three decades of the 13th century. The *Deesis*, a Byzantine image depicting Christ enthroned between Mary and John the Baptist, is depicted in the upper panel. The lower register held a Benedictine scene, little of which remains today: the figure of St Benedict is in the middle, whereas one of his disciples, St Romanus, was probably on the left; the person who commissioned the work, Abbot Rainaldo, is portrayed on the right.

427. Facing page: aerial view of the abbey.
428. Above: the crypt.
429. Below: the western portal.

Eroi, constructed in the second half of the 19th century, which today houses the interesting **contemporary art collection** with sculptures, paintings and engravings, then the extremely old **San Matteo church**, extensively reconstructed over the centuries. To the right of the parish church is the entrance to the 16th-century **Palazzo dei Filippini**, which was used as a parish dwelling until it was sold to the state in 1870. There are some beautiful beaches we might mention: for sand, the Cavalluccio, and the wide, pebbly Foce, between Punta Torre and the district of Vallevò, with the outstanding **Punta Tufano trabocco**, one of the quaintest such platforms along the coast. Here the hinterland is furrowed by gullies, with streams and natural caves, including the Fosso delle Farfalle, a Site of Community Importance, in the heart of the **Riserva Naturale Grotta delle Farfalle**. The "**Costa dei Trabocchi**" **Environmental Documentation Centre** in Vallevò exhibits photographs, documents and materials on the area's nature trails as well as the historic and art heritage of the area.

**TORINO DI SANGRO** stands on a hill on the unsound slopes of the Osento valley. The town's noteworthy monuments include the 18th-century parish **church of San Salvatore** documented from the 1300s and the interior remodelled first in the mid–18th century and then in the 1900s; **Palazzo Priori** built between the 1700s and 1800s; and the **church of San Felice**, with annexed 19th-century convent.

The town's coastal area is enchanting, with sandy and pebble beaches, with the **Trabocco**  **Punta Le Morge** emerging from a huge rock in its stunning waters. Of particular naturalistic interest is the Torino di Sangro Riserva Naturale Regionale Lecceta, a nature reserve of about 80 hectares from the last stretch of the Sangro to the coast, which protects one of the Adriatic's rare coastal forests, with precious plant and animal species, such as Hermann's tortoise, with lives and breeds here. The woods are made up mainly of tall oaks, holm oak, hornbeam and elm.

From the reserve it is easy to reach the **Sangro River War** Commonwealth War Cemetery, located on a small hill in the Sentinella district. Here there are 2,617 burials of Allied soldiers who fell during combat to break through the Gustav Line at the River Sangro during the World War Two. The cemetery was designed by architect Louis de Soissons who also designed built the Moro River Commonwealth War Cemetery near Ortona.

The town holds several events that are musts for visitors. One is held on the last Sunday in May, with the sale of "gifts" in honour of Our Lady of Loreto, and the other is on 10 December, following the vigil commemorating the Translation of the Holy House of Our Lady of Loreto, when a cantor chants the *mattina* or *viso-adorno*, verses set to music in honour of the Virgin Mary. The **Madonna di Loreto church** is the destination of the charming torchlight procession that takes place during the *Viso Adorno* event. The church is of 14th-century origins but has been modified over time and inside the

Addolorata Chapel vaunts paintings by Guardiagrele artist Francesco Maria De Benedictis, depicting the *Flight into Egypt*, the *Annunciation* and *St Alphonsus de Liguori in Prayer*.

In the nearby hills, **PAGLIETA** stands on a knoll overlooking the Sangro valley and the coast, still bearing traces of its old urban walls including the **Torre della Porta** gate into the settlement, with alongside the bell tower of the 19th-century **Santa Maria dell'Assunta church**. The fascinating **Nelli Polsoni ethnography museum** houses a large collection of objects related to farm work, sheep farming, domestic life, traditional means of transport, and crafts.

The ancient castrum of **CASALBORDINO** is on a hillslope between the low courses of the Osento and Sinello rivers. In the centre we can still see an ancient fortified village layout and some noteworthy architecture, of which the most interesting are **Palazzo Galante** and **Palazzo De Januario**. We also recommend the parish **church of San Salvatore**, built in about the mid-1700s. The tower in Via Porta Nuova is one of the surviving elements of the ancient urban fortifications. A hamlet developed around the **Madonna dei Miracoli sanctuary**, the latter built in 1962 over an existing church and popular pilgrimage destination, mentioned by Gabriele D'Annunzio in his *Triumph of Death*. The sanctuary has a large library: the Biblioteca Monastica Benedettina.

The ruins of the ancient abbey of Santo Stefano in Rivomare are near the train station. The remains of the early Christian basilica, with its annexed cemetery, and of the medieval monastery are set on a hill. The ruins of a building thought to be a *statio* (an old Roman post) have been discovered at the bottom of the hill along a Roman road, part of which was incorporated by the Aquila-Foggia sheep track. The church's original layout, which dates back to the mid-5th or 6th C., was restructured during the early Middle Ages. The presence of Benedictines has been documented since the 10th century. The abbey, which became associated with the Cistercian Santa Maria d'Arabona in 1257, has been inhabited by monks since 1380. Pillaged and desecrated in the early 15th century during the war between the partisans of Queen Giovanna II and her enemies, it was sacked again and then torched by the Turkish army in 1566.

**POLLUTRI**, built along a ridge between the Sinello and Osento rivers, in an area dotted with olive groves, still shows a typical oval layout around the parish church, with significant remains of the old fortifications. The 19th-century **Palazzo del Re** and **Palazzo D'Agostino** are notable. Inside the **SS Salvatore parish church**, of ancient origins but remodelled over time, there is a wooden statue of St Nicholas of Bari, the town's patron saint. The San Nicola chapel, dedicated to the saint, was decorated in the early 1900s by Molise painter Amedeo Trivisonno. The saint – whose cult arrived here via transhumance routes – is celebrated on the first Sunday in May, with the "throwing of taralli" and on 6 December with "the fava beans of St Nicholas", when the beans are cooked in the village square on the afternoon before.

Nearby is the **Bosco di Don Venanzio**, a rare example of a lowland forest with a large variety of trees that are particularly interesting forms of vegetation. The forest is protected by its own regional nature reserve.

430. 431. Facing page: above, the fortified walls of Rocca San Giovanni; below, the Punta Le Morge trabocco, Torino di Sangro marina.
432. 433. Below: left, Madonna dei Miracoli sanctuary, Casalbordino; right: preparation of "St Nicholas's beans".

# Pescara
and province

# Pescara

## The City

The modern city slopes from the hills to the sea, with leafy avenues and some stunning surviving pine groves, including the national nature reserve of Santa Filomena and the Pineta d'Avalos pine grove, which is a regional nature reserve and is almost all Aleppo pine. Pescara's vast sandy beaches and a marina with extensive facilities make this one of the area's most popular seaside resorts.

The city stands partially on the site of ancient Aternum, a town at the mouth of the river of that name and the origin of the name *Ostia Aterni*, by which it was known in ancient times. The site is at the meeting point between the natural course of the valley floor and the coast road. For the Vestini and Marrucini tribes, it was a maritime port in the late Republican period (1st century BC), while in the Imperial Age it became the region's main port of which significant remains have come to light. *Aternum* was destroyed by the Lombards in around 600 AD and was reborn as a port in the 12th century, when the ancient structures were refurbished. By the 13th century the population had already begun to leave, fleeing from the swamps caused by the rising river waters. In the early 16th century, before the construction of the Spanish fortress, the residential area was already in ruins and only the port continued to operate.

In the latter 19th century until after World War I, there were two towns at the mouth of the River Pescara, one called Pescara (now Portanuova) and the other Castellammare Adriatico, north of the river, which became an independent municipality in 1806. In 1927, the two towns merged to form a new Pescara, the capital city of a small province. Pescara suffered heavy bombing during World War II and was mined by retreating German troops; reconstruction evolved into a frenetic urban drift that led to the complete saturation of central areas, increasing outward expansion, and uncontrolled building along the coast that destroyed the dense pine groves. Nevertheless, Pescara enjoyed a period of growth and it developed into the region's largest city, a lively trade and tourist centre that also boasts some leading cultural institutions, including the G. D'Annunzio University.

434. On the previous double page: Ponte del Mare bridge.
435. Facing page: aerial view of the Aurum cultural centre and the Pineta Dannunziana pine grove.
436. Below: ancient map of Pescara's fortress.

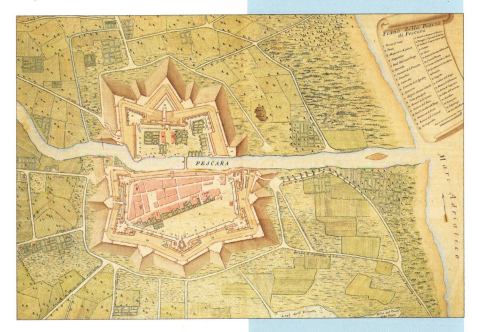

# Museo "Casa Natale di Gabriele D'Annunzio"

Gabriele D'Annunzio was born here, in the much-loved family house on Corso Manthonè, on 12 March 1863, son of Francesco Paolo and Luisa De Benedictis, growing up in the old Pescara that he evoked in his works. In 1926, the poet commissioned his brother-in-law, Antonino Liberi, a famous Pescara architect, to restore his home, which was declared a national monument the following year. His aim was to give it a solemn, monumental appearance but he fell out with Liberi and the work was then entrusted to Giancarlo Maroni, architect of the Vittoriale Lake Garda residence. From 1934-8, the refurbishment was completed to D'Annunzio's satisfaction.

The "Casa Natale di Gabriele D'Annunzio" birthplace museum was created on the first floor of the building, and in 1969 it was entrusted by L'Aquila's department for archaeology, fine arts and landscape (BAAAS). In 1963, for the first centenary of D'Annunzio's birth, an exhibition featured the mementoes and furnishings that had not been lost during the war, together with the acquisition of new material brought from the Vittoriale residence at Gardone Riviera. After the restoration in 1993, the exhibition was brought up to date to comply with new museum criteria and a series of information panels were dedicated not only to the poet but to his family, his awe-inspiring World War I feats, and the places in Abruzzo particularly dear to his heart, Pescara fortress and the urban development of the city until its fusion with Castellammare in 1927.

From the courtyard with the famous well, a staircase leads to an internal balcony and into the house-museum. The narrative of the exhibition explores the rooms remembered by the poet in the moving pages of *Nocturne*, still vaunting period furnishings – many of which are original – and the large number of tempera decorations restored by artist Dante De Carolis, brother of painter and illustrator Adolfo, a friend of D'Annunzio. The largest room is his parents' "sacred" bedroom, with its bed and the famous three steps, as well as 19th-century lithographs and a painting by Michele Cascella depicting the room. In Room VIII, interesting casts of the hands and feet of the poet by artist Arrigo Minerbi, designer of his mother's tomb in nearby San Cetteo cathedral. Some original copies of D'Annunzio's works are also on display, with illustrations by Adolfo De Carolis, Duilio Cambellotti and Giuseppe Cellini.

437. Above: house–museum entrance.
438–441. Below: the interiors of the Gabriele D'Annunzio house–museum.
442. 443. Facing page: above, cathedral of San Cetteo; below, Teatro Michetti and Palazzo Michetti–Barattucci.

Castellammare Adriatico was a cluster of hamlets that developed in the coastal area following the opening of the railway line and station (1863). By the end of the 19th century, it had become an established seaside resort. The scant remains of the residential area on the north side of the river are a few small, elegant villas, of which many more existed, built on the seafront in the late 19th century – early 20th century, when the town became popular as a summer resort. Apart from the **Madonna dei Sette Dolori sanctuary**, rebuilt from the 1700s to the 1800s over an older 1600s chapel, the 19th-century **Palazzo Mezzopreti** – now home to the Luisa D'Annunzio Conservatory – is also interesting.

The older Pescara (now Portanuova), where Gabriele D'Annunzio spent his childhood, was once enclosed by the low walls of the 16th-century fortress that straddled the river and was dismantled at the end of the 19th century. The pentagonal fortress, in a late 16th-century painting, appears to have been very imposing, with five bastions on the right-hand side of the river and two on the left. The old village took up a little over half of the area of the enclosure, and the buildings were set along three axes, still recognizable today, that branched out from so-called Piazza del Castello, now Piazza Unione; Strada di Mezzo, now Corso Manthonè (a street dedicated to Gabriele Manthonè, a Pescara-born patriot), where the **Casa Natale di Gabriele D'Annunzio Museum** is located (*see box p. 258*), in the house where the author was born in 1863; Strada dei Bastioni and Strada di Quartieri, now Via delle Caserme, the latter taking its name from the barracks located on the riverbank before the closure of the fortress, whose upper floors served as military accommodation and the ground floor was a prison.

Part of the former gaol now houses the **Genti d'Abruzzo ethnography museum** (*see box p. 260*), an anthropological narrative of the region's past, from prehistory to the 20th century.

The majestic **cathedral of San Cetteo**, near Corso Manthonè, was extensively refurbished in neo-Romanesque style after it was damaged during the last war. The construction of the new cathedral, also known as the Tempio della Conciliazione, was strongly supported by D'Annunzio. Work began in 1933 and

# Genti d'Abruzzo Museum, Pescara

The museum is found in the old Bourbon barracks, built in the 18th century in the cellars of Pescara's 16th-century fortress, and used as a gaol during the Risorgimento period. The current layout opened in 1991 and it was possible thanks to two Pescara-based volunteer cultural associations: the Archeoclub local archaeology club, and ASTRA (association for study of Abruzzo traditions), who donated their considerable collections to Pescara municipal authority. The collections were already on public display from 1973, and their fusion into a single narrative combining archaeological finds from Abruzzo's prehistoric and protohistoric sites with items from the region's crop and stick farming culture, describe the history of humankind in Abruzzo, illustrating the unique cultural continuity that exists from prehistory through to 19th-century rural and pastoral society. Exhibits in Room 1 illustrate the history of humanity in Abruzzo: from the first settlements, about 650,000 years ago, to the end of the ancient world. Significant finds from the Palaeolithic to the Roman eras illustrate the ethnic development of the populations of Abruzzo. Palaeolithic flint tools from found mainly in the Giumentina valley near Caramanico, the Foro valley and the Svolte di Popoli valley, are displayed alongside Mesolithic tools of the transition from nomadism to early forms of agriculture in Neolithic times. The finds from the latter period comprise, in particular, painted pottery from the local "cultures" of Catignano (PE) and

Ripoli (TE), with the latter illustrating the transition from the Stone Age to the use of copper. The second section of the room is dedicated to the metal ages, a time revealing the ethnic and cultural development of the region: the arrival of Indo-European peoples in Abruzzo was accompanied by the emergence of a group of shepherd-farmers with warrior temperament who then became the Italic tribes that spread throughout Abruzzo during the Iron Age. The museum includes finds from the Bronze Age, referred to shepherding, like terracotta fragments of a milk and ricotta vessel. There is also the armour of an Italic warrior from the 5th century BC, as well as a number of funeral items from the necropolises at Torre dei Passeri and Castiglione a Casauria, with others from the Jesuit sports ground in Pescara.

One of the most interesting aspects of cultural continuity in Abruzzo are the journeys to mountain environments for ritual purposes, and this is well illustrated in Room 2, where a cave simulation based on the Grotta dei Piccioni (near Bolognano) has been installed and the exterior covered with reproductions of rock paintings. Finds from different periods, from the Neolithic to the Middle Ages, are displayed in showcases. The establishment of Christianity preserved the devotional nature of ritual caves and rock shelters, while superimposing new worship on pagan cults. As is clear from the archaeological and ethnographical timeline shown in Room 3, a continuity can be traced through traditional celebrations with a Catholic stamp but rooted in agricultural cycles, and forms of pre-Christian ritual, through the survival of decorative motifs and forms in the objects used in different eras from prehistory to the 20th century. The museum dedicates the next three rooms to sheep farming, for centuries the region's main economic resource and a context that retains many of the characteristics of continuity described above. The final section is given over to traditional agricultural and production cycles, types of dwellings, furnishings and rural domestic activities, spinning in the home, and traditional dress, with a display of the most popular costumes worn in Abruzzo. There is a room devoted to arts and crafts, focusing on Castelli majolica, the region's best-known and most significant production. On the ground floor, space is reserved for the history of the Risorgimento in Abruzzo, the Museo del Gusto, and three galleries for temporary photography exhibitions.

The permanent "Armi e Guerrieri del Mondo Antico" ["Weapons and Warriors of the Ancient World"] exhibition is located at the entrance, next to the Galleria del Territorio, with panels illustrating the enormous cultural heritage of Abruzzo. The "Centro Didattico Sperimentale P. Barberini – R. La Porta" has set up three rooms for teaching workshops and a fully-equipped multimedia room. Additional services include the "Leonardo Petruzzi" auditorium for conferences and performing arts, and the "Giovanni Favetta" and "Renato Candeloro" rooms.

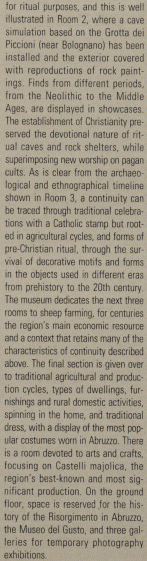

was completed in 1938, while the old San Cetteo church was demolished to make way for the **Teatro Michetti** and **Palazzo Michetti-Barattucci**, and the parish functions were moved to the Sacramento church.

The white stone, horizontal-parapet façade of the current church is cadenced by several pilaster strips that frame three doorways surmounted by round windows, with the belfry on one side and the baptistery on the other. The church has a nave, two aisles, a central apse and raised transept. It is home to the marble tomb of Luisa D'Annunzio, mother of the poet, which was designed by Arrigo Minerbi. Her remains were moved there in 1949, to comply with D'Annunzio's wishes. The poet donated a precious 17th-century painting, attributed to the Guercino studio, depicting St Francis of Assisi, and now on display in the chapel itself.

The remains of the Medieval Santa Gerusalemme religious complex stand opposite San Cetteo cathedral, built over a late-Roman, central-plan construction, confirmed by recently discovered remains of bases of three-lobed pillars and wall sections, which can be seen through the glass panels in the pavement.

Some squares are furnished with beautiful sculptures by Pietro Cascella (the famous *Ship*, in the seafront Piazza I Maggio, the Piazza Garibaldi *War and Reconstruction Memorial*), descendent of a dynasty of Pescara artists founded by Basilio. The **city's Basilio Cascella Civic Museum**, in Viale Marconi, is dedicated to this family, and is located in the rooms where Basilio Cascella set up his chromolithographic studio at the end of the 19th century. The studio became a hub for Abruzzo's artistic and cultural scene, as well as for a leading artistic and literary magazine founded by Cascella himself in 1899. First published as *Illustrazione Abruzzese*, it later went by the name of *Grande Illustrazione*, and the

444–446. This double page: an exhibit; a view of the exterior; above, an exhibition room in the Genti d'Abruzzo museum.
447. 448. Below: some of the works exhibited in the Museo Civico Basilio Cascella.

greatest Italian artists and writers contributed to it. The exhibition space houses over 500 paintings, sculptures, ceramics and graphics by Basilio, his sons Tommaso, Michele and Gioacchino, and Tommaso's sons Andrea and Pietro.

The famous **Pineta D'Annunzio** pine grove, or D'Avalos Park, is located just over a kilometre south of old Pescara. It is one of the loveliest spots in the city, praised D'Annunzio and today a protected Nature Reserve. A clearing in the dense vegetation is the site of the stele of the modern Teatro-Auditorium D'Annunzio. Behind it stands the unusual **Aurum** building, originally a meeting place designed by Antonino Liberi as the Kursaal, then taken over by the Aurum distilleries in the 1920s and used by the company until the 1960s. In the 1930s, Giovanni Michelucci designed an extension, opting for an unusual horseshoe layout, with a double order of large windows.

Neglected for years, in 2003 a plan to recover the building was put in place and endowed the city with a splendid multipurpose museum structure. Around the Pineta Dannunziana there is a series of prestigious Liberty villas, dated 1920s and 1930s, part of Antonino Liberi's "Progetto Pineta", a project to reclaim the swamps there.

Heading a short distance towards the sea, Pescara's modern, well-appointed Marina is pride of place for local pleasure craft facilities and one of the biggest of its kind on the Adriatic coast.

In the 1930s the creation of the new province brought a drive for buildings to represent the Fascist regime. The city's new architecture was erected mainly along what is now Corso Vittorio Emanuele, the largest urban street, joining

449. 450. Above: a view of the exterior and an exhibition room in the Aurum multipurpose museum complex.
451. Below: riverbank.

the two original centres by means of a bridge inaugurated in 1933.
Impressive public buildings were erected on the left bank of the river, in a new square called Piazza dei Vestini (now Piazza Italia). The square and the buildings, designed by architect Vincenzo Pilotti, were intended as the monumental city centre and modified during construction. The white stone façade of mighty **Palazzo del Governo**, the current home of the provincial council, features beautiful sculptures by Ortona artist Guido Costanzo. The works of art symbolize *River, Sea, Mine* and *Agriculture*. The interior is decorated with superb polychrome marble and Costantino Barbella's noteworthy group *Canto d'Amore*, opposite the entrance to the Sala dei Marmi, and *Iorio's Daughter*, Francesco Paolo Michetti's renowned large-scale canvas. **Palazzo di Città**, the town hall, is also by Pilotti (as was the Liceo Ginnasio G. D'Annunzio high school) and also decorated with sculptures by Costanzo, as well as paintings by Luigi Baldacci in the council chamber. A wing of Palazzo del Governo is home to the **Provincial Library**, founded in part with donations and funds from citizens. It has over 150,000 volumes, including rare 16th-century texts like Muzio Pansa's *Rime* and the L'Aquila edition of *La Storia del Regno di Napoli* [History of the Kingdom of Naples], and a *Divine Comedy* (Venetian edition, 1554). The reading and catalogue rooms are hung with beautiful paintings by Tommaso Cascella, Antonio di Fabrizio, and Elio di Blasio.
Also worthy of note in the immediate vicinity is the **church of Sant'Andrea Apostolo**, designed

452. 453. Above: left, Palazzo di Città; right, Palazzo delle Poste and Telegrafi.
454. Below: Palazzo del Governo.

by Eugenio Maria Rossi in 1964, with striking wall mosaics and a large fresco by Aligi Sassu.
Turning onto the embankment, there is the interesting **Museo delle Meraviglie del Mare** [Marvels of the Sea Museum], in Via Raffaele Paolucci. It was founded in the 1950s as the Museo Ittico [Museum of Fish] and exhibits fishing and sailing equipment, large sections on malacology (with shells from all over the world), ichthyology, and a palaeontology section of with significant fossils and cetacean relics.
Casa del Balilla (later a school) is also interesting, a splendid example of Rationalist architecture completed in 1939 to a design by Roman architects Mario Paniconi and Giulio Pediconi.
Returning to Corso Vittorio Emanuele II, there are two impressive structures: the **Banco di Napoli** bank and the **Palazzo delle Poste e Telegrafi** post office, designed by Cesare Bazzani. The new Littorio bridge was by the same architect, decorated with monumental statues, but later destroyed by German mines and rebuilt in its present form with towering steles decorated by Andrea Cascella.
Following Corso Vittorio Emanuele as far as Piazza della Repubblica, the main block of the old railway station and elegant **Palazzetto Imperato** (dated 1926 to a project by Antonino Liberi and Nicola Simeone) are still visible. The striking modern **Spirito Santo church** (architect M. Piacentini) with its unusual façade, stands on the square of the same name.
Heading for the seafront, in Piazza Primo Maggio, the very interesting **Museo d'Arte Moderna Vittoria Colonna** is installed the old university premises. Also noteworthy is the modern church of **San Pietro Apostolo**, also known as the "church of the sea", built between 2000 and 2005 to a design by architect Guido Crescenzi. The interesting **Mediamuseum** in Piazza Alessandrini is the national cinema and

455. 456. Above: left, Cascella's *Ship*; right, Museo delle Meraviglie del Mare.
457. 458. Below: left, Vittoria Colonna Museo d'Arte Moderna; right, Palazzetto Imparato.

audio-visual museum. Another artistic and cultural gem is the precious Fondazione Paparella-Devlet collection of old Castelli pottery housed in the **Museo di Villa Urania** not far from the very central Piazza Salotto. It was donated to the city of Pescara, along with the villa, by Professor Paparella Treccia.

Some recent architectural experiments are behind an interesting urban transformation process in Pescara, involving entire sections of the city, starting from the most rundown area, south of the River Pescara, the **Portanuova** district, which had developed beyond the walls of the old town.

This process engaged authentic starchitects of the building design world and the jewel in the crown is the awe-inspiring **Ponte del Mare**, the recently built bridge that has become an icon of the transformation of the urban area closely

459. 460. Above: an exhibition hall and the exterior of Villa Urania museum.
461. Below: sea procession for the feast of St Andrew Apostle.

connected to the river, in an attempt to forge a long-overlooked tie between the city and the waterway that runs through it and gives it its name. The bridge is a curved pedestrian and cycle path that joins the two "beaches" near the Madonnina roundabout to the north and the Lungomare Papa Giovanni XXIII to the south.

Designed by Bolzano architect Walter Pichler, the bold cable-stayed bridge is an eye-catching architecture with strongly expressive geometry, evident both to those crossing it and enjoying a new perspective towards the city, and also to those who look at the bridge from different observation points. The new **Ponte Ennio Flaiano** is also a monumental, cable-stayed bridge of steel and concrete but for motor vehicles as well as bicycles and pedestrians, spanning the River Pescara from Via Gran Sasso to the Torri Camuzzi building. The evocative structure, designed by the engineer Enzo Siviero and inaugurated in 2017, impacts the urban skyline with its tall mast. Here a Majella stone slab is inscribed with Flaiano's aphorism, "with feet set

firmly in the clouds" and the name of the bridge named after the Pescara writer.

Pescara artist Franco Summa's *Il Giardino Incantato* is just a stone's-throw from the courts, at the foot of the OperA residential and office complex designed by architect Mario Botta. This permanent installation comprises 16 coloured pillars, six metres high, like abstract trees arranged in symmetrical rows, characterized by their communicative use of colour typical of Summa's palette, and in close dialogue with the new architectural forms of the setting.

The Riserva Naturale Statale Pineta di Santa Filomena Filomena is a pine grove and nature reserve that stretches along the coast from Pescara to Montesilvano, hugging the shore for three kilometres. The woods comprise mainly Aleppo pine and the forestry offices have also opened a sanctuary for birds of prey there.

The extensive calendar of noteworthy summer cultural events includes the **Premio Flaiano**, a literary award of international scope, organized by the "Centro Studi Ennio Flaiano" research centre alongside the well-known film festival, in memory of this writer, journalist and scriptwriter, born in Pescara. Then there is the **Pescara Jazz Festival** and the extremely popular **FLA**, "festival of books and other things", not to mention the important sporting event, the **Trofeo Matteotti** international pro cycle competition.

Religious folklore festivals include that in honour of Our Lady of the Seven Sorrows, which takes place on the first Sunday in June at the **Madonna dei Sette Dolori** sanctuary; the **feast of the city's patron saint Cetteus**, sometime between late June and early July; and the **feast of St Andrew Apostle**, on the last Sunday in July, with the traditional procession of flag-bedecked fishing boats, concluding with the "Ballo della Pupa" and firework display, on the banks of the Pescara.

462. 463. Above: left, the Ennio Flaiano bridge; right, Pescara's artist Franco Summa's *Il Giardino Incantato*.
464. Below: Ponte del Mare bridge.

# The Coast Meets the Hills

Montesilvano, Cappelle sul Tavo, Spoltore, Moscufo, Pianella

The town of **MONTESILVANO** today comprises two nuclei. The first, Montesilvano Marina, along the coast, developed in 1900 following the growth of the fishing industry. The second is the ancient fortified village of **Montesilvano Colle**, where we should note **Palazzo Jannutti**, in particular the entrance with floral decorations, and **Palazzo Delfico**, with a 19th-century coat of arms over the entrance. The small suburban church of **Madonna della Neve** (formerly San Nicola) is particularly interesting and it also has a beautiful view of Gran Sasso.

From the current single nave layout, we can make out a structure with a nave and two aisles, and ogival round arches on brick pillars on the left-hand side. Amongst the valuable frescoes that came to light, the most important portrays a young saint standing with a slim cross in his hand, probably dating from before the late 12th century. The parish **church of San Michele Arcangelo** at the northern edge of the hill is now home to the 15th-century statue of Our Lady of the Snow, from the Madonna della Neve church. Nearby, the small church of Madonna del Carmine with its ancient layout.

Continuing inland, the town of **CAPPELLE SUL TAVO** is located on a hill, where the rivers Tavo and Fino meet. The town has been part of

The itinerary lingers through a territory enclosed by the Saline, Tavo and Fino, and Pescara rivers. Starting from the popular seaside resort of Montesilvano, directly linked with Pescara, the route continues through scenic villages, on the summits of plains overlooking the sea with the main town behind. The enchanting villages line up on hills that promise endless jewels of art and natural beauty spots, as well as being famous for the excellent quality of olive oil produced. One of the most attractive villages is Moscufo, because of the church of Santa Maria del Lago, and architectural gem, together with Pianella, with its church of Santa Maria Maggiore, known for the splendid ambo.

465. 466. On this page: right, the church of Madonna della Neve; below, Palazzo Delfico, Montesilvano Colle.

267

Moscufo since the early 1800s, and then passed to Montesilvano, only becoming a municipality in its own right in the early 20th century In the 17th century, this rural village with ancient origins was the home of a colony of Slavs from the Illyrian coast. **Palazzo de Landerset** (19th century) is worth mentioning, along with the recently restored parish **church of Santa Maria Lauretana**. To the sides and at the back, we can see parts of a masonry wall probably dating from between the late 16th century and early 17th century.

On 15 August each year the town organizes the famous **Palio delle Pupe**, a competition between outlying districts which involves large papier-mâché dolls topped with a with a firework device, managed by a dancer inside to perform an extraordinary pyrotechnical dance.

A brief detour takes us to **SPOLTORE**, on a small plain with a fantastic view over the Pescara valley. The historical centre is contained within the boundary created by the wall houses, which stretch form beyond the entrance to elegant Piazza d'Albenzio. At the top of the hill, in the Castello district, we can see the remains of the ancient fort with traces of a corner rampart to the north and a round brick tower to the south. Among the most important buildings, we should mention former **Palazzo Castiglioni** (16th–17th century) with its impressive brick entrance. The lovely parish **church of San Panfilo Vescovo** was rebuilt in the late 18th century on the site of the older Santa Maria della Porta, of which only the entrance architrave survives. The aisleless interior is graced with understated late 18th-century stuccos by Alessandro Terzani, a 1794 canvas by Giuseppangelo Ronzi dedicated to St Pamphilus, and an impressive *Madonna and Child* wood sculpture, known as "Madonna del Popolo", believed to be 15th century.

Just outside the town, the **complex of San Panfilo "fuori le mura"**, of ancient Benedictine origin, was restored in the late 15th century by the Olivetans to the original features of the nave and two aisles, separated by large round arches on columns (later modified to pillars), and closed by a flat wood roof. In 1617, the Reformed Franciscans began the large-scale project of adapting and enhancing the interior decorations. These works were followed by others during the first decade of the 1700s, which gave the inside of the church the stunning appearance of a Baroque "theatre". One of the most over-decorated of the remarkable altars is dedicated to St Anthony of Padua in 1708. The brick façade includes the 15th-century entrance, the date also attributed to the bell tower, which is closed by a 17th–18th-century clerestory. In 1912–13, eclectic alterations were made to the prospects of the convent's square cloister. The village really comes to life in June, for the cultural event "**I colori del territorio**" and in August, for the extremely popular **Spoltore Ensemble**, a music, theatre and dance review, with exhibitions and side events. Of all the religious events, the sacred Easter tradition of the "**Madonna che corre**" ("running Madonna") is the most evocative.

Turning back to Cappelle sul Tavo, we reach **MOSCUFO**, rolling down a hill dominating the Tavo valley. The parish **church of San Cristoforo** is well worth seeing, now in an 18th-century style, with interior stuccowork by Ambrogio Piazza and beautiful wooden furnishings. The design is an almost-oval central section, with a chapel built on either side, and the large choir chapel. The room is barrel-vaulted with lunettes and calottes.

467. Above: the "Palio delle Pupe" event, Cappelle sul Tavo.
468. 469. Below: left, the San Panfilo "fuori le mura" complex, Spoltore; right, the parish church of San Cristoforo, Moscufo.
470. 471. Facing page: the exterior and interior of the church of Santa Maria del Lago, Moscufo.

# The Church of Santa Maria del Lago, Moscufo

The church is mentioned in 1140 sources as coming under the jurisdiction of the bishop of Penne, but its current configuration is a result of the restoration carried out towards the mid–12th century. The Romanesque motif decorating the archlets on corbels the three semi-circular apses is particularly striking, as are the apse window frames, carved with animal and plant motifs.

The classic façade, restored in 1733, with a triangular tympanum on four pilasters, was replaced by the current unadorned wall during a more recent restoration project. The layout comprises a nave and two aisles, separated by round arches on circular brick pillars, with the exception of the two central pillars, with rectangular core and two semi–columns on either side.

The church still has a priceless 1156 **ambo** by the famous Nicodemo, of the Roberto and Ruggiero workshop. The work, ornately sculpted and still showing some of the original colours, stands on four columns connected by round arches, with one trefoil element, and a staircase with parapet on the side facing the nave. Two sides of the caisson feature the eagle of St John and the angel of St Matthew, both holding a lectern resting on the winged lion of St Mark and the ox of St Luke).

Striking late–12th-century **frescoes** depict the theme of the *Last Judgement* and here, as in Pianella, they are on the counterfaçade, which is unusual. They were recently attributed to the same artist who worked in the church of Santa Maria ad Cryptas, in Fossa. The altarpiece of a seated Madonna and Child standing on her lap is attributed to Andrea Delitio.

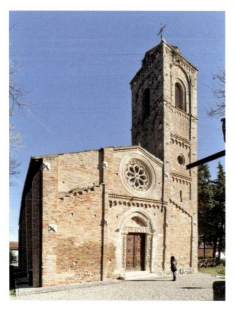

The **Sant'Antonio chapel** is quite remarkable. It is located in the street of the same name, with remains of the original brickwork and cobbled paving. Also of interest, the **church of Santa Maria della Pietà** (with a Greek-cross layout and a cupola) and the **church of San Rocco**. There are also intriguing examples of civil architecture, 18th-century **Palazzo de Ferri**.

The most important monument is just outside town: the 12th-century **abbey church of Santa Maria del Lago** (*see box p. 269*).

Having left Moscufo, we continue inland to **PIANELLA**. In the oldest part, on a hill, between the rivers Nora and Tavo, we find two of the ancient urban gates. Inside the walls there are interesting examples of civil construction dated late–16th– 18th–century. Worthy of mention are Palazzo Todesco and Palazzo De Caro with their imposing portals, as well as **Palazzo Di Felici** and **Palazzo Sabucchi**. Also worth seeing is the **church of Sant'Antonio**, completely renovated in the 18th century, and the **Carmine church**, in its 17th–18th-century guise, with the front set between two bell towers. Inside they both have beautiful late–18th-century stucco decorations by Lombard artists. Not to be missed is the church of San Domenico, founded in 1490 but renovated in the 1700s. the ancient adjoining convent is now the town hall.

In the hamlet of Castellana di Pianella, the church of **Santa Maria di Lauretana** displays a beautiful 13th-century *Madonna and Child*.

The important **Santa Maria Maggiore** (or Sant'Angelo) church is near the centre. It was built between the late 11th and early decades of the 12th century but has since been altered several times, with the beautiful entrance and rose window dated late–12th–early–13th century.The church has a simple layout with a nave and two aisles, separated by round arches on brick supports, with no transept, and ending in three apses. Despite the later addition of the bell tower, the brick façade is unusually consistent, partly due to the splendid, perfectly preserved entrance with ogival arch and elaborately engraved lintel and jambs, and the fine rose window. The interior, despite having been altered several times, retains its ancient appeal thanks to the valuable frescoes.

Particularly outstanding are the early-12th-century *Last Judgement*, unusually located on the apse walls, and the handsome **ambo** – also 12th century –, in part by the artist known as Maestro Acuto, as stated in the lectern inscription, which also mentions Abbot Roberto as the patron.

472. 473. Above: views of the exterior and the ambo inside the church of Santa Maria Maggiore, Pianella.
474. Below: Porta Santa Maria, Pianella.

# Penne and the Vestino area

The splendid town of **CITTÀ SANT'ANGELO**, within easy reach of the Pescara Nord motorway exit, is in a lovely natural location, the hills rolling from Gran Sasso down to the sea. The village retains the layout dating to the reconstruction after the 1239 destruction, and another in the 16th century. Once enclosed behind defensive walls, the town's narrow streets and fine examples of civil architecture are truly evocative. It still has its four gateways and the most important monument is the **collegiate church of San Michele Arcangelo**, rebuilt in the 14th century on the ruins of an extant building, to which the two fragments of ambo walled to the sides of the stairway probably belong. Formerly a cathedral, it became a collegiate church in 1353 and today it appears as

Città Sant'Angelo, Elice, Picciano, Penne, Loreto Aprutino, Collecorvino

This strip of territory to the northwest of Pescara is a rolling hillscape, scattered with art towns, whose economies are based on vineyards and olive production. The historic centres date to the Middle Ages in the Vestino area and are full of interesting examples of architecture and art, with similar origins and cultural identities. They are the highlight of this attraction-filled itinerary and the most outstanding of all is the ancient town of Penne with its splendid examples of Baroque architecture, highlighted by a skilful use of brickwork.

475. Below: the collegiate church of San Michele Arcangelo, Città Sant'Angelo.

it was restored in the early 18th-century restoration. A large chamber whose longest side runs parallel with the main road, with the main entrance dated 1326; the shorter right and left sides show, respectively, a semi-octagonal apse and an impressive bell tower with ogival arch portico added in the early 15th century. In the 16th–17th centuries, a lower, narrow, short room was added, connected to the main church by three large arches, and home to the 15th-century sarcophagus of Amico Buonamicizia, Bishop of Penne. The priceless 14th-century wooden statue of *St Michael the Archangel*, attributed to the Maestro di Fossa, is in the nave. Under the roof beams, hidden by the modern recessed-panel ceilings, there is a fine series of 14th-century frescoes attributed to the Maestro di Offida, probably Luca D'Atri. The inside of the **church of San Francesco**, with its 14th-century Atri-type entrance, was restored in the 18th century. The Franciscan convent (now mainly in use as municipal offices) was founded after 1240, and therefore after the reconstruction of the town that had been destroyed the previous year by order of Frederic II. The Baroque restoration of the church, in 1741, remodelled the body to a nave with barrel vaults and lunettes, and a cupola. The fragments of 14th-century frescoes are attributed to the Maestro di Offida.

There are many important examples of Baroque architecture: the **church of Sant'Agostino** is to be found at the highest point of the town. Dated 18th-century, its interior is decorated with stuccos of the same period by Como-born Alessandro Terzani. Apart from the 18th-century **church of San Bernardo**, there is also the 17th-century **church of Santa Chiara**. This has an unusual central plan, with a cupola and three chapels that place it within a triangle. The stucco decoration is by Carlo Piazzoli and Girolamo Rizza. The **Sant'Agostino Auditorium** is home to the **Moder Museum**, Abruzzo's Photography Museum, named in tribute to the Dalmatian photographer Giuseppe Moder. Nearby, the former Manifattura Tabacchi building is now a **contemporary art museum and workshop** with a large collection of works by Italian and international artists.

Continuing inland, we come to **ELICE**, on its lonely hilltop. One striking building is the parish **church of San Martino**, founded in ancient times, now seen in the Baroque refurbishment of the late 18th – early 19th century. Another is the **Castiglioni castle**, of ancient origins, dominating the village skyline. Significantly reworked, the castle is mainly brick, with an irregular floor plan, and a central courtyard. The façade overlooking the piazza is in exposed brick and would seem to be the result of a more recent intervention, with string courses and arches framed by vertical strips. The entrance leads into a hallway with vaulted sides, onto which open the rooms once used as cellars, stables, servant and guard quarters. Recent excavations in the basement uncovered a rainwater tank as well as masonry silos and tanks for storing olive oil, wheat, and farm products. On the first floor there is a large room known as "la galleria", and the chapel leading to the parish church of San Martino. Inside the church we can still see narrow openings that have since been closed off, connecting the interior of the castle, from where it was possible to participate in religious services.

The village comes to life in August for the Medieval re-enactment called *La Notte nell'Ilex* and for the *Mugnaia festival*.

Over the River Fino, we find the hillside village of **PICCIANO**, with several interesting examples of early 20th-century architecture. Two column-supporting lions, presumably salvaged from the destroyed abbey of Santa Maria in Picciano, have been recovered and installed in the **Madonna del Soccorso parish church** doorway. The church building project began in the early 19th century, to a design by Penne-born Aniello Francia, and the interior decoration was finished midway through the century. The façade (about 1846) is intriguing, as it betrays Baroque inspiration in the portal's rounded angle-irons and mixtilinear tympanum. The interesting MUTAC **Museum of Farming Traditions and Arts** is also worth a visit.

A short but winding road arrives in **PENNE**, the 16th-century capital of the Farnese state in Abruzzo, and birthplace of the famous Luca da Penne, Muzio Pansa and Cola Giovanni Salconio, as well as Renaissance patriots Clemente and Domenico De Carolis. The so-called "town of brick" is one of the region's most interesting precisely because it is almost entirely built in terracotta, featuring prominently in façades, roofs and decorative elements, but also used for paving the ancient town's steep, narrow streets. The original fortified centre ranges over the Colle Santa Croce or Colle del Castello, where the long-gone ancient fort stood. The ancient fortifications are still discernible and a few of the ancient gateways survive.

The main urban gate, **Porta San Francesco** (or San Nicola, after the adjacent **San Nicola church**, the result of a 19th-century restoration) is a striking 1780 work by Neapolitan architect Francesco di Sio, as is **Palazzo Castiglione**, on Largo San Nicola, its elegant 18th-century brick façade a backdrop to the square. The same architect is said to have constructed the beautiful **Palazzo Del Bono** on Via

Muzio Pansa, where there are other important buildings. It is perhaps the most interesting example of civil Baroque architecture in the Vestino area. The mansion can be dated to around the mid–18th century, and is characterized by a lively exposed brick façade, that harks back to Medieval tradition. Only a few details, such as the capitals and the jamb friezes, are in stone. The brick front differs from the usual Abruzzo model and is divided by rusticated pilasters on the two levels. The elegant portal is flanked by pairs of staggered columns, and overhead features a long, curved balcony. The second-floor windows are adorned with classic triangular and curved gables, with the exception of the large central window, where a split gable is used. The clever use of materials, the significant stylistic coherence and rare expertise of the language applied suggest that the

476. 477. Facing page: left, Elice; right, Madonna del Soccorso church, Picciano.
478. 479. On this page: above, the Annunziata church on Corso Emilio Alessandrini and, below, Palazzo Del Bono in Penne.

Neapolitan architect, Francesco di Sio, played a direct part in designing the building.
The nearby **church of Sant'Agostino** is well worth a visit. It is the result of radical 1756–9 transformation of an extant 14th-century building to which the ogival single-light side windows presumably belong. The wall at the back of the choir vaults a *Crucifixion* by Antonio da Atri, the only surviving trace of the 1300s building.
The **cathedral of San Massimo** is located on Colle Sacro and it is certainly prior to the year 1000. Its appearance today is the result of the restoration works carried out after it was destroyed during World War II. The only surviving part of the original nave and two aisles, and presumably three apses, is the bell tower, although it has been lowered, with interwoven arch decoration and a carved portal. The intriguing crypt, dating from before the 14th-century phase of the church, and extensively restored, retains the layout of the ancient presbytery, and is characterized by the ancient shafts of recovered columns, and by remains of frescoes probably dating from the late–13th–early–15th centuries. The cathedral façade today, modified by the post-war restoration, has a portal and a wheel window, originally located on the side. The right side has a 16th century portal, and inside there are a splendid holy water stoup with a 15th-century base, a 14th-century wooden figure of *Christ*, and a wooden *Pietà* of the 16th century brought from the church of di San Giovanni Battista. The crypt is now an integral of the **Diocesan Civic Museum** circuit and houses a significant collection of sacred art. The collection of precious metals (14th–15th centuries) and the Medieval stone material are particularly valuable

The oldest items include an interesting bas relief from the 2nd–3rd centuries AD, depicting a *gladiator contest*. There is a very fine, singular hexagonal reliquary dated 1576, made from carved ebony and ivory.
The **Museo Archeologico** is of great interest for regional history, housed in the rooms of Palazzo Vescovile, on one hand displaying archaeological materials from the excavations led by Baron Giovan Battista Leopardi, and on the other reconstructing the history of the Vestino area, using images, texts and audio visuals.
Along Corso Alessandrini, we find important buildings such as the deconsecrated Baroque **church of San Giovanni Battista**, whose stuccos by Giovan Battista Gianni are perhaps the most famous in the region. Past the Salconio porticos, we find the **SS Annunziata church**, radically restored in about 1773. The interior

480. Facing page: aerial view of Penne.
481. 482. Above: left, a detail of the frescoes that decorate the church of Sant'Agostino; right, the crypt of San Massimo cathedral, Penne.
483. Below: the bas-relief of a gladiator battle, Museo Civico Diocesano, Penne.

has a central chamber with calotte, flanked by two smaller, barrel-vaulted spans. A rectangular area houses the high altar at the end of the main block. The impressive façade, with an extraordinary strength of expression and remarkable freedom of composition, is a significant piece of Baroque architecture, despite being created at the early 19th century. The lively front features a concave wall silhouette and accentuated distance, reminiscent of Borromini's designs.

In Piazza Luca da Penne, in the heart of the town, we find the Medieval **complex of San Domenico** (the former convent is now the town hall). The appearance of the church reflects a radical 16th–17th-century restoration and was rebuilt many times over until a radical rebuilding dated 1722–30. The portal stands in an austere façade, with a 15th-century relief above it, depicting a *Enthroned Madonna with Child*, by Matteo Capro of Naples. There is a fine wooden choir carved by Ferdinando Mosca and Venanzio Bencivenga, with striking canvases by G. B. Ragazzini. Annexed and parallel to the church, we find the splendid **Rosario chapel**, started in 1613, and enhanced by an elaborate wooden caisson ceiling, a work completed between 1638 and 1641 by the carver Sebastiano Carinola of Guardiagrele. At the back looms the wooden high altar of the same period, with impressive volute columns and aedicule. The convent cloister is home to the public **epigraphic museum**. Inside nearby **Palazzo Aliprandi**, with its elaborate 17th-century portal, we find the charming, elegant **church of Sant'Antonio**, a noble chapel built in 1648 but with 18th-century furnishings.

The **church of San Giovanni Evangelista** on Corso dei Vestini is also worthy of note. Dating from the 14thcentury, today it is seen in its 16th-century reconstruction, with Baroque interior furnishings. There is a single nave with a polygonal apse, internal stuccos by G.B. Gianni and the vault was frescoed by Domiziano Vallarola. The façade features 1604 portal with a split tympanum, supported by corbels, and an architrave with frieze. On the left side, another portal, with a flat architrave, is dated 1594. The enchanting, central-plan **San Ciro oratory** is particularly interesting, as are the **church of Santa Croce**, near the gate of the same name, and the nearby 18th-century **church of Santa Chiara**.

Outside the ancient walls, on a hillside immersed in the countryside, we come to the **convent of Santa Maria in Colleromano**. The church is one of the last testimonies to Benedictine building skills, constructed between the late–13th and early–14th century. Apart from the beautiful 14th-century portal, fresco paintings dating back to the 15th-16th centuries have survived, along with a majestic, late-16th century wooden high altar. The convent, erected in the 15th century but later remodelled, is home to another small epigraphic museum and a picture gallery.

Another attraction is the nearby **complex of the old Santa Maria del Carmine convent**. It was already under construction in 1642, built on the site of an ancient hermitage. What we see today dates back to the mid–18th-century project managed by Neapolitan Francesco Di Sio and Penne-born Aniello Francia. Towards the end of the 18th century, Francia created the precious Baroque façade, cadenced by the double row of extrados columns. The interior, an outstanding regional example of a Latin cross plan, was designed by Di Sio to have a nave and side chapels, a deep presbytery and cupola transept located almost half-way down the chamber. The majestic stuccoed interiors are attributed toa Pietro Piazzola and dated 1770–73.

Part of the town is given over to the **Lago di Penne Nature Reserve**, home to the Museo Naturalistico Territoriale N. De Leone. The museum is divided into two sections, one devoted to nature, and the other promoting the local area and traditional activities.
A cultural highlight is the **Città di Penne International Literary Prize**, held in November.

**LORETO APRUTINO**, once known as *Castrum Laureti*, lies on a hill slope just a few kilometres from Penne, amidst luxuriant olive groves producing excellent EVO, mainly the PDO Aprutino-Pescarese. Loreto still has the feel of a Medieval village developed around an early site in what is now Via del Baio, with buildings of remarkable architectural quality: 19th-century **Palazzo Acerbo** and **Palazzo Valentini**, **Palazzo Treccia-Casamarte**, with its historic cobbled

484. Below: the convent of Santa Maria in Colleromano, Penne.
485. Facing page: aerial view of the historic centre of Loreto Aprutino.

courtyard, and **Palazzo Casamarte**.
Via del Baio connects impressive **Palazzo Chiola**, Francesco Valentini's 19th-century reconstruction of an extant Medieval castle, dominating the village, to the remarkable **Abbey of San Pietro Apostolo**, whose current appearance is the result of various alterations carried out over time. Some of the important works completed by Abbot Giovanni Battista Umbriani in the 16th century include a side portal (1534), the main portal (1549), and refurbishment of the choir (1551). A three-span cross-vaulted portico, with splendid mullioned windows, marks the entrance with its finely carved portal. The recently restored interior, with a nave and two aisles and a semi–circular apse, was reconditioned during the late–18th century, according to documentation of works by master architect, Ignazio Melella. A more remarkable and older feature is the chapel of San Tommaso d'Aquino, just to the left of the entrance, with its splendid altar and a wooden statue of the saint, as well as a 16th-century Castelli ceramic tiled floor. The 19th-century chapel of San Zopito Martire, with a cupola on pendentives with lantern, contains significant pieces of sacred 18th-century silverware such as the bust of the saint and a reliquary arm. The scraps of 16th-century frescoes in the first span of the right nave and the organ by Perugia-born Angelo Morettini are also interesting.

On Via Cesare Battisti, formerly Via Borea, closed off to the northwest by **Porta Castello**, we find **Castelletto Amorotti**, an unusual neo-Gothic revival constructed towards the late–19th century, home to the **Oil Museum**. Along Salita San Pietro is the **Acerbo Museum** building, with its extensive collection of Castelli ceramics, brought together from the 1930s onwards by the collector Baron Giacomo Acerbo. The valuable exhibit features chemists' jars, objects such as water stoups and tiles decorated with human figures, used in domestic worship. There are also dinner services, spanning a wide period of time from the 16th to the late–19th century. The products are from the workshops of Castelli's most prestigious masters, such as Grue and Gentili.

The Baroque façade of **Palazzo Guanciali** and the **church of San Francesco d'Assisi** are on Largo Guanciali. The latter was founded in the 13th century, the horizontal parapet façade boasting a beautiful stone portal of that time, and an impressive bell tower also in Atri style with a pyramid roof on an octagonal base, probably 15th century. The Late Baroque interior (1729) contains beautiful stucco decorations and wooden furniture.

486. 487. On this page: above, the arcaded porch of the abbey of San Pietro Apostolo; below, the Museo Acerbo, Loreto Aprutino.

# The Church of Santa Maria in Piano, Loreto Aprutino

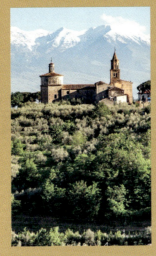

The church id documented as early as the 12th century as part of the possessions of the San Bartolomeo di Carpineto della Nora monastery. The nave is cadenced by ogival arches on semi-columns, ending in an octagonal apse, created with the mid–16th century alterations commissioned by Abbot Giovanni Battista Umbriani of Capua, as engraved on the sides of the main entrance architrave. These works include the portico added to the façade, the elevation of the impressive bell tower, work on the main Gothic portal (1599), and installation of a side entrance (1560). The segmented apse vault, with its majestic **golden altar** and lavish multicoloured statuary is protected by a cylindrical lantern with clerestory and probably dated back to the mid–17th century. The interior is decorated by a **series of fresco paintings**, mainly 15th century, with the exception of 16th-century works on the left-hand side. On the counterfaçade, we can see the famous *Last Judgement*, probably dating from the 1430s, whose right side was lost as it is covered by the 17th-century choir.

488. 489. Left, the church of Santa Maria in Piano; below, a detail of the frescoes that decorate the interior.

Behind the high altar there is a fine 18th-century organ, thought to be the work of Adriano Fedri (1745). The convent building, one of the region's oldest Franciscan settlements, has changed considerably over time. Today, it is home to the **Teatro Comunale**, recently restored, the **Museo della Civiltà Contadina** and the important **Antiquarium Casamarte archaeological museum**. This is an appropriate setting for the archaeological findings of Baron Antonio Casamarte, dating from the late–19th century. Valuable archaeological finds from prehistoric times to the Middle Ages are also on display, uncovered during the numerous digs supervised by the Archaeological Superintendency.

The large public museum network also includes the **Oleoteca Regional**, near Porta Palamolla, displaying EVO products from local oil mills.

The 14th-century **church of San Biagio** is also of great interest, restored in 1621, with its striking onion-shaped belfry. Also worthy of note is the **church of Santa Maria de Recepto**, with its elaborate wooden altar framing a *Madonna and Child*. Worth visiting in the vicinity are the **church of Santa Maria del Carmine** (or dei Cappuccini) with its fine 18th-century wooden tabernacle, and the **church of Madonna delle Grazie**, with its gilt wooden altar and a 15th-century *Madonna and Child*. A short distance from the monumental **Fontana Grande** there is the charming Parco dei Ligustri, a botanical park created by restoring an old abandoned garden.

However, it is the **church of Santa Maria in Piano**, in an isolated spot on a hill near the village, that retains the most important artistic legacies, with one of Abruzzo's foremost examples of 15th-century art (*see box p. 279*).

Since the 18th century, Whit Monday has been a traditional date in the calendar for the "genuflection" of an ox during the **Feast of St Zopitus**. A white ox adorned with coloured ribbons is ridden by a child dressed in white, then made to kneel before a statue of the saint.

The village of **COLLECORVINO** stands on a panoramic hill between the Tavo and Fino rivers, with a compact centre set around the main square. Highlights are the **church of Sant'Andrea Apostolo**, founded in the late 16th century and reworked in the late 18th – early part of the 19th century. An outstanding and unusual feature is the tall, narrow façade, crowned by small twin belfries. At the top of a hill to the north of the village, with a beautiful frescoes cloister and a central well, the monastery of San Patrignano of Benedictine origin was rebuilt from the 17th century onwards by the Franciscans.

490. 491. Above: left, the Antiquarium Casamarte archaeological museum; right, the feast of St Zopitus, Loreto Aprutino.
492. Left: the church of Sant'Andrea Apostolo, Collecorvino.

# Nora River Valley

The residential area of **CEPAGATTI**, in the River Nora valley, is a stone's throw from where it meets the River Pescara and may originate from a Roman settlement, suggested by the finding of a mediocre section of *opus reticulatum* near the 18th-century parish **church of Santi Lucia e Rocco**. The buildings then continue in a northeast direction. Dominating the village, **Torre Alex,** an imposing square tower probably dating back to the Middle Ages, even though it has been remodelled over time. Connected to many other garrisons built for the protection of the area, the tower's role was to act as a lookout post and send signals. Built in brick, it is now four storeys high and has a walkway all the way around the top, and a central room with a pyramid-shaped roof. Until the beginning of the 20th century, the walkway was open to the elements and protected by merlons.

On one side of the tower stands **San Rocco**, a chapel built by a noble family after the 1657 plague; on the other, the gate to the village with its vaulted passage. There is a connection between the tower's history and construction and that of the towers in the adjacent baronial mansion, now known as **Castello Marcantonio** and which replaced the older, fortified garrison. Work to convert the building to give it a typically residential appearance

Cepagatti, Nocciano, Catignano, Vicoli, Civitaquana, Cugnoli

The journey from Cepagatti, a short distance from where the Nora meets the Pescara, skirts the river through areas whose charm is due in no small part to the diminutive size of the towns and villages set in a hilly landscape of outstanding beauty. What makes this short itinerary really unique is the particular value of the ancient town and village centres seen in their complex stratification of different eras, and in their very close relationship with the surrounding area. The route is rendered even more interesting by monuments of undoubted value such as the parish church of Santa Maria delle Grazie at Civitaquana, one of the most important Romanesque places of worship in the region, and the parish church of Santo Stefano in Cugnoli with its extraordinary 12th-century ambo, a Romanesque masterpiece sculpted by Maestro Nicodemo in the renowned workshop of Roberto and Ruggiero.

493. Below: the Alex tower, Cepagatti, with the small church of San Rocco (left) and the Marcantonio Castle (right).

was undertaken in various stages and presumably began in the latter half of the 15th century, with the arrival of the Valignanis, an illustrious Chieti family and feudal lords of Cepagatti for generations. In the 17th century, the castle was the residence of the Marquis of Cepagatti, Alessandro Valignani and in around 1730, testified by a stone marker in the atrium, the mansion was restored by Marquis Federico Valignani. Considerable restoration work, some in the 1930s and more carried out recently, has partly modified the layout and how the complex appears from the outside.

If we continue towards Catignano and then branch off towards **Villa Badessa**, a district of Rosciano, founded around the mid-18th century, by a colony of Albanian refugees, we find the Greek Orthodox **church of Santa Maria Assunta**, erected in 1754 and the only Greek-Byzantine place of worship in Abruzzo. Inside there is a precious iconostasis and ancient icons than can be dated 15th–19th century.

Before reaching Catignano, it is worth stopping at the old fortified village of **NOCCIANO**, dating back to around the 11th century. Sitting atop a panoramic rise, its unusual compact ring shape surrounds baronial **Palazzo De Sterlich-Aliprandi**, an old castle now home to the **Museo delle Arti d'Abruzzo**, with a permanent collection of works by contemporary regional artists. The winding fortified complex and characteristic wall-houses delimit a ring layout that encircles the hill and probably developed around the original ancient isolated bulwark tower, which can still be discerned, even though it has been swallowed up by the later construction and is very much changed by the addition of windows. The bulwark tower has a splayed plinth base and typical sturdy rough-hewn cornerstones.

The parish **church of Sant'Antonio da Padova**, with its 16th-century portal (restored in the 17th century), contains interesting 18th-century canvases.

Standing apart from the built-up area we find the village's most striking monument, the Medieval **church of San Lorenzo**, with a simple rough-hewn stone gabled façade. The interior was originally a simple nave with a cross-vault apse, but an aisle was then added to the right. There are surviving remains of 14th–15th-century frescoes.

In the neighbouring village of **CATIGNANO**, it is worth visiting the parish **church of San Giovanni Battista** (also called Santa Maria della Neve), with its remarkable late 18th-century (1795) stone façade, an elegant example of Abruzzo Baroque, thought to the work of the circle of Giovan Francesco Leomporri, who designed Suffragio church in L'Aquila.

Outside the village, the **Natività monastery** was a settlement of Capuchin monks who took over the old Benedictine site. Its church, with its nave and two aisles survives and was recently restored to its former glory.

A short distance from the modern town of **VICOLI**, which developed along the road, there is the old village of **Vicoli Vecchio**, now being reclaimed, which was built around the old castle on a rise with splendid views, alongside the old church of San Vincenzo Ferrer. Walking up a steep, spectacular path from the old village's tiny square, there vistas over the gorge and the River Nora. The path leads to Parco Territoriale Attrezzato di Vicoli, an equipped park set in woods with flora and fauna.

Vicoli Vecchio's ancient **baronial mansion** is home to the nature reserve's **Ecomuseo Naturalistico**.

Turning back down towards the village of **CIVITAQUANA**, on a hill along the River Nora valley, we can still see the remains of its ancient walls. The **church of Santa Maria delle Grazie**, one of the region's most important churches, is particularly interesting, originally dating to before the first half of the 12th century. There have been several remodellings before being a stylistic restoration in 1935–8 and although this preserved original features, there are some questionable additions. The nave and two aisles have no transepts so end in three semi-circular apses crowned – like the façade – with a series of pilaster strips and pensile archlets typical of Lombard Romanesque architecture. The nave was originally cross-vaulted, then enclosed by a barrel vault, although the aisles still conserve some of the cross vault. The unusual alternating of supports shows multistyle to the left and cruciform to the right, as well as smaller circular supports. On the terracotta façade with its unusual gable there is a restored triple-light window aligned with the portal and replacing what was probably a rosette. A square bell tower has been grafted onto the left side of the

494–496. Facing page: above left, the church of Santa Maria Assunta, Villa Badessa, Rosciano; above right, Palazzo Baronale De Sterlich–Aliprandi, Nocciano; below, the church of San Giovanni Battista, Catignano.
497–499. On this page: above, views of the exterior and interior of the church of Santa Maria delle Grazie, Civitaquana; below, Vicoli.

church, presumably rebuilt in 1466 as indicated by the inscription. The top was reconstructed after the earthquake in the early 18th century. Inside we find an interesting panel depicting a male figure, set against a pillar that may date back to the Lombard era. The remnants of frescoes on the counterfaçade show a St Martin of Tours (datable to the latter half of the 15th century) and a fragment of Michael the Archangel, possibly inspired by the late–Gothic approach of the Maestro di Beffi. Also worth seeing is **Palazzo Leognani-Fieramosca**, with its handsome 17th-century façade.

The last stop on the itinerary is **CUGNOLI**, which still has traces of its old walls. The parish **church of Santo Stefano** is home to one of the masterpieces of Romanesque sculpture: the **ambo** made for Abbot Rainaldo by Maestro Nicodemo in 1166 (*see box p. 284*).

The **Carmine church**, with its central plan and cupola roof is dated early decades of the 1800s.

500. 501. Below: the external façade and the ambo of the church of San Stefano, Cugnoli.

## The Church of Santo Stefano, Cugnoli

The result of a series of reworkings, the church shows a varied façade of late Mannerist appearance, suggesting that several artisans had a hand in the creation of the 15th-century portal, with the addition of a split gable on two columns (perhaps in 1579) and the window above. The aisleless interior is decorated with 18th-century stuccoes, and has a splendid ambo, masterpiece of Abruzzo Romanesque sculpture attributed to the renowned Maestro Nicodemo. The **ambo** was built in 1166, as shown on the panel set facing the congregation, and was brought here in 1528 from the San Pietro church, no longer in existence. During the move, the stair parapet, where the mason's signature was probably carved, was lost. The square caisson ambo stands on slim octagonal pillars and is decorated with the Symbols of the Evangelists, reminiscent of the Moscufo Santa Maria del Lago ambo, also by Maestro Nicodemo.

# The Pescara Valley and its Historic Abbeys

ROSCIANO, skirted by the sheep track connecting L'Aquila to the coast of Chieti and the Tavoliere plain, is set on a height overlooking the Pescara valley. Remains of a Medieval fortification dominate the village, and include the square tower – perhaps 14th century – annexed to late-Renaissance **Palazzo Felice**.
The Assunzione della Beata Vergine Maria parish church is opposite the tower. It is likely that the layout dates to the 14th century and the interior, bell tower and the beautiful facade are 18th century (1794). There is a canvas of *Our Lady of the Rosario* (1581) brought from the 15th-century **church of San Nicola**. The interior is decorated with devotional frescoes dated 15th–16th centuries and echo the work of Andrea Delitio
Continuing inland, the ancient fortified village of **ALANNO** stands to the north of the River Pescara, on a hill strip at 300m asl. The round and square layout of the ancient fortifications are still visible in part. The compact urban fabric extends along the main road with streets branching off to form the characteristic plan.
The **Assunzione della Beata Vergine Maria parish church**, rebuilt following the 1915 earthquake, is home to valuable 16th–17th-century

Rosciano, Alanno, Pietranico, Torre de' Passeri, Castiglione a Casauria, Popoli, Tocco da Casauria, Scafa, Turrivalignani, Manoppello Scalo

The territory is of great environmental interest and lies within the Gran Sasso & Monti della Laga and Majella national parks. The River Pescara, the largest water course in Abruzzo, runs through it. Historically this was a transit area for shepherds and their flocks, and it is dotted with important monastic settlements and remarkable defensive constructions. Starting in Alanno, and crossing from one bank of the Pescara to the other, we reach Popoli, dominated by its impressive, unique fort, at the intersection of the Pescara and Gizio valleys and the so-called Via della Lana ("wool road"), that connected Florence to Naples, via L'Aquila.

502. Right: view of Rosciano.
503. Below: Aerial view of Alanno with Mount Majella in the background.

paintings, a 1300s polychrome wooden statue of Our Lady of Mercy and an ancient stone opus of St Clement. Also worth seeing, the **church of San Francesco**, annexed to the **convent of San Ludovico**, with its 18th-century interior home to stuccos and canvases by Paolo de Majo and Nicola Ranieri. The façade was rebuilt in 1880 when the convent was completely reworked.

The **Madonna delle Grazie oratory**, about 3km from the residential area, is worth visiting, as is the church of Santa Maria della Croce at Pietranico, both rare examples of votive churches built anew during the 17th century. The characteristic design of rural churches in Abruzzo, which continued past the 1550s, can be seen in Santa Maria in Valle Verde, in Celano, or Santa Maria delle Grazie, in Civitaretenga, of that time. Legend has it that the first construction dates back to sometime after 1498, following the miraculous apparition of the Virgin Mary, commemorated by two inscriptions on the counter-façade. The church was later extended, and richly decorated in the 16th–17th centuries. The church chamber comprises two bays, with cross-vaults, and two barrel-vaulted chapels on the left, while there are two altars on the right. The vaults are entirely frescoed, depicting the Holy *Trinity* as well as the *Sibyls*. The apse frescoes in the wall lunettes and the vault crowns show interesting references to Umbria-Marche expression, in particular to Marche artist Giacomo Bonfini. There is a 15th-century triptych and a 16th-century sculptural group depicting a *Crucifixion* with the *Virgin Mary and St John*.

The 16th-century portal is set into the simple arcaded façade, surmounted by a *Madonna and Child* dated early 1500s. Inside, we find admirable frescoes and polychrome stuccos, including those created in 1675 by the Lombard master, Donato Ferada. The oratory, closely linked to the nearby sheep track, is a rare example of an important Baroque construction that survives intact.

The older part of the picturesque village of **PIETRANICO,** set on the left bank of the River Pescara, retains a few examples of 15th-century buildings. The modern parish **church of San Michele** has a 1400s processional cross. The **Madonna della Croce oratory** is the most interesting construction, located just a short distance from the built-up area. The small chapel was founded after 1613 to honour the apparition of the Virgin Mary. It appears as an incomplete Greek cross, made up of squarish cross-vaulted cells with scheme arches and like the end walls of these wings, are decorated with magnificent stuccos and paintings dating to various periods of the 17th century, the work of local artists. There is an eye-catching pictorial cycle in the Madonna della Croce chapel, produced by Tommaso

Berardino Aquilano in 1628, influenced by Roman culture, who left his signature on the left-hand pillar. Also worthy of note is the Annunciazione chapel with its 1656 paintings by Antonelli de Castelli from Tocco da Casauria. Colour and gilding were added by Berardino Caldarella and his son Francesco in 1670. The stark stone façade, with horizontal coping, is enhanced by a portal with two scroll corbels supporting a tympanum and plaque dated 1618. On 2 May each year, there is a charming procession in honour of Our Lady of the Cross, the route lit by bonfires burning genista.

**TORRE DE' PASSERI** is located near the River Pescara. The town is dominated by **Gizzi** (formerly Mazara) **castle**, the result of work carried out in the 18th century by order of Smeralda Mazara, and which englobed the remains of an existing fortified structure. The building is home not only to the Dante research institute and the **Museo Dantesco Fortunato Bellonzi**, with many illustrations of the *Divine Comedy*, but also to the Biblioteca Caldora library. The façade is completed by a round-arch portal flanked by two extrados columns, and above it a balcony with central window, crowned by a tympanum with the Mazara coat of arms. Amongst the annexes we find a particularly interesting oil mill and wine cellar, with round arches, dug out of the tufa. Also worth seeing is the **Madonna delle Grazie parish church**, dating back to the late–18th century, with its unusual prospect with two side belfries, in a layout often used by European Baroque but quite rare in Abruzzo.

The **abbey church of San Clemente a Casauria** (*see box p. 288*) is a short distance from Torre de' Passeri and one of Abruzzo's most significant architectural and artistic architectures, the result of a series of interventions implemented from the end of the 12th century, up to the restoration work carried out between the late 19th century and early 20th century.

The adjacent village of **CASTIGLIONE A CASAURIA**, astride a ridge to the north of the River Pescara, is documented from the 10th century as a fortified castle. It retains characteristic buildings with beautiful stone portals and windows. The 14th-century portal of the **church of San Francesco** is worth mentioning, as is another – almost coeval – entrance of the **church of Santa Maria Assunta** on the right.

**Palazzo de Petris Fraggianni** looms over the tiny urban centre for which it was the ultimate

504–506. Facing page: above left, inside the oratory; below, the Madonna della Croce procession, Pietranico; above right, the entrance of Palazzo di Petrolio Fraggianni, Castiglione a Casauria.
507. On this page, below: aerial view of Torre de' Passeri.

# The Abbey of San Clemente a Casauria

The abbey complex consists of the church, preceded by a portico, and a convent building to its right, so it is well placed, just a short distance from the River Pescara. The abbey, built in the 9th century, was commissioned by Ludovic II, on a legendary island in the River Pescara, was renovated to its current form by Abbot Leonate, from the 12th century. onwards, and became a centre of political and economic importance for a wide area. Abbot Leonate started the work from the frontispiece, where the famous portico with the upper oratory dedicated to San Michele Arcangelo can be found. Leonate also ordered Brother Giovanni di Berardo to collect together all the papers still in possession of the abbey, accompanied by a precise chronicle of the monastery: this was the start of the *Chronicon Casauriense*, which is now acknowledged as an extraordinary source of historical news of the time. In 1182 Abbot Leonate died, very probably leaving works unfinished that he had planned to complete. His successor, Abbot Gioele, continued his work, in particular completing the bronze doors of the church's main portal. The monastery, still active towards the late–14th century, began to decline with the death of Abbot Leonate, and reached a terrible state of dereliction in the 19th century. Thanks to the commitment the scholar Pier Luigi Calore, and to the personal intervention of Gabriele D'Annunzio, who took up the cause of saving the abbey, in 1894 San Clemente was declared a national monument. The **main portal**, with architrave and lunette, shows elaborate carvings that depict scenes from life at the abbey, and is enhanced by the fine **bronze doors**. It opens onto the nave and two aisles, with a wooden roof, cadenced by different styles of pillars and ogival arches. The transept protrudes slightly from the longitudinal section, which closes in a semi-circular apse. The presbytery area, distinguished by the mighty concrete beams constructed during 1920s' restoration work, is raised up above the **crypt**, which was probably rebuilt towards the end of the 11th century, with abundant use of recovered material. In the nave, the splendid 12th-century **ambo** is flanked by a lovely **Paschal candle**. In the apse area there is a 15th-century **ciborium** protecting the altar, and an Early Christian sarcophagus that once contained the urn with St Clement's sacred remains.

The **Antiquarium** dedicated to Pier Luigi Calore was set up in the premises of the nearby convent. The collection includes many stone plaques and findings from nearby Interpromium and findings from the digs in the area adjacent to the abbey.

508. 509. On this page: the central portal and façade of the abbey of San Clemente in Casauria.
510. 511. Facing page: above, the castle; below, the church of San Francesco in Piazza della Libertà, Popoli.

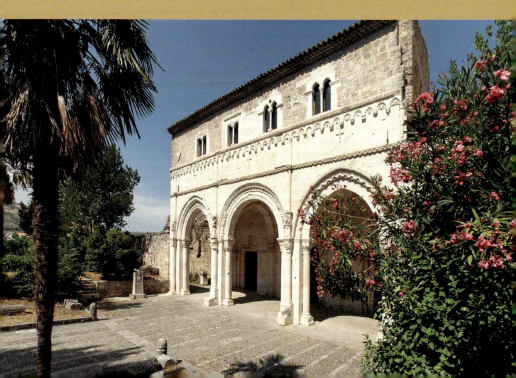

bulwark. This impressive building was transformed into a residence after it was acquired in 1620 by Nunzio de Petris of the Castiglione fief. It is on a hilltop with the town sloping beneath it. The current layout, consisting of a residential core and numerous rooms used for storing and processing agricultural products, is the result of later extensions and conversions. The extremely ancient original core comprises a section upstream, with a triangular garden. The other buildings were annexed to this (17th–18th century), forming the central courtyard we see today. Efforts are being made to restore the original building, which still retains part of its traditional architectural language, and several elements pertaining to its ancient productions, like the ancient oil mill and millstone. An ogive portal with double arched lintel opens in the inner façade, showing the typical broken stick motif reminiscent of the portico of the abbey of San Clemente. The outer portal is the fruit of 17th-century interventions. A number of rooms inside have been recovered to house the small **Museo della Comunità Agricola e Artigiana del Secolo XX Edolo Masci,** a museum of the 20th-century farming and artisan community.

Nearby, on the rocky Colle Sant'Angelo slopes, dominating the windy Popoli gorge, we find the striking Sant'Angelo grotto, a place of rock worship difficult to access. This is one of the most interesting caves in Abruzzo, a place of worship as early as Roman times, then throughout the Middle Ages, when it was dedicated to the Gargano cult, already very common in the Lombard era. With shepherds playing a part in diffusion of the cult throughout Abruzzo. In the first half of the 12th century, this ancient place of worship was given to the monastery of San Clemente a Casauria by Sansone di Teodino.

Just beyond the gorges of the same name, **POPOLI** ("key of the Three Abruzzos") stands in part on lowland and in part picturesquely along the slope. The town is on the banks of the River Aterno, which here flows into the Pescara, and is now a well-known spa, dominated by the striking ruins of the **Medieval castle** built by the powerful Cantelmo family. Here on the slopes of Mount Morrone, the first settlement dates back to the time of its fortification by Tidolfo, Bishop of Valva (1015). The ruins of the elaborate enclosed castle, once of great strategic importance, are almost triangular in shape and clearly visible, with a pentagonal stone ravelin in the upper part and towers on each of the two corners.

It has now been partially consolidated, and the remains still have considerable historical, environmental, and architectural impact. As the 15th century drew to a close, Count Restaino Cantelmo added the southern round tower, flanked by two buildings of the same period.

Popoli still has important architectural features of its noble past, above all the **Taverna Ducale**, considered to be one of the region's most interesting Medieval civil buildings, with its splendid façade graced with coats of arms and bas reliefs (*see box p. 290*).

The 15th-century **Palazzo Cantelmo** courtyard is striking, with its open staircase, a triple-arch loggia on Ionic columns, and elegant Renaissance-style portals. The main rusticated portal is superb.

The **church of San Francesco** in monumental Piazza della Libertà, in the heart of the town, is worth a visit. Presumably founded in the late 13th century, it was then rebuilt in about 1480 – a date carved into the Cantelmo coast of arms at the base of the bell tower – by order of Restaino Cantelmo. This 15th-century reconstruction work was then further modified by 18th-century Baroque decorations, and altered again by recent, very controversial, restoration work. The original layout, with no aisles, a square choir and a roof, was altered by the construction of four chapels per side and vaults, then replaced by a flat ceiling in 1958–62. The addition of the a cupola to the bell tower is dated 1714. The oldest part of this unusual façade, framed by corner responds and finished with a jutting cornice, is enriched by an

## Taverna Ducale, Popoli

Built in the latter half of the 14th century, this is one of the most typical examples of Medieval architecture in Abruzzo. It was formerly intended for the collection of tolls and tithes as we can read in the façade inscription indicating the "tolls" that the local feudal lord demanded on animals, goods and people who passed along the public street, ordered to be placed there by Fabrizio Cantelmo, 4th Duke of Popoli, who died in the early 17th century. The building was later used as an inn. Two portals open onto the street, with larger, lancet arch leading into the ground floor; the smaller portal is set above street level and led into the floor above. The scheme-arch feature of the smaller Popoli portal resembles others found in L'Aquila and especially in Naples, which are a variation of a design commonly found in Tuscany, where segmental arches were set under lancet arches. The elegant façade is in local ashlar as high as a cornice that runs along the entire front, and acts as a sill for the pair of mullioned windows with a central dividing pillar. Each two-light mullion is enhanced by small ogival arches, and fretwork or bas-relief decorations; these, together with some of the sculptures, may be recovered material. Some of the finest elements include the eight Samnite shields, alternated with decorative bas-reliefs, bearing Angevin and Cantelmo symbols, and symbols of families connected to them. On the ground floor the building houses a **museum of antiquities**, with stone relics dating from Roman times and from the Middle Ages, discovered in the Popoli area.

512. On this page: the façade of the Taverna Ducale, Popoli.
513–515. Facing page: above, River Pescara springs; below, the Maestro di Caramanico *Pietà* and the ceramic antependium by Francesco Grue, both in the church of San Francesco, Popoli.

Aquila-type 13th-century splayed portal and by a unique quatrefoil rose window with the Cantelmo and Carafa coat of arms. The prospect ends with a horizontal coping attic, a large central window, indicating 1689, and connecting side scrolls. On the 18th-century altar in the right transept wing there is a Pietà, a fresco recently attributed to the so-called Maestro di Caramanico active between in the 15th–16th centuries. In the San Francesco chapel, there is a remarkable ceramic frontal (18th century) attributed to Francesco Grue of Castelli.

Opposite Palazzo Cantelmo, the **SS Trinità church** has some remarkable 1732frescoes by Giovan Battista Gamba, and an 18th-century high altar by Nicodemo Mancini of Pescocostanzo. In the oratory next door there is a 16th-century panel painting. Rebuilt between 1716 and 1734, the church is at the top of a spectacular staircase, has an austere stone façade, divided in three by pilasters and responds on pedestals, framing the three portals. The prospect ends in a smooth double-strip frieze and a central, triangular pediment. The central church has four chapels along its axis, a cupola enclosed in an octagonal base with a terminal clerestory.

Also worth seeing is the adjacent **church of San Lorenzo**, with its beautiful 18th-century marble and wooden furnishings, in addition to the **church of San Domenico** which vaunts two 18th-century altarpieces by Neapolitan Girolamo Cenatiempo, a pupil of Luca Giordano.

Of particular interest is the **Museo della Tecnica Corradino D'Ascanio**, dedicated to the legendary inventor of the helicopter and the extremely successful Vespa scooter, who was born in Popoli, in 1891. This important engineering museum is housed in the town hall and includes a library, a multimedia library, and a conference room.

The **Riserva Naturale Sorgenti del Pescara**, and part of the Riserva Naturale Orientata Monte Rotondo, fall within Popoli's municipal boundaries.

The town of **TOCCO DA CASAURIA** is found on the state road, east of the River Pescara, on a Mount Morrone foothill, in a strategic position on the Popoli gorges. This was the birthplace of the jurist Francesco Filomusi Guelfi, the cobble-poet Domenico Stromei, and the famous painter Francesco Paolo Michetti, whose birth house is open to the

public. The old town has winding streets, adapted to the lay of the land. The remains of boundary walls are visible, generally incorporated into houses. There are interesting examples of civil constructions, notably 19th-century **Palazzo Toro** on the high street, built by Enrico Toro to house his famous Centerbe liqueur distillery. The village is embraced by two impressive buildings. One is the parish **church of Sant'Eustachio**, of ancient origins and now revealing subsequent restorations that changed its appearance from 1706, with a façade reflecting a late intervention (1846) in keeping with the original style, the work of master Gaetano Alberici; the other is the **castle** in the upper area of the village, but now derelict. Its compact configuration is evident. There are four blocks arranged around a courtyard, and four corner towers, comparable to a similar layout in Celano. The current plan is the result of the reconstruction that took place after the 1456 earthquake, and was the work of the de Tortis family, lords of Tocco. Originally designed purely for defence, it was later converted and eventually became a residence. The castle can be entered from the southeast front, through a lancet arch a portal on Renaissance-style capitals. The lower part of the castle, with a steep scarp wall, shows that great care was taken in construction, both in the use of perfectly hewn tufaceous rock, probably found locally, laid in horizontal rows, both in the laying of stone in stronger and weaker points of the construction, for instance at the corners of the towers. The upper part of the building, on the other hand, is separated from the base by a continuous string-course, and was created almost entirely from rough stone, laid in an irregular fashion, probably the result of a reconstruction following the 1706 earthquake. On the upper level, there are large stone-framed windows with geometric patterns. Some of the tower-top merlons, with their characteristic four-point silhouette, are still evident.

The elegant 1500s portal of the **church of San Domenico** (1495) was recently attributed to Pietro dell'Aquila and Bernardino Darz. The interior vaults a splendid Madonna and Child known as the *Madonna della Candelora*, a late–1400s polychrome wood statue and a praiseworthy pictorial cycle on the side altars by Chieti-born Donato Teodoro. The rural **church of Madonna delle Grazie** has a fine portal dated 1605. In the surrounding

areas, in a stunning natural environment, the **Osservanza convent** is well worth a visit, with its annexed Santa Maria del Paradiso church and 17th-century frescoed cloister, as well as a comprehensive library of codices and precious incunabula.
The Riserva Naturale del Monte Rotondo falls within the municipal boundaries.
Continuing along the state road, in Piano d'Orta there are interesting examples of early 20th-century industrial archaeology. These workshops show skilful use of elegant iron trusses and combine Majella stone with the brick decorated in Art Nouveau style.
Originally part of San Valentino in Abruzzo Citeriore, **SCAFA** stands at the confluence of the River Pescara and the River Lavino, and officially became a municipality in its own right in 1948. The use of the local asphalt rock, which began long ago, has made the town an important industrial centre. Until 1870–81 "Scafa di San Valentino" was a boat crossing point over the River Pescara. The town centre developed after that, near the wooden bridge that replaced the boats. It then grew quite significantly thanks to its industrial activities.
The **Parco Territoriale Attrezzato Sorgenti Sulfuree sul Lavino** is a few kilometres away, in De Contra. Here the sulphurous springs form lakes that are a unique shade of turquoise, creating a truly enchanting environment. Along the river the 17th-century working **Farnese mill** can be visited.
The Oasi del Lago di Alanno – Piano d'Orta protects wildlife in an area of about 160 hectares spread around the municipalities of Alanno, Bolognano, Scafa, and Torre dei Passeri, in the wetlands of the barrage at the River Pescara's third leap. From Scafa, it is just a short trip up to **TURRIVALIGNANI**, located at the top of a sandstone crag. The main natural attractions include the Ripe, a group of natural badlands protected as a Site of Community Interest. Retaining part of its historic urban centre, at one time the village was known simply as Turri but later became a

stronghold of the Valignanis, a famous Chieti family, hence the change in name. The **church of di San Giovanni Battista e di San Vincenzo**, dated 12th century, is near the cemetery. Its basilica layout shows a nave and two aisles, divided by different types of pillar, and closed by a small apse. The presbytery is raised above the ancient crypt below, with barrel vaults over a nave and two aisles. The crypt is also home to an ancient, worn statue of St Vincent, who is afforded special worship. The façade is the result of modern restoration work.
The important Cistercian **abbey church of Santa Maria Arabona** (*see box p. 294*) is found along the main road, very near to Manoppello Scalo.

516. 517. Facing page: above, Tocco da Casauria against the backdrop of Mount Majella; below, the *Madonna della Candelora* in the church of San Domenico.
518. Above: aerial view of the Lago di Alanno–Piano d'Orta oasis, along the River Pescara.
519. 520. Below: sulphur springs on the River Lavino; the Farnese mill in the Decontra di Scafa district.

# The Abbey of Santa Maria Arabona, Manoppello

The abbey was founded in around 1197 and it is a prime example of Burgundian Cistercian architecture in Abruzzo, with design reminiscent of the Lazio abbeys of Casamari and Fossanova. The construction started by 1208 and continued until the end of the 13th century, beginning with a main rectangular chevet, but for unknown reasons was never completed. Only the first bay of the church's main section was built, forming an unusual cross, with a five-span transept and ribbed cross vaults, and a rectangular choir composed of two transverse cells, with light provided by five windows arranged in a so-called triplet motif, with a large rose window above. The choir is flanked by a chapel on either side, originally used as the monks' private refectory. The central bay, with its eight-segment vault, was originally intended to support a tiburium used as a bell tower, as was the Cistercian custom, but it was never completed. The oculus at the centre of the vault was intended to allow passage of bell ropes. Instead, unusually, the bell tower was constructed at the former left transept, which meant that the rose window was off centre. On this side, we find the ancient "door of the dead", now used as the main portal. In the right transept wing, there is a door leading to the ancient sacristy and a staircase leading to the monks' dormitory, which corresponds to the beautiful mullioned window on a wall that is now closed. In 1952, the consolidation work was completed, including a nave with modern brick façade. The church portal was refitted to the new façade, whilst the communicating door between church and cloisters now opens out onto the garden. Both portals, which probably date back to the early 1300s, have a singular semi-circular archivolt with double lunette. Inside, there are beautiful frescoes by Antonio di Atri, an important 14th-century Abruzzo painter, and remarkable sculptures, including the **Paschal candle** and fine **tabernacle**, the only one of its kind in Abruzzo, both sculpted with refined symbolic motifs.

At the end of the 1700s, the Zambra barons of Chieti purchased the whole convent building, which they

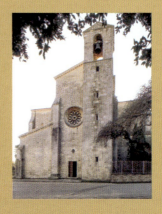

then transformed into a noble residence, adding doors and windows in keeping with the original style, a garden and a fish pond. Despite the alterations, several of the original rooms are identifiable, in particular the well-preserved **chapter room**, rare for this region, with its four spans and ogival arches resting on a central clustered pillar with eight smaller columns encircling an octagonal centre.

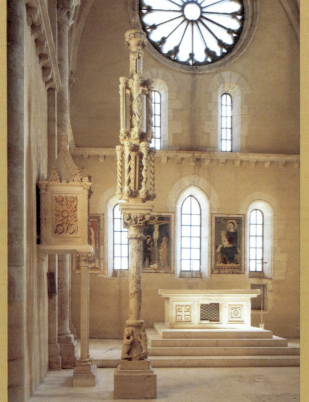

521–523. This page: right, Paschal candle and tabernacle; above, the abbey façade and a detail of the *Madonna and Child* fresco, Santa Maria Arabona.
524. 525. Facing page: above, the ex-convent of the Poor Clares; below, the Volto Santo shrine, Manoppello.

# National Parks in the Pescara Disctrect

The first part of the itinerary begins at **MANOPPELLO**, set up on a panoramic hill to the right of the River Pescara. The area is distinguished by important 18th–19th-century buildings, constructed and decorated with fine local Manoppello stone. Some of the most significant monuments include **Palazzo Marinelli** and **Palazzo Verratti**, with their important 18th-century portals, as well as Palazzo Pardi, with its small internal courtyard, and 19th-century **Palazzo Blasioli**. The most interesting features can be found along Corso Santarelli, a road named after Manoppello's famous sculp-

tor, Giovanni Antonio Santarelli (1758–1826). Here we should note the important **church of San Nicola**, dating from the 14th century but reconstructed in the Baroque style between 1844 and 1882. Traces of its primitive Medieval construction can be seen in the lower part of the façade, dominated by the elegant portal. Inside, there are a nave and two aisles, and the presbytery is raised above a large crypt, covered by a stuccoed cupola. One of the works that has been preserved is an important statue of the *Dead Christ*, attributed to Santarelli.

The **SS Annunziata church**, with the adjoining former Poor Clare convent, has a remarkable original layout; the area once occupied by the cloisters is now Piazza Portici, graced with a sculpture by Pietro Cascella, who also designed the urban furnishings. On the right side, next to a first commemorative plaque of 1958, a new stone slab was placed in memory of the victims of the Marcinelle mine tragedy. An interesting 16th-century *Madonna Adoring the Child Jesus* can be found inside the convent. The austere façade of the **church of San Pancrazio**, with its Baroque interior and elaborate high

Manoppello, Serramonacesca, Lettomanoppello, San Valentino in Abruzzo Citeriore, Abbateggio, Roccamorice, Bolognano, Salle, Caramanico Terme, Sant'Eufemia a Majella, Bussi sul Tirino, Pescosansonesco, Corvara, Brittoli, Carpineto della Nora, Civitella Casanova, Villa Celiera, Montebello di Bertona, Farindola

The itinerary, divided into two sections, crosses the province's innermost areas, located on both banks of the River Pescara, and protected by the two large national parks and by nature reserves, in the spectacular scenario of the Gran Sasso massif, and the Morrone and Majella mountains. The Pescara side of Majella National Park is harsh and isolated. Transhumance has always been practiced in this area, and it is also dotted with evidence of sheep rearing, the most authentic examples being the drystone huts, similar to tholos, which are direct derivatives of Puglia's trulli, in the areas between Roccamorice and Lettomanoppello. For centuries Mount Majella's wild, rugged slopes were the ideal place for mystics: the intriguing hermitages and spectacular grottoes, places of worship with an ancient history, located in the highest part of the mountain, provide solemn proof.

altar (1728), can be found at the end of the Corso. The **convent of San Lorenzo** is also very striking. A Franciscan church with an unusual central plan, it originally had a cupola, but is now covered by wooden planks after the roof collapsed.

Just a short distance away from the built-up area is the **Volto Santo sanctuary**, whose foundation as a Capuchin convent is traditionally dated to 1620, although the current appearance is the result of interventions from 1960 to 1965. Here the famous Holy Face relic is venerated and with the Turin Shroud it is considered the true effigy of Christ, attracting thousands of faithful to this small town in Abruzzo. The sanctuary contains a **section devoted to valuable religious art**, housed in the adjoining Treasury, where there is also an ethnology section. Another outstanding item is a precious 18th-century wooden tabernacle produced by Capuchin masters, kept in the ex-voto room.

The itinerary continues up to **SERRAMONACESCA**, built at the foot of Mount Piano di Taricca, near the River Alento, amid woods and olive groves. Here, although the parish **church of Santa Maria Assunta** is quite interesting, one of the Region's most important **Medieval churches, San Liberatore a Majella** (*see box p. 297*), once part of a vast abbey complex, is located outside the built-up area.

Near to the abbey church, in its striking natural setting, is the rock **complex of San Giovanni**, with arcosolium tombs dug into the rock, and small hermit cells opening up amidst the vegetation of the small rock wall.

Evident remains of **Castel Menardo** still dominate the Alento Valley. The castle was erected to defend the Benedictine abbey of San Liberatore a Majella and was destroyed in the late–15th century.

The only remains of the fortified village of Polegra (part of a round tower) can be seen on the right bank of the River Alento, set on the sheer cliff top, and once the property of the abbey of San Liberatore a Majella.

The **grotto hermitage of Sant'Onofrio** is well worth a visit. It is a well-known place of worship for shepherds, and ancient rituals are still practiced there. Inside the cave we find St Onofrius' "cradle", presumed to be the hermit saint's straw bed, where devout pilgrims come to lie as part of an ancient lithotherapy rite.

Returning downhill to Manoppello, the town of **LETTOMANOPPELLO** rises on a spur to the right of the River Lavino, and is famous for its stonemason workshops, which help to keep alive an ancient tradition. Apart from the **San Nicola di Bari parish church**, there is the lovely **Iconicella sanctuary** close by, as well as the stunning **Praie cave** with its stalactites, near the Garzillo Springs, and the magical **Sant'Angelo cave**, a place of worship dug from the rock. The Angel statue (found in the church of San Tommaso and now on display in Pescara's Genti D'Abruzzo ethnography museum) is presumed to be the 13th-century work of craftsmen in the San Tommaso di Caramanico area. Lettomanoppello together with the municipalities of Abbateggio, Roccamorice, San Valentino, and Scafa, was part of one of the most important mining districts for the extraction of bitumen, active from 1840 until the 1960s. In the Pilone district, traces of the ancient mining activity are still visible, almost a singular open-air museum.

526–528. This page: above, reliquary of the Holy Face of Manoppello; below, the ruins of Castel Menardo and the rock hermitage of Sant'Onofrio, near Serramonacesca.

# The Abbey of San Liberatore a Majella, Serramonacesca

The Benedictine church lay in ruins for the entire 19th century, until it was restored in 1967–71, and is one of the most important examples of Abruzzo Medieval architecture, despite the many refurbishments. The church and the monastery are documented as early as 856 as the property of the Abbey of Montecassino. Rebuilt in the early 11th century by the monk, Teobaldo, who restored both the apse area, raising it above a crypt, and the lower part of the façade, bringing it slightly further forward from its original position. Presumably before the end of 1073, Abbot Desiderio of Montecassino commissioned the renovation and completion of the church, preserving the parts that had already been finished. The current triple-apse basilica design has a nave and two aisles, divided by pillars, replacing the flat ceiling with a wooden truss version. In the 16th century, the portico was rebuilt, its traces still visible in front of the gabled façade, and the simple Romanesque single-light windows were replaced with the Mannerist windows in place today. Outside, at an angle to the right-hand corner, a square bell tower that probably dates from the 1130s. Other renovations were carried out by the Abbot Bernardo Ayglerio of Montecassino (1263–82) who commissioned the fine Byzantine-style mosaic floor – today partly relaid in the nave – and the internal pictorial decoration of which fragments of frescoes survive in the central apse and on the left side. During the 16th century other paintings were added and can currently be seen in the right aisle. The precious **ambo** dates to the early 1180s.

529. The abbey of San Liberatore a Majella.

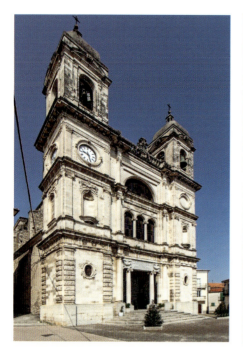

The town of **SAN VALENTINO IN ABRUZZO CITERIORE** is located further along the main road, in the hilly area between the rivers Orta and Lavinio. This settlement was part of the Farnese state until the dynasty came to an end during the first half of the 18th century. What is believed to be the original urban centre, once enclosed by town walls with towers and gates, is built on top of the hill, retaining some relics of an ancient **castle or Palazzo Farnese**, set on the southwest slopes. The castle, partially converted into a residential building, is set around a courtyard. A few sections of the impressive walls can still be seen, and, on the south side, the overhang of the ancient tower is still visible, with defence embrasures. The northeast side, where the access door is located, was presumably modified during the 18th century.

From Largo San Nicola, going down to the left, we find the charming 18th-century **Delfina Olivieri De Cambaceres house** with a beautiful portal surmounted by two heraldic coats of arms. This is home to the wonderful **Museo dei Fossili e delle Ambre**, a unique museum of its kind, exhibiting some of the oldest fossils, brought from all over the world. A splendid collection of amber is also on display, with some quite ancient pieces in many nuances.

The 18th-century parish **church of Santi Valentino e Damiano** is also worth seeing. The original ancient church was already derelict in 1771 and rebuilt in late–Baroque forms in 1777–91. The aisleless interior with cupola vaults lavish stucco decorations entrusted to Alessandro Terzani in 1795 and finished mid-way through the 1800s. The majestic stone façade with two distinctive bell towers was added to the 18th-century church in 1920–31 by architect Antonino Liberi, achieving an entirely unique expression of combined styles. In the surrounding area, there is a particularly striking **rural chapel Madonna della Croce**, located along a secondary L'Aquila–Foggia sheep track path, known as Centurelle–Montesecco. There are two interesting inscriptions, still partly visible, on the façade's ashlar angle irons: one side reads SULMONA, and the other CIVIT[A].

Noteworthy events, the characteristic **Good Friday procession** and the singular "Cornuti" procession, dedicated to cuckolds on 10 November, the eve of the feast of St Martin.

**ABBATEGGIO** is just a short distance away, located to the left of the Lavino River, in

an area of sumptuous beech and oak woods. Apart from the parish **church of San Lorenzo** and **Palazzo Simone**, with its lavish portal, the **Madonna dell'Elcina sanctuary** is also of interest. It is set on a panoramic hill, overlooking the valley, built on the spot of a miraculous apparition of the Virgin Mary on a holm oak in the 1400s. On the eve of the Madonna dell'Elcina feast, the "Stanga" pageant is held in the San Lorenzo church square. For the occasion, the honour of carrying the statue of the Virgin Mary in the procession the next day is sold to the highest bidders.

In the area around Macchia di Abbateggio, there are some interesting typical tholos drystone huts, traditionally used by Majella shepherds.

Humans have settled this area since the Palaeolithic period, as can be seen in the Valle Giumentina site, extremely important for the study of prehistory, which was explored by the illustrious scholar Antonio Mario Radmilli in the 1950s. It is considered one of the most important examples of Lower–Mid Palaeolithic in Abruzzo.

Continuing towards Majella, lovely **ROCCAMORICE** appears as if suspended from an airy rock spur. Medieval in origin, it retains all the character of a small mountain village, and for some time it was the Valignani family stronghold, who were still the owners in the late–18th century.

In the Medieval centre of lanes, narrow streets and small terraced houses, it is worth noting the ancient home of the hermit Pietro da Morrone, who later became Pope Celestine V: it is the only doorway with Celestine's coat of arms.

**San Donato parish church** is interesting, with its Medieval origins, demolished and rebuilt in 1910. Inside we find most of the works and furnishings brought here in 1807 from Santo Spirito a Majella following the closure of the Celestine abbey, including a remarkable polychrome wooden crucifix which shows late-13th-century German production traits.

Before arriving at the Belvedere, we pass the Annunziata church, formerly the Madonna del Buon Consiglio, and still known as the "baron's church" as it was

530–532. Facing page: top left, SS Valentino e Damiano parish church; top right, the castle Palazzo Farnese and the Museo dei Fossili e delle Ambre; below, the Good Friday procession, San Valentino.
533. 534. This page: above, the sanctuary of the Madonna of Elcina, Abbateggio; right, a drystone hut in Valle Giumentina.

# The Abbey-Hermitage of Santo Spirito a Majella

In the mid–13th century, Pietro da Morrone, the future Celestine V, also carried out his reconstruction work in this area.
On the wall to the left of the main altar, we see the surviving fragment of the plaque depicting the miraculous event of 1248, which led Pietro to found the abbey of Santo Spirito.
In 1586, after a long period of neglect, Abbot Pietro Santucci of Manfredonia restored the complex in the Late Renaissance forms we see in the beautiful portal that retains fragments of frescoes from the same period in the lunette. Also visible are traces of the original 13th-century church in the cross vault above the 16th-century high altar with its precious *Pentecost*, dated 1605, recently attributed to the Neapolitan painter Fabrizio Santafede (1560?–1626).
After a series of events, the 1807 suppression and the 1820 fire, the abbey was abandoned once more.

A number of artefacts and canvases, and a wooden *Crucifix*, owned by the abbey, were already saved then. The complex comprises three parts: the first is the church and sacristy annexe, as well as living quarters on two floors; the second houses the remains of the old monastery's amenities; the third were guest quarters (recently restored and called "Casa del Principe"), with the holy staircase and Maddalena oratory.
We continue along a low walkway on the left side of the church, which leads to the crypt which is made up of three small rooms. The central room is called the "Stanza del Crocifisso", while to the right of the church next to the stone fountain there is a tunnel carved into the rock and leading to the ruins of the convent. Along the way we see 17th-century stone coats of arms with bishops' insignia. At the end of the walkway, two doors open into the "Casa del principe", a stark 17th-century construction commissioned by Neapolitan nobleman Marino IV Caracciolo, Prince of San Buono, Duke of Castel di Sangro, and Marquis of Bucchianico, traditionally said to have intended to lead an ascetic life here.
A very steep stone staircase leads us to the Maddalena oratory, its name inspired by the presence of a precious late–16th-century high relief above the portal depicting *Mary Magdalene*. Inside there is a beautiful fresco of the *Deposition of the Cross* by the 18th-century Roccacasale painter, Domenico Gizzonio.
Large drinking troughs are located in the square in front of the church.

535. Below: the hermitage of San Spirito.
536. 537. Facing page: the hermitage balcony; below, the 25 August procession, San Bartolomeo in Legio.

commissioned in 1760 by Giuseppe Zambra, Baron of Roccamorice. The church was built over the ancient Medieval tower of the village's fortified walls and the outline is still discernible. After the stop at the belvedere, a high terrace offers a spectacular view of the Santo Spirito valley, carved by the River Lavino. The Sant'Anna trench leads to the opposite end of the village as far as the Medieval tower, the only trace left of the ancient fortified system.

The area is dotted with the distinctive drystone huts once used to shelter sheep and for farming purposes. Sometimes the huts were grouped together to form a community, like the impressive example at Colle della Civita, to the southeast of the town. The Region's most remarkable hermitages are to be found in the area, and the most important is the **hermitage of Santo Spirito a Majella**. It is one of the most famous of Majella's monastic complexes, and notwithstanding the many changes in use to which it was subjected over the years, it has lost none of its appeal, due mainly to its spectacular location at the foot of an impressive limestone face (*see box p. 300*).

The **hermitage of San Bartolomeo in Legio** is also magnificent, hidden by the sheer face of the rugged Santo Spirito valley. It was rebuilt immediately after 1252 by Pietro da Morrone, who lived there in 1277–88. It continues to be popular today and on 25 August each year the statue of St Bartholomew is carried through the town in a procession, after which the devout drink and collect the "miraculous" water from a spring inside the hermitage. A 13th-century fresco survives in the church façade, depicting *Christ in Blessing*.

Further along the main road, we come to the characteristic village of **BOLOGNANO**, located on a rise along the Orta valley, virtually unchanged and clustered around its Palazzo Baronale (16th century) and the Medieval **church of Santa Maria Entroterra**, with its 16th-century façade (inside see *Madonna with Child and Saints*, a 16th-century fresco whose style suggests the hand of Pompeo Cesura). The artist Joseph Beuys (1921–86) often stayed there during the latter years of his life, a guest at the

16th-century **Palazzo Durini** set on what is now Piazza Joseph Beuys, named after the artist. It is designed as an amphitheatre facing the valley and is planted with four large descending flowerbeds planted with living examples of the four symbols of Beuys' art (oak, laurel, rosemary and olive trees).

Part of the Riserva Naturale Valle dell'Orta falls within the Bolognano municipal boundaries and is also the site of the prehistoric **Grotta dei Piccioni**, one of the Region's most important archaeological caves, with extraordinary discoveries made over the last few years. One particularly impressive cave opens at 75m along the rock face of the River Orta's left bank. The cave consists of two large chamber and contains clearly identifiable layers that can be dated back to between the fifth millennium and the tenth century BC, including various stages of the Neolithic and Eneolithic eras, and the Bronze Age, up to the early Iron Age.

Skirting the parish **church of Sant'Antonio Abate** and following the itinerary, we reach the Cisterna di Bolognano, a unique natural swimming pool within the reserve.

Charming **Musellaro**, is a tiny district of Bolognano and the upper part is certainly the oldest, with the Medieval castle and annexed **Palazzo Tabassi** and **SS Crocifisso chapel**. With Salle, the village was famous for traditional production of musical instrument strings.

The itinerary continues as far as the intriguing ruins of the ancient village of **SALLE**, which was seriously damaged during the 1933 earthquake, and rebuilt just a short distance away from the old site. An interesting **museum of Bourbon history** is located on the ground floor of the castle of the Genova Barons. The origins of **Salle Castle**, now entirely reconstructed, would seem to date back to the 10th century. Today almost nothing remains of the original buildings, with the exception of part of the foundations in the court, uphill, and a few underground chambers in the garden, downhill.

The next spot we visit is the popular spa town of **CARAMANICO TERME**, on a spur between the River Orfento and River Orta valleys. The spa facilities are in an ancient building in a park. The town has an interesting **Museo della fauna abruzzese e italiana** wildlife museum. Rebuilt following the 1706 earthquake the town vaunts some of its important monuments, including the **church of Santa Maria Maggiore**, founded in the 15th century, but with evident traces of the numerous modifications carried out over time. It has a nave and two aisles, renovated in the 19th century, with the restoration of the prospect, cadenced by pilaster strips on a tall plinth and accommodating the 1476 portal, as engraved there. The lunette contains a high relief of the *Coronation of Mary*, signed by

538. 539. Below left: Santa Maria Entroterra church, Bolognano, and the Musellaro hamlet.
540. 541. Below right: Bolognano's "Cisterna" and the Baroni di Genova castle, Salle.
542. Facing page, above: the centre of Caramanico Terme.

Giovanni Teutonico of Lübeck. The apse prospect, with an attractive ashlar facing, features small statues of saints and worshippers. The cuspidate bell tower with several orders, bears the coat of arms of Francesco D'Aquilo, Prince of Caramanico, and is dated 1432.
Inside there is a wooden Christ of the German school, a 16th-century canvas of the Flemish–Neapolitan school, and the choir with 18th-century paintings by Giuseppangelo Ronzi.
In addition to elegant 18th-century buildings, other highlights are the **church of San Domenico**, with its attractive portals, and that of **San Nicola church**. The latter, in Piazza Garibaldi, has a nave and two aisles spectacular building with impressive 16th-century altars and precious furnishings.
Worth a visit at a short distance from Caramanico, out in the River Orta valley with its luxuriant pastures, the **church of San Tommaso**, with its splendid central portal and interesting interior frescoes (*see box p. 303*).
Not far from the village of San Tommaso, there is a truly enchanting location: the Luco plain with the remains of Medieval castle of Luco.
In the fascinating Valle dei Luchi the River Orta has eroded the rock, leading to the formation of the so-called "Marmitte dei Giganti", near the Santa Lucia rapids and creating canyons.
The Riserva Naturale Orientata Piana Grande della Majelletta and the Riserva Naturale Orientata Valle dell'Orfento reserves are both located in the municipal district of Caramanico, an exception among Majella valleys because of the abundance of water.
The **Paolo Barrasso nature museum**, in the **Reserve Visitor Centre**, was set up in 1986 by the Italian state forestry corps and also worth a visit. It has an active study centre with a library and screening room. The archaeological section of the museum, on the first floor of the main building, together with the nature and

## Church of San Tommaso, Caramanico Terme

The discovery of several bronzes of the god Hercules, on the site where the church stands today, is proof of the presence of an ancient place of worship dedicated to a deity loved by shepherds. Inside, a column has been worn away at the base by devout pilgrims rubbing against it, and a well of spring water in the crypt reveals the practice of ancient rituals linked to water and stone cults that are still alive today.
The late 12th–early 13th century church, clearly in Benedictine style, has a somewhat complex but disjointed layout, the result of a series of building phases. It has a nave and two aisles cadenced by two rows of pillars with round arches, a single apse and no transept. Along the right-hand row, apart from the five pillars, there is a slim presumably recycled column. The bell tower was built during restoration work after the 1706 earthquake. The 13th-century paintings on some of the aisle supports are intriguing, especially the impressive depiction of *St Christopher*. An outstanding feature is the façade, with its relief of Christ and the twelve Apostles on the main portal architrave. On the side doors we can identify on the left, St Berardo, patron of the church and abbot of San Clemente a Casauria; St Thomas is depicted on the right.

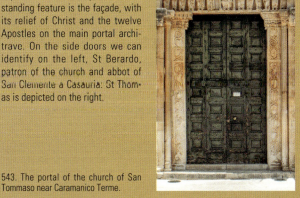

543. The portal of the church of San Tommaso near Caramanico Terme.

geology sections on the ground floor, provide a comprehensive picture of Majella, and are one of the first exhibition structures in Europe specifically designed for the blind and partially sighted. The panels dedicated to prehistoric times describe the important **Valle Giumentina archaeological site**, one of Abruzzo's main Early- and Mid-Palaeolithic sites, found on the bed of an ancient lake that dried up about 40,000 years ago. In the Decontra district of Caramanico there are several examples of drystone shepherd huts and a striking two-storey tholos hut with spiral roof, the largest to survive in Abruzzo.

The River Orfento **Area Faunistica della Lontra** includes a breeding centre where attempts are being made to reintroduce the endangered otter locally.

From the headquarters of the Reserve, a path on the hydrographic right of the valley leads to the **hermitage of Sant'Onofrio all'Orfento**. The scant remains of the church still show some sections with painted plaster. Nearby, the **hermitage of San Giovanni all'Orfento** (one of the most spectacular and inaccessible on Majella) is set into the walls of one of the Orfento's most rugged side valleys.

Continuing towards the mountain, the town of **SANT'EUFEMIA A MAJELLA** is located halfway up Mount Rapina, between Majella and Morrone, nestled in Majella National Park.

For the high environmental value of the district and the extraordinary variety of natural habitats found there, from the high-altitude breccia pits of Mount Amaro to the river valley below, which includes the most picturesque part of the upper course of the River Orta, the mountain town constitutes one of the most valuable natural oases of the central-southern Apennines and one of the most popular destinations for mountain tourism, especially in summer, with delicious dairy specialities an added attraction.

In the upper part of town, the **church of San Bartolomeo Apostolo** has a remarkable lavish 17th–18th-century tabernacle, the work of Capuchin artists.

A short distance from the town, the **Lama Bianca** beech wood is part of a dedicated nature reserve, bordering on the Riserva della Valle dell'Orfento, with special paths for disabled visitors. The reserve takes its name from a local place name that indicates a pale rugged slope (Lama), typical of Apennine and Majella chalkstone.

It is worth visiting the **Daniela Brescia botanical garden**, about a kilometre from the town, which can also be reached via the state road SS487 for Passo San Leonardo. The garden covers five hectares and has four sections, with an artificial lake, a peat bog, rock gardens, with two streams crossed by wooden bridges.

At the foot of Mount Morrone beech wood, the intriguing Medieval village of **Roccacaramanico**, abandoned during the 20th century, retains its original traits and is now being restored. The **ethnography museum** (initially "Diana e Tamara" now "Marcello De Giovanni") is located in the old town hall (formerly the church of Sant'Antonio Abate, shown in an ornamental frieze on the outside wall). The comprehensive collection of objects, tools and machines narrates the working lives of the people from this mountain district.

Roccacaramanico is a perfect starting point for relaxed walks and more demanding hikes to discover the wonderful mountain landscapes.

The itinerary returns down valley and takes the road for Popoli, turning off towards **BUSSI SUL TIRINO**, a fairly large town built on the banks of the River Tirino, 344m above sea level, set against the Pescara Valley. This is Gran Sasso–Laga National Park territory and includes municipalities in the Province of Pescara. It is possible to identify some of the layout of the older settlement, originally a stronghold, fortified with mighty walls reinforced by round towers, whose traces are still visible.

It has been suggested that a **castle-mansion** was erected over an existing fortification. The current configuration indicates that extensive refurbishments were undertaken and today's square mansion, with an elegant inner court, has a high corbelled, square tower to the north. The main entrance is highlighted by an arched portal framed by ashlars (hewn stone, often square in shape, that are visible on the wall surface).

Southwest of Bussi, there is the remarkable

early-Medieval **Sutrium triangular tower**, quite unique in Abruzzo along with the Montegualtieri tower, in the province of Teramo.

Nearby, the remains of the beautiful **church of Santa Maria di Cartignano**, documented in the early 11th century, owned by Montecassino. Its ruins were rebuilt and restored in 1968-9, with a few integrations. The nave-and-two-aisle layout is still visible, with square pillars and a semi-circular apse. The unusual façade ends in a small bell-gable tower. Armanino da Modena's 13th-century apse frescoes have been moved to the Museo Nazionale d'Abruzzo in L'Aquila. The church is also the origin of a bas relief and a polychrome *Madonna and Child* statue, now both in the church of San Lorenzo, also in Bussi.

The nearby town of **PESCOSANSONESCO**, overlooking the Pescara Valley from its foothill position is truly striking. After serious damage caused by the 1917 and 1933 earthquakes, and by subsequent landslides, the old town – Pescosansonesco Vecchio – was abandoned and its population began a new settlement. The abandoned area is intriguing, with the ruins of the Medieval castle at the top, the beautiful castle portal has been moved to the left of the entrance gate to the nearby church of San Clemente a Casauria for those wishing to see it. Above the 14th-century portal there is a coat of arms and an epigraph bearing the name of Sigismondo Cantelmo, member of the powerful family who dominated the town in the 16th century. Lower down, the 12th-century **church of San Nicola** is near the gate of the same name. The decorative details, in particular the capitals of the austere portal and in the rosette inside the lunette, of the small church show sculptural motifs inspired by the nearby abbey of San Clemente a Casauria. Inside the church there are interesting remains of the fresco of *saints Sylvester and Andrea*, as well as the Baroque wooden bust of St Nicola.

The old **Franciscan convent of Santa Maria in Coll'Angeli** is also significant, with annexed church and beautiful 16th-century. portal. The interior, enlarged in the 1600s in the Baroque style, has a spectacular painted stucco altar. Two inscriptions on the sides of the entrance

544. Facing page: the church of San Bartolomeo Apostolo, Sant'Eufemia a Majella.
545. 546. Above: the centre of Bussi sul Tirino and the ruined church of Santa Maria di Cartignano.
547. Below: Pescosansonesco.

attest to the restoration of the façade of 1744.

Nearby, the small church of Santa Lucia is worth visiting for the so-called **Fonte Romana** fountain, perhaps 16th century but restored in 1870.

In the new town, the **church of Santa Maria in Blesiano** (also called dell'Ambrosiana) was built in the 12th century and is said to stand on the site of ancient temple dedicated to Diana. The crypt is remarkable, built completely above ground, with columns cannibalized from the older complex. Inside there are the remains of an interesting cycle of 13th-century frescoes depicting the *Judgment* and attributed to the painter Gentile da Rocca. There is also a stoup, perhaps 14th-century, consisting of an ancient base and basin, as well as a 15th-century *Madonna and Child*.

At the edge of the new town we can visit the small 16th-century **church of San Rocco** with the remains of coeval frescoes inside. On the nearby Pizzo della Croce hill there are the remains of the most important archaeological complex in the province of Pescara, an **Italic-Roman sanctuary** where the Italic oath against Rome was probably sworn during the Social War.

A religious destination is the impressive **sanctuary of the Saint Nunzio Sulprizio,** a young worker born in Pescosansonesco in 1817. Pilgrims come here all year round to bathe in the waters of the miraculous spring where the saint would treat his ulcerated leg.

Continuing inland, the characteristic early Medieval village of **CORVARA** appears on the slopes of Mount Aquileo. There are surviving traces of a wall-houses and a small round tower; only the bell tower and the apse base of the parish church of Sant'Andrea Apostolo remain. In the more recent quarter, we find the late–18th-century **church of Santa Maria delle Grazie** as well as the **church of Santa Maria in Costantinopoli**, with an interesting 13th-century portal.

Once through the Forca di Penne mountain pass, the town of **BRITTOLI**, with its typical watchtower, is found midway up a hillslope between the Nora and Cigno valleys. Dating back to the early Middle Ages, it developed around the castle, whose site is presumed to stand over what is now **Palazzo Pagliccia** (15th century), whose portal bears the family coat of arms. Annexed to this early 1800s Sant'Antonio family chapel. Northwest of the complex, the parish **church San Carlo**, with a late–18th-century layout, a simple portal with split gable and central coat of arms.

Forca di Penne WWF Oasis lies between the municipalities of Corvara and Brittoli.

Nearby **CARPINETO DELLA NORA**, located on the southern slopes of Mount Cappucciata, along the River Nora, has the noteworthy **SS Agata e Carlo parish church**, with 18th-century interior and two 17th-century wooden altars. The refurbishment of the 16th-century portal is dated 1738 and bears the Borromeo coat of arms. Not far from the residential area there is the abbey **complex of San Bartolomeo** (*see box p. 309*), which is certainly worth seeing.

**CIVITELLA CASANOVA** lies along the crest of a hill, near the confluence of the Schiavone and Festina rivers. The parish **church of Santa Maria delle Grazie**, originally dated 16th century, but remodelled over time, is worth visiting for the late-16th-century fresco of *Our Lady of the Rosary*, attributed to Compassino senior. Also interesting are the **Palazzo Pignatelli** wall decorations by painter Severino Galante (c. 1750–1827). The most important monument, however, is just out of town: the **church of Santa Maria della Cona**, annexed to the cemetery, with its beautiful Renaissance portal (1529) by Pietro de Stefano and Bernardino Darz, brought from nearby Casanova abbey. Inside, a Baroque altar contains a 1515 *Madonna and Child* fresco.

The hamlet of **VILLA CELIERA** lies on a ridge on the slopes of Mount Bertona. Near the village there are the ruins of the **Cistercian abbey of Santa Maria di Casanova**, erected in 1191 as the first foundation of that order in Abruzzo, and later a flourishing economic and cultural centre. The charm of these places and the exceptional historical value of the ancient fortified monastic settlement make the ruins of Casanova one of the most important sites for cultural and environmental reasons. The

548. Facing page: Corvara.
549. 550. This page: above, aerial view of Forca di Penne; below, portal of Santa Maria delle Grazie parish church, Civitella Casanova.

original layout can be discerned despite dense vegetation, with the now-derelict but mighty watchtower, deprived of its ancient battlements with archlets and corbels, presumably in visual communication with the tower of the nearby settlement of *Bertone*, an ancient fortified village on a rocky spur, with significant surviving remains. The **Casanova tower** in hewn stone has five inner levels, connected with a stairs dug into the thick wall, with barrel vaults and characteristic embrasures. On the ground floor there are traces of a chimney and a brick cupola. Fragments of the boundary wall and the remains of the church and monastery, which would have been set around the cloister, are visible down valley. The church, which must have been refurbished, although the exact date is unknown, originally had a nave and two aisles, a transept and rectangular choir, with round archways on pillars.

In the upper section of the village of **MONTEBELLO DI BERTONA**, an ancient Farnese stronghold on a hill to the south of the River Tavo, vestiges of the ancient castle survive on the escarpment, incorporated into **Palazzo Baronale**. In the late–18th-century **church of San Pietro Apostolo** there are some interesting wooden sculptures.

**FARINDOLA**, an ancient Farnese settlement, extends over a spur to the left of the River Tavo. Worth visiting are the parish **church of San Nicola** and the remains of the **castle**. The village is famous for its excellent **Pecorino cheese**.

The municipalities of Farindola, Villa Celiera, Montebello di Bertona, Civitella Casanova, Carpineto della Nora and Brittoli are part of the Riserva naturale regionale del Voltigno e della valle d'Angri. An **Abruzzo Chamois wildlife reserve** also exists at Farindola, where a project was put in place in 1992 to bring the chamois back to Gran Sasso.

551. Facing page: San Bartolomeo abbey.
552. Above: ruins of the Cistercian abbey of Santa Maria Casanova near Villa Celiera.
553. 554. Below: the portal and interior of San Bartolomeo abbey, Carpineto della Nora.

## Abbey of San Bartolomeo, Carpineto Nora

The chronicles tell us that the ancient abbey was founded by Count Berardo of Penne, who enriched the new complex with the remains of St Bartholomew. The abbey was later rebuilt but only the church and relics of the monastery survive. The stark façade, flanked on the left by a mighty square tower, originally a Late Romanesque belfry. The interior has an atrium portal leading to a nave and two aisles, divided by round arches of equal height, on rectangular pillars. The presbytery area, influenced by Burgundian Gothic, is believed to be 13th century. It is defined by a three-section transept and flat, slightly protruding choir, with ribbed cross-vaults. The transept is thought to be the only part of the church to have retained the features of the original construction perhaps dating to the first quarter of the 1200s. Particularly fine elements include the altar, supported by four columns with sculpted capitals, and the splendid portal, originally 13th-century, decorated with lively animal and plant motifs. The complex was restored in 1970–1.

# Teramo
### and province

# Teramo

## The City

Remarkable evidence of Roman Interamnia, dating back to a time of great splendour when it became a municipality, is still evident in Teramo's urban fabric. Substantial remains of Roman buildings devoted to entertainment are to be found in the heart of the city: the **amphitheatre**, built in the second half of the 1st century BC, and the Augustan **theatre**. The southeast sector of the amphitheatre can be seen from Via Irelli, but the entire northwest sector was destroyed and replaced by the cathedral building where bas reliefs depicting armed gladiators almost certainly taken from the near by amphitheatre can be found in the curtain walls. Of the impressive oval building, 70m along the main axis and 60m along the short axis, the exterior ring of walls with brick facings are visible among the modern constructions. To the south, aligned with the main axis, there are three openings, while the most important entrance was set to the east, on the short axis.

Also on Via Irelli it is possible to admire part of the theatre, also visible from Largo Anfiteatro and Via Teatro Antico. The ancient building, which could accommodate around 3,000 spectators, still preserves parts of the *praecinctio*,

The city of Teramo, an ancient Praetutii settlement, has prehistoric roots. The city's ancient name of Interamnia (*inter amnes* = between rivers) refers to its favourable position on the table between the rivers Tordino and Vezzola. The modern part of the compact city faces towards the mountains while the well-preserved oldest part of the ancient town is on the table between the rivers.

The Praetutii town has brought forth important archaeological evidence that documents phases of protohistoric habitation and of a first urban structure that became a Roman colony in the 3rd century BC, seat of the Conciliabulum, a place where Roman administrators and the Praetutii met regularly. Following destruction and pillaging during the barbarian invasions, the city enjoyed great prosperity under the rule of the Angevin dynasty and was a lively cultural hub in the 18th century, vaunting a striking standard of artistic activity.

555. 556. On the previous double page and facing page: aerial views of the historic centre.
557. Right: the remains of the Roman amphitheatre in Via Irelli.
558. Below: the remains of the Roman theatre in Via Paris.

stage, *proscenium*, orchestra and *summa cavea*. The cavea structure was supported by two orders of arches, but only the lower order has survived. An elegant female statue recovered near the theatre, the so-called "Musa", is currently exhibited in the city's archaeological museum. Further important evidence of Roman Teramo can be seen in the stunning remains of the **Largo Torre Bruciata** *domus*, with precious frescoes and foliage decorations, upon which the ancient city cathedral (Santa Maria Interamniensis, then San Getulio) was built. The **Via di Porta Carrese** *domus* and **Largo Madonna delle Grazie** *domus*, with their dolphin-motif mosaic flooring, are breath-taking. The sensational remains of the magnificent **"del Leone" house** were brought to light at the end of the 19th century during renovation work on **Palazzo Savini**, in Corso Cerulli. The excavations uncovered the flooring of the tablinum, the main room of a Roman house, decorated with a polychrome mosaic of exceptional workmanship: the centre boasts a particularly precious mosaic, depicting a lion in combat with a serpent, was made separately and subsequently inserted. A band decorated with theatrical masks and garlands surrounds the emblem, striking for its unusual richness of colour and chiaroscuro effects.

Remains of the **hot baths**, probably built during the period when the Roman town expanded westwards, can be seen in Largo Madonna delle Grazie.

Teramo's **"Francesco Savini" Archaeological Museum** (*see box p. 315*) is found in 19th-century Palazzo del Tribunale and is undoubtedly the very heart of the city of Teramo's museum system. It is considered a veritable "territorial museum", closely linked to the archaeological sites present in the city and its district (theatre, amphitheatre, Torre Bruciata domus, Lion mosaic, Largo Madonna delle Grazie,

Porta Carrese and, outside the city, the Ponte Messato necropolis). It also provides precise references to other museums like the Pinacoteca Civica municipal art museum.

The most iconic of Teramo's monuments is certainly the splendid **cathedral of Santa Maria Assunta**, a complex and fascinating building has kept intact its true identity despite renovations, integrations and some questionable restorations (*see box p. 316*).

The **church of Sant'Anna dei Pompetti** (formerly San Getulio) is part of the ancient cathedral of Santa Maria Aprutiensis, erected in the 6th–8th centuries, and destroyed by the 1156 fire which involved the entire city. The small church occupied the ancient cathedral's atrium, which has brought to light the remains of a nave and two aisles with a central apse, in the area of an *insula* which may have been the original site of two marble columns with Corinthian capitals, recycled for the subsequent Medieval structure.

The interior is composed of three squared roofed rooms. On the right with a roof, in the centre with a ribbed cross vault, and on the left with a brick cross vault without ribbing. The most precious elements preserved here are ancient stone remains, fragments of an intrados fresco, a middle entrance, and a 14th-century fresco of a *Nursing Madonna* attributed to Giacomo di Campli.

Examples of Medieval civil architecture where the original characteristics are still visible include **Casa Francese** and **Casa Urbani**, and the outstanding **Casa Dei Melatino**, built in about 1237 over another building.

Situated right in the historical centre, in Largo Melatino, the house was the residence of the

559. 560. Facing page: above, the mosaic of the "del Leone" residence; below, one of the Roman sculptures exhibited in Teramo Archaeological Museum.
561. 562. Above: left, the remains of the *domus* in Largo Torre Bruciata; right, the interior of the church of Sant'Anna dei Pompetti.
563. Below: a room in Teramo Archaeological Museum.

## Francesco Savini Archaeological Museum

Teramo Archaeological Museum has two floors: the ground floor comprises an eight-room exhibit that retraces the urban history of the area currently occupied by the city from the 12th century BC to the 8th century AD. The findings exhibited, linked to the sites of provenance, provide precise references to the area and testify to the greatness of ancient Interamnia Italic funeral furnishings, architectural fragments of the theatre, amphitheatre and public buildings, from earthenware and everyday objects to Roman sculptures, some of excellent workmanship (for example, the solemn white marble bust depicting Septimus Severus, and the female bust thought to be Faustina Maxima, both 2nd century AD). Then the Muse statue with drapery, from the 1st century AD, recovered from the Roman theatre, and the headless statue of Aphrodite from the early 2nd century AD are simply marvellous. On the upper floor there is an exhibition dedicated to the settlement of Teramo territory from prehistory to Medieval times. The Museum is also home to the Auditorium Comunale San Carlo, used as a conference room for cultural events.

# Cathedral of Santa Maria Assunta, Teramo

The cathedral stands between Piazza Martiri della Libertà and Piazza Orsini and shows various stages of construction. It currently comprises two main structures: the older eastern part, with a nave and two aisles and alternating columns and pillars, is known as the "Guido nave", built in 1158–74 by order of Bishop Guido II; higher up, beyond the transept, the western section is called the "Arcioni nave", and dates back to the enlargement ordered by Bishop Niccolò degli Arcioni in 1332–5, and comprises six bays with ogival arches. The centre of the three-part transept has an octagonal segmented dome, of mid-northern influence and uncertain date. On the left of the transept there is the sumptuous **chapel of San Berardo**, built in 1731–76, during the Baroque refurbishment that completely reinterpreted the interior with original features, subsequently erased during the 1932–5 restoration. The exterior has a series of impressive features, such as the **main portal** dated 1332, made by the Roman sculptor Deodato di Cosma, with a round archivolt enhanced by a golden mosaic decoration, a high cuspidate tympanum decorated with statues in aedicules, and a large rose window. The two columns, one at each end, support two sculptures by Nicola da Guardiagrele. The square belfry, begun in the 12th century and finished in 1493 by Antonio da Lodi, who built the soaring octagonal structure, is softened by double-lancet and oval windows, framed by majolica tiles and culminating in a pyramidal cusp. The cathedral vaunts many masterpieces, for example, the superb *antependium*, a silver **paliotto** by Nicola da Guardiagrele, made in 1433–48, and found today on the high altar; the beautiful 15th-century marble aedicule by Antonio da Lodi; the precious Sagrestia Nuova wooden altar (1594–1632), with 17th-century paintings by Polish artist, Sebastiano Majewski. The 15th-century **polyptych** by Venetian Jacobello del Fiore can be admired on the Baroque altar in the San Berardo chapel. In the apse, we find a large round window with multicoloured glass, by Duilio Cambellotti.

564. Above: a detail of the bronze frontal by Nicola da Guardiagrele.
565. Left: the nave.
566. Facing page: cathedral portal.

powerful Melatino family who fought over the rule of the city with the rival Antonelli family for over a century. Elegant brick porticoes, once the ground floor, were walled and used as stables, shops and stores at a later date. Prestigious architectural and decorative details enhance the main façade on Largo Melatino. The four double-lancet windows are noteworthy, with their elegant stone pillars and striking protomes, two of which are wrapped in the coils of a snake with a female head. The structure is now also home to a precious collection of ancient Abruzzo majolica.

Opposite, we find the side of the **church of Sant'Antonio** (formerly San Francesco), founded in the 13th century and rebuilt in the 1300s. After various exterior alterations, the interior was modified between the 18th and 19th centuries. Of the ancient church there is a surviving portal (perhaps originally located on the left-hand side), the large, partly-occluded, double-lancet apse window, the apertures of three single-lancet windows on the left-hand side, and a short section of the coping with a hanging arch detail. Around the cloister, adjacent to the right side of the church, the convent is still recognizable despite many modifications.

In the **church of San Domenico**, founded at the end of the 13th century, there are remarkable 14th-century frescoes on the walls of the choir and the upper terminal part of the left nave wall which survived refurbishments. The

567. Above: Medieval Casa dei Melatino.
568. 569. Below: left, the church of Sant'Antonio; right, the church of San Domenico.
570–572. Facing page: above, Palazzo del Municipio; below left, the church of the convent of Santa Maria delle Grazie; below right, the portico of Palazzo Vescovile.

latter are attributed to the so-called Luca d'Atri. The 15th-century *Annunciation* by the Maestro del Giudizio of Loreto Aprutino stands out on the walls adjacent to the counterfaçade.

Certainly worth visiting is the **church of San Benedetto**, belonging to one of the most ancient Capuchin convents in Abruzzo, built over extant Benedictine constructions. A noteworthy monumental high altar with inlaid tabernacle and wooden altars in the side chapels are attributed to the 17th-century Capuchin carver, Fra Giovanni Palombieri.

Outside the ancient urban walls, the **Santa Maria delle Grazie convent** cloister is still magical, although largely modified when the church was rebuilt in the late 19th century. The interior now appears in its 19th century guise to designs by Cesare Mariani and is home to a splendid wooden sculpture of the *Madonna and Child*, recently attributed to Giovanni di Biasuccio.

The **church of Sant'Agostino**, now seen in its restored form of 1876, was home to the polyptych by Jacobello del Fiore, now found in the cathedral. Also of interest are the cloisters of the **San Giovanni convent** founded in 1384 and later restored, now home to the **conservatory** dedicated to Teramo musician Gaetano Braga. The 14th-century **Palazzo Vescovile**, with its elegant arcade on Piazza Orsini, facing **Palazzo del Municipio**, is also interesting, now seen in its 1828 restored version. Last but not least, the flamboyant, Neoclassical **Palazzo Delfico**. Certainly worth mentioning, the **Della Monica castle** dating to the late–19th century and was part of a Medieval revival driven by the painter Gennaro Della Monica, and **Palazzo Castelli** is

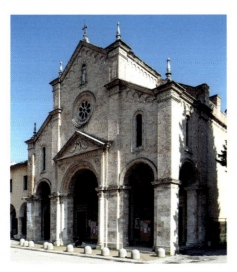

one of the most significant examples of Abruzzo Art Nouveau. 19th-century developments includes the San Ferdinando bridge over the Tordino, Palazzo della Provincia (now the Prefecture), the botanical gardens outside Porta San Giorgio, and the Piazza Garibaldi fountain. The distinguished **Melchiorre Delfico Library**, now found in Palazzo Delfico, is dedicated to Teramo's celebrated historian and philosopher (1744–1835), whose family donated a precious collection of volumes. The library is a point of cultural reference for the entire Abruzzo region, and worthy of note not only for its large collection of books, but also for manuscripts of local historical significance, such as the *Palma* Documents, and letters written by Delfico and Giannina Milli, the illustrious poetess born in Teramo (1825–88), whose commemorative bust is located in the city park. Of further note is the collection of paintings, partly displayed in the reading rooms, an expression of 19th–20th century art and culture.

The **Pinacoteca Civica**, the municipal art museum, in an elegant Neoclassical building in the city park, is of particular interest. As well as paintings of the 15th-century Teramo school and the Neapolitan, Venetian, Roman and Tuscan schools of the 16th, 17th and 18th centuries, it exhibits 19th-century Abruzzo art.

Teramo is also an important academic city, with five university faculties.

There are numerous cultural and sporting events, including the prestigious **Premio Teramo** for unpublished stories, the **Maggio Festeggiante**, the May festival of cinema, dance,

573. Below: the cathedral façade from Corso Cerulli.
574. Facing page: view of the cathedral bell tower from Corso San Giorgio.

music, and theatre, the important **Teramo Comics** exhibition, and the international **Interamnia Cup** handball tournament.

A few kilometres from the city centre, we find the **Osservatorio Astronomico d'Abruzzo**, an observatory located in the Collurania district. It was founded in 1890–93 by Teramo astronomer, Vincenzo Cerulli (1859–1927), who donated it to the State in 1917. It is also home to the **Collurania Museum** of 19th-century research instruments.

The **necropolis of Ponte Messato** unfolds along the so-called Via Sacra di Interamnia, a few kilometres outside Teramo, at Madonna della Cona. The funeral monuments are both cell-type and tempietto-type with opus incertum foundations, nucleus and enclosure, and opus quadratum travertine cladding and front; memorial stones, with inscriptions of the name of the deceased and size of the tomb, are found at the sides. The mausoleum of the illustrious *Sextus Histimennius* must have been the most monumental, as revealed by the size of the platform and burial area. The structure of the Roman necropolis is linked to cremation rites of the early decades of the 2nd century AD.

The city's surrounding areas are particularly charming with a great many villages scattered across the panoramic hills, and in valleys crossed by the River Tordino and River Vezzola. It is worth visiting Forcella, to see the "Ballo dell'Insegna" flag-throwers (23–24 September), Miano and its castle, Poggio Cono and Poggio San Vittorino, Villa Ripa, Rapino, Frondarola, Valle San Giovanni, where we can see the ruins of the **monastery of San Giovanni in Pergulis**; Colleminuccio with the small **church of San Lorenzo** and its large canvas of *St John in Patmos* by Flemish Dirk Hendricksz (c. 1544–1618) who transferred to Naples; Varano, Colle Santa Maria, San Pietro ad Lacum, and, lastly, towards the sea, Nepezzano and San Nicolò a Tordino. In Pantaneto it is worth seeing the **church of Santa Maria de Praediis**, of very ancient origins and with fine examples of carved capitals.

575. Above: detail of the 15th-century polyptych in Teramo's Pinacoteca Civica.
576. Below: the "Ballo dell'insegna", Forcella.

# The Coast from Martinsicuro to Silvi

**MARTINSICURO** is located not far from the A14 San Benedetto del Tronto-Ascoli Piceno motorway exit and is therefore extremely near the Marches border. It is a pleasant seaside resort of ancient, pre-Roman origin (*Castrum Truentum*), known for its mighty Carlo V **watchtower**, set along the main Adriatic coast road, not far from the River Tronto. The recently-restored brick tower is square-plan with scarp base, and was built for policing of river traffic, with opposite it a second tower, that no longer exists, which were just two of the many towers in the massive coastal defence system ordered by the Spanish viceroys of Naples, Alvarez de Toledo and Parafan de Ribeira, in the mid-16th century to fend off the attacking Turks. The Martinsicuro construction differs somewhat from the other vice-royalty towers, but these are the very features that make it so interesting and closer to the model of defence towers built on the coast from Latium to Campania. The tower was built in 1547, under the supervision of Captain Martin de Segura, whose name it took, confirmed by the dedicatory epigraph on the monument, now lost. The tower has two stone belt course cornices and typical machicolations supported by jutting corbels, with elegant, stone-framed windows that grace the sea-facing wall; originally the tower would have had crenelated battlements, now replaced by a span roof. The building next to the tower, evidently remodelled more than once, makes use of the old customs house and annexed lodgings.

Martinsicuro, Alba Adriatica, Tortoreto, Giulianova, Roseto degli Abruzzi, Montepagano, Pineto, Silvi

Seven enchanting riviera towns in the province of Teramo: small enough to retain a human dimension and sharing a calling for seaside tourism and seafaring activities. Fish-rich reefs and wide sandy shores are common to the area and this itinerary will wind its way through pleasant tourist towns with precious examples of art and history, relics of a splendid past that now form the ideal scenario for brilliant cultural events. Two of the most interesting old towns are Martinsicuro, with the mighty tower built by Charles V, and the art town of Giulianova, with a quite unique urban layout, designed anew in the 1400s. Then there is the well-preserved Cerrano tower, near Pineto, a fundamental element in the coastal defence system, ordered in the mid-16th century by the Spanish viceroys of Naples, following devastating Turkish raids.

577. Right: the Martinsicuro watchtower.
578. Below: a stretch of the Teramo coast.

Today the Tower and the Customs House are home to the **Antiquarium di** *Castrum Truentinum* **archaeological museum**. Also worth visiting is the **Museo delle Armi Antiche,** a display of ancient weapons found in a stately home along the Adriatic highway.

Proceeding along the coast, the next town is **ALBA ADRIATICA**, famous for its long sandy beach. A fascinating typical coastal watchtower, the **Torre della Vibrata**, has recently been restored. The 16th-century tower, which was part of the viceroyalty's coastal defence system, has the form of a truncated pyramid on a square base, without battlements but with a machicolations gallery, which is known to have played its military role as late as 1762, since it was described as a "corporal's tower".

The next town on the itinerary is **TORTORETO ALTO**, dove, where the remains of a primitive, river-pebble boundary fortification can be discerned at the base of today's clock tower, presumed to have separated, at least from the 14th-century, the two districts of Terravecchia and Terranova, which made up the town. A narrow gully ran between the two districts, installed with a drawbridge near the **clock tower**, whose base is original, although the upper section has been rebuilt. When the Acquavivas of Atri acquired Tortoreto in 1424, they ordered rebuilding of the fortifications, which englobed the old walls in the 15th-century scarp. Ample sections of the 15th-century brick walls survive along the town's northern edge, and to the east there is a round tower. The **church of Santa Maria della Misericordia** is extremely interesting for the 1500s frescoes by Giacomo Bonfini. The pictorial cycle attributed to the Ascoli artist illustrates episodes from the *Passion of Christ.*

Rebuilt in about 1534 (although the façade is the result of a 1700s–1800s reconstruction), the parish **church of San Nicola di Bari** boasts a noteworthy organ attributed to Ascoli-born Vincenzo Paci (1811–86), who also built another organ, for the **church of Sant'Agostino**. The convent structure was added to the church in the early 1500s and there is still an interesting terracotta *Madonna and Child* (although the child is missing), inspired by Silvestro dell'Aquila's more illustrious Ancarano prototype. Until 1973 the church also had an extraordinary *Baptism of St Augustine*, by Mattia Preti, now transferred to L'Aquila's National Museum.

Worth visiting at the highly popular resort of **Tortoreto Lido**, with its large beach and good facilities, including the Adriatica cycle path. Also noteworthy is the **Museo della Cultura Marinara**, a seafaring museum with a large collection of fishing equipment as well as a huge exhibition of shells, molluscs and vessel models.

The remains of a large **Roman villa** have been unearthed in Le Muracche district. The relics include parts of the dwelling section, looking out towards the sea, with plastered walls

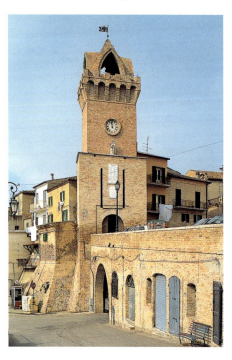

and mosaic flooring, as well as countless rooms from the rustic section.

The town of **GIULIANOVA**, built on a hill near the mouth of the River Tordino, with a splendid sea belvedere, is one of Abruzzo territory's most interesting, since it is a rare example of surviving uniform grid urban layout, designed ex-novo in the 1400s. In fact, the town was founded in the 1550s by Giulio Antonio Acquaviva d'Aragona, Duke of Atri and Count of San Flaviano and Conversano, and he installed the inhabitants of Castel San Flaviano, the older village, of Medieval origins (which had developed north of the important Roman town of Castrum Novum), destroyed in 1460. The new urban layout developed on a more defendable hillside and was settled within a four-sided fortified boundary wall, defended by round towers typical of the Teramo and Marches area.

Of the round towers that marked the corners of the curtain walls, all that survives is part of what was called the "**il Bianco**" tower, recently

restored and now home to the **Archaeological Section of Giulianova Civic Museum**. The first room exhibits are the contents of excavations undertaken near the cemetery, which brought to light structures and mosaic floors. The second room exhibits relics brought from excavations on the No. 16 highway, which served to clarify several aspects of the ancient urban plan with regard to the port layout.

In the high part of the town there is the noteworthy **church of San Flaviano**, an impressive brick construction dated post–1550 and one of the rare central plans in Abruzzo. The cathedral has an octagonal floorplan, with a unique bracket coping cornice, more typical of a fortification; the tambour cupola with clerestory, originally finished in enamelled tiles, later replaced with flat roof tiles The interior shows the results of a modern restoration that demolished the Baroque decorations and is cadenced by shallow niches, carved out of six sides of the octagon; under the church there is a large crypt, with its own entrance, characterized by an umbrella vault on pillars separating the central zone from the perimeter. The church has some interesting modern sculptures by Francesco Coccia and Venanzo Crocetti. In Via Piave, neighbouring the Belvedere, there is an

579. 580. Facing page: left, the Tortoreto clock tower; right, detail of the 16th-century frescoes that decorate the church of Santa Maria della Misericordia, Tortoreto.
581. Above: the so-called "Il Bianco" keep, Giulianova.
582. Below: Giulianova Lido.

interesting **Vincenzo Cermignani house-museum**, which exhibits the work, sketches and personal documents of the Giulianova painter (1902–71), who spent many years exiled in France. In Piazza della Libertà there is a striking monument to Vittorio Emanuele II, by the Giulianova sculptor Raffaello Pagliacetti (1852–1928). Other work by Pagliaccetti, who was a leader of the Florentine Realist Movement of the late 1800s, can be found in the noble San Gaetano da Thiene or De Bartolomei chapel, including two medallions depicting Luigi and Giovanni De Bartolomei, as well as a marble cenotaph.

The civic plaster cast located on the ground floor of the De Amicis school is dedicated to the artist.

The **Gaetano Braga House-Museum**, a Giulianova musician and internationally renowned concert performer, is worth visiting. It houses various works of art referring to the figure and life of the musician as well as plentiful documentation put together by the research of the epoymous association based here.

There are also some other interesting places of worship, including the **church of Sant'Antonio**, with its Baroque interior, and the **sanctuary of Madonna dello Splendore**, built in the 16th century, where there is said to have been an apparition of the Virgin Mary. Inside there is a 16th-century altarpiece with the *Virgin and Child in Glory and saints Peter, Paul, Dorothea, and Francis*, by Paolo Veronese. The convent, recently restored and still occupied by the Franciscans, is home to the **Museo d'Arte Contemporanea dello Splendore** (**MAS**), with 250 works on display. The corpus includes items by Banchieri, De Stefano, Francese, Gianquinto,

Sassu, Attardi, Bonichi, Calabria, Schifano, Miller and Vespignani, as well as sculptures by Bodini, Cascella and Garcia. Monumental **Palazzo Bindi**, which the Giulianova scholar Vincenzo Bindi (1852–28) donated to the town, houses a great library of 26,000 volumes, and the **public art gallery**, on the top floor of the building, all vaunting original furnishings, accessories, pottery, and sculptures. The most important collection is that of paintings from the Posillipo School, with works by van Pitloo, Giganto, Fergola, and others by the Consalvo Carelli dynasty, an outstanding member of the 19th-century pictorial movement, and Bindi's son-in-law; there are also works by local artists like Palizzi, Celommi, Pagliaccetti, Della Monica, Michetti.

The P. Candido Donatelli library, a point of reference for Franciscan and Abruzzo studies, can be found in the sanctuary garden.

Then there is the **San Francesco Cultural Centre**, with an abundant library of art, theology and medical books, which also exhibits the work of contemporary artists.

583–585. Facing page: top left, the church of San Flaviano; top right, the Pinacoteca Civica in Palazzo Bindi; below, the Madonna dello Splendore sanctuary, Giulianova.
586. 587. This page: above, the portal of the church of Santa Maria; below, the procession of fishing boats for the Madonna di Portosalvo pageant, Giulianova Lido.

At **Giulianova Lido**, a coastal town that developed from the 1970s onwards to become today's thriving seaside resort, there is the **church of Santa Maria a Mare**, presumably rebuilt in around the mid–12th century over an existing building. It was rebuilt following damage during World War II. Currently the interior has two irregular naves, divided by a pillar and three columns; the great façade features a bell gable on the right, and on the left has an elegant portal with a round arch datable to the last quarter of the 1200s, and two voussoir lions, as well as a high-relief *Madonna with Child* in the lunette.

Giulianova's modern Marina is installed in the town centre and occupies part of the southern area and the shore jetty of the port basin, which is mainly dedicated to fishing boats.

In April there is the Madonna dello Splendore event, followed in August by the Madonna di Portosalvo festival which closes with a traditional sea procession.

The characteristic Salinello coastal tower (1568) is one of the few surviving Neapolitan viceroyalty coastal towers. It is set along the Adriatic highway near Giulianova. The remains of another coastal tower, the Tordino tower (1568) are also in the Giulianova municipal district, to the left on the eponymous river and presumably destroyed by a flood in the early

1800s. Both of the towers were in signal communication with Abruzzo Ultra's neighbouring coastal towers.

The busy seaside resort of **ROSETO DEGLI ABRUZZI**, located along with the Adriatic between the mouth of the River Tordino to the north and River Vomano to the south (with marina facilities), is of recent origins. The original village of Le Quote, which developed thanks to the building of the Adriatic railway (1863), was renamed Rosburgo in 1887 and in 1927 became Roseto. Along the roads that connect the hillside to the beach, there are numerous interesting late-1800s villas. The **public art collection** is housed on the ground floor of the town hall and is noteworthy. The collection includes some precious works by the painter Pasquale Celommi.

**Montepagano**, a lovely nearby hamlet, with a splendid sea-facing terrace, was once the capital of the municipal district. The ancient fortified settlement still has one of its gates, Porta da Borea. Worth visiting, the **Annunziata parish church**, built between the late 16th century and the early 17th century (the small portal bears the date 1611), with its splendid 1600s wooden altar and an interesting 1300s *Annunciation*. The emblem of the village is the belfry of the ancient church of Sant'Antimo. A **museum of material culture** has been installed in the old town hall.

The municipal district of Roseto is home to the extraordinary **Borsacchio Nature Reserve**, which protects an area of 1,100 hectares of unspoiled beauty, with very rare coastal dunes characteristic of the stretch of beach occupied by the reserve, reaching as far as the cultivated hills and gullies.

The charming seaside resort of **PINETO**, originally the Mutignano district of Villa Filiani, became a municipality just over 60 years ago. This is a modern little town and it takes its name from the dense pine grove that was planted on the shore by Luigi Corrado Filiani. The historic municipal capital of **Mutignano** is up on the hillside and is now a district of Pineto. It has a compact elongated layout, its urban fabric dating mainly to the 19th century and modern times. The parish **church of San Silvestro Papa** has a 15th-century high altar paliotto by Andrea Delitio, depicting the *Life of Pope Sylvester*.

588. Above: the modern Piazza della Libertà, Roseto degli Abruzzi.
589. 590. Below: left, Porta Borea; right, a view of Montepagano.
591. Facing page: Cerrano coastal tower.

# Cerrano Tower, Pineto

The tower, built in 1568, has the typical shape of towers built by the viceroyalty, and its original nucleus, despite significant interventions to raise and extend the structure, is still clearly visible. The building, which continued to serve its watchtower function throughout the 16th and 17th centuries, became the property of the Marquises of Cermignano. The original tower had a truncated square pyramid base, with machicolations on sturdy corbels and three murder holes per side; in the early 20th century the second square tower with embattlements, was added. During this refurbishment, the interior of the building was also modified, and a staircase was added, with niches set into the thick walls, with porthole-type windows. The tower was further extended with the addition of an L-shaped block to the southeast, and following the 1982–3 restoration, it became the home of the **Area Marina Protetta Torre del Cerrano**, a protected area with rare dune environments and archaeological remains of the ancient port of Atri. Recent additions include a library and the **Museum of the Sea**, with modern technology.

The **Cerrano Tower** is on the southern edge of Pineto, near the Filiani pine grove. It was erected on a promontory sheer above the sea, a fundamental element in the more extensive territorial coastal defence system, ordered in the mid–16th century by the Spanish viceroys of Naples, Alvares di Toledo and Parafan de Ribeira, Duke of Alcalà, following devastating Turkish raids (*see box p. 329*).

The **Cenerone volcano geopark** opened just recently to the public, in the area in front of Piazzale Cimarosa, in Borgo Santa Maria di Pineto. It is a very interesting natural phenomenon whereby the spontaneous rise of hydrocarbons mixed with clays, liquid mud and saltwater, form a conical spout around the circular crater.

Now we are now near **SILVI**, a popular seaside resort, with a wide sandy beach, also famous for its production of liquorice. Here there are numerous late–1800s and early–1900s villas, scattered throughout the modern Silvi Marina residential area, which became a municipality in 1931. **Silvi Alta** is an enchanting location, set on a ridge overlooking the Adriatic, with a sheer terrace facing the sea. Formerly called Castelbelfiore until the 1800s, Silvi Alta's unique position is traced back to spindle-shaped acropolis layout, with a network of streets and lanes that branch out from a central axis, typical of an ancient village fabric.

The **church of San Salvatore**, Medieval in origin, is worth visiting. The façade of the original installation was set on what is now the left-hand flank and where it is possible to see the surviving, but bricked over, 1300s portal reminiscent of the portals at Atri cathedral.

During May, Silvi Alta revives its ancient "lu ciancialone" tradition. In this legend, during a siege by the Turks a young man from the town, called Leone, faced up to the enemy with a huge lighted torch. To commemorate this occurrence a tall bonfire of canes is burned as musicians and dancers perform. There are several summer events in the local calendar, including the intensive **Castelbelfiore Arti e Mestieri**, an arts and crafts event that takes place in mid-July, in the town of Silvi.

# Vibrata and Salinello River Valleys

Colonnella, Controguerra, Ancarano, Sant'Egidio alla Vibrata, Faraone, Civitella del Tronto, Valle Castellana, Sant'Omero, Torano Nuovo, Nereto, Corropoli.

The town of **COLONELLA**, not far from Martinsicuro, in a panoramic plateau position to the right of the Tronto River, offers a spectacular view of Gran Sasso, the Majella massif, the Sibillini mountains and the sea. The town, primarily 19th century and modern, shows rare traces of older buildings, while its soaring clock tower identifies it on the horizon. The **church of Santi Cipriano e Giustina**, rebuilt in 1795–1817, is worth a visit. Rebuilt on the site of a 16th-century church, it has the characteristic features of Marche Neoclassicism following work by Pietro Maggi, an architect originally from Ticino, who was particularly active in Ascoli Piceno at the time. Following his death, his son Giacinto completed the opus. The aisleless interior has a lovely canvas of the *Exaltation of the Most Holy Sacrament* by Tommaso Alessandrini of Ortona, dated 1627, and a remarkable painted, gilt wooden statue of *Our Lady of Intercession* (18th century), as well as a lovely organ built in 1833 by Quirico Gennari.

Continuing inland, the provincial road leads to the town of **CONTROGUERRA**. The remodelled **Palazzo Ducale** tower stands out in the highest part. The **church of Santa Maria delle Grazie**, now seen in the guide of its 19th-century reconstruction, has a polychrome high-relief *Madonna with Child*. The parish **church of San Benedetto Abate** (17th century) restored in the early–19th century has two respectable 17th-canvases. Outside the town walls, the small but interesting **rural church of San Rocco** is dated around 1527. The **Museo della**

The route along the Vibrata and Salinello valleys presents significant moments of history and art as it winds through charming old villages, hugging scenic plateaus along the ancient border between the Papal States and Bourbon Kingdom, marked by the Tronto River. The route, which covers an area famous for its wines and busy industries, also has some of the most important and characteristic fortifications in Abruzzo, even more remarkable for the truly scenic backdrop, where nature blends with and complements art. The highlight is the Civitella del Tronto fortress, dominating the valley and village below, considered one of the most important strongholds of the Neapolitan vice realm, followed by the evocative Castel Manfrino, located a short distance from Valle Castellana, on a rocky promontory between the Salinello torrent and Fosso Rivolta, one of the most exciting defence posts in Abruzzo, perfectly adapted to the site. The charming fortified village of Faraone, now completely abandoned, stands on high ground a short distance from Civitella del Tronto.

592–594. Facing page: top left, Villa Filiani, Pineto; top right, "lu ciancialone"; below, Silvi town.
595. Below: Colonnella centre.

**Civiltà Contadina** dedicated to rural culture is in a rustic structure in the San Giuseppe Lavoratore area and is worth a visit.
In the original fortified village of **ANCARANO**, located on a crest above the Tronto and Vibrata rivers, the outline of the walls is still visible, replaced over time by the curtain of more modern buildings. The urban layout is the result of 16th–17th-century reconstruction, with narrow roads and buildings from that period. The two characteristic gates leading into the village have been preserved: **Porta da Monte** to the west and **Porta da Mare** to the east, dating back to the end of the 14th–early 15th century, presumably spared from the 1557 assault ordered by Alvarez de Toledo, Duke of Alva. The brick Porta da Monte, located on the western slope, is characterized by a round arch, set in a more recent brick cornice (1826); in the upper part, closed by the typical projecting apparatus with corbels, it is still possible to see the bores for the drawbridge chains. The Porta da Mare, on the eastern side of the walls, has a lancet arch opening on one side, with arched stone lintel and uprights in the brick masonry, and is topped by a corbels coping similar to Porta da Monte. The epigraph located above the cornice of the Porta da Monte arch, engraved on a travertine slab, is dedicated to the Bishop of Ascoli Piceno, Giulio II Gabrielli of Rome, who had the gate restored in 1642, during his first year of office. The coat of arms of Bishop Roverella can be seen above the Porta da Mare arch.

The modern parish **church of Madonna della Pace** houses a lovely late 15th-century wooden statue of the *Madonna with Child*, attributed to Silvestro dell'Aquila.
Only the bell tower remains of the oldest parish church (documented in the 12th century), as most of it was rebuilt after the 1703 earthquake, reusing the original stones from the church. The 17th-century octagonal **Madonna della Misericordia** tempietto has some interesting fine stucco altars. The 18th-century **church of Madonna della Carità** is located in the vicinity.
The road continues towards **SANT'EGIDIO ALLA VIBRATA**, the populous and vibrant valley town with the **church of Sant'Egidio**, built in the late Middle Ages and with 16th-century portal.
Continuing towards Civitella del Tronto lies the charming village of **Faraone**, a district of Sant'Egidio alla Vibrata, located next to the River Salinello. The old part of the village, first mentioned in the 11th century, is situated on a hillock and is completely abandoned. Two gates are left of the fortified walls which once defended the village: the southern gate is built with hewn stone and masonry similar to the base of the external curtain of the **church of Santa Maria della Misericordia**, behind the gate. An ashlar on the front of the gate, added during a subsequent reconstruction, bears the date 1467. To the right of the southern gate stands the impressive **baronial palace**. The Madonna di Reggio chapel (17th century) stands at the edge of the village.
The road then leads to

**CIVITELLA DEL TRONTO**, located at an altitude of 645 m., overlooking the Vibrata and Salinello river valleys, and included in the I Borghi più belli d'Italia list. It is one of the Region's most interesting towns for the rich architectural heritage enclosed within its walls, of which large sections remain. It is famous for its extraordinary **fortress**, bastion of the Bourbons before the Unification of Italy, which dominates the mountains and sea (*see box on p. 334*).

Beyond **Porta Napoli**, the old Porta Piazza is the only remaining gate, bearing the town's coat of arms with its five towers, and leads to scenic Piazza Francesco Filippi Pepe, open on the southern side, where it is possible to enjoy a magnificent view encompassing the Fiori and the Laga Mountains, and the majestic peaks of Gran Sasso. It stands on a buttressed rampart built into the walls, and its conformation remained unchanged from the mid–16th to the early–20th century, when a building with loggia occupied the western end, facing the **church of San Lorenzo**, documented since 1153. With the late–16th-century reconstruction and subsequent expansions carried out in the mid–18th century, the church acquired its current cross configuration, with the massive cupola with an octagonal lantern tower. Expansion work and decoration were completed in 1790 as witnessed by an inscription on the vault. The simple façade, presumably restored in the early–20th century based on the form of the 18th-century model, has a double pair of giant pilasters which support the trabeation surmounted by a classical tympanum. The door, built by Ascoli Piceno craftsmen, dates back to the 16th century with 20th-century modifications and restoration, on the sides of the church, the storey with large splayed windows, added in the 18th century, is visible. The interior, decorated with large niches containing

596–598. Facing page: top left, the Porta da Monte, Ancarano; top right, the gate into Faraone; below, the wooden *Madonna and Child* statue in the Madonna della Pace church, Ancarano.
599. 600. This page: above, the access door; below, an aerial view of Civitella del Tronto.

# The Fortress, Civitella del Tronto

The Civitella del Tronto fortress, which dominates the village below from its plateau, is considered one of the most important strongholds of the Neapolitan vice realm. The building of the fort, still clearly recognizable despite subsequent maintenance and reconstruction work conducted for modern restoration, maintains the general features of the great Spanish design, started in the latter half of the 16th century. This renovation transformed the already powerful Aragonese fortress, built over an earlier, Medieval castle, into the formidable vice realm stronghold desired by King Phillip II of Spain, only partially modified and reinforced during the 19th century and recovered in 1973–1983. The complex, situated on a travertine hill, occupies the entire summit of the plateau and is surrounded by massive walls whose ramparts ensured crossfire barrage on the enemy.

On the southern side, where the town formerly protected by fortifications, stands, the defensive enceinte is doubled by a faussebraye, a low, external walled perimeter that protects the lower part of the curtain walls. The fortress, impregnable from the north and west, was more vulnerable on the eastern side, and for this reason the larger defence works were concentrated here, comprising massive ramparts at different heights and armed platforms. After "**Porta Napoli**" and the older Porta Piazza, there is a paved road leading to the entrance to the fortress, protected by the **San Pietro rampart**.

A ramp leads to **Piazza del Cavaliere**, the first parade ground, protected by the **Sant'Andrea ramparts**; a second ramp, protected by the San Paolo bastion, leads to a second parade ground, protected to the south by the **San Giovanni rampart**, ending at the west with the ruins of military barracks. The first of five large cisterns is located under the parade ground, which combined with a complex system of run-off canals, built by Philip II, made up the ingenious system for collecting and purifying rain water; the water was transferred to the cistern through two openings in the parade ground, currently protected by iron grating. The top of the plateau, on the **Gran Piazza**, is dominated by the remains of **Palazzo del Governatore** (inaugurated in 1574) and the **church of San Giacomo** (built in 1585 and consecrated in 1604), defended to the north by the rampart bearing the same name. Along the main east-west road there are the remains of the garrison's lodgings stretching as far as the Batteria del Carmine standing sheer above the rocks. Traces of the Angevin-Aragonese castle can still be seen in the remaining sections of walls and foundations behind the church of San Giacomo and in some of the aligned square blocks recognizable as officer housing, and inside the faussebraye of the fortified walls. Almost all of the surviving structures are attributed to the Spanish, after the siege of 1557, with the exception of the ramparts farthest east, modified in the 19th century.

The 16th-century restoration work seems to be part of the so-called **Calabozzo del Coccodrillo jail**, at the same height of the first access ramp, as well as the circle of defensive walls, including the faussebraye reinforcing the southern side, which bears the date 1564. In 1557, with this further reinforcement, the citadel put up a valiant resistance against the long assault by French troops, overcoming the siege of Philip II, Duke of Guise, who was aware of the strategic importance of Civitella and ordered work to build a real fortress, which continued until 1574. The renovated strategic configuration allowed Civitella not only to act as the fundamental defence for the entire coastline up to Pescara, but also as a logistical base for military campaigns towards the north, in conjunction with the L'Aquila fortress throughout the period of the Spanish vice realm. The brief Austrian occupation did not bring substantial changes to the fortress, which was instead the object of major tactical construction work during the Bourbon reign; this work enabled brave resistance from Civitella against the last two major assaults, one in 1806 during Napoleon's Italian campaign, and in 1860–1 by the Sardinia–Piedmontese army. After many years of restoration, with radical reconstruction, the fortress was reopened to the public, and in 1988 the **Fortress Museum**, located at the site's highest point, was inaugurated; it has a remarkable collection of extremely interesting old weapons, maps and documents that reconstructing the historical events of the fortress. Numerous activities are organized in the fortress: from educational workshops for schools to tours, cultural events and historical re-enactments.

601. Left: a room in the museum.
602. Facing page: aerial view of the fortress.

altars, is finished with finely-made wooden furniture and has excellent paintings, including a *Visitation* and *Madonna of the Rosary* from the latter half of the 16th century, and an *Annunciation* from the early–17th century In the left arm of the transept there is a wooden 1800s statue of St Ubald, protector of Civitella, supporting a model of the city. The lower level, where the remarkable **Confraternita del SS Suffragio oratory** is located, has a canvas depicting the *Deposition*, an interpretation of the *Pietà between saints Francis and Mary Magdalene* by Annibale Carracci. Entirely frescoed in 1944 by the painter Cesare Zunica of Civitella, the church is home to the parish museum.
Continuing along Corso Mazzini we note the striking **Palazzo Ronchi** with Marche-style rusticated ashlar portal. On the left, a glimpse the simple **San Francesco church** with adjacent monastery, founded between the 13th and 14th centuries, which is now the town hall. The Franciscan church was modified to a Baroque appearance in the 18th century but this were later removed. The original layout, which can still be seen, had a single nave and cross-vaulted square choir; during the 18th century modifications were made and the perimeter walls were raised, creating a system of vaults to cover the nave, and curved niches were built along the nave walls to house splendid altars.
The old choir was separated from the main part of the church by a wall supporting a magnificent altar. The dimensions and proportions of the horizontal-parapet façade were altered following a 17th-century elevation.

There is a beautiful 14th-century rose window and cornice engraved with foliage motifs is flanked by two semi-columns that old it in place. Traditionally the window is said to belong to the church of San Francesco, in Campli. Below there is a travertine door with moulded jambs and slightly lancet archivolt, with a lunette containing the remains of a traditional fresco depicting the *Madonna with Child and saints Ludovic, Francis and Claire*. The bell tower, developed over two orders and separated by a moulded cornice, is characterized by a belfry lightened by 4 rounded single lancet windows. The adjacent monastery, entered through a pointed arch portal along the left side of the church, was sold after 1870 to the Municipality and greatly modified in 1917–20.
**Largo Pietro Rosati** opens in front of the splendid façade of the church of San Francesco. The square was created and landscaped in various stages between the 1920s and 1940s, with the destruction of two buildings in a town-planning operation that involved gutting of part of the Medieval fabric. Th only building to survive was **Palazzo del Capitano**, whose original structure is attributed to the early–14th century, significantly modified during the 16th century and restored in the mid–17th century, by which time it was almost in ruins. To the left of the building, leaning against a simple plastered wall, is the 19th-century **marble monument to Matthew Wade**, of remarkable workmanship and in obvious Neoclassical style clearly inspired by Canova's cenotaphs. Commissioned by Francis I of

Bourbon, King of the Two Sicilies in memory of the Irish officer, Matthew Wade, ardent defender of Civitella's stronghold during the 1806 assault, it was made in 1829 by Neapolitan sculptor Tito Angelini, son of the Neoclassical painter Costanzo Angelini, of Abruzzo origins.

After Largo Rosati we meet and continue along Corso Mazzini, dominated in this section by the impressive Renaissance façade of **Palazzo Ferretti**, formerly the town hall. After Palazzo Ferretti there is a small wide stretch occupied on the northern side by the **church of Santa Maria delle Laudi**, named after the confraternity, called Santa Maria delle Laudi or degli Angeli, its presence in Civitella was originally documented in 1330. According to tradition it was founded in the early decades of the 14th century, but based on studies of the older remaining walls, it seems that the building actually dates back to the end of the 15th century However, its current single chamber appearance is

603–605. Facing page: top, view of the interior and detail of the canvas of St Ubald, church of San Lorenzo; below, detail of the marble monument to Matteo Wade, Civitella del Tronto. 606. 607. This page: above, the church of San Francesco; below, Palazzo Procaccini–Savi, Civitella del Tronto.

the result of numerous interventions and additions made over the centuries. The older nucleus, seen to the east where the high altar and choir are located, still preserves masonry remains of the early ashlar angle irons. Expanded until it reached its current dimensions, between the 16th and 17th centuries the church had a semi-circular barrel vault in the western part and cross vaulting in the eastern part, the walls on the southern side were reinforced and the interior frescoed with an elegant polychrome Renaissance-style decoration of nature, a trace of which can still be seen on the church's left wall. The highly deteriorated interior is frescoed with a pictorial cycle of religious illustrations and monochromatic arabesques from the beginning of the 19th century Mounted in the altar leaning on the right wall is a shrine containing a wooden *Deposition of Christ*, of modest workmanship, its characteristics show that it is probably a German-influenced work dating back to the end of the 15th century Lastly, a magnificent organ with Neoclassical decorations and shape is located in the loft over the entrance towers. The simple, small façade houses a severe door with smooth travertine cornices and architraves supported by the typical brackets found in Civitella,

featuring a circle and leaf, while below the cornice projections lozenge-painted bricks are noticeable, a common tradition in the town and the entire Teramo area until the 15th century. Corso Mazzini offers a sequence of interesting examples of secular architecture, including 18th-century **Palazzo Procaccini-Savi** and late–16th-century **Palazzo Graziani**.

Leaving Porta Napoli, after a few switchbacks and a short straight section, we find the **monastery of Santa Maria de Lumi**, on a hill overlooking the town. This church and monastery complex is the oldest Franciscan installation, which originated from an existing Benedictine site. Occupied in the first half of the 13th century and given to the Observants in 1466, it was often used to garrison troops who besieged the nearby fortress, so it

suffered significant damage. Suppressed first in 1811 and then in 1866, it was returned to the monks in 1882, who began major restorations in 1922-3, followed by other work in 1960. The current structure is the result of numerous transformations over the centuries, which make it difficult to identify the original layout, recently modified with the addition of a second aisle on the left and characterized by 19th-century and modern furnishings. The 19th-century Renaissance-style wooden altar has a splendid *Madonna with Child*, or *Madonna dei Lumi* polychrome wooden work, mentioned in a 1489 document, but presumed to be at least a decade older, attributed to Giovanni di Biasuccio, colleague of the younger and better-known Maestro Silvestro dell'Aquila, Abruzzo's most important Renaissance sculptor. The convent cloister is interesting, once frescoed with paintings by Sebastiano Majewski, a Polish painter who worked in the Teramo area in the 1630s and 1640s; the lower order of the loggia survives, with round arches supported by small stone pillars, and 14th–15th- century traces, but of uncertain date.

**Monte Santo abbey** is located on a wooded slope in the surrounding area. It includes the church of Santa Maria Assunta and a monastery and was once one of the Region's most prosperous Benedictine centres. The only certain source on the presence of the abbey dates it as 1064, even if tradition attributes its founding to St Benedict, in the years 540–542. The monastery, which in the 13th century was one of the most important in the territory, began to deteriorate around the end of the 15th century until it was finally suppressed in 1797. Archaeological investigations conducted

608–610. This page: top left, the convent of Santa Maria dei Lumi; top right, aerial view of the abbey of Monte Santo; below left, the wooden Madonna dei Lumi sculpture.
611–614. Facing page: above, the Salinello gorges seen from Grotta Sant'Angelo and the church of Santa Maria di Stornazzano; below, the SS Rufina e Vito church; the church of San Vito in Valle Castellana.

during recent restoration work on the abbey have brought to light ruins along the northern side of the church confirming the Medieval layout with a nave and two aisles, transformed between the 13th century and 14th century to a single nave system. The renovated building corresponds to the monument conserved to date, with the exception that the space of the original arcade and initial part of the nave itself are missing. The current church layout, with a single chamber and straight choir, facing east, has two entrances along the southern side, with a round archivolt and two slightly splayed single lancet windows. The space, covered with trusses in the nave and with cross vaults in the rectory, has a remarkable 1640 Bologna School reed organ near the altar. Outside, the Romanesque bell tower, positioned next to the older façade in the Middle Ages, is currently detached from the church and incorporated in the monastery structure which Palma's testimony says was surrounded at the time by a double set of walls with towers, traces of which remain on the southern side of the hill.

Part of the Gole del Salinello Regional Nature Reserve falls within Civitella del Tronto territory, which protects the spectacular gullies, some of the most beautiful of the Laga massif, with sheer close faces, dug out by the river between Mount Campli and Mount Fiori.

From the village of Ripe di Civitella, site of the Gran Sasso-Laga National Park Services Centre, a few meters after the church of San Pietro, a trail of about a kilometre leads to the fascinating **Sant'Angelo grotto**, primarily of interest from an archaeological standpoint for the significant Neolithic to Roman findings, as well as those left by the presence of hermits. After a ten-minute walk, the aerial hermitage of Santa Maria Scalena can be glimpsed up on the right while the Grotta di San Marco is visible on the opposite side beyond the valley. From here it is possible to climb along a scenic road set amidst the pines, up Mount Fiori, with its caves and River Vibrata springs, to reach San Giacomo di Valle Castellana, a ski and summer resort on the slopes of Mount Piselli.

The road continues to **VALLE CASTELLANA**, resting on a plateau at the foot of the Laga Mountains, surrounded by a surprising natural habitat, scattered with interesting historical and archaeological testimonies. The charming **church of Santa Maria di Stornazzano** (or dell'Annunziata), is just out of the town; it was founded in the Middle Ages but restored in the early–16th century (the crypt dates back to the 11th–12th century). The **church of San Nicola di Bari**, in the village of Colle Pietralta, has a Renaissance ciborium and, even more important, the **churches of Santa Rufina** and **San Vito**, in the villages of the same names, both formerly property of Farfa Abbey, and dating back to the 12th century. Originally built by the Benedictines

as simple nave and apse, with exposed truss ceiling, the structure was altered significantly during the 1930s by the addition of a new, perpendicular nave. The church maintains its most significant characteristic, however, a bell tower, used as the entrance to the church, is set against the façade and aligned with the chamber. An unusual solution for Abruzzo but common in other Farfa properties, with a clear transalpine influence. The bell tower makes this building, formerly considered minor and marginal, quite unique. The unique, eclectic **Bonifaci castle** is located in the village of Vallinquina. The high altitude and severity of the sites denote their primarily military function, at the border with Ascoli Piceno territory, making **Castel Manfrino**, near Macchia da Sole, one of the most fascinating defence posts in Abruzzo. The strategic garrison (*Castrum Maccle*) is located a short distance from Valle Castellana, on a rocky promontory between the Salinello torrent and Fosso Rivolta. The current structure, enclosed in walls fortified by three watch and defence towers, including one in a central position, still easily recognizable, occupy the entire spur, adapting to the impassable orography; it is believed that the construction may be situated on a 13th century fortress, and is attributed to the Swabian King Manfred, probably built at an altitude of 936m, at the northern border of his kingdom, as a defence against claims by Ascoli Piceno and Angevin invasion. After Charles I of Anjou defeated Manfred, the castle and its surroundings came under Angevin rule. The remains of a keep, recognizable from its square shape, are among the rare remains of the early Angevin period. The considerable strategic role played by Castel Manfrino in the kingdom's defensive chessboard continued until the end of the 15th century and ended only when new military techniques were introduced.

There are interesting rock places of worship at San Francesco alle Scalelle, Santa Maria Maddalena and Sant'Angelo in Volturino, concentrated in the valley between Mount Fiori and Mount Campli. Heading back towards Civitella del Tronto, we soon meet the village of **SANT'OMERO**, on a small plateau, with its elegant Porta del Castello Gothic arch and fine ashlar arched lintel. The bell tower of the old **Misericordia church** (rebuilt in the 17th century and now called "Marchesale") is unique and built on the wall scarp. The present-day **church of SS Annunziata**, with its three-part facade dated 1754, is decorated with niches and altars as well as lively plaster medallions. The furnishings include important works such as a late 16th century wooden cross, an 18th century majolica of St Anthony Abbot and a Baroque organ and choir. The town is interesting mainly due to the presence of the nearby **church of Santa Maria a Vico**, which is traditionally dated back to a period before 1000 (*see box p. 341*).

**TORANO NUOVO**, a town on the left bank of the River Vibrata, is primarily 19th century is style with an interesting **Madonna delle Grazie church**, first mentioned in the 17th century, although modified by 18th–19th-century restoration work. The most important monument is the **church of San Massimo**, in the Varano district, dating back to the 11th century, although its current appearance is the result of restoration work in around 1565. Traces of the Romanesque building can be seen on the rear, where the older round arch portal entrance was located, and in the masonry of the two sides of the church, with two splayed single lancet windows. The interior has a 16th-century altar with the Acquaviva family coat of arms. The **church of San Martino**, in the village of Torri, is also interesting: mentioned in sources as early as the beginning of the 16th century, it has frescoes that may be dated between the end of the 16th century and 1620s. The **Museo d'Arte Sacra** is a recent addition.

In nearby **NERETO**, a lively industrial and commercial town in the heart of Val Vibrata, the parish **church of Madonna della Consolazione** (its current appearance is the result of restoration work completed in 1848) stands on the site of the older church of

# Church of Santa Maria a Vico, Sant'Omero

This fascinating church has long been famous as Abruzzo's only surviving monument prior to 1000. Nevertheless, many doubts have been raised as to the early Medieval origin of the building, suggested by the modest nature of the construction as well as the unique stone transennae at the windows and *opus spicatum* applications on the façade. Although it cannot be excluded that it was built in the Dark Ages, its construction is currently placed at the end of the 11th century and first half of the 12th century. Despite numerous reconstructions, the building seems to match the original church, with a nave and two aisles separated by round supports, with the exception of the first two after the façade, which are square, ending in a single, semi-circular apse at the nave, with an exposed wooden truss ceiling. Its interior has fragments of frescoes from the late 14th century, which point to extensive work being carried out, probably because of static instability. The bell tower was erected at that time and the façade, which has a horizontal parapet that reflects 14th-century models. The rose window was created during 19th century restoration work.

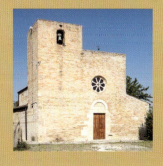

615. Facing page: the ruins of Castel Manfrino, near Macchia da Sole.
616. 617. This page: the façade and interior of the church of Santa Maria a Vico near Sant'Omero.

Sant'Antonio, documented in the 1700s. On the night between 30 April and 1 May, Nereto celebrates its **May Tree** tradition, and the custom is also documented in Val Vibrata villages: a group of men plant a felled poplar in a hole dug in the town square and celebrate the event with wine.

A short distance from the town lies the **church of San Martino**, fulcrum of the old village of Galianum. Documented as 12th century, but its current appearance is the result of subsequent rebuilding. The portal has a lovely relief of *St Martin and the Beggar*.

The fortified village of **CORROPOLI** is quite near, with surviving sections of walls along the western slope and the vaulted passageway of the eastern gate. The parish **church of Sant'Agnese** dominates, its current appearance the result of a 16th-century expansion and 19th-century restoration work by architect Carlo Maggi. The Atri-type brick bell tower is part of the old church, with octagonal coping and cusp with majolica covered bricks. The single nave interior has a vaulted ceiling with 19th-century decoration, an early–14th-century wooden *Madonna Majulana*, set in an 18th-century throne from the abbey of the same name. The **abbey of Santa Maria a Mejulano** is on a plateau to the north of the town. It is documented as 1018 but the current church is the result of a stylistic restoration; the bell tower survives from the Medieval building.

The now-derelict **church of Sant'Antonio di Padova** is of great interest for its relief decoration. It was once part of the Montagnola monastery, in the district of the same name.

Ripoli is a very well-known locality, where a Neolithic village was explored, and which gave its name to a particular culture known for its painted striped pottery.

618. 619. Above: the bas-relief depicting *St Martin and the beggar* on the portal of the church of San Martino, Nereto; detail of the wooden *Madonna Majulana* high relief, Corropoli.
620. Below: Corropoli town hall, right, the bell tower of the parish church of Sant'Agnese.

# Tordino Valley

The village of **Montone**, a district of Mosciano Sant'Angelo, is a few kilometres outside Giulianova and overlooks the Salinello Valley. Three brick towers and wall fragments remain of the 14th-century fortifications. The most imposing tower, with characteristic corbels, is at the highest point of the village and is similar to Mosciano's Acquaviva tower. Recent restorations left the original structure unaltered and part of the wall is still visible on the south side. The tower is set against the **church of Sant'Antonio Abate**, which has the late–14th-century funeral monument of the Montone nobleman, Bucciarello di Jacobo, as well as two modest 1600s canvases.

Further inland, **MOSCIANO SANT'ANGELO** lies on the southern ridge of a hill between the Tordino Valley to the south, and Salinello Valley to the north. The original nucleus of Mosciano emerged the 9th century, with the first Benedictine settlement; the village, subsequently fortified, developed around the convent of Sant'Angelo. Plentiful evidence and the study of ancient maps has allowed has retraced the structure of the fortified wall, which presumably had seven towers of various shapes, one in each of the four corners and one in the centre of each wall, with the exception of the east wall where the entrance can still be seen. **Torre Cardelli**, restored in 1925, and the recently remodelled **Torre Marini** are pentagonal, like a third tower demolished in about 1935; the central tower on the south wall was probably similar to Torre Marini, like the now-demolished tower near Palazzo Civico. On the eastern side there are still two rounds towers, including **Torre del Belvedere**. The more recent **Torre Acquaviva**, in the highest part of the village, stands to the left of the façade of the **San Michele Arcangelo parish church**. This coincides with Mosciano's original nucleus near Largo Del Castello, near today's Largo del Castello and in the spot where the original Mosciano stood. It was built in 1397 by Brother Matteo di Angelo of Morro, a Benedictine monk and church provost at the time of Andrea Matteo I Acquaviva, Duke of Atri and Count San Flaviano, inscribed on the plaque on the monumental tower's east wall.
With the subsequent enlargement of the adjoining parish church, the Torre Acquaviva lost its original defensive function and was converted into the church belfry, with the addition of large arched windows under the

Montone, Mosciano Sant'Angelo, Bellante, Campli, Torricella Sicura, Rocca Santa Maria, Cortino, Crognaleto

The small towns encountered through this itinerary are truly interesting, first along the coast and then turning inland, crossing the splendid Tordino Valley, where the urban centres and constructions share similar roots and cultural identities. The itinerary will wind its way through a territory of unique charm, bordering with Latium and the Marches, embraced by the Gran Sasso and Laga Mountains National Park. These are enchanting locations that combine a large number of outlying districts, some quite distant from one another, set amidst chestnut, pine and beech woods, and no lack of abundant waterfalls, with an untainted habitat generous with mushrooms and fruits of the forest. The starting point is Giulianova, to continue through Montone and reach Mosciano Sant'Angelo, which is one of the Region's loveliest examples of a fortified town; beyond Bellante there is splendid and authentic art town, Campli, set on its hillside between the Fiumicino and Siccagno Valleys. After Teramo, and beyond Torricella Sicura, it is possible to reach Rocca Santa Maria, concealed in the green woods of Bosco Martese. Also from Teramo, taking the Valle San Giovanni fork, it is possible to explore the Tordino Valley, towards the Laga Mountains, and reach Cortino with its ancient fir woods, and continue as far as Crognaleto, set in its untouched environment.

621. Below: Torre Marini, Mosciano Sant'Angelo.

343

jutting battlements with corbelled archlets. The square tower was built almost entirely of bricks, except for stone blocks at the corners and at the top of the base; the walls show putlog holes and are surmounted by battlements. With the construction of Torre Acquaviva, the fortified walls may have been extended east, along the hill crest; at this level, corbel remnants on the curtain wall were found and suggest the presence of machicolations.

It is worth visiting the **Natural Science Museum**, with with palaeontology, mineralogy, and meteorite sections, found in the **Colle Leone observatory** and planetarium. Also worthy of note in the surrounding area there is the **Santissimi Sette Fratelli convent** with its beautiful wooden ceiling, dated late–17th–early–18th-century, and a valuable 16th-century wooden *Madonna del Casale* statue. On the border with Ripattoni, at the top of the San Felice hill, we find the splendid Neoclassical **Villa di Selva de' Colli**, immersed in the greenery of a monumental 19th-century garden, abounding with refined botanical specimens.

Found on a spur between the Tordino and Salinello rivers, the ancient fortified village of **BELLANTE** still vaunts a section of wall and the beautiful turreted gate crowned with typical brick corbels. The charming parish **church of Santa Maria della Misericordia**, refurbished in the late–18th century, has a Renaissance portal, Baroque stucco interior, valuable paintings that include a late–16th century *Adoration of the Magi*, attributable to the Neapolitan Fabrizio Santafede, a leading figure during the 16th and 17th centuries, as well as canvases by Ascoli painter Nicola Antonio Monti (1735–95), not to mention wooden statues and a silver cross. Turning towards the main road, **Ripattoni** is dominated by a soaring square brick tower with corbels, next to the **church of San Giustino** with its large canvas of *Our Lady of the Rosary*. Outside the village we find the ancient **church of Santa Maria de Erulis** in the guise of its 16th-century renovation but with fine 14th-century frescoes attributed to the Maestro del Giudizio Universale of Loreto Aprutino.

Beyond Bellante and towards the Sant'Onofrio junction, along the scenic Piceno-Aprutina route between the Gemelli Mountains and the sea, we reach historic **CAMPLI**, on a hill between the Fiumicino and Siccagno rivers. In the well-preserved urban fabric of this true art town, characterized by ancient porticoes and remarkable secular and religious buildings, the **collegiate church of Santa Maria in Platea** in the town square is a must to visit (*see box p. 346*).

Opposite Santa Maria in Platea, impressive **Palazzo del Parlamento**, also known as **Palazzo Farnese**, is one of the most interesting civil buildings in Abruzzo, despite numerous reconstructions and demolitions that slightly altered its original appearance. It is a long, two-storey building: on the ground floor there is a pillared portico with seven round arches under six three-light lancet windows, interspersed with two large windows set lower than the other apertures. Some decorative and architectural details date the first structure to the late 14th century, although a tufa ashlar in the façade suggests the building was significantly restructured in the early 1500s. The

622. 623. Below: left, the turreted gate of Bellante: right, Ripattoni square tower.
624. Facing page: aerial view of Campli.

# Collegiate Church of Santa Maria in Platea, Campli

This church, once a cathedral and raised to collegiate status in 1395, was originally a nave layout and acquired two aisles following a refurbishment in the 15th–16th centuries. The nave has a fine **wooden ceiling**, painted in the early 18th century by Teodoro Donato of Chieti with the *Stories of the Life of St Pancras*. The belfry, built in the 14th century, terminates with an octagonal prism and cusp, added subsequently, and then rebuilt in 1893. The **portal** and today's façade, added in 1793 by Giovanni Fontana of Penne, is surmounted by a niche containing a stone *Madonna with Standing Child on Her Lap* datable pre-1525. There are also excellent paintings: a *Madonna with Child and Saints*, by Ravenna-born Giovan Battista Ragazzino (1577) and the *Visitation*, a homage to Raphael's more celebrated canvas. In the crypt there are some admirable frescoes, remnants of a far larger cycle of the early 1300s, which may well have covered all five aisles and the 15 bays that still constitute the **crypt**.

The frescoes, attributed to Niccolò di Valle Castellana (the same miniaturist that created the St Francis), depict the four *Evangelists*, *Resurrection* and *Pentecost*, *St Helen touching the True Cross* and *St Ursula with her Virgin Companions*. The Evangelists are painted in the cross vault of one of the nave bays; the other illustrations are distributed across the walls of the terminal bays. The **SS Sacramento chapel** and 1532 altar by Sebastiano da Como are particularly striking. At the centre of the altar we see the *Madonna dei Lumi*, executed in 1495, probably by Silvestro dell'Aquila, the most important L'Aquila sculptor of the Renaissance. On the sides, two panels with saints on a gold background comprise the early–16th-century work by Cola dell'Amatrice.

625. 626. Campli collegiate church of Santa Maria in Platea and a detail of one of the panels painted by Cola dell'Amatrice.
627. 628. Facing page: Campli's Holy Stairs.

monument was in fact partially demolished and reconstructed, beginning with the ground floor vaults; Gothic windows were replaced in the façade and two large windows were inserted. The Palazzo, already seriously damaged by the 1703 earthquake, declined under the first French invasion. From 1820 to 1888, a series of reconstructions and restorations give Palazzo Farnese its present appearance.

Behind Palazzo Del Parlamento, the **Holy Staircase** set against the church of San Paolo attracts many pilgrims. Pope Clement XIV's bull of 21 January 1772 accorded the same indulgence to the Holy Staircase being built here as that enjoyed by the Holy Staircase in Rome. The staircase has 28 olive wood steps rising upwards and 19 to descend. The walls are decorated with paintings of the *Passion*, *Death* and *Resurrection of Christ*. The stone portal comes from the former monastery of Sant'Onofrio.

Worthy of note is the 14th-century **church of San Francesco**, with its original austere structure mainly unaltered and typical of mendicant churches, with a fine portal carved with human faces and animal figures. The church's wooden truss nave, without a transept, is connected by a large pointed arch to the square rib-vaulted choir, rebuilt in an early 20th-century restoration. The placement of the two chapels is unique, set against the counter-façade whose vault is decorated with fragmented, yet magnificent, 14th–15th-century frescoes. These paintings are similar in style to those found in the crypt of Santa Maria in Platea and are fine examples of the work of an unknown painter active during the mid-14th century in the inland areas of northern Abruzzo. Over time, numerous side altars were installed, but only the 17th-century Ascensione altar remains. The incomplete *Pietà* fresco in the aedicule adjoining the choir is remarkable. The work constitutes another precious contribution from the brilliant master who, trod in the footsteps of Ottaviano Nelli and the Salimbeni family, and painted the famous Santa Maria in Piano frescoes of Santa Maria at Loreto Aprutino during the 1420s and 1430s.

The church is home to a mid-13th-century painted stational cross and Cola dell'Amatrice's wooden painting of the *Madonna with Child and Saints*. The church has a square belfry, but repeated damage has brought it barely to the level of the church roof. Only two cross-vaulted porticoed wings of the 15th-century cloister remain, one with an elegant doorway with a polyfoil ogival arch flanked by two-light lancet windows. In the restored rooms of the former convent of San Francesco, we find the **National Archaeological Museum** (*see box p. 348*), which exhibits precious findings from the protohistoric Campovalano necropolis, occupying situated 50 hectares on a plateau at the foot of Mount Fiori, in the municipality of Campli.

In nearby **Campovalano** there is the early-Medieval **church of San Pietro**, rebuilt between the late-11th and the 14th centuries, and readapted extensively in subsequent centuries. It is home to a fine *Madonna and Child with Two Angels*, an 18th-century polychrome clay statue.

# Campli National Archaeological Museum

The Museo Archeologico of Campli, located in the restored former convent of San Francesco, near the church of the same name, contains some very valuable exhibits from the protohistoric necropolis of Campovalano.

The Museum has been set out in four sections and offers a fascinating overview of this well-known archaeological site. Some findings shown in the first room, and alongside relics of fauna, prove the existence of the first settlement on the Campovalano plain as early as the 14th–13th century BC, but from the 10th century BC until the 2nd century BC, the site was used as a burial ground, and over time not only the funeral furnishings but also the actual tombs changed. From the first excavations in 1967, work has continued almost uninterruptedly to bring to light an extensive and important necropolis of over 600 graves.

The Museum path has been designed to include the most significant funeral furnishings, comprising objects of daily or symbolic use, where weapons and trinkets reflect the economic and social condition, age and gender of the deceased. A series of explanatory panels describes the relics and makes it possible to reconstruct the social and economic revolution of Campovalano's Piceno community, from its most historic phases (10th, 9th and 8th centuries BC) right up until the necropolis' final historic period (late 5th century–early 3rd century BC), which corresponds to the time when the Romans conquered the territory. There is a particularly intense section dedicated to the necropolis' moment of greatest glory (7th–6th century BC), when barrow tombs with stone circles began to be affirmed and funeral furnishings became more sumptuous and extensive.

The funeral furnishings of the golden age include some extremely precious items: for instance, in male graves it was common to find weapons, iron swords and sauroteres (lances), and even the remains of battle wagons, whereas women's graves typically contained trinkets, brooches (fibulae), cowrie pendants, glass beads, and several instruments for weaving, including reels, spindles and bobbins. Common to all the tombs are the vases, in all shapes and decorations, in bronze or in pottery, some made in a typical blackish Etruscan paste, called "bucchero". Recently there was a quite spectacular discovery of a trousseau from a young girl's grave, which included a gold necklace of over 60 gold leaf beads of different sizes and designs, with two gold female heads. there was also a noteworthy multicoloured glass paste head, typical of Phoenician production.

Audiovisual aids and a systematic collection of anthropological data derived from the study of the remains of Campovalano are available to complete the rigorous exhibition itinerary.

In the surrounding area, beyond the Fiumicino torrent, the **convent of San Bernardino** is sited on the hill of Santa Lucia. One of the oldest Observant settlements to survive without significant alterations now lies abandoned. The convent was apparently founded by Vicar Giovanni Da Capestrano in 1448 and completed around the latter half of the 15th century and following the 1813 and 1863 suppressions it was abandoned by the Grey Friars, who returned until the earthquake of 1950 forced them to leave the convent for good. The church, with a truss-roofed rectangular nave, has the typical mendicant order cross-vaulted choir. Traces on the walls of now-derelict vaults are all that remain of the Baroque alterations. The charming cloister preserves its original character in the double order of arches on stone and brick supports. The pictorial decorations are of particular interest: the church door lunette has been attributed to Matteo Campli; the 18th-century cloister painting depicting scenes from the life of St Giovanni da Capestrano are signed by7 the Flemish artist Paolo Giovanni Auche.

In the ancient fortified village of **Castelnuovo**, now part of the municipality of Campli, the **Porta Orientale**, also known as the Angoina or San Giovanni, is a well-preserved gate, presumably built in the 14th century and it is one of the most interesting fortified structures on the territory. On the exterior, an ogival arch with palmette-decorated lintel opens in the compact wall built

using stones from the nearby Ioannella quarry, whilst remnants of the ancient fortified walls are found on either side. The structure is completed by an elegant corbelled overhanging structure of three progressively jutting stone brackets. The belfry of the adjoining **church of San Giovanni Battista**, with its unique dual nave structure, dates back to the mid-14th century Fragments of votive frescoes, mainly 14th-century, survive on the walls, including a Madonna and Child attributed to Giacomo da Campli. There is also a *Pietà* attributed to Paolo De Matteis, an important master of Southern Italian painting active between the end of the 1600s and 1728.

**Nocella**, now part of the municipality of Campli, was one of the four quarters that composed Campli in the latter half of the 16th century Located on high ground, it is strongly characterized by the historical **Torre dei Melatino**, built in 1394 in compliance with the wishes of Roberto IV Di Melatino, as we read on the tower inscription. The tall tower is clearly visible from a great distance and was originally a lookout point, subsequently converted into the belfry of the church of San Mariano, which no longer exists. Two stone stringcourses separate the three levels of the tower, with local travertine edging and a warm red brick exterior.

Beyond Teramo, towards the Laga mountains, we reach **TORRICELLA SICURA**, a village straddling a ridge and with a magnificent view of the Tordino Valley. The curved Baroque-style façade of the lovely **San Paolo parish chuch** - seen in its 16th–17th-century returbishment – is enclosed by two concave, recessed wings. Inside there is an altarpiece by Sebastian Majewskj with the *Madonna and Child with Saints* (1627), and a 17th-century stoup from the older church.

The Villa Popolo district is home to the **church of San Bartolomeo** with its magnificent painted wooden ceiling (17th century). In Ioannella, famous for its stone quarries, there is the **church of Santa Maria Assunta** in its late–16th-century guise and traces of the early 18th-century restoration. The 1590 trussed ceiling is striking, with tiles decorated with red geometric, flora, fauna, and sacred symbol motifs. Among the furnishings, there is an outstanding gilt, painted 17th-century Baroque altar, with a beautiful central *Madonna in Adoration* but lacking Child Jesus. In the Costumi district, there is the **church of San Pietro in Azzano**, built in the 14th century and restored in the 1400s; the round-arch portal presumably dates back to the first half of the 1300s.

**ROCCA SANTA MARIA** is a charming group of small outlying hamlets (part of the municipality of Imposte) immersed in the verdant Bosco Martese woods. Lovely excursions to the Laga Mountain peaks start from Ceppo. Near Tavolero, ruins of the late–13th-century church of San Flaviano are sited on the ruins of an extant religious structure of which some elements (11th–12th century) may have been reused in the façade portal and single lancet windows.

629. 630. Facing page: Campli Archaeological Museum; below, one of the exhibits.
631. 632. Below: left, the church of San Pietro, Campovalano; Torre dei Melatino, Nocella.

349

Again from Teramo, moving towards L'Aquila and the Valle San Giovanni junction, we can admire the ruins of the Romanesque church of San Giovanni in Pergulis, then through the Tordino valley reach **CORTINO**, with its many districts, in an extremely interesting natural scenario. The splendid surrounding area includes the village of Elce, starting point of the Sentiero Natura dell'Abete bianco leading to the **Abetina di Cortino** where rare silver firs can still be found. Further ahead there is Altovia, semi-deserted with charming ruins of the church of Sant'Egidio. In Pezzelle we find the interesting **church of San Paolo** with frescoes datable 15th–16th centuries.

The next stop is **CROGNALETO**, set deep in the splendid scenery of the Gran Sasso and Laga Mountains, surrounded by numerous outlying hamlets. Mainly 19th–20th-century buildings typify the village but there is the 16th-century **church of Santa Caterina** and, in the high area, the charming **church of Madonna della Tibia**, built on a rock spur in the early 17th century.

Among the many districts, Senarica is worthy of a visit, with its interesting stone buildings dating back to the 16th–19th centuries, as is the **church of Santa Maria Apparente** with its 14th-century frescoes, in the hamlet of Alvi. In the pure environment of Cervaro, a tiny village on the precipice of a torrent ravine, we note the **church of Sant'Andrea** with its splendid 18th-century painted wooden ceiling. The municipality offers one of the most charming sightseeing tours through the **Valle delle Cento Cascate** falls along the Fosso Dell'Acero, past waterfalls and age-old beeches; the valley can be reached via the hamlet of Cesacastina; the parish **church of Santi Pietro e Paolo** can be visited in the village.

The ruins of the Rocca Roseto fortification are found on the peak of a rock spur at 1,258m above sea level, overlooking the Tordino and Vomano valley. Although most of the structures now lie in ruins, the 100m-perimeter fortress is known among Abruzzo fortifications as one of the most striking from a landscape, structural and architectural point of view, especially considering that it is presumed to have originally been part of the vast Swabian defence system, claimed and strengthened by the Angevin dynasty.

633. 634. Above: Valle delle Cento Cascate valley and SS Pietro e Paolo parish church, Cesacastina.
635. Left: the church of Sant'Andrea, Cervaro di Crognaleto.
636. Facing page: aerial view of the church of Santa Maria di Propezzano, near Morro d'Oro.

# From the Vomano Valley to Gran Sasso

Morro d'Oro, Notaresco, Castellalto, Castelbasso, Canzano, Montegualtieri, Cellino Attanasio, Cermignano, Penna Sant'Andrea, Basciano, Castel Castagna, Castelli, Isola del Gran Sasso, Colledara, Tossicia, Montorio al Vomano, Fano Adriano, Pietracamela

In the municipality of **MORRO D'ORO**, built on a hill to the left of the Vomano valley, a short distance from the Roseto A14 motorway exit. Its 15th-century fortified village structure is still visible, later extended during the 1800s. It is worth visiting the **church of San Salvatore**, built in about 1331 over an existing site, remodelled several times over the centuries including 17th-century interventions to the façade, with a gabled stone portal, beaded bracket and cornices. The right-hand flank in brick with a stone portal, four single-lancet windows with unique decorative motifs, and the rear with one single lancet windows and surviving bell gable, are said to be from the original structure. The rectangular-plan building has a nave and two aisles cadenced by square pillars on abutting semi columns. The interior has a precious polychrome terracotta *Madonna*, dated 16th-century and refined 17th-century canvases by Francesco Ragazzino.
A **Museum of Rural Culture and Arts** has been installed in the cellars of historic **Palazzo De Gregoris**, with about 300 exhibits in nine themed showrooms.
In the **Vaniglie** district there is a surviving 1300s portal in the church belonging to the Sant'Antonio Abate convent, later converted into a farm. There is also a precious lunette fresco.
The **church of Santa Maria di Propezzano** and annexed Benedictine convent are built near the town. The complex was assigned to the Observant Order in 1580 (*see box p. 352*).
In nearby Guardia Vomano, a district of

The itinerary winds its way through the lovely Vomano valley, certainly one of the most beautiful in the entire Apennine range. Historic mountain villages are rendered more precious by important works of art, alongside those of neighbouring Val Mavone (or Siciliana) and, together with surviving traditional crafts, create a unique location for the curious and enthusiastic visitor. Turning inland from the coast, up to the hills, there is a triumph of vineyards, then continuing along the valley we reach the Laga Mountains, which together with the Gran Sasso massif, constitute one of the most spectacular and lavish national parks as far as natural habitat is concerned. This is the area where artistic and popular religious references include Santa Maria di Propezzano (Morro d'Oro), San Clemente al Vomano (Notaresco) and Santa Maria di Ronzano (Castel Castagna), some of the Region's loveliest Romanesque churches, not to mention the sanctuary of San Gabriele dell'Addolorata (Isola del Gran Sasso), a centre of a deep-felt devotion. One of the most important destinations for artistic crafts is Castelli, the "town of ceramics", whose flourishing pottery workshops ensure the historic tradition does not die out. The territory offers numerous attractions for tourists, its appeal ranging from nature to landscape, architecture to art, not to mention history and culture, not to mention traditions and food and wine.

Notaresco, we might well visit the monastery **church of San Clemente al Vomano**, which dominates this fertile valley from a hilltop position (*see box p. 354*).

The ancient layout of **NOTARESCO**, also called Civitello, can still be seen in the characteristic tower-houses protecting the village. It also has interesting pieces of 19th-century civil architecture. **Palazzo Devincenzi** and the **churches of SS Pietro e Andrea** and **San Rocco**, with a precious early–16th-century *Madonna with Child* terracotta sculpture, are worth visiting. The **G. Romualdi Civic Museum**, hosted in Palazzo Romualdi, in the central square of the town, is of interest, with exhibits that include relics from the Roman settlement in the Grasciano district.

**CASTELLALTO**, built on a hilltop dividing the Vomano and Tordino Rivers, still has traces of its Medieval fortifications. The **church of San Giovanni Evangelista**, with a 1584 portal and 1700s canvases, and the **church of Madonna degli Angeli**, with a valuable Baroque altar and 18th-century paintings are significant.

The striking village of **Castelbasso**, perched on the hill between Castellalto (of which it is a district) and the other district of Castelnuovo, with the River Tordino to the north and the River Vomano to the south, stands out among the various settlements on municipal territory. Despite various modifications, Castelbasso still has the original layout of a fortified village,

637–639. Above, left to right: the walls of the village and a display room in Palazzo De Sanctis, Castelbasso; the church of San Salvatore, Canzano.
640. 641. Below and facing page: the brick cloister and view of the exterior of the church of Santa Maria di Propezzano.

## Church of Santa Maria di Propezzano, Morro d'Oro

Today's layout of a tall, wide nave and two smaller aisles, without transept or apse, is configured as 15 round arch bays, set on composite pillars. All of this is the result of the 1300s reconstruction of the previous church, which was much older and had a single nave with semi-circular apse that are still discernible. The church has cross vaults but the ribbing only in the far presbytery area. The façade illustrates the various stages of construction perfectly as it was involved in extensive remodelling in the latter 1400s: the addition of the straight coping to the façade at the nave and left aisle. The unbalanced prospect is preceded by a roofed portico set against the Romanesque façade, which survived the 1300 expansion, although the oculus was covered and another opened higher up, aligned with the façade. During the 1969–70 restoration, the ancient oculus was reopened. There is also a lovely square cloister with two orders of brick columns, decorated in the 1600s by the workshop of Giovan Battista Spinelli. The unique *Madonna del Crognale* fresco in the lunette of the main portal is linked to the legend of the foundation of the church.

the old Acquaviva fief. With its typical ring plan, surrounded by strong walls reinforced by a counterfort and towers (of which traces survive), the village also had access gates, of which two are still in use. We enter by the **Porta Sud** gate, a round arch in mixed masonry including rough-hewn stone and slim bricks, with a second order, pulled back from the lower arch and probably added during a later transformation. Its structure is crowned by swallowtail merlons of different sizes that mark a recently restored, rear terrace. The **Porta della Fonte** gate (1467), or Porta della Marina, accessed by a ramp close to the walls, is a characteristic local tower-gate. The rectangular stone and brick tower is framed by the defensive walls on one side, and by an 18th-century building on the other.

The machicolation and murder hole system is characteristic and there are three large flat-top merlons closing the structure, delimiting the walkway at the top of the fortifications. The upper part of the gate features typical embrasures.

At the highest point there was an imposing castle, dominating the Tordino and the Vomano valleys, but only the curtain wall base survives.

Civil architecture is noteworthy, especially 16th-century **Palazzotto Costantini Cancrini**, as well as **Palazzo De Sanctis** and **Palazzo Clemente**.

Of the religious buildings, the **church of SS Pietro e Andrea** is noteworthy. A direct homage to the Propezzano church, has an elegant 14th-century portal with two lions on the jambs and higher up a *Madonna and Child*, attributed to the same hand as the portal. The church was consecrated in 1338 and has a nave an two aisles, with barrel vaults on round arches. Inside there are a baptismal font dated 1589, fine stuccoes produced during the Baroque restoration, and 17th–18th-century canvases. In the choir there is a precious organ by Adriano Fedri.

In summer all Castelbasso becomes the amazing scenario for a prestigious cultural event that brings together the most important figures of contemporary art.

Heading inland we encounter **CANZANO**, an important Medieval village set in the mid Vomano basin. An embattled round tower survives, although it has been remodelled. **Palazzo Taraschi**, with its imposing stone ashlar portal, is the most interesting of the 18th–19th-century buildings.

The **church of Santa Maria dell'Alno**, built in 1592 and restored in the mid–1700s, with 15th–18th-century paintings and furnishings, is worth seeing, together with the important **church of San Salvatore**, near Canzano cemetery. The church has ancient origins and has been heavily refurbished, now presenting a unique inserted belfry in the right aisle; inside, where the presbytery is lower than the entrance, there are fine cycles of frescoes, the oldest attributed to Maestro d'Offida.

We then reach a district of Cermignano, **Montegualtieri**, by turning back to the valley line

road. The village lies close to a soaring 14th–15th-century triangular tower, similar to the Sutrium (near Bussi, in the province of Pescara) structure, which are rare in Abruzzo. The tower is on a rocky spur and controls a huge territory, so it was a major element in the Vomano valley's warning system. Coming down Via del Torrione it is possible to see the 18m triangular tower, perfectly integrated with the surrounding environment. It was built for defence purposes and stands on a sloping sandstone base, reinforced with brick buttresses; at the top there are typical corbel-supported machicolations finished with fine embattlements, partly restored in 1976, and still well-preserved.

The mighty round brick tower – typical of the Marche coast – and fragments of another tower and a section of walls, are what remains of the late–15th-century Acquaviva fortification that encircle the charming village of **CELLINO ATTANASIO**. It can be reached by continuing along the southern hillslope between the River Vomano and the River Piomba. The section of stone scarp walls is crowned by brick swallowtail battlements added in the early 20th-century restoration. One of the two mighty round brick towers is scarpless, with flights of putlog holes with embrasures and loopholes, and conventional, elaborate corbel-supported machicolations on round scheme arches.

Two massive square stone towers must have been part of the older walls, one of which has been englobed by the Santa Maria la Nova parish church bell tower, while the other is incorporated in the apse of the church of San Francesco.

The **church of Santa Maria La Nova** is the most precious building in the town, with its

## Church of San Clemente al Vomano, Notaresco

The church and annexed monastery, which already existed in the 9th century, were radically restructured in the Romanesque period; the remains of the coenoby and today's church date back to that time, with a nave and two aisles on hybrid supports, and exposed wooden ceiling, three semicircular apses, no transept and an presbytery set over a crypt. The refurbishment is traditionally dated as 1108, the year etched into the lovely portal's left-hand jamb and which was the bone of much contention amongst numerous scholars.

The dating of 1108 could correspond to the construction phase of the presbytery while the nave may have been built between the fourth and fifth decade of the twelfth century. The church, subsequently used only as a cemetery chapel, underwent important restoration and the structures brought to light are referable the 9th-century monastic complex, whose remains are now visible through a transparent floor installed in the church. The interior has a rich, valuable **ciborium**, dated mid–12th century, erected on the altar by the famous workshop of Ruggiero and Roberto; the structure is supported by marble columns with sumptuous capitals. There is also a precious intarsia **marble altar** and a fresco of the late–13th century.

642. Above: Montegualtieri tower.
643. 644. Below: views of the interior and façade of the church of San Clemente in Vomano.

fine 15th-century portal. Documented in 1330 for the first time, the parish church was modified extensively in the 1800s, after the roof collapsed in 1824. The interior shows two irregular aisles with a restored wooden roof, but originally had a nave and two aisles. In the right aisle there are traces of 14th-century frescoes on the brick columns, supposed to be part of the 1300s layout. The layout has a massive square tower, with a stone lower section surmounted by a brick belfry. Inside, there is the 1383 Paschal candle shaft, a 1472 stone tabernacle on the right of the sumptuous Baroque altar, both attributed to the workshop of Andrea Lombardo, and the 1496tomb of Giovan Battista Acquaviva d'Aragona, attributed to a Veneto artist of the Pietro Lombardo school. The stunning façade has a lavish rose window and a fine 1424 portal by Matteo Capro of Naples, with multiple reliefs using small, embedded columns and a round archivolt, inspired by Aquilan models.

Continuing towards Penna Sant'Andrea we reach **CERMIGNANO**, set on a hill ridge between the Vomano and the Piomba rivers, surrounded by a group of charming villages. The hilltop areas vaunts the noteworthy **Santa Lucia parish church**, with a 1700s' reconstruction including an impressive hexagonal drum cupola and soaring belfry, as well as a handsome inflexed façade that is not common in Abruzzo. There are 18th-century paintings inside.

On the outskirts of Cermignano, the aisleless **church of Sant'Eustachio** (1678), which belonged to the convent (1672) and which has been remodelled but is in a good state of repair. The interior retains a lovely Baroque altar in carved walnut, by Capuchin artists and 1600s' paintings by Giacomo Farelli.

**PENNA SANT'ANDREA** is a lovely little village set on a ridge along the Vomano valley, in ancient Adriatic Sabine territory. The mother **church of Santa Maria del Soccorso** is well worth seeing, probably founded in 1500s but now showing restoration undertaken in the latter 18th century Inside visitors notice

645. 646. Above: the round tower and the façade of Santa Maria La Nova church, Cellino Attanasio.
647. Below: Cermignano.

the 1700s stuccowork and a particularly precious paliotto and 1600s gilt, painted wood tabernacle. The municipality is also home to the Castel Cerreto Riserva Naturale Guidata, with a tourist information office in Contrada Pilone. The archaeological findings (on display in Chieti's Museo Archeologico Nazionale) from a necropolis, including three illustrated, inscribed steles, are fundamental for understanding Sabine Italic society at the time it went from the monarchic era to the aristocratic republics. The village organizes the traditional *Laccio d'amore* maypole event and in August the **Folklore International Folklore meeting**.

The itinerary returns downhill and then uphill towards **BASCIANO**, on its panoramic site to the right of the River Vomano. The original settlement, in the northwest, is still identifiable, clustering round the site; the entrance is at the **Porta Penta** gate, with its looming San Giorgio tower leading to Via del Torrione. At the top of the built-up area we can discern the remains ever keep and defensive structures. In the old part there is the interesting **church of San Flaviano**, documented as early as 1065, but radically changed in 1500. The gate 1582 is etched into the portal. The **church of Santa Maria a Porto Lungo** also called **fuori le Mura** is very interesting, with its majolica-tiled ceiling and a splendid gilt wooden altar dated 1646.

Following the Mavone valley, in the municipality of Castel Castagna, we encounter the striking **church of Santa Maria di Ronzano**, solitary on its terrace to the right of the river (*see box p. 357*).

Quite close by, **CASTEL CASTAGNA**, set against Gran Sasso's northern slope, has some precious examples of civil architecture woven into the urban fabric. The places of worship include the **church of San Pietro Martire**, mentioned in existence in the 14th century, and restored in the early 1500s, which is the period of the handsome Renaissance portal.

Proceeding, the next stop is **CASTELLI**, on its spur at the foot of Mount Brancastello, between River Leomogna and the Rio canal. Despite a prevalently 19th-century and modern appearance, there are still some 16th-century buildings. Entering the town, we encounter the **church of San Rocco**, with a Renaissance portal; inside there are still 1400s frescoes of *Our Lady of Tears*, attributed to Andrea Delitio. The parish **church of San Giovanni Battista** has a characteristic, handsome façade portal dated 1601, with a split gable and a centre niche with the statue of a saint. The three-bay interior is divided by mighty columns and is home to a priceless wooden *Madonna with Child*, said to be 12th century, as well as a splendid 1647 majolica altar front, by Francesco Grue, depicting the *Madonna of Loreto and Saints*. On the right wall we can admire the *Martyrdom of St Matthew*, painted in 1620, and signed by the Florentine artist Bernardino Monaldi. There are some interesting fragments of a 12th-century ambo, brought from the derelict abbey of San Salvatore and walled into the façade.

This tiny town is famous for its artistic production of pottery which earned it international fame, especially from the mid–1500s to

648. Above: Porta Penta gate, Basciano.
649. 650. Below: Penna Sant'Andrea and the traditional "Laccio d'amore" maypole dance.

# Church of Santa Maria di Ronzano, Castel Castagna

The church was built before 1180, which is presumed from the priceless apse frescoes dated 1181. In 1183 a fire caused sufficient damage to leave traces that are still visible, causing calcination of the pillar limestone ashlars. The layout is one of the earliest expressions of mature Romanesque passing to Gothic: there is a nave and two aisles, with roof, and split by round arches on square pillars with abutting pilaster strips; these, and others in corresponding positions on the perimeter walls, betray the former existence of vaults or arches in the aisles. The sheer height of the presbytery, internally split into three cross-vaulted bays, emerges from the nave section, and is cadenced by a round arch motif on pilaster strips. The rear facade, conceals the outer apse curve behind a straight front, proposing motifs commonly found in Apulian churches, which also offer inspiration for the elegant frieze around the rear single-lancet window, originally completed by nine human heads of which only two still survive. The church features one of the most significant cycles of Medieval painting. The year 1181 is certainly the date of only the frescoes in the great apse, the *Christ* in the apse bowl, *Apostles with Evangelists* and *Annunciation* in the first order beneath, *Stories of the Childhood and Passion of Christ* in the last two. Surviving Old and New Testament stories on the right-hand transept head, are of the same era as the apse frescoes, but are painted by a different hand; the isolated "head of a saint" fresco on the right-hand pillar of the triumphal arch is attributable to the same artist that painted the most significant sections of the apse frescoes. Fragments of the *Last Judgment* found in the left transept head are referable to the 13th century, and for style and iconography resemble the frescoes at Santa Maria ad Cryptas, near Fossa (AQ); what remains is probably the reproduction of an older Last Judgment that would have closed the 1181 iconographic cycle lost during the blaze.
Among the later frescoes in the side apses, the rare illustration of *St Norbert of Xanten* is an important work by the Maestro di Offida.

651. 652. This page: detail of the frescoes and external view of the church of Santa Maria di Ronzano.

the mid–1700s, and still continues with a healthy number of artisans. It is certainly worth visiting the **Museo delle Ceramiche**, in the old Franciscan convent with a collection the includes a huge legacy of objects made by the greatest master potters, including figures of the calibre of Carlo Antonio and Francesco Antonio Grue, the Gentile, Cappelletti, Pompei, and Fuina families. The F. A. Grue state art institute is home to the **International collection of Contemporary Ceramic Art**.

The lovely **church of San Donato**, erected near the Franciscan convent, was built in the early 17th century, on the site of the smaller church known as the "cona", and is graced with a splendid majolica ceiling that stands as one of the most significant contributions to early 17th-century Abruzzo culture, earning itself the name of the "Sistine Chapel of Italian majolica". Castelli's potters had originally decorated an older church with a painted tiled ceiling in the 1500s replaced in the 17th-century renovation. The town's guild of potters created a ceiling whose surface covers about 100sqm, comprising more than 800 majolica tiles, dated 1615–17. This sloping truss ceiling is divided into sections where the rows of tiles are aligned and held in place by joists. This work of art was radically restored in 1969-70, when missing or ruined tiles were replaced.

**The Mostra Mercato dell'artigianato Ceramico Castellano**, a trade fair of local ceramic crafts, is held in Castelli every August, concluding with the characteristic "lancio di piatti", when plates are hurled from the Belvedere down steep slopes towards the Leomogna torrent.

The ancient fortified village of **ISOLA DEL GRAN SASSO** is located near Castelli, on the northeast slopes of the Gran Sasso massif. The original layout still be seen in the "isola", an island wedged between the River Mavone and

653–655. This page: above, the interior and majolica ceiling of the church of San Donato; left, parade plate by Francesco Grue found in the pottery museum; below, Castelli with Mount Camicia in the background.
656–658. Facing page: left, the historic centre of Isola del Gran Sasso and Andrea Delitio's fresco in the shrine of San Sebastiano; right, church of San Giovanni ad Insulam.

the Ruzzo torrent, included boundary walls, of which some sections are still visible, although they have been mainly absorbed by later construction work, when dwellings were built. The oldest sources regarding the settlement are dated mid–11th century, referring to the Adelberto's donation of the "fortified village of Isola" to the cathedral of Santa Maria, Teramo. Along Via Duca degli Abruzzi there is a surviving *castrum* gate, **Porta Canapina**, and here it is also possible to identify several sections of ancient sloping walls, similar to those on the eastern perimeter; here the forepart of a tower concludes in double order of four arches (the upper order was added later). Along Via Romea there is a massive, remodelled defence tower, which has a round arch gate known as **Porta del Torrione**, and near by there is a parish **church of San Massimo** whose structures absorbed sections of the existing fortifications.

The church of San Massimo offers an elegant 1420 portal by the renowned Neapolitan sculptor Matteo Capro, the interior including a number of precious works like the 1529 Renaissance chapel and baptistery. Also worthy of note is the **cona of San Sebastiano**, with 1400s frescoes attributed to the school of Andrea Delitio, and the **church of Santa Lucia** with a portal dated 1450 and the remains of an early–1500s fresco of the *Annunciation*.

This is also the location of the important **church of San Giovanni ad Insulam**, dated 11th–latter–12th-century, and modified in the late 13th century The church interior falls into two sections: the ample chamber with roofed bays, cadenced by rectangular pillars, and the presbytery with underlying crypt, divided by several small, round supports, closer together and with variable section. The unit of space achieved in the front area is noticeably accentuated by the subsequent raising of the aisles. The main prospect is lovely – one of the first in Abruzzo to be graced with a horizontal coping façade, sadly blemished by the addition of a campanile. The façade is enhanced by a decoration of vaulted arches on brackets, continued along the flanks and recovered on the apse semicircle; the portal, with an archivolt framed by a cusped aedicula, has jambs decorated in elegant bas relief figures. On the apse basin there are 1400s frescoes attributable to a follower of Andrea Delitio.

The fascinating remains of the ancient castle of the Counts of Pagliara are found on a steep slope at 980m asl. This was the illustrious family of St Berardo, Bishop of Teramo, and of many other important personalities. Today's remains betray the layout of the ancient castle, laid along a rocky ridge; it still has mortared Medieval structures and traces of later remodelling. Set against the castle are the historic remains of the **church of Santa Maria a Pagliara**, rebuilt by the hermit monk Nicola

Torretta, and today almost intact. On the Sunday after Easter the faithful make their way to the hill to celebrate this Madonna.

About 4km from Isola del Gran Sasso, after passing the district of Pretara and continuing along the steep path through the woods, we reach the **hermitage-church of Santa Colomba**, at 1234m, also restored by the hermit monk, Fra' Nicola, and the destination of a pilgrimage for the 1 September festivities. There is also the **hermitage-church of San Nicola** di Fano at Corno, a few kilometres from the district of Casale San Nicola and near the San Nicola springs; then there is the **hermitage of Fratta Grande**, just beyond Pretara, built by Fra' Nicola in about 1850, where he died in 1886.

If we return down valley, we find one of the most important and popular sanctuaries in Abruzzo, **San Gabriele dell'Addolorata**, near Isola del Gran Sasso, where the convent is also home to the **Stauròs Museum of Contemporary Religious Art**; the paintings and the sculptures on show include the Fieschi Collection, donated by the artist in person. The older sanctuary enlarged the small extant church dedicated to the Immaculate Mary, annexed to the SS Annunziata Franciscan convent (suppressed in 1809, and now run by the Passionist Fathers). The remains of St Gabriele dell'Addolorata (Francesco Possenti) are buried here: a saint born in Assisi in 1838, who died before taking holy orders, in 1862, at Isola del Gran Sasso, canonized in 1920, and co-patron of the Italian Young People's Catholic Movement, as well as being patron of Abruzzo. The neighbouring convent has the two cells occupied by St Gabriele at the end of his life, and a Museum, with the saint's memorabilia and documents, as well as those of his family, with ex votos and relics. Construction of the new sanctuary, which could accommodate 10,000 worshippers, began in 1970; for part of the year the urn with the saint's remains is kept here.

Continuing towards Montorio al Vomano, we reach the municipality of **COLLEDARA**, in the Mavone valley, surrounded by several districts, of which the most noteworthy is Ornano Grande, with the interesting **church of San Giorgio**, with a bell gable and 16–1700s interior. **Castiglione della Valle**, once the location of the town hall, is a very interesting location: it is almost completely uninhabited and retains sections of its boundary walls. The **church of San Michele Arcangelo** is especially interesting. The building's current configuration is the result of an extension built in an unspecified period, standing as a second block

659–661. This page: above, the hermitages of San Colomba and Fratta Grande; below, the sanctuary of San Gabriele dell'Addolorata.
662–665. Facing page: above, the church of San Giorgio, Ornano Grande and the church of San Michele Arcangelo, Castiglione della Valle; below, the portal of San Sinforosa church and Tossicia Palazzo Marchesale.

alongside the older main unit, closed by a straight wall that once had a single-lancet window (now only visible from the outside), and which corresponds to the shorter, left-hand aisle. The main portal is crowned by a round arch lunette, with two typical small heads supporting the archivolt, bearing a close resemblance to that of the church of Santa Sinforosa, at Tossicia (1438). Inside the church there are some especially interesting fragments of a stone frieze, and traces of several frescoes, visible to the right of the high altar, presumably part of an early 1500s layout. Other frescoes, a Baroque altar, wood ceiling dated 1762, the choir organ set above the secondary entrance, are all part of later interventions. In the hamlet of Villa Petto, the parish **church of Santa Lucia** inserted in the mighty stone walls, remains of fortifications probably dating back to the 14th–15th centuries. Inside the church there is a 1568 stoup and an 18th-century wooden tabernacle.

The municipality of Colledara is home to the splendid Fiume Fiumetto Parco Territoriale Attrezzato, safeguarding the lovely Fiumetto river, whose brief four-kilometre course is a cross-section of tiny wetlands, falls and river-bank vegetation of willows and poplars.

**TOSSICIA**, on the ridge that spans the Mavone and Vomano river basins, is characterized by prevalently 1700s architecture, with some hints of the previous era. The parish **church of Santa Sinforosa**, with handsome 1400s portals worth seeing, was originally called Santa Maria Assunta. It has two bays and a simple façade with a smart, intricate portal, whose door is decorated with two vibrant heads, the work of a 15th-century Abruzzo sculptor. Another 15th-century portal is installed on the other side, surmounted by an inflexed arch lunette, and with figures of the Archangel Gabriel and Virgin Mary of the Annunciation on the door.

The precious furnishings in the church include a 1400s wooden *crucifix*, the facing of the 1570 stone altar and, at the back of the presbytery, the polychrome wooden group of the *Madonna with Child* dated late 1400s–early 1500s. Until the 2009 earthquake, the wooden statue of the *Madonna of Providence* or "*Reclining Madonna*" (late 14th–early 15th century) was found here but is now in the San Gabriele sanctuary.

Outside town the **chapel of the Madonna della Neve** or Santa Teresa cona is an interesting work dated early–16th century and attributed to Girolamo da Vicenza.

The **church of Sant'Antonio Abate**, with its magnificent 1471 portal attributed to Andrea Lombardo, taking up almost the entire façade, is also worth seeing. The portal is surmounted by a pointed tympanum set with a round window. The symbols of the *Evangelists* are set into the edges of the architrave, *St Anthony Abbot* in the lunette, and *Angel musicians and the Eternal Father* in the architrave; the jambs and small, side columns are decorated with lavish figured capitals and small heads. Inside there is a wooden 1400s *crucifix*.

Palazzo Marchesale is home to a **Museum of craft traditions**, exhibiting numerous copper items, furnishings and tools.

Finally we reach the lively craft and trade centre of **MONTORIO AL VOMANO**, at the mouth of the upper Vomano valley, with oldest buildings laid on a hillside dominated by the remains of the San Carlo fortress. The remains of the Italic **temple of Hercules** are of great archaeological interest. In the town centre, on Piazza Orsini, there is the **church of San Rocco** (16th century), whose interior is fitted with precious Baroque wooden altars and a fine 16th–17th-century canvas of the *Resurrection of Christ*, by Vincenzo Pagani.

The splendid **SS Concezione convent** of the Minor Observants or "Zoccolanti", founded over an ancient Clareno installation, is located next to the River Vomano. The impressive complex features austere external façades and is set around a rectangular cloister, with round arches and a small, central well. Subsequent refurbishment projects altered the convent's architectural and structural traits. The church retains stuccowork by Carlo Piazzoli.

The SS Annunziata or Cappuccini convent was built on the edge of the town, and is now derelict, but the **Santa Maria della Salute church** survives, with its lavish wooden high altar, is still officiated. The civil buildings include **Palazzo Pantealoni** and **Palazzo Martegiani**, the old town hall, **Palazzo Camponeschi-Carafa** in Piazza Orsini, and the splendid 1500s façade of **Palazzo Catini**, with its lion portal.

The Fiume Vomano Parco Territoriale Attrezzato park, the largest of this type of protected area, lies completely within the confines of municipal territory, and comprises the course of the river that flows through Montorio to Vomano.

Worth seeing on the afternoon of Ash Wednesday is the *Carnevale Morto*, a traditional ancient event and unique in its kind in Abruzzo.

Now we turn back to the upper Vomano valley to **FANO ADRIANO**, which stretches along its right flank. The most significant monument

666. Above: Montorio al Vomano.
667. 668. Below: left, Montorio al Vomano's traditional Carnevale Morto event; right, detail of the portal of the church of San Pietro, Fano Adriano.
669. 670. Facing page: above, Fano Adriano; below, Pietracamela with Mount Intermesoli in the background.

in Fano is installed in the old town and is the parish **church of San Pietro**, seen in its 16th-century guise. The austere façade, in local sandstone, features a sumptuous portal, with Castelli majolica tiles set into the lunette, with the year 1693 inscribed. The interior of a nave and two aisles still has lovely Baroque furnishings and a handsome wooden false ceiling dated 1608.

At the top of the San Marcello hill, with a magnificent view over the Gran Sasso range, we find the tiny **SS Annunziata church**, called a "cona", which includes the walls set to the north of the remains of older square sandstone block walls. On the left-hand entrance the date 1597 has been engraved into a stone block then set into the wall; inside there are interesting traces of frescoes of folk tendency, and an altar dated 1785.

An **Ethnography Museum of Folklore and Popular Traditions**, with collections of shepherds' tools, ex voto and craft devices, has been set up in the tiny district of **Cerqueto**.

Just a few kilometres uphill we find ourselves in Medieval **PIETRACAMELA**, which was built compact against the slopes of a rock spur, amidst dense woods, in the heart of the Gran Sasso-Laga Mountains National Park. Opposite the ancient boundary wall tower (with the year 1550 marked on one of its window frames), now the canon's accommodation, there is the Medieval **church of San Leucio**. An original 1500s holy water stoup, with quatrefoil basin, sculpted with marine animals, can be seen in this church; a fine 1700s organ and, above all, two precious processional

crosses attributed to Nicola da Guardiagrele.
The centre of town preserves its ancient urban fabric, and here we can see the **church of San Giovanni**, built in about 1432, as indicated by the inscription on the portal; the **church of San Rocco**, in the higher part of town, has a stone portal and architrave inscription that indicates the year 1530. The **ethnography and ancient crafts museum** been set up in the town hall and the **museum of mountaineering** in Prati di Tivo, dedicated to the history of exploration on Mount Gran Sasso are both worth a visit.

After the town's last houses, there is a short nature trail that leads to the **chamois wildlife reserve** that allows observation, study and repopulation of this herbivore, fundamental to the ecosystem.

Pietracamela is the gateway to the marvellous Pietracamela Corno Grande Nature Reserve, which stretches for over 2,000 hectares, including the formidable Corno Grande, Corno Piccolo and Pizzo d'Intermesoli peaks. The Reserve is managed by the Abruzzese delegation of the Italian Alpine Club. A unique natural phenomenon is the **Calderone glacier**, concealed amidst the Corno Grande peaks, at 2,700m in height, the Apennine chain' s only glacier and most southern in Europe.

671. Above: Prati di Tivo with Corno Piccolo in the background.
672. Below: Calderone glacier on Corno Grande.

# Fino River Valley

**ATRI** is a jewel in the centre of Teramo province, on a ridge between the Vomano and the Piomba rivers, with magnificent sea views. The area is clearly dominated by the distinctive badlands, protected by the **Calanchi di Atri regional nature reserve**.

The town was probably a pre-Roman fortified settlement and the numerous findings that have come to light over the last few years show the importance and vitality of life there at the time of the Roman town and the urban layout of the time also created the matrix for later building modifications that took place as late as the 19th century, inside the town walls. Atri became a free commune in the mid-13th century and came under the control of the Acquaviva family at the end of the 1200s. Early in the 16th century, the Acquavivas made it the capital of a vast district that stretched from the River Tronto to the River Pescara, remaining stable until the latter half of the 18th century. The most obvious signs of Roman Atri date back to the imperial period, one of the town's most glorious eras and the time when the urban plan was redesigned. The main findings relating to this period were made in what is now Corso Elio Adriano; nowadays its route

Atri, Castilenti, Castiglione Messer Raimondo, Montefino, Bisenti, Arsita

The route runs through one of the most beautiful areas in the province of Teramo with a wealth of traditions. One of the prime attractions is Atri: its numerous monuments and particularly attractive town centre make of it a real gem and one of the most important tourist destinations in the Region. One feature of the Atri hills, with views ranging from Gran Sasso down to the sea, are its unique badlands, accentuated forms of erosion that run through the sandstone, the most famous being at the feet of the pretty town, and which cast unique colours and fantastic effects on the landscape.

673. Below: aerial view of the Calanchi di Atri regional nature reserve.

links, as it did then, the two main sections of the town, Piazza del Comune, where the old Forum was; what is now Piazza dei Duchi d'Acquaviva, and Piazza Duomo. The Renaissance courtyard in the town hall is home to inscriptions and funeral stones dating from the late Republican era to the end of the Imperial period, and record the construction of public works; the beautiful sarcophagus fragment, showing the meeting between Bacchus and Ariadne, dates back to the 3rd century AD.

The remains of the **Roman theatre** are of particular interest; going by the building techniques adopted, it can be attributed to the Augustinian era (1st century AD). The building was identified in the cellars of **Palazzo Cicada**, an orphanage that has now closed. The structure had a diameter of 70m and seated about 10,000. The interesting **mosaic** is found set into the outer wall of a building at the corner of Via Ferrante and Piazza Duomo, dated 2nd or perhaps 3rd century AD. It probably decorated a *triclinium* in a *domus* and comprised black and white tesserae laid in refined geometrical motifs. Worth visiting is the **De Galitiis-De Albentiis-Tascini civic archeological museum** in the 18th-century complex of buildings going by the same name, with three display rooms. Certainly, a fascinating visit is guaranteed to the so-called "grottos" located just outside the old town centre, in the direction of the main road. The narrow tunnels, reached by taking a very steep staircase, were probably originally used as shelters and became cisterns in Roman times, as can be seen by the impermeable *opus signinum* walls.

Little survives of the late 13th-century fortified boundary walls, restored and reinforced the 14th and 16th centuries, then mostly dismantled in the 19th–20th centuries. The only surviving gate is the San Domenico, restored around 1528 and still in good condition. The gate, with ogival arch, is surmounted by a plate with three stems dating back to Angevin times. Close by, Piazzale del Belvedere, with its permanent exhibition of contemporary sculptures creating a truly magical atmosphere.

The Capo d'Atri keep was closely linked to the town fortifications and remains of the polygonal rampart's imposing structures with brick scarp wall, can still be seen. The ancient fort, built near the end of the 14th century, was destroyed by the people of Atri in 1414.

The magnificent ducal mansion, **Palazzo Acquaviva**, on the highest point in the town, is worth a visit. It is built around an elegant porticoed courtyard and is now the town hall. The Acquaviva family rebuilt the mansion in the 14th century on the site of an even older building, and it was again transformed in the 1500s. The complex's square plan and central court 14th-century remains can be discerned in the main frontage and in the lower order of the courtyard, with its four wide ogival

674. Below, left: the door and the church of San Domenico.
675. 676. Below, right: remains of the Roman theatre and courtyard of Palazzo Acquaviva.
677. Facing page: aerial view of Atri.